HOMOPHILE STUDIES
IN THEORY AND PRACTICE

Books By W. Dorr Legg

Homosexuals Today 1956: A Handbook of Organizations
& Publications (Los Angeles: Publication Division
of ONE, Incorporated, 1956)

Annotated Bibliography of Homosexuality (Co-Editor)
2 vols. (New York: Garland Publishing, Inc.,
1976)

HOMOPHILE STUDIES

IN THEORY

AND PRACTICE

Written and Edited
by

W. Dorr Legg

Associate Editors
David G. Cameron
Walter L. Williams

Managing Editor
Donald C. Paul

Co-Publishers:

 institute press

 PUBLISHERS
San Francisco

Published in the United States by
ONE Institute Press and
꿺 Division, GLB Publishers
P.O. Box 78212, San Francisco, CA 94107 USA

Cover by Curium Design

Publisher's Cataloging in Publication
(Prepared by Quality Books Inc.)

Homophile studies in theory and practice / written and edited by W.
   Dorr Legg ; associate editors, David G. Cameron, Walter W.
   Williams ; managing editor, Donald C. Paul.
      p. cm.

      1. One, Inc.--History. 2. Homosexuality--United States--
History. 3. Homosexuality--United States--Study and teaching.
I. Legg, W. Dorr. II. Cameron, David G. III. Williams,
Walter W.

HQ76.2.U6H65 1994   305.9'0664
                             QBI93-22657

First printing, May, 1994
10 9 8 7 6 5 4 3 2 1

ABBREVIATIONS

CA	*ONE Calendar*
CONFI	*ONE Confidential*
LTR	*ONEletter*
MAG	*ONE Magazine*
QTLY	*ONE Institute Quarterly of Homophile Studies*
SCI	*Science*
TDY	*Homosexuals Today 1956: A Handbook of Organizations & Publications*

NOTE: Where citations indicate, unpublished original documents are preserved in the ONE, Inc. Archive, a special collection of ONE, Incorporated, Blanche M. Baker Memorial Library and Archives.

Pseudonyms and identifications are from Bullough *et al*, *Annotated Bibliography of Homosexuality*, "Index of Pseudonyms," vols I & II, New York: Garland Publishing, Inc., 1976.

HOMOPHILE STUDIES
IN THEORY AND PRACTICE

TABLE OF CONTENTS

Preface   i

Introduction   1

PART I
Transition from General Education
Purposes to a Graduate School

Chapter 1
How ONE Institute Began   9

Chapter 2
Educational Methods and Curriculum   23

Chapter 3
Supplementary Educational Projects   52

Chapter 4
The Graduate School   70

PART II
Homophile Studies: An Overview

Chapter 5
Homosexuality in History   80

Chapter 6
Homosexuals in American Society:
The Sociology of a Sub-Culture   117

Chapter 7
Psychology   153

Chapter 8
Law   179

Chapter 9
Religion   193

Chapter 10

   Biology 215

Chapter 11

   Anthropology 238

Chapter 12

   Literature and the Arts 262

Chapter 13

   Philisophy 288

PART III

         ONE Institute Today

Chapter 14

   Homophile Studies: Summary 317

Chapter 15

   What of the Future? 327

PART IV

       Appendix, Index and Topical Guide

Appendix 337

Index and Topical Guide 457

PREFACE

Since the opening of ONE Institute in 1956, thousands of men and women have attended its Extension and Graduate School classes in Los Angeles, Chicago, Detroit, Long Beach, New York, Phoenix and San Francisco. They have shaped and tested the adventurously innovative and probing new perspectives in the study of homosexuality which we call Homophile Studies.

In days when newspaper articles, broadcasts and books were focusing public attention on sit-ins, parades and confrontations, which the media find so irresistible, ONE Institute quietly kept working to change society's attitudes toward the topic.

A Los Angeles chief of police might silence protesters to great acclaim by saying, "I will never sit down to confer with criminals," for such was the legal status of homosexual men and women in all parts of the United States thirty-five years ago. In the same vein a large New York publisher could gain both respect and profit by publishing Bergler's *Homosexuality: Disease or Way of Life*?

In a climate like this, ONE Institute stubbornly rejected such attitudes and launched its lonely assault against virtually the entire scholarly and academic establishment, charging them all with sheer ignorance. More than this, it also called for each and every one of the major fields to step forward and defend itself. Defend itself? Could anything be more preposterous?

Thirty-five years later most scholarly disciplines are undergoing major revisions in their understanding of homosexuality and universities from coast to coast are offering courses in "gay studies."

While ONE Institute makes no claim to have brought about such a revolution single-handedly, it insists that the persistent efforts and research work of its dedicated faculty and far-flung student body have played a significant role in these changes. It furthermore asserts that, important as civil rights campaigns and political lobbying may have been, genuine social change does not come about until broad and systematic educational foundations have been laid. News of the day make it painfully clear that myths, legends, and superstitions will arise again and again until they have been exposed and laid to rest by careful and patient education. This book is a tribute to the vanguard which at ONE Institute began to blaze trails of enlightenment thirty-five years ago, trails over which growing numbers are marching today.

i

This ONE Institute Press project has gone through three phases: (1) Early in 1990 start-up funding for which the largest donors were Victor Burner, Christopher Street West, Henry Glazier, Henry Tate, and Joe Weaver. The hiring of Garry Doran, then, Clay Brown, put the text on paper. (2) In 1991 months of frustrating delays arose in the search for someone who would and could do the next and more careful steps. Delays were ended (3) when two ONE members, Calvin Cottam and Reid Rasmussen, brought forward a recently retired aerospace librarian and computer professional, Donald Paul, whose quietly efficient efforts as volunteer Managing Editor have at last brought more than four hundred pages of difficult text and fractious footnotes under control.

Associate Editors David Cameron, working as eagle-eyed proof reader, and Walter Williams have provided sterling assistance in preparing the work for publication.

The watchful and tireless safeguarding of this Editor's time and well-being by John Nojima has provided the working environment without which the job could not have been completed.

W. Dorr Legg
September 6, 1993

INTRODUCTION

E arly in 1950 in Los Angeles, a little group of men and women met to discuss the difficult, seemingly insurmountable problems they had to endure every day of their lives. It was hard enough, they said, for same-sex couples to make a go of it in a disapproving society, but for couples, one white, one black, the situation was much worse.

At that time public attitudes toward blacks appeared to range from passive unconcern and indifference to aggressive dislike and intolerance. The Civil Rights Movement was not politically strong. It would be five years before Rosa Parks refused to move from that bus seat and civil rights for blacks picked up momentum.

Attitudes toward homosexuals were still lower. Even the American Civil Liberties Union officially declared that civil rights did not apply to homosexuals. It would be fully fifteen more years before the Southern California Chapter of ACLU became the first to frame a "Statement of Policy" acknowledging that homosexuals were American Citizens who had Constitutional Rights.[1] It would be nearly twenty years before a police raid on the Stonewall Bar in New York City created a journalistic perception of an event which has been incorrectly called "The Birth of Gay Liberation."

Homosexual acts were legally criminal in every one of the United States in 1950, a legacy of English Common Law which had itself descended from early ecclesiastical law. Churches were virtually unanimous in condemning homosexuals on Biblical grounds. Medical and psychological dogma defined homosexual behavior as ranging all the way from deviance to total pathology. Small wonder, then, that hostility and harassment were the daily lot of inter-racial same-sex couples in 1950.

Knights of the Clocks. One of the little group who had been talking about their problems was a brilliant young black man, Merton Bird, whose idea was that by coming together to form a mutual aid society the group could at the very least offer each other encouragement. The decision was to form a California non-profit corporation and call

---

[1] "Statement of Policy Regarding Sexual Behavior Submitted to the American Civil Liberties Union of Southern California," MAG XIV:1 (January, 1966), pp.4-8. The Statement was authored by Vern L. Bullough, Ph.D., Chairman of the ACLUSC's Committee on Sex and Civil Liberties, and a Director of ONE's affiliate foundation, the Institute for the Study of Human Resources.

it the Knights of the Clocks, a deliberately ambiguous title. In doing so they had established the earliest of the "Gay Community Centers," which are now found all across the country. In addition, it was officially co-sexual and interracial.[2] The Knights continued in active existence for several years and had an official presence at a public meeting of similar organizations as late as 1966.[3]

Mattachine Society. Also in Los Angeles in 1950, Harry Hay and quite a different group had been struggling to establish a program which would include civil rights and political concerns. In November of that year, they launched the first Mattachine Discussion Group which held regularly scheduled meetings.

Sometime later, Dale Jennings, one of the members of that group, was arrested and charged with "lewd conduct," a catch-all term the police often employed at the time. He chose to fight back, admitting in open court in June, 1952 that he was homosexual, but denying that the charge was true. Such unprecedented and brash behavior created quite a stir. The case was eventually dismissed, which amounted to a considerable victory for those days. The news spread rapidly. Soon the original Discussion Group became two, then divided again. Meetings sprang up all over the Los Angeles area. Before long, hundreds of men and women were joining in excited discussion and argument in a veritable flood of social protest and calls for action throughout Southern California.

"Missionary expeditions" were then sent to the Bay Area. Earliest interest and acceptance were found in Oakland.[4] San Francisco joined in later. Fuller accounts of this remarkable social uprising can be read

---

[2] TDY ed. Marvin Cutler (pseud. for W. Dorr Legg) (Los Angeles: ONE, Inc., 1956), pp.93-94. See also Appendix Introduction: Invitation, Knights of the Clocks Social Event, 1951.

[3] Richard Conger (pseud. for W. Dorr Legg), "Where the Mainstream Flows: An Account of the Exciting, High-Quality 1966 Midwinter Sessions of ONE, Traditional Top Event of the Homophile Movement Since 1955," *MAG* XIV:2 (February, 1966), pp.6-12. See, in particular, the list of participant organizations, p.8.

[4] A letter from the Mattachine Society, December 20, 1953, gives its addresses as P.O. Box 1925, LA 53, and P.O. Box 851, Oakland 4, the only Mattachine locations listed as of that date. (Mattachine Foundation Archive, ONE's Baker Memorial Library & Archives)

elsewhere.[5]

ONE, Incorporated. In October, 1952 a third Los Angeles organization was born.[6]   Meeting in The Studio Bookshop on Hollywood Boulevard, founders voted to incorporate as a California non-profit body on November 29, 1952.[7] Martin Block was elected President, Dale Jennings, Vice President, and Don Slater, Secretary. The first two were, or had been, Mattachine members. Two other signators were Merton Bird and W. Dorr Legg, both of them founders and officers of the Knights of the Clocks at the time. The remaining two signators were Antonio Reyes and Bailey Whitaker, whose name appears in documents as Guy Rousseau.[8]

The name this group chose for itself was ONE, after a quotation from Carlyle, "A mystic bond of brotherhood makes all men one."[9] Its primary aim would be to provide public information about homosexuality by means of magazines, books and other printed material. Like the Knights, it would also provide social services. In addition there would be educational programs and research, both in-house and in collaboration with others. More details about this organization can be found elsewhere.[10]

A number of recent books have offered more detailed accounts of

---

[5] TDY pp.9-60.

[6] TDY p.64; also *MAG* VI:10 (October, 1958), p.4,5.

[7] *CONFI* III (March, 1958), p.7.

[8] Martin Block: a writer with a New York background and owner of The Studio Bookshop in Hollywood; Dale Jennings: a professional advertising writer who had traveled extensively as a juvenile violin prodigy; Don Slater: a graduate in English with considerable library work experience; Merton Bird: an accountant; W. Dorr Legg: a landscape architect specializing in urban planning who for several years was Assistant Professor of Landscape Architecture at Oregon State College; Antonio Reyes: a designer of ceramics and an occasional dancer in Mexican night clubs; Bailey Whitaker: a young black man who later earned a Ph.D. in speech therapy for children with learning problems.

[9] Each of the Founders was asked to submit names for the new organization's title. After many had been rejected, Bailey Whitaker proposed the Carlyle quotation. It was unanimously approved at once.

[10] TDY pp.61-86.

the three organizations from the early 1950s described briefly above. It is the purpose here to focus as much as possible only upon development of the educational programs of ONE, Incorporated, leaving general history of the Movement to others.[11]

Four chapters written by W. Dorr Legg make up Part I of the Table of Contents. Chapter 1 traces the four years (1952-1956) during which the somewhat general terms setting forth educational purposes in ONE's Articles of Incorporation[12] gradually brought greater focus and detail to those general purposes until the structure of a formally organized community college type of institution had been developed and was ready to open.

Chapter 2 describes the opening of ONE Institute of Homophile Studies in October, 1956 and covers the period through 1980. Included are the Extension Lecture Series, Extension classes given in other cities, classes given jointly with California State College, Long Beach, the Midwinter Institutes and projects conducted jointly with the Institute for the Study of Human Resources (ISHR).

Chapter 3 describes the launching of ONE Institute Quarterly of Homophile Studies, the issuing of several bibliographic publications and overseas programs.

Chapter 4 outlines the steps leading to the authorization by the California State Department of Education Office of Private Post-Secondary Education in 1981 to offer the M.A. and Ph.D. degrees in Homophile Studies.

The nine chapters of Part II, the major section of this book, consist of selections from papers by ONE Institute faculty and students. These provide an overview of the theory and methodology of Homophile Studies.

These nine major areas of scientific and scholarly investigation have been chosen because each of them makes strong claims to having definitive contributions to offer toward understanding the phenomena of same-sex attraction between humans. The claims made by these scholarly fields are then placed under examination on several different levels. How does each field define itself? What are its goals? Is there a

---

[11] Wayne R. Dynes, *Homosexuality: A Research Guide* (New York: Garland Publishing Inc., 1987), pp.185-192.

[12] See Appendix,1-1: ONE, Incorporated. Articles of Incorporation & By-Laws, 1953.

general consensus that these goals are being met? Specifically, what does each field say about human same-sex attraction and behavior? To what degree do the methods of each of the disciplines qualify for studying human same-sex phenomena? What are the limits of the competency of each? Is there a hierarchy of competencies between the various disciplines? How are criteria for such judgments to be determined?

Homophile Studies asks these and many other questions of each of the nine core areas of general scholarly inquiry, always narrowing the focus to form something of "an independent audit" of what each field says it does, what it has done, and what it is contributing to an understanding of the specific populations and behaviors which are the concern of Homophile Studies.

It is these methods and viewpoints of Homophile Studies which define them as a unique field of specialization owing allegiance to none of the existing established professional disciplines listed in Part II. This approach is both adversarial and a quest for clarification. For example, does sociology adequately explain society as a whole? Can history that makes little or no mention of millions of men and women and their actual lives qualify as being "real" history? The attitudes of various world religions toward a major segment of humanity pose fundamental challenges toward definitions of the very word "religion." The aim of Homophile Studies is to try to clear pathways through areas which many in the past have chosen to ignore and leave unexplored.

The selections presented from ONE Institute faculty and student papers give some indication of what progress has been made and how much more there yet remains in defining this new field for study and research.

The first of the two chapters of Part III, written by W. Dorr Legg, brings together the current theoretical positions in Homophile Studies as they have been developed since the Institute opened in 1956. These are presented mainly in summarized form for easy reference.

The chapter on future directions gives a review of options for creating an ongoing relationship between the Institute and its alumni in the development of standards in the field of Homophile Studies. More general concerns are for the physical facilities of the Institute and its long-range funding. The second part of the chapter is devoted to the Center for Advanced Studies. Plans and expectations for this body are presented in some detail.

The Appendix includes documents, statistics, and archival material not readily available elsewhere.

PART I

TRANSITION FROM

GENERAL EDUCATION PURPOSES

TO A GRADUATE SCHOOL

CHAPTER 1

HOW ONE INSTITUTE BEGAN

A new era regarding homosexuality and homosexuals began in the United States in 1950, the era in which we live today. New eras usually come about as the result of a long period of small changes and the slow decay of timeworn customs and attitudes. This new era had its origins nearly a century earlier in some seemingly unrelated events in Germany. Only recently has their significance been given increasing notice and evaluation.[1]

Some Trends From Germany

To suggest that certain mid-19th century European archaeological and literary matters might have some connection with events in Los Angeles one hundred years later may seem to put a heavy strain on plausibility.

In archaeology of that period the name of Heinrich Schliemann (1822-90) is relevant; he was a German businessman who rose from humble beginnings to become very wealthy. His good fortune enabled him to do whatever interested him, such as travel. That pursuit happened to bring him to California in 1850 just as it was being made a State of the Union. Whether on a whim or whatever, he became an American Citizen at that time and remained so for the rest of his life.

Schliemann had great talent for languages, including both Ancient and Modern Greek. Reading this literature gradually became an obsession with him, especially that of Homer and the stories of Troy. To try to find the ruins of Troy became his lifework.

Schliemann's large archeological expeditions, his diggings, and his immense finds of gold, silver, ivory, and ceramics, soon became legendary and fired the imaginations of people all over Europe. British Prime Minister Gladstone was but one of his devotees. His many books describing various discoveries and methods of working became widely

---

[1] Wayne R. Dynes, *Homosexuality: A Research Guide* (New York: Garland Publishing Inc., 1987), pp.7-17, passim.

read.[2]

Greek literature, Greek art, and Greek ideas became fashionable. Large public buildings in the Greek style were built all over Germany. The Romantic Movement had already made Germans familiar with Greek ideas partly through the widely publicized role of Byron, who had died during the campaign for the liberation of Greece from Turkey somewhat earlier.[3] The strong homoerotic element in German society dating from Frederick the Great[4] and earlier found reinforcement from Greek precedent. The writings of Karl Heinrich Ulrichs (1825-95), published from 1864-70, referred at length to male/male relationships in Greek literature.[5]

German universities were becoming centers for scholarship and learning at the time. Students came to them from all over the world. German became the internationally accepted language of research; even in the United States, anyone studying for a doctorate was required to learn German.

Intellectual vigor and zest for discovery in many directions seemed to be in the air. Medical men were busily identifying diseases previously unknown. Patterns of human behavior, including sexual, began to attract study. "Contrary sexual feelings," tribadism, hermaphroditism, and bestiality were some of the topics being dealt with in German scientific journals.

These journals proliferated rapidly. By the end of the century more than 150 such publications in German were giving extensive attention

---

[2] See for example, Heinrich Schliemann, *Ithaka, der Peloponnes und Traja* (1870); *Troy and its Remains* (1875); *Mycenae* (1877); *Traja* (1884).

[3] Louis Crompton, *Byron and Greek Love: Homophobia in 19th-Century England* (Berkeley: University of California Press, 1985).

[4] Noel I. Garde (pseud.), *Jonathan to Gide: The Homosexual in History* (New York: Vantage Press, 1964); see 'Frederick the Great.' See also Gabriel-Honoré de Riquetti Mirabeau, Comte de, *Histoire Secrète de la Cour de Berlin* (Paris, 1789), 2 vols.

[5] Michael A. Lombardi, "The Translation of the Writings of Karl Heinrich Ulrichs with Special Emphasis on Research on the Riddle of Man-Manly Love," unpublished Ph.D. dissertation (ONE Institute of Homophile Studies, 1984). See also Lombardi, trans. *The Complete Writings of Karl Heinrich Ulrichs* (Jacksonville, Florida: Urania Manuscripts, 1988).

to such topics.[6] Books by anthropologists and medical men were bringing these themes to an increasing audience.[7]

In 1886 German physician Richard von Krafft-Ebing's massive *Psychopathia Sexualis* was published. It was an immediate success. New editions were issued almost yearly well into the next century. There were shorter editions, translations and expurgated versions, although Krafft-Ebing had carefully left many explicit parts of the book in Latin. He and his books soon achieved status as the standard authorities for the newly developing field of sexology, and remained so for many decades. Terms such as paranoia, sadism, masochism and fetichism [sic] have been attributed to Krafft-Ebing. His influence was undoubtedly a major force in establishing what has since been called "the medical model" for defining homosexuality, an attitude which lingers on to some extent even today in psychology, psychiatry and some of the therapies which are concerned with homosexuality.

Emigration to America. At the same time that these developments were occurring in Europe during the latter half of the 19th century, large-scale emigration of German-speaking people to America was underway. Many settled in the states of the Midwest. As late as the 1980 U.S. Census, the largest ethnic group in the populations of eight Midwestern American states was of German ancestry. Cities such as Cincinnati and St. Louis, the latter originally French, became Germanized. German-language newspapers, large Lutheran churches (note the Lutheran Missouri Synod of today), vigorous musical institutions and scholarly bodies were established.

Physicians among the newcomers brought their medical and scientific training, including sexology, with them. Both St. Louis and

---

[6] *An Annotated Bibliography of Homosexuality*, Vern L. Bullough, W. Dorr Legg, Barrett W. Elcano, and James Kepner, eds. (New York: Garland Publishing Inc., 1976), Vol. I, pp.xxiii-xxxvii; II, pp.viii-xii.

[7] See for example, Johannes Ludwig Casper, *Handbuch der gerichtlichen Medicin* (Berlin: Hirschwald, 1856-58), rev. Carl Liman (1881); Albert Eulenberg, *Sexuelle Neuropathie* (Leipzig: Vogel, 1895); Norbert Grabowsky, *Die mannweibliche Natur des Menschen mit Berucksichtigung des psychosexuellen Hermaphroditismus* (Leipzig: Max Spohr, 1894); Gustav Jager, "Colibat," *Handworterbuch der Zoologie, Anthropologie und Ethnologie* (Breslau: Eduard Trewendt, 1880); L.S.A.M. Von Römer, *Untersuch ungen über der Libido sexualis* (1897).

Cincinnati soon had medical journals of their own.[8] Major universities existed in both cities by the mid-19th century.[9]

Emphasis has been given here to the years before 1900, which are sometimes overlooked or given little mention in favor of the period from 1900 up to World War I, when the writings of Magnus Hirschfeld and his associates at the Institute for Sexual Science (medical research) in Berlin became widely known. Iwan Bloch, August (Auguste) Forel, Benedict Friedlaender, and Edward Westermarck are but a few of the names which became prominent during this later period.

They were soon overshadowed, however, by another German importation whose influence upon the lives of homosexuals and public attitudes toward homosexuality in America remains yet to be fully examined: the "Age of Freud."

As a witness in person to virtually the entire span of this period in the United States, some personal recollections are included here of both the rise and decline of Freudian influence and authority.

When first read as a teenager, *The Interpretation of Dreams*[10] seemed arcanely interesting, but had something of an otherworldly aura of seeming not quite real. This reader felt none of the thunderclaps and great insights which some said they were experiencing. Instead, there was frustration and impatience as other Freud works came into the bookstores. "What do they say to me?" was the question. "Does this somewhat wordy man offer anything more than an unending series of speculative hypotheses?" Having read some of the earlier books cited above had perhaps taken the edge off Freud for this teenage critic.

However, Freud was being widely read and talked about in many circles. Repression, sublimation, the unconscious, transference – what later has been called psychobabble – entered the language. Neuroses, fixations, complexes, infantile sexuality and penis envy were the slightly dangerous topics often discussed during the 1920s.

Too many novelists and playwrights put Freud into their writings, it was said. Eugene O'Neill was accused of leaving the Freudian

---

[8] *Alienist* and *Neurologist*, St. Louis; *Lancet*, Cincinnati.

[9] University of Cincinnati, founded 1819; Washington University, St. Louis, founded 1853.

[10] Sigmund Freud, *The Interpretation of Dreams*, trans. A.A. Brill (London: Hogarth Press, 1913).

machinery all too visible in his plays. The tortured characters of D. H. Lawrence were nothing but the author's own unresolved sexual problems, according to some armchair Freudians. Freud's writings did provoke and without any doubt bring the long-forbidden topic of homosexuality ever closer into the open.

Then came the Great Depression of the 1930s. Sheer survival became the most important subject during much of that decade. Political disputation and social changes largely usurped public attention.

The Rise of Nazi Power. A social change which was intruding into public notice with ominous force toward the end of the decade was the rise of Nazi power. Its unrelenting pressure against non-Aryans and anyone accused of associating with non-Aryans grew ever more intense. Just four months after Hitler became Chancellor in 1933, Hirschfeld's Institute for Sexual Science in Berlin was vandalized, and the contents of its massive Library, accumulated through many years of effort, were thrown into the square and torched with great celebration. While Hirschfeld and other staff members had already fled, 29-year-old Christopher Isherwood witnessed the event and described it to us years later at ONE Institute.[11]

As World War II loomed, then swept over all of Europe, incredulous disbelief gave way to virtual panic. From Warsaw to Vienna there was an exodus of writers, artists, musicians and, above all, psychiatrists, psychoanalysts, psychologists, many of them Jewish professional men and women. To England, to Argentina, and to the safety of the United States they went by the hundreds, if not thousands, in a Diaspora eclipsed in public memory only by the far larger dimensions of the Holocaust which followed.

Many of those coming to America stayed in New York. It is less well-known that the Los Angeles area ranked second as a destination.

---

[11] Christopher Isherwood first spoke at ONE Institute on February 7, 1965, later serving from 1976-84 as a Director of ONE's affiliate foundation, the Institute for the Study of Human Resources. At ONE, Inc.'s 30th Anniversary Celebration and the first ONE Institute Graduate School Convocation, January 30, 1982, the Graduate School conferred its first honorary Doctor of Letters degree (Litt.D.) on Isherwood. See also Christopher Isherwood, *Christopher and His Kind*, 1929-1939 (New York: Farrar, Straus Giroux, 1976), much of which was researched in ONE Institute's Blanche M. Baker Memorial Library and Archives.

It has been well publicized that world celebrities like Stravinsky, Schoenberg, and Heifetz had homes in Los Angeles, but they were far outnumbered by writers, lesser musicians, artists, and great numbers of professionals: the medical people, psychologists and psychotherapists of all persuasions, Freudian and other. Telephone books from that time listed more psychoanalysts in Beverly Hills than any other city except New York.

Some of the newcomers found placement in local universities. Others joined the staffs of hospitals and correctional institutions. Some cynics said that the principal qualification for status as an "authority" in psychotherapy and sexual matters was a thick German accent. The effect of this importation of European professionals upon the lives and well-being of homosexuals has not yet been given the careful study and investigation it merits.[12]

The Kinsey Effect

In 1948 a book from the Midwestern heartland hit the scientific world, jolting public notice like an earthquake. Studies of sexual matters would never be the same again. For that matter, neither would many time-honored scientific methods.

Sexual Behavior in the Human Male[13] by Alfred C. Kinsey, Wardell B. Pomeroy, and Clyde E. Martin had a 21-page bibliography containing two Sigmund Freud entries and several by Magnus Hirschfeld. Other German sources were given duly respectful notice, but the wide range of numerous newer names, along with the innumerable statistical tables and graphs derived from thousands of interviews, gave clear notice of a change in methods. These cool and dispassionate

---

[12] Jarrell C. Jackman, and Carla M. Bordman eds., *The Muses Flee Hitler: Cultural Transfer and Adaptation, 1930-1945* (Washington: Smithsonian Institution Press, 1983).

[13] Alfred C. Kinsey, Wardell B. Pomeroy, and Clyde E. Martin, *Sexual Behavior in the Human Male* (Philadelphia: W.B. Saunders Co., 1948).

procedures suggested new ways of studying human sexuality, and seemed to imply that some of the older approaches were deemed no longer adequate.

Most jarring of all the Kinsey findings to the general public was heavily–documented evidence that in terms of "physical contact to the point of orgasm, at least 37 per cent of the male population has some homosexual experience."[14]

The enormous impact of this book on American public consciousness has been compared to the effect of Darwin's *The Origin of Species* in 1858. As a witness to some of the innumerable sermons delivered in churches of many denominations, as well as the countless scientific and pseudo-scientific attacks against the book itself, its findings, and the authors, was to become aware of the deep changes of consciousness on sexual matters the Kinsey book had set in motion. No in-depth analysis of the specifically homosexual aspects of the Kinsey impact has been readily available, although it would have been welcome to have had such a book.

Before 1950 there were no ongoing organizations in the United States serving the needs and interests of homosexual men and women, although two brief earlier attempts can be documented.[15]

The Kinsey book and the public attention it aroused, particularly concerning homosexuality, were without doubt very important factors in preparing the way for the successful organizations which did appear in 1950.[16]

---

[14] Kinsey, p.623.

[15] TDY pp.90-91. See also "The Feminine Viewpoint, By and About Women," *MAG* VII:6 (June, 1959), pp.8-10; Henry Gerber, "The Society for Human Rights – 1925," *MAG* X:9 (September, 1962), pp.5-11; Jim Coughenour, "The Life and Times of an Ordinary Hero," *Windy City Times* (June 22, 1989), pp.60, 62.

[16] See Introduction.

As Educational Objectives Evolved

The main focus here is to point out the steps by which the original rather generalized statements of educational purposes set forth in Section Two, Article B of ONE's 1952 Articles of Incorporation[17] evolved by successive stages over a four-year period into the community college type of facility, ONE Institute of Homophile Studies.

The main source for tracing these steps can be found in the pages of *ONE Magazine*, which premiered in January, 1953. The only other publication circulated by ONE during this time was an advertising flier.[18] The attention and energies of ONE's founding group were more than fully taken up with the enterprise of publishing a 32-page periodical once a month.

A selection of articles appearing in *ONE Magazine's* first year had no specific reference to formal education. The principals still gave no signs of thinking in such terms.[19]

An important move taken during 1953, however, was the renting of an office in an old building in downtown Los Angeles open to the public during regular business hours. As a result of this visibility and accessibility, ONE gained in reputation. No other organization in the United States had taken such a step nor, so far as is known, had any comparable organization in Europe. This move greatly enhanced the new organization's outreach to a wide range of social and ethnic contacts, evidence of ONE's firm commitment to its objectives.

The second year brought several additions to ONE's staff, most notably two gifted women: Irma "Corky" Wolf, who became an Editor writing as Ann Carll Reid,[20] and Joan Corbin, who began a 10-year career as *ONE Magazine's* Art Director, signing her work as Eve

---

[17] See Appendix 1-1: ONE, Incorporated. Articles of Incorporation & By-Laws, 1953.

[18] See Appendix 1-2: Advertising Flier, pub. 1952.

[19] See Appendix 1-3: *ONE Magazine*, Representative Articles, v.I, 1953.

[20] *MAG* V:10 (November, 1957), p.16-19.

Elloree.[21] These two women attracted writers, artists and many other women drawn to ONE's often exhilarating and always challenging environment. Some became Directors and Officers of the Corporation, making essential contributions to the work of the organization. A full account of "The Women of ONE," as they called themselves, remains yet to be written.

What is clear, however, is that by 1954 *ONE Magazine* became better looking, as longer and more interesting articles became available to the Editors, and the Editorial Board was enlarged. Despite the innovative changes underway, the topic of formal education still had received no direct mention in the monthly's Tables of Contents until October 15, 1954, the second anniversary of ONE's founding, when it was announced that ONE's Voting Members had adopted a motion "To hold a series of forums dealing with scientific, philosophical, legal and social questions pertaining to homosexuality."[22] This was the first action implementing the educational objectives of ONE's Articles of Incorporation, although it did not significantly move beyond the relatively diffuse intent of ONE's founders. Just five days after this vote had been taken, the United States Government served notice that the October, 1954, issue of *ONE Magazine* had been impounded by the Postmaster of Los Angeles as obscene, and unmailable.[23]

ONE promptly responded to what it viewed as a flagrant violation of Freedom of the Press, as provided for by the U.S. Constitution, and brought suit against the Postmaster of Los Angeles. The litigation sought to compel him to release the impounded copies of *ONE Magazine* and deliver them in performance of his duty as an employee of the citizens of this country. It should be noted that this action was taken by ONE as *Plaintiff*, rather than as *Defendant* entering a plea for relief. These two moral and philosophical positions are in radical opposition to each other: at issue was the long-standing legal assumption which held in essence that homosexual men and women as deviants or perverts were not full citizens with Constitutional Rights. ONE's suit was in total opposition to such a legal fiction.

---

[21] *MAG* V:6 (June/July, 1957), cover.

[22] Minutes, ONE, Inc. Board of Directors, October 15, 1954. (ONE's Baker Memorial Library & Archives) See also Appendix 1-4: *ONE Magazine Representative Articles*, v.II, 1954.

[23] Minutes, ONE, Inc. Board of Directors, November 12, 1954.

Psychiatrist Blanche M. Baker, M.D., Ph.D.

Legal skirmishes not withstanding, ONE's little downtown office continued to be open as usual. One morning a woman of impressive appearance came in and introduced herself as Blanche M. Baker, a psychiatrist from San Francisco. "I have been hearing of your work," she said. "It is very interesting to me. My own profession has been at a dead end for 20 years. I have come to learn." With this astonishingly unconventional preamble, a warm and friendly two-way learning relationship began which continued during the rest of her life.

First Midwinter Institute. Early in discussions with her, she agreed to take part in one of the "forums" ONE's officers had so recently authorized. Other program details were quickly scheduled, announcements sent out, and on January 29, 1955, in Los Angeles' Biltmore Hotel, the first of ONE's Midwinter Institutes was held.[24]

No one who was there will ever forget that event. It was not only the talk by Dr. Baker, a dynamic woman whom her husband, physical therapist William F. Baker, referred to as Brunhilde. Nor was it her dramatic opening statement, "I am Blanche M. Baker. I have come here from San Francisco to be with you because I am impressed with what you are doing and I want you to know that my husband and I are *ONE* with you." There was a general feeling that they were witnesses to a very special and, as it later proved, a historic occasion. "Where did you get this woman?" UCLA Professor of Clinical Psychology Evelyn Hooker whispered to one listener.

There was loud applause and an excited buzz as Dr. Baker ended her talk. A number of teachers and other professional people were in the audience, as well as Eric Julber, ONE's brilliant young attorney, Gerald Heard, an English writer of the Huxley-Isherwood-Auden circle, and a clergyman or two. ONE had moved beyond the "little organization" stage into a much broader arena.

---

[24] See Appendix 1-5: 1955 Midwinter Institute. Letter of announcement and invitation.

Education Division of ONE, Incorporated. While the Voting Members had already given official status to ONE's Education Division as one of ONE's organizational components,[25] the Division gave no report at the 1955 Annual Meeting.[26]   Dr. Baker's talk and her comments at both the Luncheon and the Dinner Banquet that evening were a catalyst for bringing into focus ideas and discussions which had been floating around for some time.

Education soon became a major topic of discussion, not only at ONE, but with others. Suggestions for an educational structure were received on May 17 and May 19, 1955, from the Mattachine Society's Harry Hay.[27]   ONE's Officers did not feel, however, that his ideas fitted in with those which Dr. Baker's talk had stimulated them to start developing.

They prepared a roughly sketched, undated proposal, apparently completed in early June, 1955, somewhat recklessly proposing that ONE's Education Division immediately embark on a "Summer Term, 1955," giving attention to "The Homosexual and Society" for the professional and nonprofessional student. The plan called for 12 weeks of sessions, June 28 - August 4, 1955, viewing the main subjects in terms of History, Sociology, Anthropology and Psychology.[28]

Enthusiasm, however, was soon tempered by prudence. No sessions were held in 1955. The Education Division was directed back to the drawing board with the recommendation to proceed with more discretion, and to return to the Directors only after a thorough analysis and a comprehensive plan had been prepared. As a result of this injunction, the most practical approach turned out to be the staging of another Midwinter Institute, which was held January 27, 1956, in conjunction with ONE's Fourth Annual Meeting.

The report of the Annual Meeting and Midwinter Institute published

---

[25] N.b., *MAG* III:4 (April, 1955), cover verso.

[26] "Report of the Annual Meeting," *MAG* III:2 (February, 1955), pp.6-7; "Report from the Library," p.16; "Report on Social Services," p.17.

[27] See Appendix 1-6: Suggested Prospectus for Division of Education.

[28] Proposed announcement: 1955 Summer Term. (ONE's Baker Memorial Library & Archives)

in *ONE Magazine*[29] shows a much more complete and detailed program than in the previous year.

Merritt M. Thompson, Ph.D., Emeritus Professor of Education

The most important part of the day, however, was not in the printed program at all. During a break period, this writer noticed a distinguished senior gentleman sitting by himself, and spoke to him. He was Merritt M. Thompson, Emeritus Professor of Education at the University of Southern California.[30]   Dr. Thompson expressed great interest in the day's events and offered to help the fledgling Education Division.

The Pivotal Relationship. Thus began the pivotal relationship in moving ONE's still somewhat unfocused program of educational activities into becoming a unique and carefully designed college. In playing this role, Dr. Thompson helped create, literally from the ground up, an institution which stands alone in the world, its purpose, goals, and methods carefully well-defined.

A renowned scholar, Dr. Thompson came to ONE at the age of 72.   Although retired after 50 years as a teacher and University Professor, he was full of energy. During meetings and discussions, both at ONE and at his home, we came to learn more about Dr. Thompson's remarkable and varied career.

It began in 1905 at a rural school in New Jersey; then, as Supervising Teacher of Primary Schools in the Philippines, where from 1906 to 1908 he took part in establishing a national school system for the Islands, a U.S. Government project.   He told us about many

---

[29] "Fourth Annual Meeting [and] 1956 Midwinter Institute," *MAG* IV:1 (January, 1956), p.4.

[30] "65 Club Biographies," University Archives, University of Southern California (n.d.). Recollections provided by ONE Institute faculty. All articles authored by Merritt M. Thompson in ONE publications were signed Thomas M. Merritt.

decisions and policies which had to be developed to fit those unusual situations and circumstances.

Fifty years later this writer has asked taxi drivers and others in Manila how they had learned English. The answer invariably was, "It is the language of instruction [in the schools]," a policy that was established in 1906, Dr. Thompson told us. In the Philippines his natural ability with languages enabled him to become fluent in the native Tagalog.

From 1911-15 and later in 1919-1921, Dr. Thompson was assigned to Peru to help reorganize a chaotic school system there. Already fluent in Spanish, he also learned the native Quechua.

Other languages in his command included French, Italian, Dutch, German and the Scandinavian languages. At ONE, these skills enabled him to provide abstracts and full translations from the many overseas publications which were already coming to ONE's Library by the mid-1950s.

At USC from 1921, eventually becoming a Professor of Education, Dr. Thompson chaired the School of Education's Committee on Admission to Doctoral Candidacy for many years and contributed to Graduate Seminars in education, sociology, psychology and philosophy. Among his many off-campus activities were involvement with the John Dewey Society, the American Civil Liberties Union, and the Humanist Society. Most notable among his many publications is *The History of Education*,[31] which while written in 1933 was still going through many reprintings in the 1960s.

During the Spring and Summer of 1956, meetings with Dr. Thompson continued to refine details for what it was then realized must become a specialized college in a radically new field. "Structure the field," Dr. Thompson kept saying over and over. "Define your terms, for you are setting them," he told those who took part in these discussion sessions, which continued on through the Summer of 1956. Some dropped out, but the core group of those through all the meetings were Merritt, as he preferred to be addressed, Julian Underwood (Woody), Jim Kepner, and this writer.

Woody's degree was in mathematics and philosophy. Many of his articles will be cited in Part II. Jim was writer of the monthly "Tangents" column in *ONE Magazine*, as well as articles on Whitman,

---

[31] Merritt M. Thompson, *The History of Education* (New York: Barnes & Noble Inc., College Outline Series, 1933).

religion and other subjects. These too will be cited in Part II.

Merritt's calm guidance and vast erudition patiently steered the core group through endless argumentative and sometimes wildly impractical sessions. The spirit of John Dewey was often present, for the USC School of Education was a stronghold of Dewey-influenced theories of "modern education." Insights which Merritt contributed from his many years of work in the Third World added a special flavor that made the meetings endlessly fascinating and stimulating.

This writer's own years of college teaching gave him a special appreciation of just how remarkable these meetings were, and the great good fortune by which we could take part in them. A growing realization of the newness of what was being developed, as well as the excitement of exploration and discovery, never slackened.

In late Summer, ONE's Board gave these meetings formal status as the Division of Education Planning Committee. The minutes of the September 25, and October 4, 1956, meetings summarized decisions of the preceding months and recommended a nine-week Fall Term pilot project open only to members of ONE's staff.[32]

ONE's Voting Members adopted the Committee's recommendations on October 15, 1956, the fourth anniversary of ONE's founding. The project was given the name "ONE Institute of Homophile Studies." It would have "a Dean in charge of academic matters, a Director to handle administrative affairs, and a Secretary – all officers of the Institute."

The first class was held October 22, 1956, with fourteen persons present. ONE Institute of Homophile Studies had opened its doors.

---

[32] Minutes, ONE, Inc. Board of Directors, September 25, and October 4, 1956. (ONE's Baker Memorial Library & Archives)

CHAPTER 2

EDUCATIONAL METHODS AND CURRICULUM

W hat does the phrase Homophile Studies mean? This volume's purpose is to define them: what they are, what they do. Each of the chapters in Part II will focus upon and amplify one of the areas relating to the field as a whole. A critical step-by-step examination is necessary in defining this new academic discipline.

Problems of Terminology. The problem of terminology has existed as long as there have been written records, and as long as both male-to-male and female-to-female intimate bodily contacts have been observed. An immense lexicon of terms used to describe these contacts has made its way into print from the various cultures of the world. A veritable Babel of religious, nationalistic, historical, occupational, mythological, literary, bawdy, and other sources has contributed to the confusion. *Tribade, sodomite, fricatrice, pederast, invert, pervert, Dioning, lesbian, fellator, catamite, sapphist, Urning, bugger* and *androgyne* are but a very few of the troubled words in an almost endless glossary.

When specialized studies of sexual behavior began to emerge in the mid-19th century, notably among the German-speaking parts of Europe,[1] tidy systematists threw up their hands at such an unmanageable situation. A physician, variously calling himself Kertbeny/Benkert, is credited with coining the word "homosexual" in 1867. This attempt at improving matters rapidly acquired widespread scientific and eventually general usage. It remains listed today in more bibliographies and indexes than any other term, although rejected by some scientists almost from the start as "a barbarously hybrid word." [2]

Somewhat later the word "Homophile" made one of its earliest appearances in scientific literature. There is no indication that this use of the word was intended as an improved alternate or a replacement for homosexual. It occurs in Magnus Hirschfeld's *Die Homosexualität*, sometimes called "Encyclopedia." In a section classifying sex-object preferences, he writes, "We could call one type Homophile: those who

---

[1] See Chap.1, pp.10ff above.

[2] *Oxford English Dictionary*, Supplement (Oxford: Oxford University Press, 1971), p.472. The characterization is attributed to Havelock Ellis (1859-1939).

seek their own mirror images as sex objects."[3]   This definition of Homophile does not seem to have found wide acceptance in sexological literature. Kurt Hiller's comprehensive summaries do not mention it,[4] nor do Kinsey's indexes.[5] The mirror-image concept did find its way at a later date into the writings of psychologists such as Edmund Bergler and others who have been given more popular than scientific acclaim.

The works of Hirschfeld and many other sexologists enjoyed a period of considerable acceptance and renown. In England the writings of Edward Carpenter, Havelock Ellis, and Norman Haire, among others, were also being widely circulated, but the increasingly public visibility of homosexuals themselves took place largely in the Germanic parts of Europe. *The Berlin Stories*[6] of Christopher Isherwood well described some of this period. Marcel Proust's novels portray a somewhat veiled description of homosexuality in Paris around the same time.[7] During the 1920s and 1930s there were many organizations for homosexuals established on the Continent and elsewhere; some had publications which achieved substantial circulations for many years. All of this began to change with the advent of Nazi power in 1933.[8]

---

[3] Magnus Hirschfeld, *Die Homosexualität des Mannes und des Weibes*, 2nd ed. (Berlin: L. Marcus Verlagsbuchhandlung, 1920), p.1027. See also "Classification of Homosexuals as to Age Preferences and Sex Acts," trans. Henry Gerber, *QTLY* V:1 (Winter 1962), p.20-29. Gerber's translation includes Hirschfeld's definition of "homophile" as well as passages from the 1st edition (1914).

[4] Kurt Hiller, "Zur Frage Bezeichnung," *Der Kreis*, XIV, No. 8 (1946), p.2-6.

[5] Kinsey et al, *Sexual Behavior in the Human Male* (Philadelphia: Saunders, 1948) pp.612-617.

[6] Christopher Isherwood, *The Berlin Stories* (New York: New Directions, 1946).

[7] See, e.g., Marcel Proust, *Cities of the Plain*, trans. C. K. Scott Moncrieff (New York: A. and C. Boni, 1927).

[8] Johannes Werres, *Keine Zeit für gute Freunde. Homosexuelle in Deutschland, 1933-1969* (Frankfurt: Forster-Verlag, 1982).

As noted,[9] magazines, books and printed matter of any sort referring to sexuality in other than traditional terms were suspended throughout Europe from the time of the Nazi ascension until the end of World War II, even in England. Only neutral Switzerland withstood the onslaught. Its well-edited *Der Kreis*, a monthly magazine produced in German by an organization of the same name, continued in Zurich without any break. French and English sections were added at later dates.

C.O.C. and the Word Homophile. After the second defeat of Germany and the end of World War II, many of the homosexual organizations which had been driven underground by the Nazis became active again. Among the earliest of these was in Amsterdam, where in September, 1946, members of a pre-war group resumed their former activities, calling themselves the *Cultuur en ontspannings Centrum* (C.O.C.). Shortly afterward they started the monthly *VRIENDSCHAP*, with articles, news, commentary, and artwork. It continued publication for around twenty more years, many issues of which are preserved in ONE's Baker Memorial Library. C.O.C., the organization, continues today and issues several different publications.

In 1946 the use of the word homosexual was greatly criticized by many. Coined in the 1860s by a physician, half-Latin, half-Greek in derivation, its medical connotations of mental illness, abnormality, and pathology had long been found objectionable.[10] Yet no suitable replacement had been found.

During the next three years there were many discussions and an extensive exchange of letters between various persons in the C.O.C. and elsewhere aimed at finding a better term.

The word Homophile which was finally chosen is based upon two Greek roots, *homos* (the same) and *philos* (love for), in contrast to the opposite term, *heterophile*, love between those opposite genders.

Use of the word spread rapidly in many parts of Europe, where it continues today. In America the first issue of *ONE Magazine* in

---

[9] See Chap.1, pp.13ff above.

[10] For a summary of such objections see Jean-Claude Féray, "Un Histoire Critique du Mot Homosexualité," *Arcadie*, No. 325 (January, 1981), pp.11-21; No. 326 (February, 1981), pp.115-124; No. 327 (March, 1981), pp.171-181; No. 328 (April, 1981), pp.246-258.

January, 1953 used the word.[11] In 1956 ONE's organized educational
activities were given the name ONE Institute of Homophile Studies.
There has been so much misunderstanding and confusion surrounding
the meanings and history of the word that facts which can be verified
are presented here.

The most reliable source of information is two Dutch writers,
Warmendam and Koenders.[12] These authors indicate that Jaap Van
Leeuwen (who wrote as Arent van Santhorst) is "probably not" the
originator of the word, as has sometimes been claimed. They suggest
that he may have found the term in *Hetero und Homophilie*, a 33-page,
1924 pamphlet by Karl-Guenther Heimsoth, whom they describe as a
Dutch psychoanalyst. However, they do not document that Van
Leeuwen had either read or even seen the Heimsoth work. Thus the
Heimsoth connection is entirely conjectural.[13]

What they do produce are letters between Van Leeuwen, Schorer,
the Swiss *Der Kreis*, and memos to Engelschman (who wrote as Bob
Angelo), extending back as far as 1937.[14]

They give no information or dates about associations Van Leeuwen
had with Hirschfeld and his famous *Institut* in Berlin, or whether he
knew of Hirschfeld's use of the word "Homophile" as early as 1920,
perhaps earlier.

The record is clear, however, that Niek Engelschman made the
actual decision to use the word Homophile in the August, 1949 pages
of *VRIENDSCHAP*. Therefore, neither Van Leeuwen nor Heimsoth
can be said to have "introduced the term" into wide public use.

Whether any of those at C.O.C. realized in 1949 what a radical
thing they had done is not known. With a simple linguistic gesture they
had swept away perversion, inversion and pathology. They had moved
discussion away from the endless pages of medical speculations which
existed, into basic and non-judgmental considerations of relationships,
love relationships.

It was a Declaration of Independence empowering a hitherto stigmatized segment of society to define itself in its own terms. The word
Homophile lifted discussion out of the age-old grip of medical, psycho-

---

[11] "Die Insel," trans A.E. Galbraith, *MAG* I:1 (January, 1953), p.5.

[12] Hans Warmendam and Pieter Koenders, *Cultuur en ontspanning, het
COC 1946-1966* (Amsterdam: 1987), tr. Willimien Ruygrok.

logical and theological obloquy onto the levels of philosophical, moral, and ethical discussion, properly befitting full-fledged members of society.

Copies of *VRIENDSCHAP* in ONE's Baker Memorial Library show that by 1950 the term Homophile was being used without any need for definition. In Zurich, *Der Kreis* was doing the same. *Arcadie*, founded in Paris in 1954, officially called itself "Mouvement Homophile de France." The word continues in regular use all over Europe today. For example, a recent issue of *Fritt Fram* in Oslo contains such headlines as "Homofile har rett til" and "Homofile I Fjellveggen."[13] Even more significant is the fact that teen-agers in the streets of Amsterdam today will say, "I am Homophile," lest there be any doubt as to their identities. Without question the word has acquired an oral as well as written currency in large areas of the world today. Those who, like historian John D'Emilio and other exponents of the concept of a so-called "Homophile phase" in history, may not persuade everyone that the phrase "in the United States" gives their concept validity. The continuing activity of ONE Institute and its *Quarterly of Homophile Studies*, lectures, symposia and international conferences are not to be so lightly dismissed.[14]

An Introduction to Homophile Studies. The very first course offered at ONE Institute was entitled *An Introduction to Homophile Studies*.[15] The word Homophile has been embedded in the curriculum ever since. Fourteen staff members met in nine weekly sessions of two or more hours each. At each session, syllabus/outlines were made available. These presented aspects of the educational theory embodied in Homophile Studies, covering individual disciplines at the stage of development each had achieved at that time.

---

[13] *Fritt Fram* (July/August, 1989), pp.5, 10; also pp.13, 46.

[14] John D'Emilio, *Sexual Politics, Sexual Communities: The Making of a Homosexual Minority in the United States, 1940-1970* (Chicago: University of Chicago Press, 1983).

[15] *CONFI* I (November, 1956), p.3. Instructors for the first term were Merritt Thompson, Jim Kepner, Julian Underwood, Harry Hay, anthropologist Don Leiffer, and this editor.

The First Session[16] focused upon biology and medicine, briefly outlining its areas of concern and relevance. A modest bibliography was included.

The Second Session was concerned with history. "The purpose of this and future sessions is to find for the homosexual a place in history," stated the syllabus. A bibliography was included which gave clear indication that investigation of Homophile History must look beyond Europe and North America to include Asia, Africa and Latin America. A critique of much existing historical writing was already implicit.

Session Three on psychology was much more detailed in presentation, a natural result coming from the personal experiences of everyone in the class. Several were not at all hesitant in citing long lists of the sins of omission and commission from their own reading and contacts with therapists and psychologists.

The Fourth Session provided a substantial outline and bibliography for the disciplines of sociology and anthropology. A number of full courses based on the pioneering perspectives of this first effort were developed in subsequent years at ONE Institute, most notably the classes on various aspects of the *Sociology of Homosexuality.*

Session Five on law also involved all class members on a personal and emotional level, either because of their own disastrous conflicts with the law or the experiences of close friends. To many at that time, law was the problem, legal reform the solution.

Religion, the topic of Session Six, again evoked the emotional involvement of nearly every class member. Religion and the Church were charged with intolerance, hypocrisy, and arrogance in laying claim to infallibility and the authority of Higher Law.

Literature and the Arts, topic for the Seventh Session, fared better in that there was some agreement that writers who tried faithfully to reflect their own times might be trusted to be more honest than exponents of some of the preceding topics.

Between the Seventh and the concluding Sessions, the Division of Education Planning Committee convened to review the progress of the class work to that date and to make plans for the future. The structure of ONE, Inc. itself was examined, and the work of the Education

---

[16] An Introduction to Homophile Studies. Class Outlines for the Initial Term: 1956. (ONE's Baker Memorial Library & Archives)

Division spelled out in some detail. Non-professional and professional courses were differentiated and an extensive roster of ONE Institute publications proposed.

The Eighth Session on philosophy evidenced the professional hand of Dr. Thompson. The syllabus asked, "What does the Homophile need and/or expect from philosophy?"

Session Nine was entitled "Programmatic." It examined "The Future Programs of the American Homophile, of ONE Institute, [and] of ONE Incorporated," raising important questions about the relationships of each of these to the others. Several pages of outlines reviewed such questions in the light of what had been achieved during the first ONE Institute class term.

It was the ONE Midwinter Institute in January, 1955[17] which marked ONE's inaugural venture into the field of education. Earlier pages here have given notice also of the 1956 Midwinter Institute events,[18] which fortunately led to Merritt Thompson's long and central role in the development of an institution of higher education at ONE.

The January 26-27, 1957, Midwinter Institute sessions, with the theme "The Homosexual Answers His Critics,"[19] continued the pattern of having papers read, round-table discussions, community involvement, a banquet and theater performances, the blueprint which has characterized so many of these Midwinter Institute events.[20]

The Midwinter Institutes have been regarded as forming an integral and important part of ONE Institute's class work. They were placed within the Division of Extension and Special Programs, along with the ONE Institute Sunday Afternoon Lecture Series, as a means of meeting general interest in homophilia at a non-degree level.

Each succeeding year has seen several hundred persons attending these ONE Institute programs as "short-term students." This form of mass adult education is found today as part of the non-degree programs

---

[17] See Chap.1, p.18 above.

[18] See Chap.1, pp.19ff above. Also see Appendix, 2-1: 1956 Midwinter Institute and Fourth Annual Meeting. Letter of announcement and invitation.

[19] See Appendix, 2-2: Program, 1957 Midwinter Institute, "The Homosexual Answers his Critics."

[20] "1957 Midwinter Institute and Fifth Annual Meeting," *MAG* V:2 (February, 1957), p.11.

of hundreds of colleges and universities across the country. For Homophile Studies their importance can hardly be overestimated. They provide a way of helping large numbers of men and women "come out of the closet." They also are a reliable, non-judgmental source of information for the community at large. These Extension Division events have drawn substantial attendance and contributed greatly to the improving social and legal status of the Homophile Community which exists in Southern California today.

On February 6, 1957, the Planning Committee again held a meeting, this time to complete preparations for the ONE Institute Spring Term, which had started the day before. ONE Institute's second semester of classes repeated *An Introduction to Homophile Studies*, opening it for the first time to "outside" students. Among other items dealt with by the Committee was the need for a "glossary for immediate use of ONE Institute students." There also was discussion of the possibility of translating Hirschfeld's "Encyclopedia," a copy of which had been presented to ONE's Library by Dr. Thompson. Also proposed was the development of an *Encyclopedia of Homosexuality* by ONE Institute. The Committee recommended that an extracurricular Sunday Afternoon Lecture Series to supplement the survey course be initiated and that it be offered to the public.[21]

The Planning Committee held three more meetings: February 27, March 1, and March 4, 1957. The February 27 meeting was devoted mostly to detailed proposals for the administration and conduct of ONE Institute. An expansion of the 1957-58 academic year to 36 weeks was proposed, with the survey course extended to two semesters for better coverage. Suggestions for extension classes in other cities, correspondence courses, and the development of a "quarterly" publication for the presentation of scholarly articles were proposed as well.[22]

On March 4, 1957, the final meeting of the Planning Committee was held. A report was prepared and submitted to ONE's Directors which listed detailed proposals for Institute Administration, Faculty and

---

[21] Minutes, Planning Committee Meeting, February 6, 1957. (ONE's Baker Memorial Library & Archives)

[22] Minutes, Planning Committee Meeting, February 27, March 1, and March 4, 1957. (ONE's Baker Memorial Library & Archives)

Curriculum.[23]   In recommending that the elected Directors of ONE, Inc. become the governing body of ONE Institute, the Planning Committee dissolved, its duties completed.

On February 5, 1957, then, ONE Institute's second semester began its eighteen-week term. A detailed listing of class schedules is not intended here. What will be noticed is the first presentation of each new course in the order of its being added to the curriculum. This incremental method will document the steps which have been taken in expanding and defining Homophile Studies from the earliest classes until today.

During that busy 1957 spring semester, an article in *ONE Magazine*[24] gave an overview of what had been somewhat quietly going on with ONE Institute's formal educational programs and the thinking behind them. By that time 3,000 subscriber and newsstand copies of *ONE Magazine* per month were being read by a considerable multiple of that number of people. It was felt that it was high time to tell this larger audience that adult education for Homophiles was very much a topic of the day and that Homophiles needed to learn more about themselves, as well as their brothers and sisters all over the world.

Homosexuality in History.   The first new addition to the curriculum was *Homosexuality in History*, a two-semester course given first in the Fall of 1957 and Spring of 1958. Its content was described in the first catalogue, *Announcement and Schedule of Classes,* as, "Contrasting social attitudes in Paleolithic and Neolithic times; emerging customs and institutions. Attitudes toward homosexuality in Mesopotamia, Egypt, India and China. Greece and some of its great Homophile figures. The rise and decline of Rome. The clash of pagan and Christian sex attitudes. The story of Inca and Aztec homosexuality. Modern European history. Homophilia in United States."

As can be readily understood, a range of such scope as described above could be only sketchily presented in a two-semester course. It was later expanded as a four-semester survey, with a number of one-semester classes added to give more detailed examination to periods

---

[23] Ibid.

[24] W. Dorr Legg, "Education Badly Needed," *MAG* V:5 (May, 1957), pp.7-9.

of special interest.

The aim of *Homosexuality in History* has been to examine aspects often omitted from "standard histories," or presented in so abbreviated a form or with such euphemistic terms as to be essentially unintelligible. Students soon discovered that an immense amount of revision would be required before it might be said that history could itself claim some solid degree of credibility.

Problems such as correct and accurate translations of ancient and classic texts were soon encountered. Names and genders were found to have been transposed. Even Plutarch has often been heavily censored, and passages have been omitted from the records of many other sources in the interests of "propriety."

Despite such obstacles, enough long-hidden lore has been brought to light, making it clear that drastic rewriting both of many periods and of much historical theory is needed.

Extension Classes. Earliest outreach of ONE Institute's classes from Los Angeles was *A Symposium: How Homosexuality Fits In*, for the Daughters of Bilitis in San Francisco.[25] There were eight sessions, November 11-17, 1957, all held in the spacious home of Dr. Harry Benjamin.

Provocative session titles such as "Squaw-Men & Amazons," "The Glory That Was Greece," "Mores & Morals," "Is Your Body Homosexual?" "Disaster, or Decadence in Germany" and "The Curse of Eve & The Curse of Sodom," were designed to stimulate the students to release themselves from long-held psychological, medical and religious clichés about homosexuality. Their attention was then directed to contemporary anthropological, sociological and non-traditional ethical views of the topics listed.

Twenty-five women maintained a sustained interest in the classes throughout the week with lively and often somewhat startled discussion. This was the earliest of the many examples of cooperative projects between men and women which characterized those early years in the Homophile Movement.

Instructors for the Symposium who came from Los Angeles for the sessions were ONE Institute faculty members Jim Kepner and this

----

[25] See Appendix, 2-3: ONE Institute. Presenting a Symposium: How Homosexuality Fits in, November 11-17, 1957.

Editor. ONE Institute Extension Classes took place subsequently in other cities.

ONE's Midwinter Institutes functioned not only as "short courses" for greater numbers than were ready to enroll in full semester classes, but as pilot explorations into new areas of study. In this way they served as tryouts for several of the full-length courses which were added to the curriculum at later dates.

The Midwinter Institute of February 1-2, 1958, undertook major inquiries into several areas which were given full semester treatment in succeeding ONE Institute years, such as law, sociology and ethics. As one commentator put it, "At least the homosexual was not just sitting around listening to a lot of people telling him things, but that instead he was doing his own thinking, announcing his own conclusions, passing his own judgments on homosexual and heterosexual alike." [26]

The sessions were packed with intellectual and emotional highlights, of which the cool and brilliant banquet speech on ONE's U.S. Supreme Court victory by ONE's attorney Eric Julber, and the moving dramatic reading by actress Rachel Rosenthal of the Spartan Love Feast Scene from Naomi Mitchison's *The Corn King and the Spring Queen*, were but two.

The next Midwinter Institute, January 31 - February 1, 1959, moved boldly into "enemy territory" as so many homosexuals regarded psychology, psychiatry and the attitudes widely held at that time by most of those professionals.[27] Attendances were large, discussions lively. The scope of the sessions ranged more widely than in any previous year, testimony in part certainly to the greater perspectives and assurance ONE Institute's ongoing classes were giving both faculty and students.

Notable among the presentations were the latest contribution from ONE's friend, iconoclastic psychiatrist Blanche M. Baker, the scholarly Dr. Mario Palmieri, speaking from his profound background in Greek literature and philosophy, and the truly impressive afternoon presen-

---

[26] "Homosexuality: A Way of Life," *MAG* VI:3 (March, 1958), p.8; also see Appendix, 2-4: Midwinter Institute [1958] Theme: Homosexuality - A Way of Life.

[27] See Appendix, 2-5: Business Meeting [Agenda and Program] 1959 Midwinter Institute "Mental Health and Homosexuality."

tations of Homophile Poetry and Drama.[28]

Without any doubt, however, the top event was the last public appearance of this sort by the much beloved Merritt Thompson, whose mellow and graceful speech entitled "Accepting Middle Age" brought a standing ovation from the entire gathering in tribute to him as a role model, as well as for his great contributions to the Homophile Community, which he had done so much to help bring out into its rightful standing in the world. A remarkable occasion, a remarkable man.[29]

Sociology of Homosexuality. Not until the Fall and Spring Semesters of 1959-60 was the exploration of another new area of academic studies undertaken, *The Homosexual in American Society* or *Sociology of Homosexuality*. An earlier "tentative class outline" had been prepared for use in the four sociology sessions of *An Introduction to Homophile Studies*.[30]

In preparing for the 1959-60 course more than one hundred sociology textbooks were reviewed with some care and extensive notes taken. A depressing uniformity in the treatments of the topic as "deviance," or "social deviance," was found. Thus homosexuality was classified along with prostitution, drug abuse, alcoholism and other anti-social patterns of behavior, characterized variously all the way from passive deviance to aggressively active criminality.

The subject was sometimes given no mention at all or only a few cursory sentences with what seemed to be almost total professional agreement that homosexuality was a topic of minimal sociological concern, hardly "a real topic" at all.

There was one honorable exception. In his 399-page textbook

---

[28] Don Slater, "Mental Health and Homosexuality," *MAG* VII:4 (April, 1959), pp.15-16.

[29] Dr. Thompson was not able to appear at later Midwinter Institutes, although taped greetings from him were played at the 1963 and 1969 Midwinter Institutes. He continued as a valuable consultant until his decease in November, 1970.

[30] *QTLY* I:1 (Spring 1958), p.22,23.

Sociology of Deviant Behavior,[31]   Marshall Clinard included a discussion of homosexuality, which was "probably the first general textbook in sociology to do so," according to Thompson.[32]

Like most of his colleagues of the day, Clinard included a section on "Deviant Behavior" with a chapter on "Murderers and Sex Offenders." A copy of *ONE Institute Quarterly'*s review of his book was sent to Professor Clinard at his University of Wisconsin office. He responded by expressing bewilderment that so little notice had been given to the major arguments in so large a textbook and so much attention given to the few pages dealing with homosexuality.

The real bewilderment was on the part of ONE Institute's faculty that virtually total institutional blindness should be found in an entire scholarly discipline in 1957. Yet the profession possessed a vast body of statistical records, surveys, and vigorous intellectual enterprise, all the way from Comte, Durkheim, Sumner, and other Founding Fathers, to the charts of the Chicago School and the elaborate theoretical constructions of Sorokin, Talcott Parsons and others.[33]

In view of the shortcomings in sociology textbooks as noted above, no embarrassment was felt in devising somewhat unorthodox teaching methods for this ONE Institute class. The basic procedure was to utilize a composite outline based upon several then current college textbooks, briefly sketching in their main topics. Each textbook heading was then evaluated using "field observations," of which each student had a great abundance. This procedure turned out to be in close accord with John Dewey's "bring theory into the life experience of the students," which Dr. Thompson had been so strongly urging. This was well before "relevancy" had become one of the most overused slogans of the politicized later 1960s.

Results were lively beyond expectation, a true "Sociology of Relevance" at the level of experience. Who is homosexual? The married man who tricks out on the side? Or can only those who are

---

[31] Marshall B. Clinard, *Sociology of Deviant Behavior* (New York: Rhinehart & Co., 1957).

[32] Merritt Thompson, "A Sociologist Looks at Homosexuality," *QTLY* I:2 (Summer 1958), pp.48-49, 64.

[33] Not only ONE's faculty have felt bewilderment at "the myopia in sociological studies." See Princeton's Mary Douglas, "The Effects of Modernization on Religious Change," *Daedalus* (Summer 1988), p.458.

heterosexually virgin be included? What significance does the Kinsey Scale really have? Is there such a thing as a flight from homosexuality? Can homosexual behavior be observed by a functional analysis? Is there really such a thing as a "community?" What about arrest and the social consequences, social conflict, and accommodation?[34]

A seminar class attended primarily by faculty members was *Homosexuality in Modern German History: From Frederick the Great Through Hitler*, given during the 1959 Fall Term by Jim Kepner. The homoerotic aspects barely hidden under the surface in German Society were noted: the virtually all-male court of Frederick; Goethe's references to the topic; the careers of Winckelman, Stefan Georg, and his literary circle costumed as Classic-Age Greeks; Barons Krupp and von Gloeden and the "Capri Period;" the Eulenberg and Redl scandals; then, unprecedented freedoms under the Weimar Republic; Roehm, his "Brown Shirts," and the "final solution" or Homosexual Holocaust executed by Hitler. This initial full semester focusing upon a particular historical "problem" was later followed by several other courses exploring enigmatic trends so conspicuous throughout German history.

The four-day program of the January 28-31, 1960, Midwinter Institute on the theme, "The Homosexual in the Community," represented an expansion of these traditional events. It opened with an invitation for visitors to attend the Thursday evening closing ONE Institute session of the 1959-60 Fall Semester, the final class of *Sociology of Homosexuality*. The next day was an Open House for the "Friends of ONE," and featured slide presentations and a workshop highlighting the activities of local Homophile organizations.

Saturday was filled with panels and papers read, most notably the first Midwinter Institute appearance of Evelyn Hooker, U.C.L.A. Professor of Clinical Psychology, whose researches into male homosexuality had already made her a national celebrity. Also featured was an address by Dr. Eason Monroe, Executive Director of the American Civil Liberties Union of Southern California. This was five years before this A.C.L.U. Chapter itself had the courage to act openly

---

[34] See Appendix, 2-6: January 28-31, 1960, The Education Division of ONE, Inc. Presents its Sixth Midwinter Institute, Theme: "The Homosexual in the Community."

upon the questions of the civil liberties of homosexuals.[35]

Readings and short dramatic scenes had in earlier years been presented at Midwinter Institutes. However, 1960 marked the first production of a play with scenery and costumes, James Barr's *Game of Fools*, which ONE had published in 1955 in a handsome, numbered edition.[36]

Another seminar class primarily for faculty members met during the 1960 Spring Term. Those attending took turns in leading a virtually word-by-word exegesis of Freud's *Three Essays on the Theory of Sexuality*, first issued in 1905. The class used the 1949 Imago Publishing (London) translation. Their general conclusion was that Freud has not been well served by many, if not most, of those professing to be his followers.

This exercise in critical analysis greatly reinforced the "accusatorial style"[37] for which ONE Institute has frequently been faulted by partisans of more conventional academic ways. For a classic statement of the accusatorial approach in educational method see Rousseau, particularly *Emile*, a founding authority in such techniques.

The accusatorial approach at ONE Institute is based upon what has been perceived as a "Conspiracy of Silence" observable throughout much academic scholarship, whether literary, historical or other. The Institute's continuing accusation has been: "Why are clearly documented records concerning Homophile behavior throughout history and world societies not given due notice? Can scholarship which ignores the lives and the presence of millions of men and women claim legitimacy?" Homophile Studies poses these questions and continues to do so.

The Gay Novel. Also given for the first time during the 1960 Spring Term was a class taught by *ONE Magazine* Editor Don Slater on *The Gay Novel*. Originally announced as covering a broad historical span, it focused mainly on a period beginning with *The Well of Loneliness*, continuing with works by Vidal, Baldwin, Barr, Compton

---

[35] Ibid.

[36] Don Slater, "Editorial," *MAG* VIII:3 (March, 1960), 4; *CONFI* V (February, 1960), pp.1-3; (March), pp.1-2.

[37] Jean Starobinski, "The Accuser and the Accused," *Daedalus* (Summer 1988), pp.345-370.

McKenzie, and a selection of other novels which had been reviewed in *ONE Magazine*. Variations of this course were given in later years. The only exception was a semester on Whitman's *Calamus* (Spring 1973).[38]

Homophile Education Project. Added to the curriculum in the 1960 Fall Term was a new course unlike anything previously offered. Until then all of the classes had fallen within established fields of academic study: History, Literature, Sociology, Psychology, and the ever-popular general survey, *An Introduction to Homophile Studies*. In line with the ONE Institute's practice of using the Midwinter Institutes for experimentation in theory and practice, something far more venturesome would be tried out. Developed as "A Group Participation Project in Homophile Education," the intent was no less than an attempt to define the goals and the very nature of Homophile Studies.

The venture into unmapped territory generated energy and momentum which would continue for the next ten years, making new discoveries along the way.   This critique of existing academic scholarship opened up new boundaries in the field, the dimensions of which have been by no means fully explored. Once again a Midwinter Institute became an experimental laboratory.

At that time civil rights and law reform had become major concerns all over America, in part because of widespread interest in Britain's Wolfenden Committee's *Parliamentary Report on Homosexuality* and a ground swell of black activism in the United States. With the approval of ONE's governing body, ONE Institute selected the theme "A Homosexual Bill of Rights" for the sessions of the 1961 Midwinter Institute. If our nation had its greatly revered Bill of Rights, why would not its homosexual men and women be entitled to equal protections under the law? Flagrantly conspicuous violations of their rights marked almost every aspect of their lives at the time. Why not then explore the theoretical and the practical aspects involved in staging such an event? What more natural than to conduct a class during the weeks before January 1961 to work out the details?

The mildly interested little group of students who met on September 12, 1960, for the first session of *The Theory and Practice of Homophile*

---

[38] See Appendix, 2-7: ONE Institute of Homophile Studies, 1959-1960 Announcement and Schedule of Classes.

Education and produced over the next sixteen weeks the planning documents for "A Declaration of Homosexual Rights,"[39] as well as conducted the first nationwide survey of Homophiles by Homophiles,[40] had no inkling of the controversy and Movement history their work and the following Midwinter Institute would spawn.

For starters, their class meetings would spin off at least eight more semesters of classes and almost a decade later another Midwinter Institute.[41] Who could have predicted that what was being planned as a laboratory exercise in group participation would result in vigorous and noisy public protests by the Daughters of Bilitis and other lesbians which would mark the start of the almost total withdrawal of participation in ONE's work by women? Nor could anyone have foreseen the shock waves that resulted in the gradual drifting away of assimilationists and all those claiming that "we are just like everyone else except for what we do in bed."

Allegiances and commitments began to fragment. A Movement previously having at least nominal consensus as to aims and goals began splitting apart. A couple of days before the Midwinter Institute started, Jim Kepner, a charter member of the ONE Institute Planning Committee, resigned.[42]

The Midwinter Institute Program[43] may give some clues as to why so many ideological disputes were brought to the surface. Was this some kind of watershed in a movement trying to discover and define itself?

---

[39] See Appendix, 2-8: ONE Institute of Homophile Studies...Presents Its Seventh Midwinter Institute, Thursday, January 26-Sunday, January 29 [1961], Theme: "A Homosexual Bill of Rights."

[40] Ray Evans, Ph.D., and Julian Underwood, *A Study of 388 North American Homosexual Males: Preliminary Findings* (Los Angeles: Institute for the Study of Human Resources, 1970). See below, p.130ff.

[41] See below p.187ff.

[42] See also "To The 'Friends of ONE,'" *CONFI* V (September, 1960), p.1; "Homosexual Rights," (October, 1960), p.1; "To The 'Friends of ONE,'" (December, 1960), p.1; "That Midwinter Institute," VI (February, 1961), pp.1-4; W. Dorr Legg, "ONE Midwinter Institute," *MAG* IX:4 (April, 1961), pp.4-10.

[43] See also *CONFI* VII (January, 1962), p.1.

The *Library Workshop*, first given in the 1961 Fall Semester and a number of times subsequently, provided discussion and lectures as well as practical application, working with both non-fiction and fiction materials in ONE's then one-of-a-kind Library.

The *Advanced Survey of Homophile Studies*, given in Fall 1961 and Spring 1962, was an expanded version of *An Introduction to Homophile Studies*.

The 1962 Tenth Anniversary Midwinter Institute[44] was a three-day affair packed with speakers and meetings. The featured speaker was Edward Sagarin (who wrote as Donald Webster Cory), who had come from New York for the occasion.
The Institute concluded with "An Afternoon at the Theater." Presented in one of Hollywood's smaller playhouses, the "Afternoon" offered an extensive program, mainly drawing from Los Angeles' rich Latino community of singers and dancers, but offering also memorable songs from Lisa Ben, the "gay folk singer" who edited and produced the unique magazine *Vice Versa* in 1947-48.

The *Drama Workshop*, given in Fall 1962 and Spring 1963, was made possible by the retirement to Los Angeles of actor Morgan Farley, who had been well-known on the New York and London stage.

The 1963 Midwinter Institute[45] followed the, by this time, traditional format. "Star events" were the speeches by brilliant San Francisco attorney Morris Lowenthal and the charismatic Episcopalian Father James Jones of Chicago, who quite literally stopped the Annual Luncheon, all of the cooks and kitchen helpers standing in a row entirely transfixed by what this handsome priest was saying about "Man's Laws and God's Laws."

Midwinter Institutes in 1964 and 1965 were deferred to permit both

---

[44] See Appendix, 2-9: Tenth...Midwinter Institute, Los Angeles, California, January 26-28, 1962.

[45] See Appendix, 2-10: The Education Division of ONE, INC., Presents Its 1963 Midwinter Institute, Theme: "New Frontiers in the Law."

students and faculty to catch up with the wide range of experimental educational additions to the ONE Institute curriculum which had been evolving. Works on the *ONE Institute Quarterly of Homophile Studies* and on the early stages of the bibliographical project[46] described below were coming to the fore also, leaving well-established classes continuing to serve newcomers.

Institute for the Study of Human Resources. In the latter months of 1964 a step was taken which would profoundly affect ONE Institute's work from that date onward: the incorporation of a foundation, "The Institute for the Study of Human Resources," whose primary objective has been supporting ONE Institute's research and educational programs.

ONE Incorporated, parent body of ONE Institute, while a nonprofit California corporation, had not been able to gain nonprofit status for technical legal reasons. This problem greatly handicapped its fund-raising abilities. The new foundation, on the other hand, which was able to move steadily ahead to achieve the favorable tax-exempt foundation designation, had been formed at the urging of Louisiana philanthropist Reed Erickson, who from that date and for many years following provided financial support for ONE Institute projects. Among such were the California State University Long Beach/ONE Institute joint four-semester project[47] and the two volume *Annotated Bibliography of Homosexuality*, edited by Bullough, Legg, Elcano, and Kepner (New York: Garland Publications, 1976).[48]

In 1981 the Institute for the Study of Human Resources (ISHR) joined with ONE Institute in obtaining authorization from the California State Board of Education to confer the M.A. and Ph.D. degrees in Homophile studies, as described in Chapter 4.[49]

Homophile Ethics. Two additions to the ONE Institute curriculum were made in 1965. *Homophile Ethics* was announced as examining "Standards of morality and ethics applicable to male and female

---

[46] Bibliographical Project Papers. (ONE's Baker Memorial Library & Archives)

[47] See below, p.145.

[48] See below, p.53.

[49] See below, p.73ff.

homosexual behavior. Value systems for the individual's own pattern of life conduct toward his fellows, and society in general, viewed in the light of various philosophical and religious teachings." [50]

The views of three writers were given special notice: Joseph Fletcher's books and articles on Situational Ethics, Helmut Thielicke's *The Ethics of Sex* and Rene Guyon's *The Ethics of Sexual Acts*.[51] The *Journal of Pastoral Care* afforded occasional useful discussion points. Unfortunately, almost everything on the topic in print was so heavily oriented toward "The Heterosexual Assumption" (a ONE Institute phrase) as to be of almost no value in the study of *Homophile Ethics*. The course was given slightly different titles in later catalogs.

Psychological Theories. The first major assault on the entrenched psychological establishment was mounted in 1965 by faculty member Julian Underwood, *Psychological Theories of Homosexuality*. His detailed and carefully constructed weekly class guides took Bieber's *Homosexuality* and Marmor's *Sexual Inversion*[52] as targets for critical analysis. While the latter text came off somewhat better, Bieber received withering critical dissection at Underwood's highly-trained, mathematical/philosophical hands. In fact, he reported that some of Bieber's statistics betray damaging evidence of having been "adjusted" to better fit Bieber's arguments. The course has not been repeated since that Spring 1966 semester. Not many students were willing to keep the pace, and Woody scorned those less dedicated.

The January 28-29, 1966, Midwinter Institute, "Where the

---

[50] "Institute of Homophile Studies Catalog for 1968-69," p.13. (ONE's Baker Memorial Library & Archives) See also "A Report to Members," *CONFI* XII (May, 1967), p.1.

[51] Joseph F. Fletcher, *Situation Ethics: The New Morality* (Philadelphia: Westminster Press, 1966); Helmut Thielicke, *The Ethics of Sex*, trans. John Doberstein (New York: Harper and Row, 1964); Rene Guyon, *The Ethics of Sexual Acts* (New York: Alfred A. Knopf, 1934).

[52] Irving Bieber, et al, *Homosexuality: A Psychoanalytic Study* (New York: Basic Books, 1962); *Sexual Inversion: The Multiple Roots of Homosexuality*, Judd Marmor ed. (New York: Basic Books, 1965).

Mainstream Flows,"[53] again broke new ground by bringing together a large number of representatives of past and present Homophile Organizations from all over California and across the country. A notable presentation was made by world-famous writer Ray Bradbury, who wittily and with impish charm evoked the universality of human-to-human bodily responses. At the Banquet, prominent Chicago attorney Paul Goldman movingly told of Illinois' successful efforts in 1961 at becoming the first state in the Union to decriminalize homosexual acts between consenting adults.

Actress Rachel Rosenthal and her Instant Theater cast once again brought the weekend to a dramatic conclusion.[54]

Counseling the Homosexual. The Fall, 1966, class *Counseling the Homosexual* became another Institute first. The subject matter was drawn from the extensive Social Service Division files of ONE, Incorporated, which virtually since ONE's founding in 1952 had been thrust into developing an entirely new field of Peer Counseling, making ONE the earliest "Community Services Center" in America by many years. Thousands of male and female homosexuals, bisexuals, parents, teachers, transsexuals, transvestites, and others came to ONE's offices during business hours and rang ONE's telephones around the clock seeking help with their personal, religious, housing, employment, military, legal and other problems. The entire staff found itself unavoidably drawn into what often were critical emergency situations.

During many years of such experiences, staff sessions, and discussions, as well as the unrelenting demands from those who did not know where to turn, many of them having already failed at getting help from all manner of psychologists and other therapists, staff members arrived at some rough guidelines. They learned how to tell which cases required professional referrals and which could best be dealt with by resources from within the Homophile Community itself.

The conclusion at which ONE's Social Service Division staff arrived was that in the great majority of cases, neither medical nor "psychologi-

---

[53] See Appendix, 2-11: 1966 Midwinter Sessions.

[54] Richard Conger (pseud. W. Dorr Legg), "Where the Mainstream Flows: An Account of the Exciting, High-Quality 1966 Midwinter Sessions of ONE, Traditional Top Event of the Homophile Movement Since 1955," *MAG* XIV:2 (February, 1966), pp.6-12.

cal" problems were at issue. Rather, confused and unhappy individuals found themselves trying to cope with situations and problems brought upon them by strains and pressures arising from hostile and oppressive societal attitudes. ONE's Peer Counselors welcomed the supporting research conclusions of Evelyn Hooker which confirmed that the subjects she studied were very little different from the rest of society in their degrees of adjustment, some better, some worse than others, but mainly quite average.[55]

The wise counsel of psychiatrist Blanche M. Baker, and many conferences with her, also gave the Peer Counselors great encouragement. Her pioneer column of advice entitled "Toward Understanding," which appeared in *ONE Magazine* from January, 1959 through June, 1960, afforded ONE's Counselors many insights. She was embarrassingly laudatory of their work, at times suggesting that Homophiles had special gifts in such directions.

True or not, ONE's Social Service Division Counselors were unhappily aware that psychologists, psychiatrists, and other professional therapists of the time were so deeply imbued with value systems derived during their own training that "treatment" all too often tended toward the goal of readapting their clients to fit into the social norms of the day. In that connection, some of the ONE Counselors found Robert Lindner's *Must You Conform?*[56] a useful resource.

From time to time several professionals attended 1966-67 *Counseling the Homosexual* classes. One local psychiatrist attended regularly during both semesters. A problem, which still remains unresolved regarding the practice of many later psychotherapists who are themselves Homophile, concerns the breadth and scope of their own in-group training with regard to goals and value systems. Staff members have not found themselves reassured that in all instances such professionals have added more than a degree of empathy and values derived from their own life experiences to their backgrounds. Perhaps the day of specialized training for counseling Homophiles is something to be hoped for in the future. This editor's "Manual: Counseling the

---

[55] Evelyn Hooker, "The Adjustment of the Male Overt Homosexual," *Journal of Projective Techniques*, XXI (1957), 18-31.

[56] Robert Lindner, *Must You Conform?* (New York: Holt, Rinehart and Winston, 1972).

Homosexual," written 1966-70, remains in manuscript form with fifteen chapters and eight appendixes based upon approximately 7,000 office cases and around the same number of cross-country telephone calls. Extensive counseling by correspondence was also handled at the ONE Community Services Center.

Only brief mention will be made here of the seminar class, *A Bibliography of Homosexuality*, given in the 1968 Spring Semester.[57]

After another two years without Midwinter Institutes, the January 31-February 2, 1969, Midwinter Institute "New Insights Into Homosexuality"[58] was notable for the breadth of participation by members of the "Councils of ONE" from Chicago, Detroit and New York. Also notable was the large number of participants from the professions of psychiatry, sociology, and psychology. They were present as respondents to the two major scientific papers which were delivered: the sociological *A Study of 388 North American Homosexual Males*,[59] a ONE Institute research project paper by faculty member Julian Underwood, and the psychological "Studies in Personality Characteristics of Several Hundred Homosexual Males," by U.C.L.A. Assistant Professor of Psychology Peter Bentler.

Among the panelists were psychiatrists Richard Green, Martha Kirkpatrick, and Richard Parlour, sociologists Barry Dank and Howard Fradkin from California State College, Long Beach, sociologist Kenneth Poole of Santa Monica City College, clinical psychologist Fred Goldstein, and Professor Fred Selden of the University of Indiana.

Interchanges between panelists were reported as being hot and heavy at times, but psychiatrist Parlour said that both he and Dr. Green commented that the presentations were a lot better than many they had heard at scientific professional meetings.[60]

---

[57] Seminar: A Bibliography of Homosexuality, Spring 1968. (ONE's Baker Memorial Library & Archives)

[58] See Appendix, 2-12: The Education Division of ONE, Inc., Institute of Homophile Studies, Presents Its 11th Midwinter Institute, Theme: "New Insights into Homosexuality," January 31-February 2, 1969.

[59] Ibid.; see also below, p.130ff.

[60] *LTR* XIV:2 (February, 1969), pp.2-7.

The 1970 Midwinter Institute broke no new ground in educational theory or practice. The traditional pattern was followed with one exception, that being the holding of one of the sessions at the distant San Gabriel Valley clubgrounds of the Society of Anubis. It was felt that this remarkable newer organization with its innovative social and community programs deserved a salute and would provide a valuable educational experience.

Probably the largest Homophile Organization in the United States at the time, with nearly a thousand members, the Society had fully-integrated, co-sexual administrative leadership, as well as a rustic ten-acre mountain location, the organization thus having created a novel and innovative niche for itself in the development of the Homophile Movement.

A more complete account of the Society of Anubis is not intended here, but its place in a textbook on Homophile Education is well-deserved.[61]

So too would be the work of Homophile filmmakers, with ONE Institute student Gordon Meyer's April, 1970 *Drama Workshop* project among the notable efforts.[62]

Law and Law Reform. The 1970 Fall Semester class *Law and Law Reform* rapidly reviewed laws of early Near Eastern, Egyptian, Greek and Roman times. Considerable attention was given to the growth and expansion of ecclesiastical laws and pandects. The very different North European tribal laws, the foundation for English Common Law, which has so greatly affected the lives of countless Homophiles, were noted. The Napoleonic Code framed in the 19th century by the Homophile Cambaceres, which has since prevailed in Latin countries, was given special notice. Some Far Eastern codes were also cited, one such, a Hindu code which atypically punished lesbian conduct much more severely than male homosexuality. The role of French jurist Rene Guyon in modernizing legal codes in Thailand was described. Some time was spent on examining contemporary, so-called

---

[61] "To the Friends of ONE," *LTR* XV:2 (February, 1970), pp.1-3.

[62] Drama Workshop, 1970. (ONE's Baker Memorial Library & Archives)

"administrative law," the rather vague, somewhat extra-legal area which so often affects nearly everyone.

The program of the January 28-30, 1972, Midwinter Institute with the theme "The Gay Community: 1952-1972,"[63] included major sessions on "The Gay Challenge to Religion and the Churches," "Counseling Homosexuals," and "An Indictment of the American Educational System." Each of these sessions presented a summary of ONE Institute's general positions on those topics.

Present and participating was a group of senior and graduate psychology students from California State College, Long Beach, one of the educational innovations of 1972. Also participating once again was Professor Peter Bentler who had been assisted by ONE Institute in one of his research projects, ONE having supplied nearly one thousand subjects for his study.

A 1972 addition to the curriculum was the Spring Semester *Near Eastern Foundations of Biblical Morality* taught by Savina Teubal, a scholar with broad knowledge of ancient Hebrew, Aramaic and other languages. Her knowledge of the tangled record of the many different manuscripts upon which modern and older translations of the bible have been based was encyclopedic.

Variant Sex Behavior. The next major public event was not technically a Midwinter Institute. However, it was arranged and staffed almost entirely by ONE Institute faculty and personnel. The June 7-9, 1974, "Forum on Variant Sexual Behavior"[64] was funded in part by the Erickson Educational Foundation, Baton Rouge, Louisiana. This assistance made possible the addition of several features, as well as widespread advance publicity. Large numbers of physicians and other professionals came from all over the West Coast and from as far away as New York City. Attendances were much larger than in any previous year.

The highlight of the Forum was the deeply emotional introduction of Evelyn Hooker by Christopher Isherwood, who had been a close

---

[63] See Appendix, 2-13: 1972 Midwinter Institute, Program.

[64] See Appendix, 2-14: Institute for the Study of Human Resources, Forum on Variant Sex Behavior, June 7-9, 1974.

friend to her at the start of her famed research. Her presentation, "Reminiscence and Forecast," was a brilliant recounting of the beginnings, the problems, the opposition to her methodology, and the eventual triumph of her massive studies of male homosexuals and their psychological adjustment, which could never be forgotten by the large audience who heard her.

Boston Institute of Homophile Studies. An unexpected outreach of ONE Institute was the catalogue received from the Institute of Homophile Studies at 419 Boylston Street, Boston, in 1974.[65]   The catalogue contained the following acknowledgment: "We are grateful to ONE Institute in Los Angeles, California for providing us with material about their program upon which we have largely based our own." ONE Institute faculty took special notice of the listing of a class *Historical Perspectives on Homosexuality*, taught by John Boswell, described at the time as "a doctoral candidate at Harvard."

The later history of this Boston Institute of Homophile Studies is not known.

Sex, Role and Gender. Another program similar to the 1974 Forum took place March 7-9, 1975: the theme, "Sex, Role and Gender." [66] A feature new to such sessions was a series of Field Trips. Attendees broke up into smaller units of their own choosing, each with a Group Leader. Each Field Trip group then visited several locations, choosing from a site list which included a gay male bar, a gay male dance club, a lesbian bar, a transvestite bar, a bar for older gay males, and a gay restaurant. Students who wished to receive one hour of credit through California State College, Northridge, were required to turn in written reports.[67]

The main speaker for the closing event was Christine Jorgensen who drew an attendance of several hundred people to hear her tell her own experiences with role and gender changes.

---

[65] *LTR* XIX:1 (January, 1974), pp.1-6.

[66] See Appendix, 2-15: Institute for the Study of Human Resources, Seminar: "Sex, Role & Gender," March 7-9, 1975.

[67] "Seminar: 'Sex, Role & Gender,'" *LTR* XX:3 (March, 1975), pp.3-5; "Sex, Role & Gender Seminar Concluded," *LTR* XX:4 (April, 1975), pp.2-4.

The January 27-29, 1978, Midwinter Institute explored the theme "A Search for Our Roots: Gay Life and Liberation – 1860-1960."[68] Low key for the most part, but intensely interesting, the programs were primarily in-group accounts. Always popular was *ONE Magazine* writer Harry Otis and his accounts of his early days among the cowboys in Colorado and later contacts with New York's 400, many of whom visited the speakeasy he ran for Texas Guinan's brother. ONE Institute's Archives has tapes of some of his adventures. The next and possibly last Midwinter Institute was a salute to the new and incoming decade, held January 25-26, 1980.[69]

Summing up and looking toward the future were such topics as "Our Goals as Citizens in Society," "Our Needs and Goals as Human Beings" and "Our Outreach to Society." A wide range of local Homophile organizations, including Gay Democratic and Republican Clubs, took part. The Banquet Speaker was Richard Kaplan, Co-Chair of the large and influential Municipal Elections Committee of Los Angeles (MECLA). The event, held in a prominent hotel, was a far cry from some of the tiny, half-furtive gatherings of the early 1950s.

Within another year ONE Institute would have added a Graduate School and a new phase for Homophile Studies would have started.

More Extension Classes. News reports about ONE Institute classes brought early inquiries from cities interested in inviting Extension Classes to their own areas. Already mentioned was the first of all Extension Series, held in San Francisco in 1957. The visit to Denver in 1959 by an Institute faculty member made possible a somewhat shorter series in that city. In 1960 the Mattachine Society of San Francisco sponsored an ambitious Extension Series in that city.[70] A five-day Series in Chicago in 1963 led to the organizing of ONE of

---

[68] See Appendix, 2-16: ONE's 1978 Midwinter Institute, "A Search for Our Roots, Gay Life & Liberation - 1860-1960," January 27-29, 1978.

[69] See Appendix, 2-17: ONE Annual Meeting [and] Program, [1980] Midwinter Sessions.

[70] See Appendix, 2-18: Mattachine Society, Inc. Department of Education, presents a series of lectures and a panel program by the ONE, Institute of Homophile Studies, Education Division of One, Inc., Los Angeles. Mattachine Seminar Series, San Francisco – August 12 to September 2, [1959], inclusive.

Chicago,[71] which had a long and impressive history of its own,[72] a second Series being held in 1971.[73] On December 3, 1965, ONE Institute Lecturer Chet Sampson gave a ONE Institute Extension Lecture for a group in Detroit. Action was then taken to organize ONE in Detroit. This group proposed to assist ONE's bibliography project by means of access to the many large university and other libraries in the Detroit area.[74] This group continued for several more years, with an active program of radio and television appearances, as well as meetings with psychiatrists and public officials. A book collection of substantial size was maintained.[75] In like fashion the 1968 New York Series led to the opening of ONE in New York.

In Southern California the energetic, newly-formed ONE in Long Beach sponsored Extension Series classes during the years 1971-73 as full semesters. A 1973 Series in Milwaukee did not, however, result in the establishing of a ONE branch in that city.

The monthly ONE Institute Sunday Afternoon Extension Lecture Series in Los Angeles, proposed in 1957 and formalized during the 1958-59 academic year, has presented an impressive roster of writers, clergy, and professional people from all over the United States and Europe uninterrupted since its inception. This Extension project will be given further notice in Part II. The more than 300 Lectures logged will be described under the various topics of specialization, that is, law, psychology, sociology, religion and all the others.

---

[71] See Appendix, 2-19: One Institute Comes Again - to Chicago ... 1971.

[72] See Appendix, 2-20: ONE of Chicago, Goals and Objectives, Adopted March, 1967.

[73] See also Appendix, 2-21: ONE of Chicago presents a Lecture by Mr. Antony Grey of London, England, on Sex, Morality and Happiness.

[74] Chuck Thompson (pseud. Chet Sampson), "ONE's Outreach Program," *Annual Report for Year 1965* (Los Angeles: ONE, Inc., 1966), p.9.

[75] "ONE Institute Comes Again," *LTR* XVIII:10 (October, 1973), p.6; Jim Kepner, "Midwest Journey," *LTR* XVIII:12 (December, 1973), pp.1-6.

Summary

What has been the ONE Institute record, beginning with that first Midwinter Institute in 1955 and the 16 Special Programs which have followed? What also of the carefully organized semesters of classes from 1956 to today?

The entire curriculum of those semesters has been carried on at a community college level of instruction, and always from the Homophile Studies point of view. This has involved a determined and tenacious effort to probe the "Conspiracy of Silence" or collective failure of traditional scholarship either to note or to evaluate the social and other implications of the fact that millions of Homophile men and women have lived and have been making their mark throughout all recorded history.

CHAPTER 3

SUPPLEMENTARY EDUCATIONAL PROJECTS

During the years that ONE Institute curriculum expansion was being developed and tested, several other educational projects began to take form. Earliest of these resulted from the urgency of the need for bibliographic resources for ONE Institute students and faculty. Adequate bibliographical resources are the very cornerstone of teaching and research today. Consequently, the almost complete lack of resources adapted to so new a field as Homophile Studies called for early attention.

There was also the need for a publication to act as a forum for scholarly articles and debate, to present new insights and raise issues. This was felt to be no less urgent a need, especially in view of the conspicuous dearth of such materials being published in scholarly journals at the time.

Only somewhat less noticeable was the growing understanding that homophilia is a worldwide phenomenon found among peoples and cultures in every part of the world. Very few books dealing with homosexuality during the mid-20th century even mentioned this, much less what educational steps might be taken in response.

ONE Institute
Quarterly of Homophile Studies

In the February 27, 1957, minutes of the Education Planning Committee, it was proposed that there should be a "quarterly to consist of scholarly articles."[1]   As soon as ONE's Board of Directors gave authorization for such a publication, an Editorial Board was appointed with James L. Kepner, Jr., as Editor, W. Dorr Legg as Managing Editor, Merritt M. Thompson as Consulting Editor, and Dawn Frederic as Art Director.

Decisions had to be made as to page size, type faces, choice of

---

[1] Minutes, Education Planning Committee, February 27, 1957 (ONE's Baker Memorial Library & Archives)

paper, number of pages per issue, and so on. The contributions of Dawn Frederic in all these matters were outstanding. Her boldly arresting designs for the covers of the *ONE Institute Quarterly of Homophile Studies* brought much favorable comment for their taste and distinction.

In Volume I, Number 1 of the *Quarterly*,[2] Editor Kepner wrote that the "editorial essence of the task is to critically examine the various systems of thought, to compare their formulations to the verifiable data of history and the sciences." Kepner was Editor for the first eight issues, Spring 1958 through Winter 1960. This writer then served as Editor for the next 14 issues, the last published in 1970. There have not been further issues since.

Part II following consists so largely of material selected from the *Quarterly* that further discussion of it and its policies at this point would seem redundant.

Bibliographical Publications

ONE Institute had not yet come into existence when the first plans were announced for "an extensive bibliography."[3] In ONE's 1955 Annual Report, this was projected as "a classified bibliography on the subject with annotations."[4]

Actual work on such a publication was not immediately undertaken. ONE's Library did not at first provide a working-size collection and demands by ONE Institute classes had not become pressing. However, Library Workshops in Fall, Spring and Summer semesters during 1961-64 did offer "practical work in cataloguing and bibliography" given by *ONE Magazine* Editor Don Slater.

In July, 1964, an unexpected offer of funding for a bibliography came from the then newly-organized Erickson Educational Foundation

---

[2] *QTLY* I:1 (Spring 1958), p.3.

[3] Minutes, ONE, Inc. Annual Meeting, January, 1954 (ONE's Baker Memorial Library & Archives)

[4] "Report of the Annual Meeting," *MAG* III:2 (February, 1955).

of Baton Rouge, Louisiana. An ambitious three-year program to be headed by Don Slater, with professional consultant John D. Gibson, was prepared.[5]   Several months of work were done in late 1964 and early 1965. These ended with the withdrawal of Slater from ONE.[6]

Work was resumed in the summer of 1965 by ONE Institute faculty member Julian Underwood, with this writer assisting. Examination of a number of existing bibliographies, most of them found in medical and psychological texts, was continued for some months.

A more complete account of the work done from that time through 1966 includes some "Sample Bibliographic Entries."[7]   This was followed by publication of *An Annotated Bibliography of Homosexuality* prepared as a prototype for a more comprehensive publication at some later date.[8]

Work was suspended for a time when it was learned that the Institute for Sex Research of Bloomington, Indiana, had been awarded a large grant for the publication of a major bibliography. This was published in 1972 with a focus and content so unlike ONE Institute's project that the way was open for resuming work again.

Some study had been continuing in the Spring 1968 ONE Institute seminar class, *A Bibliography of Homosexuality*, announced as "based on biographical, historical, scientific and other non-fiction materials to contribute to an annotated bibliography of Homophile topics." [9]

The decease of Underwood in 1970 after several years of failing health was a great loss, but fortunately a strong addition was that of California State University, Northridge, Professor of History Vern L. Bullough. The dimensions of the bibliography project were greatly en-

---

[5] *LTR* XXVI:9 (September, 1981), p.1-6.

[6] Those interested will find details in *CONFI* X (July, 1965), pp.1-3, and "ONE Inc. vs. Donald Rutherford Slater, et al," *CONFI* XII (May, 1967), pp.1-15.

[7] R.B. Evans, W. Dorr Legg, and Julian M. Underwood, A Bibliography of Homosexuality. (ONE's Baker Memorial Library & Archives)

[8] W. Dorr Legg and J. M. Underwood, An Annotated Bibliography of Homosexuality (ONE's Baker Memorial Library & Archives)

[9] "Institute of Homophile Studies Catalog for 1968-69," p.15. (ONE's Baker Memorial Library & Archives).

larged by his offering to contribute two thousand entries accumulated during his own historical researches.

Professor Bullough also offered an immense, though jumbled, collection of many thousand notes on scraps of paper which had been given him by Gershon A. Legman, whose *Horn Book*[10] and other books on erotic bibliography and folklore contained many valuable entries. Deciphering the Legman notes, many of them in a kind of hieroglyphic, scientific German, was a very time-consuming challenge.

Professor Bullough joined the project in 1974 as an Editor, along with this writer and Barrett Elcano, a bibliographer in the California State University, Northridge, Oviatt Library. James L. Kepner, Jr., became an Editor during the completion of Volume II. A summary of the two-year labors of the staff members involved in completion of the project can be found in the *Bibliography* itself.[11]

The completed 2-volume work contained 12,794 entries classified under eighteen subject headings: anthropology, history, psychiatry, law, religion, drama, poetry, etc. Assigning titles under those headings was supervised by ONE Institute faculty members to emphasize the multidisciplinary nature of Homophile Studies.

Proofreading and the actual typing of so great a number of entries on machines in ONE's offices at times seemed like an endless task. When the Garland Publishing presses in New York finally issued the volumes in 1976, immediate praise was forthcoming. There was also criticism for the numerous typos, proofreading errors, and other lapses.

In praise, one scholar wrote, "this monumental work (almost 13,000 entries) opened a new era in research horizons in its subject,"[12] which had been ONE Institute's intention from the outset in undertaking such a project. The volumes were an immediate publishing success, with another printing needed in less than a year.

Confirmation of the important role of bibliographic work in Homophile Studies such as this has led to continued work on bibliographical research and the issuing of a *Manual of Bibliographic*

---

[10] Gershon A. Legman, *The Horn Book: Studies in Erotic Folklore and Bibliography* (New Hyde Park, New York: University Books, 1964).

[11] *An Annotated Bibliography of Homosexuality* (New York: Garland Publishing, 1976), pp.vii-xxii.

[12] Wayne Dynes, *Homosexuality: A Research Guide* (New York: Garland Publishing, 1987).

Style for Entries in Homosexuality.[13] It was prepared and written by David G. Moore, who was the full-time librarian in ONE's Baker Memorial Library for several years at times when funding was available. This *Manual* represents another important scholarly contribution to Homophile Studies.

ONE Institute Overseas

The first Overseas Tour organized for ONE Members was in 1964, a first of its kind by any Homophile Organization. In serving as escort for many of these annual events, this writer saw first-hand that homophilia is a worldwide phenomenon with a very long history. These contacts between 1966-81, with cultures and traditions ranging from the most technologically advanced to others still living within traditional folk patterns, provided fifteen years of field observations. These have led to a high degree of skepticism toward some of the theories of the social constructionists and essentialists in circulation today. Cross-cultural exposure is a valuable adjunct in Homophile Studies, and an indispensable brake against hasty generalizations.

Observations in the Field

Denmark.[14] Landing in Copenhagen the group from ONE was met by representatives of the Forbundet av 1948, a name expressing their early recovery from the dark Nazi years. At a dinner in the evening, each American was seated next to a charming Dane, small Danish and American flags crossed at each place setting. Speeches of

---

[13] David G. Moore, *Manual of Bibliographic Style for Entries in Homosexuality: A Comprehensive Bibliography* (Los Angeles: Institute for the Study of Human Resources, 1980).

[14] Denmark Tours: 1966 and 1974.

welcome and response were followed by an evening of dancing. American music was tactfully alternated with Danish folk dances, enthusiastic evidence that these attractive young Scandinavians preferred their own complicated steps to the packaged American product. The next day discussion about their books and other publications made it clear that, although Danish law was relatively liberal, this group and its branches across Denmark and Norway felt a strong need for in-group identity and a sense of community.

On a return visit, further discussions and an evening in their highly successful PAN Club, an indispensable source of their income, reinforced the impression that Forbundet was in no way politically activist. It appeared that their concerns were for a pleasant social life and possibly a lowering of the age of consent, if that might be achieved without great effort.

Switzerland.[15] In Zurich the group was met by Rudolf Burckhardt, who in 1958 had spent a week in Los Angeles and given several lectures for ONE staff members and Institute students on "The History of the Homophile Movements of Europe," as well as his own recollections of Magnus Hirschfeld and other Movement figures. In Zurich Rudolf was English Language Editor of *Der Kreis*, the Swiss publication founded in 1933 which later added sections in German and French.

The head of the large Der Kreis organization was one of Switzerland's leading actors, Karl Maier, who used the name Rolf. He had successfully piloted the group throughout the Nazi period when all other European Homophile Groups had gone underground or had been wiped out.

Homophile behavior had been decriminalized in Switzerland many years earlier, yet to the astonishment of the visitors from America, the editors of *Der Kreis* took it entirely for granted that all of their highly literate and well-written manuscripts, fine artwork, and photography should be submitted for police approval before publication.

During a return visit to Zurich, ONE had commissioned Los Angeles cinematographers Pat Rocco and Brian King to make a travel film of "Homophile Lifestyles" in the various countries visited. This writer found himself roundly berated in public for escorting such an unseemly project, so socially irresponsible and in such bad taste, as the

---

[15] Switzerland Tours: 1966, 1972, and 1976.

Swiss deemed it. However, this did not dampen the proverbial Swiss hospitality, such as large social gatherings and a chartered double-deck bus tour through the countryside, each visitor seated next to an English-speaking member of Der Kreis.

A visit later to the Der Kreis branch in Basel confirmed that their ruling policy seemed to be: achieve the good life, make it a very good life, as the Swiss know how, but do it with minimal ruffling of the existing order of things.

France.[16] When first visited, Arcadie in Paris had by no means become the large and successful organization of later years. Its meeting place was hidden away up a winding staircase across an obscure court-yard. The welcome was warm, with an indefinable Gallic tone very much unlike any of the preceding encounters. Return visits found Arcadie housed in a former theater made over like a Paris nightclub on the ground floor, a visitor's gallery in the balcony above. Unlike the disapproval of the movie project in Switzerland, an audience of 600 cheered with romantic fervor the showing of several Pat Rocco short films, then greeted the Rev. Troy Perry's fiery speech in rapt silence and tears of gratitude for release from the bonds of their traditional religious backgrounds.

Yet despite all the marks of success and their handsome monthly journal *Arcadie* in tasteful French literary style, the Arcadie premises had an unmarked door. Admission was by giving the proper signs. There was little open evidence of socially public goals. Arcadie in later years sponsored several impressive seminar programs, not only in Paris, but in other French cities. Access to French radio and television programs came a dozen or more years later than those in which such communication had become commonplace with ONE and other American Homophile Groups.

Holland.[17] The short distance from Paris to Amsterdam brought ONE's group into a much different Homophile world. The C.O.C.[18]

---

[16] France Tours: 1966, 1971, 1972, and 1976.

[17] Holland Tours: 1971, 1972, 1974, 1976, and 1981.

[18] See p.25 above.

occupied offices in a large business building. Some blocks away their social activities took up three floors near the famous Rijksmuseum, facing a busy and popular public square.

The American visitors were introduced to two of the C.O.C. founding members and many others who had come from other Dutch cities to greet them. There also were representatives from German and English Homophile groups, including Johannes Werres, who often wrote as Jack Argo, and Antony Grey, prominently identified with English sex law reform movements. During several busy days the American visitors began discovering how the C.O.C., by far the largest organization of its sort in the world, had long become a quasi-public social-service agency with specialized resource groups for women, for pedophiles, and even for younger men who found themselves compulsively attracted to dirty and aged vagrants.

Return visits to C.O.C. included numerous meetings with C.O.C. personnel and opportunities for observing the work of the organization. A few random incidents tell much in few words. In 1972 after asking to see their Library, they pointed out two or three shelves which contained some scattered volumes, a mere fraction of ONE's growing Library collection even at that early date. Reference works and a library were plainly not given a C.O.C. priority at that time.

Another telling incident came during a frank and extended discussion with one of the C.O.C. officers. "Tourists come to Amsterdam and believe they have found paradise," he said. "The bars, the dancing, the same-sex couples walking arm-in-arm on the streets, shopping as pairs. To us who live here it is not paradise at all, but hell." When asked why he felt this way, he went into detail about the sociopolitical theoretical framework underlying their hopes for a state closer to socialism, with Homophiles more integrated into society, and seeking social amalgamation. Individuals ought to be judged as total persons and not as to their ratings on the Kinsey scale, he felt. Also revealing was the hooting and derisive laughter at Pat Rocco films by a C.O.C. audience, the same films the French had so greatly admired and liked.

The C.O.C., now renamed *Nederlandse Vereniging tot Integratie van Homosexualiteit* (COC), has become associated with some academic institutions and taken part in several international gatherings of Homophile scholars. It now functions as a highly-efficient, well-organized service organization with considerable public funding, having a mature and bureaucratic status appropriate to its many years and the society in which it functions.

England and Scotland.[19]   London offered a very different range
of Homophile organizations. Unlike any seen during many years of
overseas travel was a group for deaf Homophiles. Neither ideological
nor political, nor merely a social group, it provided for them a haven.
Their problems were those of literal survival, as well as avoidance of
being victimized and exploited by street people who often tried to prey
upon them. It was a highly emotional experience to see these men and
women of all ages, from those barely teen-aged to gray heads, all of
them painfully oppressed by their double minority status. The leader
of the group was a remarkable Australian man, uncannily gifted in lip-
reading, who had earned a university doctorate in social work despite
all obstacles.

Quite dissimilar was a lively meeting with a gathering of women
who called themselves the Minorities Research Group. Their quirky
little magazine *Arena Three* came to ONE's Library for many years.
In describing the group to American audiences, one comment offered
was, "They sound to me like a bunch of good old-fashioned lesbians."

The Albany Trust, which was also visited, represented socially concerned men and women of unstated individual orientations who had
organized to work for reform of England's very anti-homosexual laws,
and to support the Wolfenden Committee's recommendations[20] to
Parliament. In addition they maintained an active program of social
services, including counseling, and an educational monthly, *Man and
Society*.

Later visits to England were to the offices of the *Gay News* staff,
a well-edited paper which succumbed at last to in-fighting problems
such as have faced so many groups in England. A different, more
societal situation was noted in Bath. There, taboos and English reserve
made the members barely able to speak about their difficulties and
needs, seemingly tongue-tied with fear, guilt and self-doubts.

Similar situations were found in several other smaller English cities.
Only in Edinburgh was there found a vigorous and active organizational
presence with a fine bookshop of its own. The members seemed not

---

[19] England and Scotland Tours: 1966, 1976, and 1980.

[20] See p.38 above.

at all tongue-tied or fearful. While offering much of interest to observe, neither the Americans nor the British seemed to provide many new or useful insights in matters Homophile to each other.

Germany and Austria.[21]   Hamburg had many Homophile Institutions ranging from bawdy, wide-open bars and houses of prostitution, to ideologically-oriented groups and publications of strongly Marxist persuasion. On that basis Gay Bars were viewed as capitalist rip-offs dedicated to class oppression. The handsome, large magazine *Him,* with color photos of men dressed and undressed, claimed to be totally dedicated to the elimination of all social or legal distinctions based on sexual behavior. Yet each month's pages carried many columns of Personal Ads of the "want-to-meet" sort.[22]

In the Rhineland cities, Frankfurt and Cologne, attitudes appeared to be much less doctrinaire. Homophile Organizations had existed in both cities both before and after the Nazi period. Anti-homosexual laws and public attitudes have made their histories very difficult, the groups transitory.

Munich, despite being in Catholic Bavaria, had a small Homophile Group which received the ONE visitors most hospitably. Heavily political emphasis, as farther north, was in little evidence there. Munich night life was, however, nearly as boisterous as that in Hamburg.

In Berlin, where Hirschfeld's *Institut* had flourished and so much Homophile history was made,[23] the Weimar Republic's past and Christopher Isherwood's *Berlin Stories* seemed still very much present or perhaps only temporarily on hold. Characters right out of *Cabaret* could be seen on the streets. It was hard to believe that Hitler's hordes had ever been able to subdue so vivid and individualistic a city. Its active Homophile population was much in evidence.

Vienna had some struggling organizations with which ONE had been in correspondence, but lingering traces of the Holy Roman Empire

[21] Germany and Austria Tours: 1966, 1971, 1972, 1974, and 1981.

[22] Not German, but with similar attitudes toward homophilia, was Stockholm, just across the Baltic. In this respect, at least, it seemed less Scandinavian than German.

[23] See p.13; also Johannes Werres, "Die Kugel," Banquet Speech, *LTR* XXI:9 (September, 1976), pp.1-3. Werres began official participation in the German Homophile Movement in 1950.

days were still strong. On the one hand, there was an almost obsessive, waltzing gaiety. Music from Strauss to Lehar to Mozart could be heard on all sides. On the other hand, there was the revealing incident of an evening re-encounter in a Gay Bar of the day's charming and highly-competent tour guide, who went stonily silent when spoken to.

Greece.[24]   Greece inevitably evoked echoes from classical literature and tales of the flamboyant erotic adventures of the gods and goddesses in that literature. To see men and women today on the streets of Athens, Delphi, or in the villages of the Peloponnesus who could have stepped right down from marble friezes, gave the lie to accounts of the decline and dilution of the classical race reported by some writers. When an Athenian ONE member assured the visitors, "Under the right circumstances, every man in Greece could be available," the current existence of few active Homophile organizations became a thing of secondary concern. Reports from tour members varied, but few or none were unfavorable. One evening, in a large nightclub on the Plaka, the entire cast of singers and dancers mischievously directed the whole show to the ONE group. And why not? After all, the *hilarodia* was a Greek invention.

During one visit, Athens was busy with details of a pedophilic scandal high in Orthodox Church circles. The guide to Delos, who looked like Merlina Mercouri, offhandedly identified a group of pillars as "the home of Demetrios and his boyfriend Alexis." Such incidents made it easy to think that Greece could well have been the birthplace not only of Homophilia, the word, but the very acts themselves.

Islamic and Other Lands. In Morocco and Turkey there was no mistaking that Islamic influence and culture created an understanding gap of almost unbridgeable dimensions for the short-time visitors. Italy, Portugal, and Spain also presented social climates so deeply marked by religious tradition and rigidities left over from recent dictatorships as to be almost impenetrable for ONE's Overseas Tour members in regard to homophilia.

---

[24] Greece, Other European and African Tours: 1972 and 1975.

Japan.[25]   Merely to set foot in Japan is to start a whole process of value system revision and of questioning cultural assumptions inherited from Euro-American sources. The charming folkways and ritual politeness, so conspicuous in Japan, were soon seen as masking an almost implacable ethnocentric racism. One charming native host and highly knowledgeable historian forewarned the visitors that out of well over 1,000 Gay Bars in Tokyo they would find a welcome in not more than 20. As the guide for several days through this immense and complex city, his prediction was discovered to be true.

On one occasion, when the group did manage by its own efforts to locate a much advertised place in Shin-ju-ku, they found three attractive Japanese bartenders and a roomful of frustrated Americans looking at each other in disappointment. There were no Japanese customers.

The flourishing Homophile establishment, Barazoku, publisher of the large monthly magazine of the same name and housed in a modest headquarters with a library, was found with a number of their employees artistically deployed around the premises. One of them engaged in interesting and perhaps well-rehearsed discussion. Then, interview concluded.

In visiting the 20 cross-culturally oriented places mentioned above, ONE's group was warmly received, yet found the differences in expectations and traditions to be very real.

Highly industrialized, with conspicuously modern trappings everywhere, their traditional Shinto and Buddhist attitudes in Homophile matters were unmistakable. So also was their admiration for persons of ample girth and years past middle age, a radical contrast with the American fetish for slimness and youth.

The ancient capitol of Kyoto, solidly sure of its own traditions, seemed to be more comfortable in its Homophile interests than was commercial/industrial Tokyo, and quite relaxed in its reception of the *gajin* visitors from America.

Taiwan.   Taiwan was a striking contrast of bustling modernity everywhere, but few historical monuments. Taipei is quite a new city, strictly American in plan, with broad boulevards and straight streets unlike most cities in Asia.

The kind hospitality of a native Chinese ONE Member opened all

---

[25] Asian Tours: 1973 and 1977.

doors for the ONE group, a most fortunate circumstance. Less Buddhist, more Confucian, Homophile reactions were unlike those in Japan, far more romanticized and unrestrained than might have been expected. While the family is paramount, as everywhere in Asia, Westernized guilt and phobias seemed to be little in evidence. It could be wondered just how Freud might have dealt with all this, how many books it might have taken. William James might have found their pragmatic inclinations and "Why not?" attitude easily understood.[26]

Thailand. While also deeply Buddhist historically, individual Thais today might profess more faith in free enterprise. Homophilia exists barely beneath the surface everywhere, freely available in a sort of *laissez-faire* way that once again wreaks havoc with whole bookshelves of Western psychology.

At least two tendencies may be easily identified: one, what might be called a "situational homophilia" as fugitive and quickly forgotten as the tropical flowers which are everywhere; the other, an implicit interpretation of the theory of role inversion found in folk traditions and mythologies in so many parts of the world.

The Philippines. Although the people of Luzon are ethnically and historically very much a culture of their own, the two culture patterns described above can also be seen. What, though, of the following scene, which is left to the reader or the field work of future students to interpret? The setting, a picturesque mountain village not yet used to the idea of paper money, where a ONE group stopped for an *al fresco* lunch under a palm-thatched sun shelter.

Gathering unobtrusively during the luncheon, like an audience filtering into a theater, was the following cast: a semicircle of what to a Western eye would look like barefoot, shirtless young boys. Behind them was a semi-circle of very pretty and shy young girls. Farthest in back were mothers plaiting palm leaf articles.

After lunch the visitors were invited to use the beautiful rock swimming pools of mountain water nearby.

Returning to reclaim their clothes and dress, the visitors faced a

---

[26] Hong Kong and Singapore are two interesting but artificially created cities which might be said to have internationalized cultural identities rather than strongly indigenous ones.

huge tree. There the young boys were perched in the branches. A native managerial sort of person made it clear that these "flowers" were there for the picking.

Was this folk prostitution? Child molestation with parental approval? Some kind of expression of Philippine admiration for Americans so much evident during those years?

Having no pedophilic interests at all, this editor walked through the garden paths nearby to wait for the rest of the group and was thinking about all this when, from behind a shrub, a big-eyed urchin, who in the United States might have been all of nine, stepped out and said, "You no like me?" [27]

Colombia and Ecuador.[28] Colombia is a startlingly beautiful country whose flowers can match the finest produced anywhere. Unfortunately, political and social conditions have long been unstable. So it was remarkable to meet in Bogota a small and courageous group trying to establish Homophile Rights against all such odds. The current status of this group is not known.

Ecuador is even more beautiful, if possible, with one of the finest collections of Colonial Spanish architecture to be seen anywhere in the Americas, a veritable 17th-century area in Quito lovingly and conscientiously preserved today.

Brazil. Brazil is as big and brash as advertised. A modest Homophile organizational presence was found in Rio, but São Paulo was much more noteworthy for the ONE visitors. Huge and bustling with massed skyscrapers to rival Manhattan, it makes no claims to postcard beauty. What it does have is a vibrant, close-to-the-surface homophilia that feels little need for organized activity.

To this editor no city in the world today is so close to the spirit of adventure and boundless hopes for the future as the São Paulo of the 1980s, a contemporary echo of pre-Depression New York.

---

[27] An evening floor show featuring young go-go dancers in a Manila private club provided one insight into Philippine urban homophilia. The recent Lino Brocka full-length film "Macho Dancer" more fully explores the call boy and male prostitution institutions of Manila.

[28] South American Tour: 1978.

Residents gave a "field report" of the recruiting of Indians from Amazon regions for the booming labor market in road and subway construction. Some admirers who stopped to watch their brawny skills might find themselves asked, "You want me to come live with you?"

The Amazonians, it was reported, proved to be completely trustworthy and dependable, an unexpected side effect of civic progress for many a *Paolista*, if that is their proper designation.

Argentina. Argentina was a textbook example of a nation blessed with every possible natural resource, and which had managed to mishandle everything badly and ruin the country. Fear and suspicion were everywhere. Conspicuous government agents lurked in hotel lobbies, hostile employees were encountered at every turn. A Buenos Aires ONE member met the group with conspiratorial caution, then justified the situation as being necessary and a good thing.

What can be said of a city where only Spanish is spoken, that yet calls itself another Paris and boasts of the European purity of its population, a population which was very similar to what one might see on the streets of Omaha. "We have no Indians here," is their proud claim. The country is still locked into colonial levels of complete subservience to European standards, and brags about it. More recent news does not offer much evidence of hope for improvement.

Paraguay. Passing reference should be made to the native musicians in Paraguay. In South America they are praised as being the best. An evening visit to one of their primitive nightclubs, found down a dirty unpaved street, confirmed that this was true. Their singing and virtuosity on native versions of the Irish harp produced such infectious rhythms as to bring the entire large audience to its feet, some even standing on the dinner table tops and singing.

Peru. Peru has been left to the last because in all of South America it had so much to offer the ONE visitors. First, the Indian presence appears still to be a majority, an indication of its vitality. Inca structures quite put to shame the generally second-rate Spanish Colonial buildings found in much of South America.

The cultural arrogance of the Spanish invaders shows on many Peruvian streets, especially in Cuzco where the impressive pre-Columbian stonework, which stands two or three stories high, has been topped by commonplace Spanish stucco walls.

The native people, looking like ancient carvings come alive, seem impassive at first sight. After closer acquaintance and gaining their confidence, a sparkling and impish humor emerges.

Their high sense of dignity and honesty appears to come from strong identification with their ancient past. One tour guide explained that honesty was an Inca tradition inculcated by a carefully calibrated range of penalties: one finger joint removed for certain infractions, other breaches covered by a detailed and memorable list of procedures.

In the great sprawling city of Lima inhabitants pray, "Earthquakes we can endure, but spare us from dreadful rains." Rain is so rare there that houses are virtually roofless. Grass and trees are only for the very rich. All water must be brought down from the Andes. It is plentiful, but costly.

Lima was a headquarters of the Inquisition for the Americas. Skeletons of some of the victims, along with the torture equipment, can be seen. However, this and the large cathedral, as old as many in Europe, are not of central concern in these pages.

What is significant here is a very extensive semi-private museum in Lima, with thousands upon thousands of fine ceramics and other artifacts dating back through layer upon cultural layer for some thirty centuries. A separate building houses the so-called "sex museum." This is a large collection of ceramic, wood, and other objects, virtually a visual *Kama Sutra*, illustrating every possible variation of sexual behavior.

Erotic museums can be seen elsewhere, of course. What makes this collection so distinctive is that while many, perhaps all, other comparable collections emphasize the mythological, bizarre, or fearsome aspects of the topic, the Andean peoples apparently had entirely different concepts. The styling of all their objects was very human and above all humorous, playful, and sportive for both hetero and Homophile behavior. To the Andeans sexual behavior seems to have been neither frightening nor mysterious, but human and healthy.

In the middle 1950s, Dr. Alfred C. Kinsey was attempting to have some Andean materials of this sort shipped to his Institute in Bloomington, Indiana, when it was stopped by U.S. Customs and threatened with destruction.

He made a special trip to Los Angeles to confer with ONE, Inc. shortly before his death in 1956. His case against Customs was in Court at the time. ONE's own case against the Postmaster of Los Angeles, which was also pending at that time,[29] had alarmed him. He feared that it might in some way jeopardize his own case and hoped that ONE might drop its suit. ONE's victory in the U.S. Supreme Court in 1958 was a total triumph with nationwide and lasting legal impact. The Kinsey case was eventually won, but only in a New York court which gave it a much more narrow legal significance.

ONE Institute Overseas in Review

Is Europe "The Old World?" Old, as compared to what? In global terms Europe is simply a relatively small area of modest population density which extends out from the far larger land mass of Asia. Asia has population concentrations which are truly "old."

The Chinese "Middle Kingdom" is often cited as the archetype of ethnocentrism. Has not Europe studied and restudied itself endlessly, as if the "Western World" were all "the world" that mattered? Homophile Studies must necessarily take a larger view because homophilia is found wherever there are humans.

In such a frame of reference, homophilia among North European peoples relatively recently emerged from their tribal beginnings, Viking and other, have retained certain Northern European cultural patterns. The Warm Brotherhood concept of Germany is one such. The folk patterns seen in Scandinavia are another. The British Isles also developed in their special ways.

Perhaps European studies of sexual behavior should be regarded as more useful for the questions they raise, than as having broader and definitive applications.

In Asia homophilia varies from Japanese stylized Homophile traditions dating back for centuries, as even today the younger man turns erotically to a senior. Women turn to each other in compensation for their social position. China has virtually two histories: that of the courts and the elite and that of the more earthy pragmatic peasantry. Homophilia in these cultures has had but little study thus far.

---

[29] See Chap.1, p.17; also *MAG* IV:9 (September, 1956).

In South Asia, peoples ethnically unlike those to the North often regard homophilia in religious and prescientific terms. Sex role reversal behavior based upon mythological models can often be noted.

In this Review, the Americas turn out to be not a New World at all, but a very Old World with answers and solutions for sexual behavior that are uniquely their own. Andean traditions seem to have survived the Spanish invasion to a surprising degree. Some Atlantic American countries are strongly African, particularly Brazil, the largest. As for the Northern Atlantic countries, Canada and the United States, the monolithic European overlay imparted when the Northern Europeans first landed continues to weaken, as ethnic diversities keep increasing.

CHAPTER 4

THE GRADUATE SCHOOL

College credit for classes was not a matter of great concern in October, 1956, as the earliest ONE Institute Semester opened. Content of the course, bibliographical references recommended, term paper requirements, and many other such questions absorbed the energies and time of students and faculty alike for the next several years.

When the subject of college credit for courses did arise on occasion, faculty members with university teaching experience were quick to point out the many obstacles standing in the way. For instance, would it be likely in view of the negative tone of most academic books about homosexuality that universities would welcome giving credit for study of such a topic? Would university administrations be eager to face public and political criticism or brave the Anita Bryants and frequent anti-homosexual legislative and other campaigns by sponsoring such an idea? Would Gay Liberation's obstreperous and noisy campus sit-ins and other demonstrations of the 1960s and 1970s be likely to have created a very receptive attitude toward giving university credit for so controversial a subject? These and similar arguments effectively brushed aside further discussions for many years.

As described in earlier chapters, classes went right on and subjects were added to the curriculum. Class-record books through the years logged the students attending, many of them faithfully following through with a wide range of the subjects offered. The Sunday Afternoon Lecture Series events, held the first Sunday of the month during the academic year, presented a remarkable array of economists, writers, theologians, psychologists, aspiring politicians, clergy of many denominations, and others, a line up of literally hundreds of contrasting and controversial educational topics.

Some European Homophile organizations referred to ONE Institute as "the world's first homosexual university." While maintaining its work at "university levels," ONE Institute had never claimed university status. It was not formally organized for the offering of degrees within the framework of established training programs and curricula leading to such degrees. It sought, instead, through the presenting of one to four-semester survey courses, to explore nine scholarly fields to discover the levels of relevance each might provide, leading to a better understanding of homosexuality as a human condition. These nine fields

– biology, anthropology, sociology, history, religion, law, psychology, literature and philosophy – have each in turn given fresh insights and clarifications of long-debated points of view and corrected much misinformation.[1]

It was not until the May 4, 1980 Sunday Afternoon Lecture that Dwain E. Houser, an administrator and faculty member at Los Angeles' Pacific States University, prodded the audience: Had not a quarter century of "explorations and probing" been stalled too long to remain at such a level? Had the time not come for moving boldly forward to stake out the right to speak authoritatively in the field of Homophile Studies? Why should the Homophile Community hesitate any longer to assert its claim to take its own higher education into its own hands? Was it presumptuous to assert "the need for a Cal Tech" type of institution which would be highly specialized and adapted specifically to the needs of our own sexual minority?

The presentation and discussions which followed were mind-boggling, controversial, and audacious. Having anticipated that such would be the case, ONE's staff taped the Houser lecture, for the record and the benefit of those who were not present.

In response to the Houser challenge, "An Ad Hoc Committee on Education" (Legg, Houser, David Moore) further explored the proposal, making a report of its findings at the July 16, 1980, Trustees meeting of ONE, Incorporated.

In summary the report recommended that if degree-granting authority was to be implemented, it should be limited to graduate work along well-established lines: M.A. and Ph.D. degrees in Homophile Studies. It was further recommended that 36 standard college units should be required for a Masters. Specific recommendations for doctoral and post-doctoral specialization were left for later examination.

Questions of governance were of considerable concern. It was noted that ONE Institute had a record of academically-organized classes with catalogues and class outlines on record. It was also pointed out that the Institute for the Study of Human Resources (ISHR) had an established record as an "operating foundation" since 1964,[2] and a corporate format likely to be acceptable to the educational authorities

---

[1] *LTR* XXV:5 (May, 1980), p.1.

[2] See above p.41ff.

in Sacramento." [3]

Among other participants at various Meetings of the Ad Hoc Committee on Education, in addition to Legg, Houser and Moore (Librarian of ONE, Incorporated's Baker Memorial Library), was Professor of Sociology Laud Humphreys, Pitzer College, Claremont, California, Professor of Art History Wayne Dynes, Hunter College, New York, and Los Angeles psychotherapist Brian Miller.

To further develop interest in ONE Institute's proposed educational expansion, an entire issue of *ONEletter*[4] was devoted to the Institute's history, curricula and course listings.

First formal action to implement this interest was taken at the Annual Meeting of the Institute for the Study of Human Resources (ISHR) held January 24, 1981, on a motion "unanimously adopted that: The Board of Directors of this foundation goes on record as approving the establishment of an Institute of Graduate Studies under the direction of ONE, Incorporated and will lend all possible support to that effect."[5] Directors voting were Humphreys, Legg, Bob Mitchell, Professor of Sociology, Howard Fradkin, California State University, Long Beach, and Gene Touchet, English Department, Los Angeles Unified School District. Others participating in the discussion were David Moore, Herbert Selwyn, Esq., and Professor of History Walter Williams, University of Cincinnati.

Final formal action on the proposal was taken at the February 1, 1981, 29th Annual Meeting of ONE, Incorporated, which unanimously adopted a motion, "That the Trustees authorize the Education Committee (with the approval by the Board of Directors of ONE, Incorporated) to take all steps necessary for securing the right from the State of California to give credit for ONE Institute classes." [6]

The Trustees further unanimously approved the following: "Be it

---

[3] Letter to ISHR Board of Directors (August 29, 1980), p.1. (ONE's Baker Memorial Library & Archives)

[4] *LTR* XXV:10 (October, 1980).

[5] Minutes, ISHR Annual Meeting, January 24, 1981. (ONE's Baker Memorial Library & Archives)

[6] Minutes, ONE, Inc. Annual Meeting, February 1, 1981. (ONE's Baker Memorial Library & Archives)

moved that the Trustees gratefully accept the offer of the Institute for the Study of Human Resources (ISHR) to assist such a project in any way it can." [7]

With these several actions the two official bodies of ONE, Incorporated, senior Homophile Organization in the United States, and the Institute for the Study of Human Resources, a foundation which since 1964 had established a solid record in educational and charitable fundraising, had made history. Their proposal for a two-part entity to conduct Graduate Classes in Homophile Studies was daring and unprecedented. It remained to be discovered whether the California State Department of Education Office of Private Postsecondary Education would sanction such an unusual administrative structure in a field of studies without any parallel. All of those who were going to have to prepare the applications and deal with the State officials were understandably more than a little nervous.

Having received their marching orders, the Ad Hoc Committee on Education now became a Task Force for exploring unknown territory and very possible opposition for bringing into reality something that had never before existed. There were times when they all wondered if they could succeed, but get to work they did by stealing from their already full-time duties.

For months, Moore and Legg plodded through the seemingly endless tasks set by a State Board of Education which had set out to clear away a widespread reputation that California was overrun by "diploma mills." Through countless drafts and redrafts, typings and retypings, the two ONE staff members prepared the required papers.

Among the papers and forms:
- Statement of Philosophy and Purpose
- Policies of Governance
- Degrees to be Conferred
- Graduation Requirements
- Admission Requirements
- Descriptions of All Courses to be Offered
- Faculty and Their Vitas
- Definition of Unit of Credit
- Core Course Requirements
- Officers of Administration
- Committees of Administration

---

[7] Ibid.

- Educational Rights and Privacy
- Admission Procedures (and Forms)
- Assistantships and Scholarships (and Forms)
- Registration Requirements (and Forms)
- Obligation of Payments
- Tuition Refunds
- Grading System Standards
- Dimensions of All Classrooms and Their Uses
- List of All Equipment and Furnishings
- Valuation of All Equipment and Furnishings
- Instructional Materials (and Samples)
- Valuation of All Instructional Materials
- Full Financial Disclosure (of ONE and ISHR)
- Class Catalogue

The harried staff members were guided and assisted throughout the entire lengthy endurance contest by the knowledge and skills of Dwain Houser, who as mentioned above[8] was an administrator and faculty member of a nearby technical school.[9]

By midsummer in 1981, the masses of papers and filings had been duly sent to the proper authorities in Sacramento, and the State Board of Education Visiting Committee had scheduled August 11, 1981, to examine the physical plant.[10] In a Press Release issued August 18, 1981, it was announced that the Office of Private Postsecondary Education, California State Department of Education, had authorized ONE Institute Graduate School to offer a program of courses leading to the Master of Arts and Doctor of Philosophy degrees in Homophile Studies.[11]

---

[8] See p.71 above.

[9] At the time of his first lecture for ONE Institute, March 2, 1969, Houser was already assisting the highly-respected Chouinard Art Institute to make the transition into The California Institute of the Arts, an undertaking made possible as a result of substantial funding from the Walt Disney fortune.

[10] Minutes, ISHR Board of Directors, August 2, 1981. (ONE's Baker Memorial Library & Archives)

[11] *LTR* XXVI:8 (August, 1981), p.1.

"The establishing of the ONE Institute Graduate School of Homophile Studies in Los Angeles with official authorization by the State of California to offer master's and doctoral degrees in the study of Our Community BY OURSELVES and on our own behalf is a breakthrough in intellectual and social history whose far-reaching implications will in time be appreciated and understood as a major contribution.

"No such institution exists elsewhere. No such institution has ever existed elsewhere. Strange as it may seem, until now it has not seemed intellectually possible to consider Homophile phenomena and the millions of men and women around the world who have Homophile inclinations as warranting scholarly attention or comprising a discrete population and specific patterns of behavior.

"As indicated above, the new ONE Institute Graduate School will devote its energies to studying Homophiles and their behavior, not as deviants or aberrations from 'normal humans,' but as making up in their own right a valid 'field' for study and research. As such class study proceeds, the Graduate School confidently expects to stake out its own areas of expertise." [12]

The opening term of the new Graduate School, October 5, 1981, to January 18, 1982, was devoted appropriately enough to *Homophile Studies 500*, "the Basic Core Course required of all the Graduate School students. It provides in outline form an overview of the multidisciplinary approach to the field of sex variance followed in Homophile Studies," and was taught by this editor.[13]

The 1982 Spring Trimester, which began February 1, 1982,[14] offered a fuller schedule, repeating *Homophile Studies 500* and adding *History 500 - Sexual Variance in Prehistory and Early Civilization* by Legg, *Literature 500 - The Homophile Vein in American Literature* by Touchet, *Philosophy 510 - Questions of Morality and Homophile*

---

[12] *LTR* XXVI:8 (August, 1981), pp.4-5.

[13] See Appendix, 4-1: ONE Institute Graduate School of Homophile Studies... Philosophy 500 Homophile Studies, an Analytic Method, 1981 Fall Schedule.

[14] See Appendix, 4-2: ONE Institute Graduate School of Homophile Studies, [History 500] Homosexuality in History: Outline. [Spring 1982]

Lifestyle by Houser,[15] and *Sociology 500 - Theoretical Concepts in the Sociology of Homosexuality*[16] by Humphreys and Miller, all of these presented within the now-developed framework of Homophile Studies as focused toward graduate work leading to a professional degree in the field.

The Summer 1982 Trimester[17] offered *History 501 - Homosexuality in the Classical World* by Legg, *Sociology 550 - Seminar in Community Studies: Service Organizations* by Gary Steele and Steve Schulte, and *Sociology 580 - Methods of Social Research* by Humphreys and Miller.

The 1982 Fall Schedule[18] offered *History 502 - Homosexuality from the 7th century through the Renaissance* by Legg, *Religion 500 - Religion and Sexual Minorities*[19] by Houser, *Sociology 501 - The Homophile Community: An Ethnographic Approach* by Humphreys and Miller, *Literature 501 - Homophile Literature: Prehistoric to Medieval* by Touchet and Richard J. Follett, and *Homophile Studies 500.*

The Spring Schedule 1983 offered repeats of earlier courses with the addition of *Psychology 565 - Homosexuality and Psychotherapy* by Miller,[20] and *History 560 - Germany Since the Mid-19th Century:*

---

[15] Class Outlines and Syllabi for Spring 1982 Scheduled Classes: History 500, Literature 500, Philosophy 510. (ONE's Baker Memorial Library & Archives)

[16] See Appendix, 4-3: ONE Institute Graduate School of Homophile Studies, Sociology 500 (600) Theoretical Concepts in the Sociology of Homosexuality.

[17] Class Outlines and Syllabi for Summer 1982 Scheduled Classes: History 501, Sociology 550, and Sociology 580. (ONE's Baker Memorial Library & Archives)

[18] Class Outlines and Syllabi for Fall 1982 Scheduled Classes: History 502, Sociology 501, and Homophile Studies 500 (ONE's Baker Memorial Library & Archives) See also Appendix, 4-4: Literature 501.

[19] See Appendix, 4-5: ONE Institute Graduate School, Religion 500 / Religion 600, Religion and Sexual Minorities.

[20] See Appendix, 4-6: ONE Institute Graduate School of Homophile Studies, [Psychology 565] Homosexuality and Psychotherapy.

A Study of Political Pathology by Legg.[21]

There is no intention here to give an exhaustive sequential listing of Graduate School classes, but rather to report the much-expanded class offerings and enlarged roster of faculty.

With the first "Awarding of Degrees Ceremony" January 29, 1984,[22] the groundwork of ONE Institute in its present form had been established comprising: the Non-Degree Courses, as regularly presented since 1956, the Graduate School since 1981, and the Division of Extension and Special Programs, Public Lectures, Midwinter Institutes, and other special events.

Examples of Homophile Studies themselves, papers by faculty and students in the nine fields which form the central focus of the discipline, taken from earlier to more recent years, make up the body of Part II. These selections are the first unified presentations of the field available in a single volume. It is hoped they may awaken widespread interest and encourage participation by others.

---

[21] See Appendix, 4-7: Course Outline, 1983: History 560 Germany Since the Mid-19th Century: A Study of Political Pathology.

[22] See Appendix, 4-8: Awarding of Degrees Ceremony [January 29, 1984].

PART II

HOMOPHILE STUDIES: AN OVERVIEW

SELECTIONS FROM ONE INSTITUTE
FACULTY AND STUDENT PAPERS

Part I described how the various parts and structure of ONE Institute gradually evolved from the simple early statements of general educational purposes found in the Articles of ONE, Incorporated to become a full-fledged specialized Institute with non-degree programs and degree-granting curricula.

In Part II the nine central study areas which are the basic framework and main focus of Homophile Studies have each been given a Chapter. Faculty and student papers selected to illustrate the methods used in defining the field of Homophile Studies are offered in each Chapter. It has been possible to quote only the very shortest papers in their entirety. In most cases excerpts have been chosen to illustrate the specific points felt to be most relevant for understanding the methods used in Homophile Studies. Footnotes are cited as shown in the original text. It is recommended that readers obtain the complete texts whenever possible.[*]

The nine following chapters illustrate the interaction of each upon the others. Their mutual interdependence, once seen, will gradually make apparent the full dimensions of the implicit assumptions found throughout traditional academic scholarship, assumptions challenged by Homophile Studies.

The academic conspiracy of silence has had the effect of rendering Homophile phenomena virtually invisible and in too many cases incomprehensible. The aim of Homophile Studies is to bring this world of phenomena out into the light and to begin the task of exploring and understanding it.

---

[*] Copies of *ONE Magazine, ONE Confidential* (later, *ONEletter*) and *ONE Institute Quarterly of Homophile Studies*, still in print, are available from ONE Institute Press. By special arrangement, photocopies may also be obtained from ONE's Baker Memorial Library & Archives.

CHAPTER 5

HOMOSEXUALITY IN HISTORY

The first course added to the curriculum after the initial *Introduction to Homophile Studies* was *Homosexuality in History*. The 1957-58 two-semester tryout was admittedly a hasty effort more notable for its challenges than as a pattern to be followed. It was later expanded to a four-semester sequence.

Egyptian and German history have also each been given full semesters, as have the European and American Homophile Movements.

The earliest student paper still found is dated September 30, 1957, its title "Heliogabalus: Libertine," by Jack Roust, then in his early twenties. He and his partner attended classes during 1957-58. Excerpts from his text are quoted at some length because of its early date:

Heliogabalus: Libertine

In the year 218 A.D. amidst general intrigue and plotting for control of the Roman Empire, including a minor battle between two Roman generals in Syria, the nominal emperor Macrinus lost control of the military, was overthrown by them, and succeeded by Heliogabalus.

Accounts of his appearance indicate that he was extremely beautiful in dress, form, and countenance. He was compared favorably with a beautiful picture of the young Bacchus. He was always dressed in silken Oriental clothes for he thought Greek and Roman clothing coarse. Jewelry and amulets enhanced his beauty, but his use of eye makeup and other cosmetics detracted from his natural attractiveness. Fond of dancing, he loved to perform publicly, especially for the Troops.

To the tinkling of his jewelry and the rustling of his silken gowns, a perfumed and painted Heliogabalus descended on the town at night for a little fun. His versatility was commented upon by historians as being novel to Rome where homosexuality was usually associated only with pedication [sic] and only in pairs. Heliogabalus loved prostitution. He finally set aside a room in the palace for this purpose. He would stand nude in the doorway in the time-honored stance of prostitutes, rustling the curtain which was fastened by gold rings and soliciting customers in a soft and melodious voice. He had other prostitutes engaged at this brothel [and] boasted that he had more lovers than they and took in more money.

This is not to imply that the Emperor frittered away his daylight hours. There were always games and festivals. It was at a chariot race that – during the height of the race, one of the chariots spilled its driver just opposite the Emperor. The beardless youth so ignobly dumped into the imperial presence lost his helmet in the fall, exposing a wondrous crown of yellow hair. He was carried away to the palace where he spent the night with the Emperor. He was a Carian slave named Hierocles.

As for Aurelius Zoticus, a native of Smyrna, he incurred the sovereign's thorough love and thorough hatred, and consequently his life was saved. This Aurelius had a body that was beautiful all over, as if ready for a gymnastic contest, and he surpassed everybody in the size of his private parts. The facts were reported to the Emperor by those who were on the lookout for such features, and the man was suddenly snatched away from the games and taken to Rome, accompanied by an immense procession [and] appointed *cubicularius* before he had been even seen by the Emperor. Heliogabalus on seeing him rose with modesty, "Call me not Lord for I am a Lady."

Hierocles began to fear that Zoticus would bring the Emperor into a greater state of subjection than he himself had been able to effect. Therefore he had the wine-bearers, who were well-disposed to him, administer some drug that abated the visitor's ferocity. After a whole night, being unable to secure an erection, he was driven out of the palace, also out of Rome, and this saved his life.

Heliogabalus' struggle was suddenly lost when he was attacked and killed by soldiers who then threw his body into the Tiber. Despite the brevity of his reign, Heliogabalus made contributions to history. [For example:]

1. He introduced monotheism officially into Rome.
2. He was the first to give the Christians imperial recognition, though prudish scholars attribute this to Constantine.
3. He introduced culinary prizes for gourmets.

Among Roust's bibliographic citations were: Herodian's *Historia V*; Cassius Dio's *Historia Romana* (LXXIX and LXXX); Aelius Lampridius' *Life of Elagabalus*; Otto Kiefer's *Sexual Life in Ancient Rome*; H. L. Mencken and George Jean Nathan's play *Heliogabalus: A Buffoonery in Three Acts*.

What is Maturity?

Attendance at the ONE Institute Lecture Series[1] has long been an integral part of the student class work. The following report[2] of the May 1, 1961, Lecture #50, "What is Maturity?" given by British historian and philosopher D. B. Vest (pseud.), is by Stella Rush, who often wrote as Sten Russell. She was a ONE Institute student for several terms.

The report is reprinted here for its intrinsic interest, evidencing the adventurous tone and range found in the ONE Institute Lectures, and also to document the academic and instructional purpose these Lectures have exhibited.

 3000-4000 years ago began the *Heroic Age* and a new problem faced the world: that people had begun to think and feel themselves to be individual. Ulysses and his Odyssey, the great legendary example of *physical courage* and the saga of "The Hero-Soldier." This pattern collapsed about 600 B.C., although the Soldier still typifies the Heroic in our culture. The Hero-Soldier in psychological terminology exemplifies the *Nor-Adrenalin Type*: child-like, paranoid, berserk, rage of battle, projection. Whereas the *Schizoid Conscious of Pure Adrenalin* is all turned inward to blaming oneself.

As human consciousness changed, the hormone balance changed. Whereas the *first* pattern of prestige had been physical courage, the *second* pattern of prestige became *moral courage*. Renaissance Man and Ascetic Man represented aspects of this new pattern of prestige. Ascetic Man held a belief in celibacy based on the concept that it was criminal to procreate and bring children into such a sinful, terrible world to perpetuate more sin and terror.

The *third* pattern of prestige was typified by the *Humanist* who believed that one should obey the traffic rules, but other than that, the individual should be left alone.

The Modern Age is over! It ended about 1910 and not many

---

[1] See Chap.2, p.50.

[2] Sten Russell, "What is Maturity?" *CONFI* VI (May, 1961), p.3.

people are aware that it is over. At that time a sudden change took place in the human mind – a mutation – and no mutation like this has taken place in 2500 years: it is an awareness of *the unconscious*. This newly–mutated man lives by "interest and meaning." There is a little man in our heads who [is] not at all interested in "social consciousness," "money," or "appetites." We don't see ultra-violet rays, but we're affected by them. We're a creature that *thinks*, but still uses the senses of an animal.

We need a new Pattern of Prestige which has nothing to do with "Maturity." "The Organizer," "the little man in the head we're not aware of," is subtly altering the human machine without our knowledge. The "population bomb" has had something to do with this. We have had to produce a type that didn't breed. Mr. Vest believes that there has been an increase in homosexuality because of this need. Also, new viruses are appearing to kill people. "Things are changing at a hell of a pace." We have had to produce a type that is very late in growing up. Man is not a polymorphic pervert from three years on per Freud but a Pan-aesthetic transit, a creature which feels all over.

In our society we need seers (eyes), managers (heads), technicians (hands), and people (feet). Seers we are lacking in sufficient quantity. Prescience is *not* enough. Pre-cognition comes only from the seer type. We must start with the best raw material for training seers. The best raw material are people who are unstable, charged with irresponsibility, deeply interested in fantasy, can't adjust, do not have a goal or purpose and yet feel that they must have it to live. This kind of a human creature is typified most by the Isophyl. The Isophyl is of a homosexual nature and has reciprocal love affairs with those of his or her kind who are equal or at a similar stage of development intellectually and emotionally.

In the question period, Mr. Vest made some intriguing statements. For instance, since women have been emancipated, we no longer have the classic situation of the male and the female (the lock and the key), we have *two keys*. Another: we are not up against "communism," but the concept of the four-fold state: the seer-scanner, manager-planner, technicians, and the mass.

Regarding some of the religious movements which have caused a change in the conduct, character, and consciousness of its members (the Jesuits and the Quakers), Mr. Vest made this striking statement which we all could use, "A perfect sense of belonging drives out fear."

Syllabus and Bibliography

No syllabus or study outline was in existence at the time of the earliest semesters of *Homosexuality in History*. No textbook on such a topic existed. Therefore, the classes met week by week, the instructor exploring through countless reference books, hunting for leading passages which would be relevant, also to keep ahead of the classes.

Given this situation the problem of bibliographical support at once became apparent. As the *History* course went through changes from a two-semester sequence in 1957-58 and 1958-59, during the next thirty years it evolved into a four-term sequence: I – Prehistory, Mesopotamia, Egypt, China, India and the Andes; II – Mycenean, Minoan, Greek and Roman to "The Fall;" III – Byzantine, Islamic, the Dark and Middle Ages; IV – Renaissance Europe through the 19th century. During those years, some clear demarcations were established to define the scope for such a sequence.

It was not military history and it was not the political history of reigns and dynasties. Nor was it economic history, except when such influences impinged directly upon Homophiles and their lives. The history of religions, myths and emerging scientific thinking came closer than most other areas of focus, yet only to the extent of their direct relevance: castrate priesthoods of various Mother Goddess cults, for example.

A bibliography for so vast a field: a word or two here and a sentence there throughout the centuries of social changes would become meaninglessly clumsy. More useful perhaps to anyone not actually enrolled in a specific class term is a listing of works which have been influential in a broad sense, with some indications of why.

For the earliest periods, detailed descriptions of Mesopotamia by Chiera, S. Kramer, H. Frankfort, T. Gaster, and the bibliographies they cite are very useful. Valuable also are as many versions of the *Gilgamesh Epic* as can be found: variations between versions and gaps are highly significant. The Durant books are valuable in succession for their bibliographies and citations. Their candid inclusion of references to homosexuality is a welcome contrast to others more prudish. V. Gordon Childe provides many leads which are worth following. Anything on the cave paintings is worthwhile, less for the texts than for close examination of the paintings themselves.

Egyptian history provides an immense literature quite easily accessible, with special focus upon their various religious developments, myths, and gods. Set and Horus call for close notice, also phallic symbols in art and architecture. Unfortunately, without access to such photographic evidence as has been provided by Homophile tourists showing the systematic defacement of phallic art by Christian and other latecomers, central aspects of Egyptian sexual theory might be glossed over.

On the other hand, Indian art readily provides keys to understanding much of the sexual bases of Indian mythology and philosophy. The *Kamasutra* provides some direct assistance. Indian temple art bears close study, especially the Black Pagoda and other Tantric examples. Countless phallic monuments standing in India today call for explanation. The writings of Joseph Campbell are valuable as sources for mythology worldwide. Though not in favor today, James Frazier's multi-volume *Golden Bough* still provides many trails to follow.

For the classic periods, Hans Licht's *Sexual Life in Ancient Greece* offers a wide range of themes and leads, although it needs to be used carefully. However, Licht prepares the student to find more recent works such as K. Dover's 1978 *Greek Homosexuality* helpful. The *Musa Puerilis*, or *Greek Anthology*, is a basic work for the Hellenistic and later periods.

Kiefer's *Sexual Life in Ancient Rome* has some value but the Durants are more useful. N. I. Garde's *From Jonathan to Gide* is often unreliable. Various Roman writers – Juvenal, Virgil, Petronius and many others – provide useful clues.

Homosexuality in History[3]

This editor's article "Homosexuality in History" dealt with theory in Homophile Studies. Excerpts follow which have been selected to call attention to issues relating to basic theory. No attempt should be

---

[3] W. Dorr Legg, "Homosexuality in History: Introductory Chapter for a Proposed Textbook," *QTLY II*:3 (Summer 1959), pp.93-8.

made at reading the excerpts other than as non-sequential passages, such as might be used as a basis for class discussion. This is the way they were used when *Homosexuality in History* was next offered in 1960-61.

Homosexuality is known to have occurred as far back as recorded history goes. Much older myths and legends contain frequent references to this type of behavior among nearly all of the world's peoples.

Concerning still earlier times, archaeology, paleoanthropology, and study of the higher mammals give so much evidence of its presence that the conclusion seems warranted that homosexual behavior far antedates the emergence of man, being innate in the animal kingdom as a whole.

Why, then, have historians generally paid so little attention to the subject?

Types of Historical Theory. To begin at the beginning, more than four thousand years ago, what has been called the oldest known example of historical writing was recorded.[4] It describes a boundary dispute between King Entemena of Lagash, and Mesilim, King of Kish. The forces of Lagash are depicted as being led into battle by Ningirsu, the city's patron deity, and further reinforced by the divine sanction of Enlil, himself king of all the Sumerian gods.

In later centuries, a neighboring people, the Hebrews, faithfully adhered to this particular historical tradition, always imputing supernatural leadership to their armies. "The Lord of hosts mustereth the host of the battle,"[5] is one way they expressed this idea.

The theory of history which saw divine intervention in all events found unquestioning acceptance in many literatures, achieving great elaboration through the works of Augustine, bishop of Hippo in the early fifth century, A.D., followed by innumerable later Church historians. Recently, Tillich, Christopher Dawson, Toynbee, as well as many others, skillfully perpetuate the theological approach.

Also, in Sumeria, with the *Gilgamesh Epic*, may be observed the beginnings of quite a different tradition. The gods are always present and acknowledged to be greatly influential, but they do not hold the center of the stage. Instead, there is a Great Man, or several. Their deeds and exploits, their virtues and vices, form the principal subject

---

[4] Samuel N. Kramer, *History Begins at Sumer* (New York: 1959), p.41.

[5] *Isaiah* xiii, 4.

matter. Removed thus at least part of the way from heaven to earth, greater audience identification was afforded and the method's immense popularity insured.

Achilles and Agamemnon, David and Goliath, were the mythohistorical prototypes of the subjects of this type of biographical history. The well-known predilection of Great Men for combat in various forms, military or political, made it only natural that Xenophon, Thucydides, Livy, Tacitus, Josephus, and so on down to the ever-popular writers on the American Civil War, should interpret all things in terms of conflict. (p.93-4)

There have been anthropological, sociological, and even psychoanalytic historians who see the Oedipus Complex under every event. A major recent movement has taken to itself the name *historicism*. This school rejects both the teleological approach of the Church historians and the equally teleological theories of Hegel, Marx and Spengler, its aim being nothing less than an examination of "human life in its totality and multiplicity." [6] (p.94)

If there are any who still may feel that the whole undertaking is without sufficient justification, they should refer to the tenet of historicism that the totality of human life is proper subject matter. If this be granted, how then can man's sexual behavior possibly be excluded?

This being the case, may historians be exempted from giving serious attention to the sexual aspects of history merely because Aristotle or Ranke did not do so? It is hardly required that one subscribe to all of the Freudian articles of faith to admit that it might be possible that man's sexual drives may have done as much to determine the course of history as all his other drives together. (p.95)

Translations, Definitions and Other Problems. The problem of definitions is one encountered at the very outset. For instance, is it admissible to speak of "homosexuals?" If so, how may they be defined? What definition is adequately inclusive to cover such cases as Oscar Wilde, a well-known "homosexual," yet a husband and father, and Marie Antoinette, also married and a mother, who had considerable homosexual experience, or Aristotle, whose homosexuality may have been either sporadic or short-lived? (p.96)

The whole question of translations out of ancient tongues is a vexed one, full of pitfalls. For instance, an Egyptologist may, in all sincerity labor over some obscure passage, coming up with a rather generalized religious statement about the god, Set. A specialist in

---

[6] Hans Meyerhoff, *Philosophy of History* (Garden City, New York), p.10.

Homophile studies, were he also an Egyptologist, might on the other hand have at once discerned that the scholar's translation problems arose because of his unfamiliarity with homophilia, the passage being a satirical, or a symbolic, or other indirect reference to homosexuality.

The difficulty of achieving adequate translations is further complicated by the censorship which in many cases has been exercised by scholars and scribes in the interests of whatever code of nicety prevailed at the time. This practice has, unfortunately, so riddled much of the ancient literature with euphemisms designed to conceal, rather than reveal, the facts as to completely pervert the true meaning. In some cases, the nicety code has persuaded otherwise honest men to actually alter the sexes of persons so that the fact would not appear that one man was lover of another man.

By such means much of history has been seriously distorted. An example familiar to readers is that of Plato's *Symposium*. It would be almost impossible to compute the number of pages of discussion about this famous work that have been written down the centuries, the great majority of them blandly assuming the position that Plato was discussing love between men and women or, with still less justification, some intellectual abstraction. Yet, the scholarly translator of a recent edition of the work states, "The love with which the dialogue is concerned, and which was accepted as a matter of course by all the speakers, including Socrates, is homosexual love." [7] (p.96)

Turning to still another aspect of our topic, the question must unavoidably be asked if it is possible to understand homosexuality today without knowing what happened yesterday, and the days before that. Ortega y Gasset has well put the point in saying, "History is a system, the system of human experiences linked in a single inexorable chain. Hence nothing can be truly clear in history until everything is clear."[8] (p.97)

It is confidently believed that a general textbook on homosexuality in history, however grave may be its shortcomings, will fill a need, serving many useful purposes. The listing alone of the numerous focal points or history-nodes, around which expressions of homosexuality have clustered in times past, should stimulate considerable thought of a practical nature, if pragmatic justification be deemed necessary.

---

[7] Plato, *The Symposium*, trans. W. Hamilton (London: Penguin, 1951), p.12.

[8] Jose Ortega y Gasset, *Toward a Philosophy of History* (New York: 1941), p.222.

From the pages to follow, a listing of some of these focal points may, it is hoped, suggest to the reader certain of the lines along which the work will develop. Among such important history-nodes, rich in homosexual implications, have been:

1. Such institutions as the shaman, the medicine man, and the witch doctor, from many cultures
2. Priesthoods of the Mother Goddess cults, often transvestite and castrate
3. The eunuch
4. Religious orders, both pagan and Christian
5. The theater, itself religious in origin
6. Warrior-brotherhoods during various Heroic Ages, and elsewhere
7. Military castes, as in Sparta, feudal Germany, medieval Japan
8. The tutor and student axis
9. The master and slave axis
10. Music, the arts, and ballet, particularly since the Renaissance. (p.98)

Background Aspects of the Sodom Story[9]

The following excerpts from the paper by Henry Hay, a lecturer at ONE Institute, do not attempt to give a digest, or abstract, of the writer's thinking, but are given as selections to call attention to historical records such as the Sodom story and others which relate directly to Homophile Studies. Space limitations have made excerpting Hay's closely argued text difficult. Readers should consult the original.

Critic French historian Marc Daniel raised strong objections to Hay's scholarship and methods in the pages of *ONE Institute*

---

[9] Henry Hay, "The Moral Climate of Canaan at the Time of Judges," *QTLY* I:1 (Spring 1958), pp.8-16, and I:2 (Summer 1958), pp.50-9. The article subhead noted, "This article is excerpted from a study in preparation: 'The Homophile in Search of an Historical Context and Cultural Contiguity' – subsection, 'David and Jonathan Revisited'."

Quarterly,[10] to which Hay responded with equal vigor.[11]

The first Egyptian conquest of the Semitic lands of Asia Minor, (between 2000-1800 B.C., during the crisis and disintegration of the Sumerian Empire of Ur under the combined onslaught of the barbarian Amorites and Elamites and before the resurrection of Semitic civilization under Hammurabi of Babylon) largely destroyed the inland city states and laid waste the native semi-sedentary villages. Palestine proper, and in particular, Transjordan, reveals archeologically every evidence of enormous decimations in this period. (p.8)

In the late thirteenth century, then, the period generally assigned by most modern scholars to the Mosaic infiltration is approximately 1230 B.C., the face of Palestine is that of two divergently productive and acculturated regions – both evidencing areas of great cultural advancement simultaneously interlaced with areas of desolation and cultural impoverishment. Both areas are subject on their fringes to frequent raids of spoilage by indigent barbarian inhabitants of the hill-country known to the Amarna records as Apiru. One of these raiding leaders by the name of Yashuya apparently raided and burnt Jericho approximately one hundred years before the so-called Exodus. In North Palestine, or the Israel of the Old Testament, tilthism and craft-merchantilism largely prevailed: semi-sedentary herding intermixed with garden-culture and caravan-mercantilism largely held sway in the South, or Judah. Israel was an area subject to river irrigation and seasonal rains – Judah an area harassed by infrequent inundations and unpredictable oasial conditions. (p.9)

The cycle of life throughout the whole of the Fertile Crescent of Asia Minor was Lunar. The Moon was the emanation of the Great Mother – herself both the womb of all nature and at the same time the genius of her unknown and unimportant fertilizer; or the Moon, who signaled menstruation in women and thus, according to so late a source as Aristotle, the true source of fertilization; the Moon who, according to Pliny "brings forth the dews and moistures which the sun consumes," (George Thompson, *Studies in Ancient Greek Society*, London, 1951, p.215). In some societies as the Matrilocal patterns succumbed to Androcratic usurpations, Sun-goddesses and Moon-goddesses subordinated their prerogatives to their Consorts (in common

---

[10] Marc Daniel, *QTLY* IV:2 (Spring 1961), pp.56-8.

[11] Henry Hay, *QTLY* IV:2 (Spring 1961), pp.58-62. See also *MAG* VII:5 (May, 1960), pp.5-11.

Hebrew Shemesh, the name of the sun deity, could be either masculine
or feminine); in other societies, where the Great Goddess was too
identified with basic survival patterns to be undermined, She was mas-
culinized. As W. Robertson-Smith in his *Religion of The Semites*
(London, pp.58-9) says, "Not seldom religious tradition refused to
move forward with the progress of society; the old Goddess retained
her old character as a Mother who was not a wife bound in fidelity
to a husband." Even so, in the case of Ishtar and Athtar, or Ashtar
– Ashtar became only a minor deity; according to Theodore Gaster
in his essay "Religion of the Canaanites," Ashtar was the "genius of
artificial irrigation (c.f. Arabic - "athari"-artificially irrigated soil).
(p.10)

In Sumer, as in Arabia, ba'al was used in the sense of "husband-
man"; as W. Robertson-Smith in *Religion of the Semites* (p.94) says,
"it is not used of the relation of a master to his slave, or of a superior
to his inferior." Ba'al-berith at Shechem, in ordinary Hebrew, meant
"possessor of covenant." Since, under the village commune, women
enjoyed many rights within the household phratry superior to the men
– and even under the Semitic Code of Hammurabi enjoyed many
protections including the rights to hold allotments of land as members
of the community, (Henri Frankfort, *The Birth of Civilization in the
Near East*, New York, 1956, pp.65, 67) – it must be seen that the
frequent interpretations that Semitic women were the properties of
their husbands or ba'als are inaccurate. Actually, Matriarchy and its
prerogatives were not defeated, and women legally declassed, in Israel
until the Deuteronomic Codes were railroaded through around 550
B.C. (p.13)

Modern Biblical scholarship, authoritatively summarized by Dr.
Robert Pfeiffer in the 1948 revised edition of his *Introduction to the
Old Testament*, has largely eliminated the familiar foundations and
landmarks supporting the general public's conventional images of Old
Testament times prior to the Babylonian Exile. In the first place, it
is pretty definitely established that the genealogies and chronicled
itineraries of the Patriarchs were first conceived and fictionalized not
earlier than the Tenth Century (ca. 950 B.C.), or about the time of
Solomon. As Dr. Pfeiffer puts it (abridged ed., *The Books of the Old
Testament*, New York, 1957, p.40), "It was during the united monar-
chy that the genealogical scheme was devised and the patriarchs,
originally with little in common, were joined together into a single
family; it was then, or shortly before, that Yahweh had taken the place
of the local deities of Canaanitic legends, and that events of past
history, relations with neighboring nations, and pride in national
achievements were read into the adventures of legendary heroes."
In the second place, our earliest sources of the Pentateuch have been

sifted out of the garbled and deliberately rewritten histories of the Deuteronomic Reformation as three early documents known as the J, the S, and the E documents. Dr. Pfeiffer says (p.38), "The genuine traditions of ancient Israel are confined to the stories of Joseph, Moses, and the invasion of Canaan. The rest is an adaptation from Canaanitic and other sources." (p.50)

Ba'al, the bull of fertility initiating increases to flocks, herds, and crops, was not to be compared with the *numen par excellence* whose mountain throne was grander than the great palaces of Tyre, whose garden groves were taller than the cedars of Lebanon (see, e.g., Theodor H. Gaster, "The Religion of the Canaanites," in V. Ferm, *Ancient Religions*, New York, 1950, pp.119-22). The primeval bull-inseminator of all life in the earth–sea–sky, whose stamping charge was the dynamic of heavenly storms, whose bellow the breath that stirred mighty oceans, was surely the only prototype of the thundering fire-breathing God who had led the Israelites across the wilderness to Canaan. El, the great golden bull, through his mythical wonder-working priest Aaron (see, e.g., A. Powell Davies, *The Ten Commandments*, New York, 1956, pp.52, 100), was the only possible *numen par excellence* for Israel. Note, in passing, that Aaron does not appear at all in the J document. His only mention is in E. (p.51)

The Ba'al of Judah was then the serpent, found coiled and entwined, in numberless archeologically–retrieved figurines and reliefs around the limbs of Asherath and Ashtarth who, in many cases, wore their hair in two long spiral ringlets identical to those of Hathor, Mother Goddess of the Egyptian Delta, also identified with Mut and Isis (see, e.g., Albright, *The Archeology of Palestine*, London, 1954, p.106). (p.52)

A brief summary of the *Deuteronomic* garbling, redacting, and rewriting of the Kadesh episode of *Exodus*, reveals the problems facing the modern scholar, and yields a clue to the more germane comprehension of moral horizons in this period. The Oasis of Kadesh, also known as En-Mish-Pat (the fountains of judgment), was an already ancient oracular sanctuary on the well-traveled overland route from the Egyptian Delta to Canaan-Syria-Hatti-Harran and Mesopotamia, a sanctuary whose very names *Kadesh* – dedicated or devoted, *Meribah* – waters of controversy, *Enmish-pat* – fountains of judgment, proclaimed a working priesthood who interpreted divine pronouncements from invoked signs in the waters. We have already discussed this phenomenon in relations to the stewardships of the local Ba'als. We need remember only that the Ba'al was the regent-administrator of justice, the oracular pronouncements themselves were those of his mistress, the Great Earth Matron, whose intercessor priests were the quedoshim of the shrine. Kadesh was then a well-known hospice for caravans and armies traveling to and from Egypt, and therefore a most probable place for a respite during the Exodus. Dr. S. A. B. Mercer, in his essay, "The Religion of Ancient Egypt" (in *Ancient Religions*, ed. V. Ferm, New York, 1950, p.31), mentions *Kedesh* as a West Asiatic Goddess of love and beauty, "The divine harlot of The Gods" – as an acculturated deity accruing to the Egyptian Empire. She may have been the Mother Goddess of Kadesh-Barnea, as an aspect of Asherath. But why, then, wasn't she *Kedeshath* (feminine) instead of Kedesh (masculine)? Chances are she was an androcratic anthropomorphic personification of the Sanctuary's traditional function, a deification of an abstract idea common to Egyptian theology. (pp.52-3)

Note that nowhere here is there any implication that homophilic or homoerotic practices as such bear any onus whatsoever. (p.54)

The first startling fact that confronts one, upon viewing the four stories of *Genesis* and *Judges* **as a category**, that is, Canaanitic folk tales and ballads so widely circulated that they had lost much of their original character, is the realization that the tales of Sodom in *Genesis* 19, and of Gibeah, later to become Saul's native city in *Judges* 19-21, are but **variants of the same plot** out of the folk oral tradition. (p.55)

Now Sodom and Gomorrah were not the only "cities of the plain;" such also was the designation of the flourishing and fertility-ritual-practicing cities of Canaanitic Ezdraelon, and the basis for the above stories is admittedly Canaanitic. Ballads of earthquakes, fiery volcanoes, the fall and impact of flaming meteorites, figure prominently in the tags and snatches of the myths of Hither Asia. (pp.56-7)

In *Genesis* 38:7-10, we have one of the few perfect examples of the Curse Code in action, "And Er, Judah's first-born, was wicked in the sight of Yahweh; and Yahweh slew him." Onan, Er's brother, performed interrupted coitus – spilling his seed upon the ground, "and the thing which he did was evil in the sight of Yahweh: and he slew him also." In the case of Er we must accept on faith that Yahweh found secret transgression in Er's heart. But what of Onan? Under the codes and proscriptions listed above, is Onan guilty of transgressions? Here, as with the Sodom and Gibeah tales, we must wash our consciousness clear of the clutter of Pentateuchal Codes in which we have been conditioned; we must recall that of all the existing three codes contemporary to *Genesis* 38, the only ones within our context are those forbidding ritual opportunism (necromancy or sorcery), bestiality, and those proscribing the violation of communally-protective taboos such as hospitality and "holiness." In regard to the latter, we must recall that the soil covering of earth was the Theophany of the Mother Goddess, and also that "seed" was in itself one of the most vital of ritual unguents. Was, then, Onan guilty of transgression under the code? The answer of course is yes – *but not of such a transgression as currently bears his name.*

The evidences of communal clan existence all point to the assumption that sexual intercourse at this stage of social consciousness was still nominally bound by the disciplines of ritual purity and/or largely seasonal in manifestation, a testimony of which within *Genesis* 38 itself is Judah's connection with Tamar, whose name incidentally meant "date-bearing palm" – an aspect of the Mother Goddess as bearer of the food so essential to nomads. In such terms of cause and effect, Onan therefore committed sacrilege *as uninvoked* (unconsecrated) sodomy! In the latter act, when properly ritualized, one dispensed one's vigor and seed, as a command upon, and simultaneously a gift-of-life-force to, the Goddess without incurring other than blessed and constructive social consequence.

In Onan's case, he anointed the Theophany (the earth-image) of the Mother Goddess directly with the gift of his life-containing holy unguent. The process was a variant one, but the taboo was the same in that supernatural consequences were automatically unleashed for which no ceremonial or sanctifying protections had been prepared, except as he personally might have contrived, and about which we are not told. Whether, indeed, the individual could have so arranged is immaterial; if he could, and did, his action would have to be construed as antisocially contrived, and therefore sorcery. And since the only person ostensibly present to condemn him "out of the mouth" was his brother's wife who, under the code, could not bear witness, the heavenly thunderbolt of the Anathema Curse was automatically his reward. The Deuteronomists had no cause, in inserting this tale into *Genesis*, to alter the story because it so perfectly illustrated their proscription of *Deut.* 20:2-3 concerning those who passed their seed unto Molech. Be that as it may, let it be recorded that Onan's act is the only instance in the entire Testamental Canon where sodomy was judged by the lightning furies of supernatural dynamics. Thus exited Onan, illustrating not a bad story but a sad story, not the ominous sorcerer but only the witless apprentice.

Summarizing the foregoing, we might say that whereas the Sodom variant (of a popular plot in public domain) reflects Yahweh's divine retribution for not only secret sins **but for the collective refusal to abide by the responsibilities to witnessing** (i.e., *Deut.* 27:26), with the Onan story as a variant, that the Dannite and Benjamin variations of the same theme in *Judges* 17-21 represent a more primitive ethical horizon (or again a debased retrogression) in which justice is quantitative rather than qualitative. Thus the S author reveals that the semi-isolated region of Edom in the Tenth Century is familiar with the advanced ethic of the Curse Code while Judah and the Judahitic author of *Judges* 17-21 are not. Dr. Pfeiffer seems inclined to postulate that the early author of *I Samuel* and the author of *Judges* 17-21 are the same. But, as we will later show, the author of *I Samuel* is also familiar with the Anathema Code, albeit a form more equitable with the first stages of comprehension than with the fuller synthesis sustained by S. (pp.58-9).

Homoaffectionalism: The Civilizing Factor[12]

Paul Hardman's 1985 248-page ONE Institute Ph.D. dissertation of that title is notable for its scope. It contains Chapters on the Gilgamesh Epic and the Code of Hammurabi, including its precursors.

On Hammurabi, Rabbi Dr. Charles Ber Chavel quotes the Biblical text, "There shall be no kideishah of the daughters of Israel (one who is devoted to and always prepared for illicit intercourse) nor shall there be a kadeish of the sons of Israel (one who is always ready for pederasty)." There is no doubt that Chavel considers the temple boys to be catamites (Chavel p.30). Chavel also writes, "With reference to the Code of Hammurabi then, we may conclude that homosexuality was certainly not forbidden." [13]

Hardman's lengthy chapters on: "The Hittites," "Greek Ambivalence," and "Rome, a Sense of Guilt" are too detailed for quotation here. In "Christianity, The Decline," his examination of the development of Roman marriage and family law and the patriarchal doctrine of *patria potestas* calls for special notice. "As late as 445 B.C. there was still no regular marriage." (Hardman, p.120) "As late as the fourth century

---

[12] Hardman, Paul. *Homoaffectionalism: The Civilizing Factor.* Ph.D. Dissertation, 1985. (ONE's Baker Memorial Library & Archives)

[13] Charles Ber Chavel, *Commentary on the Torah* (New York: Shilo Publishing House, 1976), p.32, cited in Hardman (1985).

A.D. the Christian church had little influence on marriage." (p.122) Hardman offers a lengthy examination of the development of homophobic attitudes, both by Justinian and his empress Theodora. "It was only in 249 A.D. that the Emperor Phillip abolished the *exsoleti*, mercenary catamites." (p.125) Hardman covers the homosexual liaisons of Augustine, which are usually mentioned only in passing. (p.153, *et seq.*)

In "Europe After the Fall," discussing Visigoths and other "tribal Europeans," Hardman notes that, "Essentially sex habits were of small concern to the state." (p.172)

In "The Middle Ages," Hardman indicates, "Although beyond the scope of this study, it is noteworthy that the recognition of homosexual feelings as "natural" could still be found among the peasants in remote and rural parts of England as late as the 17th and early 18th centuries." (p.180) Hardman cites at length a peasant case from 1716 as illustration. (p.180, *et seq.*) The chapter on "Sodomia" gives detailed examination to the development of meanings of the term preceding current usage.

His concluding chapter, "The Mamlukes," gives close attention to this little-known pederastic, military Islamic caste in 10th century Egypt and later. Hardman writes, "Thus, when the sultan Saladin declared the end of the Fatamid khalifate in 1171 A.D., mamlukes were well entrenched in the system. (Alan) Moorehead, like others, takes notice of the origins of the mamlukes as being purchased as children." (p.206) Hardman comments, "What we have here is a unique phenomenon in history, young boys are purchased, then trained to be companions and the eventual heirs of a master who truly cared for them. The bond between the mamlukes themselves and their masters can in fact best be described as homoaffectionalism." (p.207)

Enough sources have already been mentioned to indicate the wealth of reference material which is available. As the centuries move closer to our own time, sources grow more plentiful. Only two more names will be mentioned as examples: Boswell's *Christianity, Social Tolerance and Homosexuality*, with many mediaeval sources, and Marc Daniel's *Hommes du grand Siècle*, with directly relevant 17th and 18th century materials.[14]

The aim of this text is not to be a compendium of reference materials or study guide. Its purpose is to illustrate faculty and student work done at ONE Institute and the theoretical framework in the works that have been created.

Homophilia in Germany

The January, 1953, first issue of *ONE Magazine* included an article translated from *Die Insel*, the German Homophile publication. This clearly indicates ONE's early recognition of the international nature of the Homophile Movement, and also the role of German-speaking peoples in that Movement. Soon after the opening of ONE Institute in 1956, faculty member James Kepner, Jr., writing as Lyn Pedersen, published a two-part article, "The Ordeal of Prince Eulenberg"[15] based on extensive pre-World War I newspaper accounts. *ONE Magazine* published a lengthy interview with "Rolf," editor of *Der Kreis* in Switzerland, conducted by long-time German Homophile Activist Johannes Werres, who often wrote as Jack Argo.[16]

Correspondence and exchanges of publications between *ONE Magazine* and *Der Kreis* resulted in a two-week visit to Los Angeles in May, 1958, by Rudolph Burckhardt, editor of the English-language section of *Der Kreis*. During his stay he gave three lectures for ONE Institute faculty and students: "Homophiles in German and Swiss History," "The Homophile Movements of Europe" and "Magnus Hirschfeld in Germany."

Burckhardt's broad educational background, including several years residence in England, gave his lectures an impressive range and scope.

---

[14] See also *QTLY* IV:3 (Summer, 1961), pp.77-93, and IV:4 (Fall 1961), pp.125-36.

[15] *MAG* IV:8 (October/November, 1956), p.4-11; IV:9 (December, 1956), p.4-8.

[16] Johannes Werres (writing as N. Weissenhagen), "Interview With Rolf," *MAG* V:8 (August\September, 1957), pp.4-7. Werres is a recognized Swiss/German Homophile Movement historian for the period beginning in 1933.

His own personal encounters with Hirschfeld provided unvarnished views of the famed sexologist not found in the official biographies.

In September, 1959 a visit by Floris van Mechelin, an officer of C.O.C. in Amsterdam, then (as now) the world's largest such organization, provided two lectures: "The Homophile Movement in Holland" and "Social Backgrounds of the Homophile Movement in Europe." His witty insights into political strategies and aspects of C.O.C. success in Holland were much enjoyed, and also of practical value in ONE's own administrative operations.

Both lecturers provided first-hand accounts of the Nazi vs. Homophile confrontations during World War II. Both men had lost relatives in the Nazi/Homophile Holocaust, as well as many close personal friends. At the time of their lectures in Los Angeles, the story of Pink Triangles and all the atrocities that followed their imposition were essentially unknown in the United States, certainly not widely comprehended. Their official access to the records of two of the oldest and largest European Homophile organizations and personal acquaintance with hundreds of individuals scattered all over Europe gave them unmatched knowledge of the whole Nazi period.

In effect, they both said that it is likely there were more homosexuals murdered during the Holocaust than there were Jews for the simple reason that there were so many more of them.[17]

Ever since those lectures there has been much skepticism at ONE about the books and articles dealing with that period, some authored by conscientious, well-meaning writers, as well as others having mixed motives. In view of the above speakers' accounts, recent figures given

---

[17] The reports by Burckhardt and von Mechelin represent a unique supplement to ONE Institute coursework. Both the topic and the first-person accounts were given additional notice at ONE Institute Public Lecture #244 (May 7, 1978) entitled, "Gays and the Holocaust: Can It Happen Again?" which brought together a panel featuring moderator Joe Killian, California State University Northridge Professor of History Vern Bullough, former ONE Institute faculty member Jim Kepner, occasional ONE Institute lecturer Bishop Mikhail Itkin, U.C.L.A. German Department Graduate Student Michael Lombardi and Dr. Robert Orndorff. Excerpts from Itkin's paper "Silent No More: The Pink Triangle," published in the *Christopher Street West Gay Pride Celebration* (1977), were reprinted in *LTR* XXIII:5 (May, 1978), pp.1-6.

for the number of Homophiles murdered by the Nazis must be viewed as being far from definitive. For instance, should it be found surprising that statistics about a disfavored, stigmatized population might be less accurate than those kept by an ethnic community desperately trying to record and save its own very identity as a people? This question calls for careful examination.

The Fall 1959 seminar *Homosexuality in Modern German History*[18] was a natural outcome of the visits from the two European Homophile Movement leaders and the interest they had aroused. The ONE Institute four-part *Homosexuality in History* courses continued to give substantial attention to early and medieval German history, as well as the sexual aspects of German social customs and German influences upon the American Homophile Movement in this century.

Earliest known of such influences was the 1924 organizational attempt in Chicago by Henry Gerber as recorded in an article he wrote for *ONE Magazine*.[19] Direct contact with Gerber came through Monwell Boyfrank, for many years an elected officer of ONE. He had known Gerber in his and Gerber's years of service in the U.S. Army. Boyfrank often referred to Gerber's successful exploit in conducting a small "pen pal" publication of contacts circulated among servicemen and others (1930-39). Frederic Frisbie, one-time Chairman of ONE's Board who had known Gerber in New York City in the 1930s, has provided more details.[20]

Gerber's translations for ONE Institute's *Quarterly of Homophile*

---

[18] See Chap.2, p.36.

[19] Henry Gerber, "The Society for Human Rights – 1925," *MAG* X:9 (September, 1962), pp.5-11. Also, p.15 above.

[20] Frisbie's recollections were recorded audiovisually at ONE Institute Public Lecture (March 1, 1987), entitled "A Bold Pioneer of Gay Liberation," and reported in *LTR* XXXII:3 (March, 1987); also available in Audio-Visual Collection, ONE, Inc. Archive, Baker Memorial Library. See also Jim Coughenour, "The Life and Times of an Ordinary Hero," *Windy City Times* (June 22, 1989), pp.60, 62, for an accurate account including partial reproduction of the 1924 Illinois Certificate of Incorporation of the Society for Human Rights, and Jonathan Katz, *Gay American History: Lesbians and Gay Men in America - A Documentary* (New York: Thomas Crowell, 1976).

Studies[21]   included portions of Magnus Hirschfeld's famous *Die Homosexualität* (Berlin: 1914, 1920), his so-called "Encyclopedia of Homosexuality." These are the earliest and, so far as is known, the only translations into English from this influential work.[22]

The Writings of
Karl Heinrich Ulrichs

Some extracts from the 1984 ONE Institute doctoral dissertation by Michael H. Lombardi, *The Writings of Karl Heinrich Ulrichs*, are given below.[23]

> Karl Heinrich Ulrichs was a nineteenth-century Homophile activist trained in law and theology. He devoted the middle years of his life to the reinterpretation of early legal codes which dealt with the regulation of sexual behavior. His writings became a point of departure for Homophile theories and activism.
> The late Jay Hayes called Ulrichs' works "seminal" and stated that "for readers without fluency in German (many of us) and for

---

[21] Excerpts from Magnus Hirschfeld, *Die Homosexualität des Mannes und des Weibes*, 2nd ed. (Berlin: L. Marcus Verlagsbuchhandlung, 1920), trans. Henry Gerber, "Chapter 15 - Classification of Homosexuals as to Age Preferences and Sex Acts," *QTLY* V:1 (Winter 1962), pp.20-9; "Chapter 23," V:2-4 (Summer-Fall 1962), pp.31-54; "Chapter 30 - The Role of Homosexual Men and Women in Society," VI:1-2 (Winter/Spring 1963), pp.22-30.

[22] At ONE Institute Public Lecture #145 (September 21, 1969), "My Reminiscences of Famed Sexologists," Harry Benjamin, M.D., recounted his contacts with Hirschfeld, Freud and many others in early 20th Century German medical circles for ONE Institute's audience. Notable also was his account of the extensive exchange of letters he had with Dr. Alfred C. Kinsey during Kinsey's work on *Sexual Behavior in the Human Male* (1948), in which Kinsey cites two Benjamin research papers. An extensive collection of Dr. Benjamin's papers is housed in ONE's Baker Memorial Library.

[23] Lombardi, Michael H. *The Writings of Karl Heinrich Ulrichs*. Ph.D. Dissertation, 1984. (ONE's Baker Memorial Library & Archives)

those without access to the documents (most of us) Ulrichs' theories and appeals are not available for study." (p.1)

In my studies of German Homophile literature, I noticed that the life and works of Ulrichs, in particular, were available only in quotations in secondary literature. After reading his works, however, I discovered his great importance to the Homophile Movement.

Some of the early writers who read and were influenced by Ulrichs' works were Richard von Krafft-Ebing (1840-1902), two British philosophers, John Addington Symonds (1840-93) and Edward Carpenter, and Nicolo Persichetti (1849-1915), an Italian historian and archeologist. The first person ever to mention Ulrichs' theories in a publication was Karoly Maria Kertbeny (1824-82), who coined the word "homosexual." (p.18)

Much of the work written by Hirschfeld in the *Jahrbuch für sexuelle Zwischenstufen* (Annual for Sexual Intermediaries) (1899-1923), the first scholarly annual of Homophile studies, was based on the writings of Ulrichs. Hirschfeld also adopted the third-sex theory and the idea of the congenital nature of sexual orientation.

Carpenter and Persichetti were inspired by Ulrichs' literary worth. In 1883 Carpenter rendered Ulrichs' definition of the Gay disposition into a poem, "O Child of Uranus," and his book, *The Intermediate Sex*, written in 1908, relies heavily on Ulrichs' theories. (p.19)

Ulrichs is, perhaps, the first to give a Homophile interpretation of the poems of Hafis, a thirteenth century Persian poet. In the Persian language, the pronoun for "he" and "she" cannot be translated out of context. In one of his own reference works, Ulrichs suspected that the German translator had tried to hide the fact that some of Hafis' poems were about Homophile love. (p.32)

Another literary influence that made a great impact on Ulrichs was the poetry of Count August von Platen-Hallermuende (1796-1835). Ulrichs commented that a single reading of Platen's poems would convince the reader that Platen was an Urning. Ulrichs used the latter's poems to illustrate that Uranian love relationships transcended social status.

Researchers and students of sociology in the field of Homophile studies will find Ulrichs' works indispensable. Each of his writings may be considered as a rich source of material for the important aspects and issues in relation to the social life of German Homophiles living in the nineteenth century in particular, and also of Homophiles everywhere and at all times in general.

Besides his many other occupations, Ulrichs worked as a newspaper journalist, and, in his writings on Uranism, he included newspaper articles, sometimes word for word, that reported contemporary events or issues dealing with the lives of Homophile men and women. (p.39)

Ulrichs tried to dispel the myths surrounding Homophiles by making a plea to the legislators for a rational discussion of Uranism. When he stood before the Assembly of German Jurists on August 27, 1867, in Munich, to advocate publicly the legal sanction of Uranism, the audience tried to silence Ulrichs' speech, simply because some members believed the subject of Uranian love was too vulgar to discuss. (pp.39-40)

It was not actually until 1879, the year of the completion of his twelfth and final piece of non-fiction, *Kritische Pfeile* (Critical Arrows), that Ulrichs became involved in psychology *per se*. Up to that time he had referred to "psychic hermaphroditism." But now he began to make comments on the theories of Homophile sexuality in psychological terms that were being introduced by sexologists such as Karl von Westphal (1833-90) and Krafft-Ebing.

Ulrichs criticized the then more recent scientific treatment of the subject of Homophile sexuality for being brought into too close a relationship with pathology and social disturbance. (p.40)

Other political factors which actually did directly affect Ulrichs were the Austro-Prussian War of 1866, when strict Prussian anti-Gay laws began to be imposed, and the Franco-Prussian War of 1870-71, which ended in the unification of Germany and the beginning of the Second Empire, in which a unified anti-Gay law, Paragraph 175, was enforced for the next one hundred years throughout the entire Empire; this included even Bavaria, where, since 1813, Homophiles had enjoyed virtually no discrimination. In 1871, Paragraph 175 forbade any sexual acts between members of the male sex.

Ulrichs commented that if all of the German states were to be united, then, in the matter concerning Uranism, he would prefer the general application of the liberal laws of Bavaria over all of the united Germany.   Ulrichs wanted the more liberal laws concerning Homophile activity to apply to the new union.

As it was, Ulrichs left Hanover in 1866, not because he wanted to, but because he did not want to be subject to the Prussian anti-Gay laws.   In that year, the Prussian Army moved south and entered Hanover, which before then had been a sovereign state. (pp.45, 6)

For that reason, in 1880, nine years after the Second Empire had been established with Prussia as the dominant force, Ulrichs left Germany and settled in Italy, never to return to his native country. (p.46)

Lengthy commentary upon Ulrichs' work is unnecessary now that

Lombardi's translations to English make them generally available to scholars for the first time.[24]

Ulrichs' controversial propositions, which have been collectively called the Third Sex Theory, should be noted because they have been so widely disseminated in scientific and popular writing since his first presentations in 1863.

As Lombardi notes (p.18) the Third Sex Theory profoundly influenced "first generation" sexologists and countless others of those following. The concept of a Third Sex offered great journalistic appeal with its seemingly common-sense interpretations for patterns of human sexual behavior which had been both misunderstood and viewed with distaste by many.

Espousal of Ulrichs' theories by Krafft-Ebing, Hirschfeld, and others through their voluminous writings and forceful personalities, spread throughout the German scientific world with a force far more influential than Ulrichs' own writings ever achieved.

The scientific world at that time was in the midst of many revolutionary developments. Darwin had been shaking the ground in one direction, new discoveries in genetics in another. Study of hormones did not yet have an adequate technology. Psychology was not yet entirely free from theories of magnetic currents and phrenology. The word "homosexual" had not yet been coined.

Thus, Ulrichs' intuitive approach to the mysteries of same-sex physical attraction provided a point of beginning seized upon by many major figures of the day.

A brief digest of Ulrichs' writings in the order of Lombardi's translations follows:

Vindex, primarily addressing contemporary German legal codes, arguing that Uranian feelings, a word adopted from Venus Urania, mythological mother of male/male lovers, are entirely natural and congenital, hence not accessible to legal action. Ulrichs was an "essentialist."

Inclusa, with extensive references to precedents from classic literature in terms which today would be called examples of "gay

[24] See also, Hubert Kennedy, *Ulrichs: Life and Works of Karl Heinrich Ulrichs, Pioneer of the Modern Gay Movement* (Boston: Alyson Publications, 1987).

sensibility."

Vindicta, a civil rights tract citing the freeing of the slaves in Greek and Roman times. Only much later did any general theory of Homophile Civil Rights develop.

Formatrix (formed by Mother Nature), medical aspects of the question, by definition rejecting treatment or cure.

Ara Spei, morality, ethics and argument that Uranism is in no way contrary to Christian teaching; references (Lombardi, pp.190-94) to the Uranian poetry of classic Persian writer, Hafiz.

Gladius Furens, arguments for justice giving extended reporting of his August 29, 1867, speech to 500 at the German Assembly of Jurists meeting in Munich which caused much heckling and uproar. This may have been the earliest known social protest-type event. Ulrichs called for penal code reform citing frequent suicides, as well as citing the more permissive examples of the French Code Napoleon and liberal Bavarian laws.

Araxes (name taken from a poem by Virgil), in 1870, first public use of his own name, superseding Numa Numantius previously used; strongly refuted public belief in pathology and child molestation. These claims sound much like many of the discussions emerging with the advent of AIDS in the 1980s.

Summarizing Ulrichs' general theory: Uranism is congenital in terms used almost verbatim by transsexual theory today. This was the most logical interpretation he could find for male/male, female/female attractions a century before psychology had demolished the supposed connections between hormones and object choices.

Studies for a century have not yet clarified whether or not such attractions are properly sexual in nature at all. Biologists still seem unable to entertain the thought that not every function of genital body organs must necessarily be procreative.

Not all Homophiles feel themselves to be housed in a body inappropriate to their subjective feelings. What has not yet been explained is the problem that, while many Homophiles do relate to each other as male to male, there is clear indication as far back as Greek literature that many have subjectively seen themselves in a female role, as do some so-called "queens" today.

ONE Institute History courses continued presenting German History. In Spring 1983 a Graduate School class, *Germany Since the Mid-19th*

Century: a Study of Political Pathology,[25] enrolled a deeply interested
group of students. Excerpts from some of these term papers follow.

Pink Triangles and the Lavender Menace:
Lesbianism in the Birkenau Concentration Camp
by Deborah A. Coates

Oddly enough, it is commonly known and accepted that there
was a goodly amount of homosexuality (if not "homosexuals" *per
se*) among the officers and soldiers of the Third Reich. It is also
known and accepted that a great many professed gay people were
summarily stamped with the pink triangle and killed. But what of
the hundreds (if not thousands) of closeted, or non-practicing, or
unaware gay people who were caught up in the war behind the wrong
lines?

What of the female prisoners who, by virtue of their femaleness,
may have received marginally better treatment? Was their sexual urge
"generally absent" also? And if it wasn't, what did they do about
it? (Female inmates, except for a few specially chosen ones, were
prohibited from having sex with their captors.)

In order to obtain answers to these questions, it is best to examine
a sample population with the requisite characteristics: a group of
female concentration camp inmates who, for whatever reason, were
able to survive, if not thrive, as an intact group. Such a group was
the Women's Orchestra at Auschwitz-Birkenau.

The Women's Orchestra at Birkenau was the brainchild of Höss,
the camp commandant, who wanted the screams of those burned alive
to be masked by music. Eventually, though, the orchestra became
a favorite plaything of the camp officials, and became so well-known
that it performed for Himmler, Reichsführer of the SS. At its "peak"
(if that is not an inappropriate word), the group consisted of 47
"orchestra girls" whose average age was 20. One of these girls was
Fania Fenelon.

Fania Fenelon was a Parisian cabaret singer who was very popular
with the Nazi nightclub set (who dubbed her "Kleine Sangerin," or
"Little Singer"). However, Fenelon's popularity did not prevent her

---

[25] See p.77 above. Also, Appendix, 5-1: History 561 German Homophile
Movement, Syllabus.

from being incarcerated when she admitted to being half Jewish (her real last name was Goldstein). As a result, Fenelon spent over two years in the camps, much of it at Birkenau, where she became one of the guiding forces in the Women's Orchestra. Her involvement with the group undoubtedly saved her life, though Fenelon herself had an incredibly strong instinct for survival. In the years following liberation (April 15, 1945), Fenelon wrote an account of her time in the Birkenau Women's Orchestra, called *Playing For Time*.

It is doubtful whether Fenelon herself was aware of the extent of inherently lesbian encounters that she included in her book; indeed, she herself seems to have had a marked Homophile tendency, and encouraged it in others. However, because she fluctuates between commenting on overt lesbianism and remaining silent on obvious, but undeclared, lesbianism, the author of this paper has chosen to delineate examples by utilizing two different categories: "latent" lesbianism (in which it is apparent that the women are attracted, but nothing is done about it, or at least there is no account of any action taken) versus "blatant" lesbianism (where it is an obvious and accomplished fact).

Not surprisingly, many of the "latent" lesbian encounters in *Playing For Time* involve Fenelon herself. For example, she speaks movingly of her young friend, Clara, "a girl of about twenty, with a ravishing head. There was an immediate rapport between us; we swore never to leave one another, to share everything." Later, when Fenelon was chosen to be in the orchestra, she was taken to a room "closely resembling paradise. There was light, and a stove; in front of me pretty girls were sitting, well-dressed. No one spoke, no one moved, but all those charming young ladies were looking at me. It was an exceptional, divine moment." Subsequent offhand references to late-night neck- and back-rubs, as well as exchanges of "confidences," allow even the most marginally astute reader to draw the obvious conclusion.

However, latent lesbianism was not found solely among the camp inmates; there were at least a few "Nazi dykes" at Birkenau also. Fenelon wrote of one official, Grese, thusly: "Grese smiled vaguely. Her pure, innocent eyes settled curiously on Florette (one of the orchestra girls), her slim black riding whip tapping her leather boot imperceptibly. Numerous stories were told about her. She was said to be sensitive to feminine charms, and Florette, something of a tomboy with astounding green eyes, was very beautiful." The "blatant" lesbianism that Fenelon recounts is just that – blatant. She writes humorously of a fight that breaks out in a lesbian "menage à trois" when "Marila, the legal wife" discovers that "Wisha, the fellow" is cheating on her with another Polish woman, "Zocha, the mistress." The ensuing row, while disturbing everybody's sleep, provides them all with some much-needed amusement.

Fenelon writes less charmingly of the "black triangles" (the camp whores), all of whom were evidently lesbians. She writes disparagingly of two of them, "Hilde, the kapo (boss) and Inge, her lover, quite slender-looking beside her stubby friend, crafty, damp-eyed." She admits, though, that a third, Georgette, "made us all laugh a lot because, unlike the other fellows of the block, who forced their voices down so as to sound more virile, she had the piping tones of a castrato, which made for a certain comic effect."

Fenelon provides an interesting sociological insight in the following description of a "black triangles" private party: "The roles were clearly differentiated in this curious assembly of women. Evening dress was *de rigueur*: the boys were in silk pajamas – presents from their girl friends – and the ladies, in their turn, wore ravishing transparent blouses, misty muslins, black lace negligees bordered with feathery clouds of pastel swansdown." Among other things, role-playing was obviously *de rigueur* also.

However, the most convincing and poignant account of "blatant" lesbianism concerns the budding romance between two of the orchestra girls: Marta, an aristocratic cellist, and Little Irene, a left-winger who plays the violin. At the commencement, Marta confesses her feelings to Fenelon:

> Fania, I'm worried, something's happening that I don't understand. I love my sister Renate very deeply, but when I think of her I don't feel any of those contradictory feelings I have when I think of Irene. The other evening her hand brushed mine and I wanted to seize it, to kiss it. I'd never want to do that to my sister – or anyone else. All I think about is her. Do you know what I dream of? Irene puts her hand on mine, and we never leave one another again.

Fenelon then comments, "It was perfectly clear: Marta was in love with Little Irene. It didn't surprise me. *In Birkenau, one couldn't long remain ignorant of homosexuality; it was rife; it offered the women satisfaction for their fantasies, allayed their solitude, their sexual needs* [emphasis added]." Subsequently, Little Irene makes a similar confession to Fenelon, and eventually the two (Little Irene and Marta) become lovers, and remain so until the camp is liberated (much to the disapproval of the other orchestra girls, who nevertheless grudgingly accept them).

Given the above quoted statement and the various examples cited throughout this paper, it can be stated uncategorically that there was indeed lesbian activity (and lesbians!) at the Birkenau concentration camp. And if it occurred at Birkenau, it probably occurred at the other camps, also. As the old saying goes, "Where there's a will, there's a way;" and as a somewhat newer saying goes, "We are every-where!"

Johannes Werres:
An Account of the Homophile Movement
in Post-War Germany
by Gary Booher[26]

The American Homophile movement was not an isolated phenomenon, but had its parallels in other countries, especially in Western Europe. Germany was one of those countries. The Homophile movement in Germany was particularly significant because of the traumatic repression and annihilation of homosexuals during the preceding Nazi era. How the homosexual emancipation movement picked itself up from the ashes of post-war Germany is especially important today for developing a broader understanding of the interface of history, culture, and human rights advocacy.

Following the cataclysm of World War II, Germany lay in ruins: economically, politically, socially, and physically. From the ashes, the German people were to rebuild, but not without the strict direction of the occupying powers. Unfortunately this occupying influence slowed the reformation of Paragraph 175:

When the allied powers had conquered the Nazi ideology of Germany and had begun to erect a democracy after 1945, many people in Germany were filled with a new hope. Among the famished sacrifices of the Nazi regime returning from the concentration camps were many homosexuals. But this group of the suppressed were to be shamefully disappointed: the Western Allies would not revise the laws against homosexuality. Only the Russians within their occupation zone changed the laws and reduced them to the status they were before 1933. In West Germany the Germans themselves were re-

---

[26] See complete paper of this title. (ONE's Baker Memorial Library & Archives)

sponsible for changing the laws or not, but nobody expected what happened: the laws under Hitler intensified, were more intensified by the Federal Republic. A complaint before the supreme court on a constitutional question has not been decided or even answered in four years – a request which quotes that paragraph 175 StGB disagrees with the new German constitution.[27]

Despite this repressive period, the emergence of the Homophile movement in other countries also had its influence in Germany. During the early fifties, numerous publications emerged in Germany in spite of the laws prohibiting the street sales of homosexually-oriented publications. Publications proliferated as they would dodge the law and temporarily operate in one city, and then be chased to operate in another town. A sample of known publications (and their dates and locations of operation) during this period is listed as follows:[28]

> *Amicus-Briefbund* (1950-?), Berlin
> *Freund/Die Freundin* (1952-?), Hamburg
> *Die Gefährten* (1953-1954), Frankfurt
> *Der Grosse Wagen* (1958-?), Saarbrucken
> *Hellas* (1953-1954), Hamburg
> *Humanitas* (1953-1955), Hamburg
> *Die Insel* (1951), Hamburg
> *Junglinge* (1954), ?
> *Der Neue Ring* (1958-?), Hamburg
> *Pan* (1951), Hamburg
> *Der Ring* (1956-?), Hamburg
> *Vox* (1953), Hamburg
> *Der Weg Zu FreundSchaft Und Toleranz*
> (1952-1959), Hamburg
> *Zwischen Den Andern* (1956-?), Hamburg

An important resource for understanding the German Homophile movement is one of its contributors, Johannes Werres. To understand the historical perception of Johannes Werres, one must also understand

---

[27] *TDY* p.125.

[28] Bullough, et al, *Annotated Bibliography of Homosexuality*, II, pp.334-50.

a little of the background of the man.[29]   Johannes Werres was born
in Cologne, Germany, (September 12, 1923) and was raised Roman
Catholic.

The "coming out" of Johannes Werres was similar to that of many
others of that period and even today.   As a journalist, he often
appeared in Homophile publications under the pen name, Jack Argo.

After moving to Hanover, Werres wrote articles for *Der Kreis*
(The Circle) of Switzerland, and kept contact with a new group in
Reutlingen called *Die Runde* (*The Round*), since there was no gay
group in Hanover. Meanwhile, the ICSE (International Congress for
Sexual Equality) in Amsterdam approached Werres in 1956, and
helped fill the void of no central Homophile organization in Germany:

> The Dutch were willing to try to do something for Germany
> from the outside. Our country seemed to be isolated, cut
> off from factual and objective information about homosexual-
> ity. German gay groups had become less important, had only
> few members, and therefore no money at all. They were
> unable to start activities to inform the general public or to
> take part in parliamentary law reform; most of them did not
> even dare to do such things openly. ICSE was willing to
> publish a regular monthly press service in German to be sent
> to papers in Germany and Austria free of charge. Since I
> was a journalist, I would do the job of editing, if I were
> agreeable. I did so enthusiastically.[30]

Johannes Werres edited *ICSE-PRESS*, beginning in 1956, first
in Germany, and later in Amsterdam, Netherlands, until January, 1958.
Werres felt that this period was most instructive for him, noting that
the Dutch were far ahead of the Germans in the Homophile movement.

Werres instead pursued a research relationship with Willhart S.
Schlegel, M.D., which had developed while involved with ICSE.
Werres became an assistant to Dr. Schlegel at his institute in
Hamburg, later in Kronenberg, and participated in the preparation of
research activities for several books published by the Schlegel Insti-
tute:

---

[29] Johannes Werres, unpublished personal letter (May 25, 1955) (ONE's
Baker Memorial Library & Archives).

[30] *LTR* XXII:9 (September, 1977), p.3.

Die Sexualinstinkte des Menschen (Human Sexual Instincts)
Der homosexualle Nächste (The Homosexual FellowMan)
Sexualle Partnerschaft (Sexual Partnership)
Das grosse Tabu (The Great Taboo)
Lexikon der Sexualität (Dictionary of Sex)

These books were published between 1962 and 1969, and continued Schlegel's theory that homosexuality had a constitutional origin. Through his first book, *Korper und Selle* (Body and Mind), he became widely known for his studies.

One reviewer called him the "German Kinsey," which seemed to be true if one considers that Schlegel had investigated some 20,000 men and women of all ages, among them more than 600 homosexuals. Today, this number has increased to almost 30,000, and among these, an increasing number of members of other races and foreign nations from all over the world is included. Therefore, one might say that Schlegel's method has proved to be at once universal and global, and in many ways represents a reliable application to other cultures and times.[31]

In 1967 Werres contributed a chapter on gay organizations in *Das grosse Tabu* (The Great Taboo). Werres felt that this work, as with previous works of Schlegel, was influential in the German Homophile movement.

Johannes Werres became increasingly distant from the gay liberation movement because of increasing ideological and theoretical differences, but continued promoting Dr. Schlegel's theories which had now fallen completely out of favor with gay liberationists:

In Germany it has been clearly proven that the gay question cannot be solved by the homosexual alone; it must be done within the framework of society as a whole. Whoever believes that this fight can be won by provocations and confrontations is wrong: he has not understood the psychology of this problem. We should all encourage research and clear the way for it, with tolerance between the different schools of thought. While sociology and psychology may predominate in research into homosexuality, the natural sciences should not be excluded, not should there be resistance against such sciences as biology, human genetics, human ethology and constitutional biology. Their findings

---

[31] Ibid., p.15.

should be made known without delay to students in the elementary and high schools, in colleges and universities; they should be presented and discussed via the media. Adults should also be informed so that, while new generations are better informed and become adults without prejudices, everyone can be made aware of these findings and steadily perfect the laws to the end that education may move ahead without legal hindrances.[32]

Apart from his contributions to the Homophile movement in Germany, a debt is also owed Johannes Werres for his record of the activities and viewpoints and issues of that era. Documentation and analysis of this past era of the Homophile movement provide additional insight for recurrent activities and view-points and issues of today's movement.

ONE Institute Extension Lectures:
Historical Topics

It has been earlier mentioned[33] that the Sunday afternoon Extension Lectures are considered as supplementary to the curriculum. The following list includes lectures on history notable both in terms of their scholarship and their seminal contribution.

January 31, 1959 (#26) "Classical Boy Love and Modern Civilization" by Dr. Mario Palmieri. A frank recounting by a highly conscientious lifetime exponent of the Platonic ideals, the pattern as given in Greek classical literature.

January 27, 1962 (#59) "The American Homophile Movement" by such Movement founders as *Vice Versa's* Lisa Ben, Lorenzo Wilson of the Knights of the Clocks, the Mattachine Foundation's Harry Hay and Wallace de Ortega Maxey, the Mattachine Society's Hal Call and Don Lucas, and Helen Sanders and Jaye Bell of the Daughters of Bilitis.

---

[32] *LTR* XXII:10 (October, 1977), p.2.

[33] See Chap.2, p.30.

February 2, 1964 (#85) "Folklore of American and European Heritage" by Richard Chase, folklorist and author of *Jack Tales* and other books.

November 7, 1965 (#100) "The Mattachine Society: 1953-65" by Hal Call, for many years President.

May 4, 1969 (#143) "Communication: Step One." A large public confrontation of politicians, the press, church and business leaders held at Baces Hall, a Hollywood, California auditorium, and continued on June 1, 1969 (#144) with "Communication: Step Two," held in ONE's Assembly Hall.

September 21, 1969 (#145) "My Reminiscences of Famed Sexologists" by Harry Benjamin, M.D., speaking of Hirschfeld, Havelock Ellis, Freud, Edward Carpenter and others he had known.

November 7, 1971 (#165) "Candidate Forum," with an appearance by a California State Assembly candidate, later elected, who was questioned by officers of Homophile Organizations.

January 29, 1972 (#171) "Pioneers of the Homophile Movement" by this editor.

January 27, 1973 (#181) "Politicians View Homosexuality." Two candidates for the Los Angeles City Council speak and present their qualifications at ONE's large Hilton Hotel banquet.

January 27, 1973 (#182) "Homosexuality in Egypt: Yesterday and Today." Banquet attendees were given a lecture on Egyptian mythologies, with attention given to wall paintings as contrasted with revealing photography made by recent travelers.

November 4, 1979 (#255) "National March on Washington for Lesbian and Gay Rights" reported by Don Amador, anthropologist and assistant to Los Angeles Mayor Tom Bradley.

June 2, 1983 (#288) "The Making of the Modern Homosexual" by Greg Sprague, with slides and newspaper materials of early Chicago.

October 2, 1983 (#290) "Origins of Homophobia in History" by Paul Hardman, ONE Institute Doctoral Candidate.

July 8, 1984 (#298) "Homophobia in 18th Century England" by Louis Crompton, University of Nebraska. The lecture was given at the facility of the International Gay and Lesbian Archives, and followed on July 9, 1984 (#299) with "The Greek Revival and English Education in Byron's Day," and (#300) "Shelley on Homosexuality."

January 6, 1985 (#304) "Karl Heinrich Ulrichs: A Hero for the 1980s" by Dr. Michael H. Lombardi, ONE Institute Ph.D. recipient.

May 5, 1985 (#308) "A Long Beach Sex Scandal in Grandfather's Day" by David Cameron, Esq. A report on 30 men arrested in an early example of gay resistance (court acquittals of two). The word "homosexual" was used by the *Los Angeles Times* and other California newspapers in reporting on the 1914 events.

June 1, 1986 (#319) "Coming Out in the '30s and '40s" by Martin Block, an early member of the Mattachine Society and, later, a co-founder of ONE, Inc.

February 1, 1987 (#324) "ONE Documentary," a film report of ONE, Inc.'s 30th Annual Meeting in 1982, highlighted by the presentation of the ONE Institute Graduate School's first Litt. D. (Hon), given to Christopher Isherwood. Gore Vidal and other notables were present to hear Isherwood's acceptance speech.

March 1, 1987 (#325) "A Bold Pioneer of Gay Liberation" by Fred Frisbie, friend of Henry Gerber. Frisbie tells of New York and the Harlem scene in the 1920s.

November 1, 1987 (#330) "The National March on Washington" by David Cameron, ONE Institute Dean of Extension and Special Programs. Cameron's lecture described the October, 1987 March, reporting on the hundreds of thousands participating. Cameron was joined by a young Los Angeles activist who described his sit-in at the U. S. Supreme Court.

December 6, 1987 (#331) "The Movement: Past, Present and Future" by Jim Kepner, Movement activist since 1954.

April 2, 1989 (#343) "Women-Loving Women." A memorial and video history of two late ONE members including their recollections of the 1920s and their roles in World War II.

October 7, 1990 (#355) "One Institute Looks to the '90s." Panel: Jesse Jacobs, W. Dorr Legg, Walter Williams, David Cameron.

November 5, 1990 (#356) "Telling It Like It Was" by Vernon C. Mitchell, founder of the earliest health clinic for the gay community, Fall 1967.

May 5, 1991 (#362) "Harry Hay at Milbank Mansion." The '20s and '30s and his 1950 founding of the Mattachine Society.

December 1, 1991 (#366) "When the Coup Hit Moscow, I was There" by Luis Balmosedn, Librarian, ONE's Baker Memorial Library.

January 5, 1992 (#367) "Highlights from ONE's Tenth, Twentieth and Thirtieth Anniversaries." An audiovisual cassette program.

January 26, 1992 (#368) "Fortieth Anniversary of ONE, Inc." Audiovisual cassette available.

February 2, 1992 (#369) "In Memory of Vernon Mitchell."

June 7, 1992 (#370) "*Vice Versa* Was the Forerunner." Audiovisual cassette program of Lisa Ben talking and singing.

In addition to the excepts from faculty and student papers cited in this chapter, additional history sources are available on video cassettes in the Audiovisual Collection of ONE's Baker Memorial Library as follows, each of them more than an hour long:

#290   Lisa Ben recounting her founding of the pioneer lesbian periodical, *Vice Versa*.
#304   ONE, Institute Ph.D. graduate Michael Lombardi, "The Life of Karl Heinrich Ulrichs, German Nineteenth Century Pioneer."
#308   David Cameron, Esq., "A Long Beach Sex Scandal in Grandfather's Day." A fully documented account of a pre-World War I homosexual purge in Long Beach, California.
#317   Charles Rowland, a Founder of the Mattachine Society in 1950, giving a detailed account of the period and his work at ONE.
#319   Martin Block, a Founder in 1952 of ONE, Incorporated, on "Growing Up and Coming Out in New York in the 1930s."
#325   Fred Frisbie relates his contacts with Henry Gerber and at the Harlem Balls in the 1920s.
#331   Jim Kepner on experiences in New York and San Francisco in the 1930s and in Los Angeles from 1953.
#356   Vernon Mitchell, Los Angeles activist and founder in Los Angeles in 1967 of the earliest U.S. health clinic for homosexuals; also his donation "March on Washington" banners and memorabilia to the

Smithsonian Institute.

#362   Henry (Harry) Hay on the social setting in Los Angeles in the 1920s and his founding of the Mattachine Society in 1950.

Further Reading

Brown, Juanita "Dr. Mary Walker Walked Alone," *MAG* VI:11 (November, 1958), p.20.   Dr. Walker was the only woman ever awarded a Congressional Medal of Honor.

Legg, W. Dorr "The Sodomy Rite: A Tentative Reconstruction of Certain Paleolithic Magical Practices," *QTLY*, I:3 (Fall 1958), pp.98-101.

Pedersen, Lyn (pseud. James L. Kepner, Jr.), "England and the Vices of Sodom," *MAG* II:5 (May, 1954), pp.4-17.

———— "Roger Casemont: Traitor, Martyr or Pervert," *MAG* VII:3 (March, 1959), pp.18-9.

Starr, J. P. (pseud. Monwell Boyfrank), "Some Historical Incidents," *MAG* V:8 (October/November, 1957), p.17; and VI:1 (January, 1958), p.25.

———— "Ancients and the Greek Cult," *QTLY*, V:2-4 (Spring/Fall 1959), pp.55-9.

CHAPTER 6

HOMOSEXUALS IN AMERICAN SOCIETY:
THE SOCIOLOGY OF A SUB-CULTURE

A two-semester course with this title was added to the ONE Institute curriculum in 1959-60.[1] Sociology was chosen as the second addition to the curriculum because two sociological propositions had been debated endlessly, often rancorously, almost from the moment when the organized Homosexual Movement began in the United States: (1) There is a homosexual minority; (2) There is a homosexual culture.

The earliest statement of those propositions in the United States may have been made by Harry (Henry) Hay in his 1948 "ten-page encyclopedic brochure" intended "to prompt the social reemergence of the Homosexual Minority."[2] Tangible evidence of such "reemergence" did not appear until "in November, 1950 the Mattachine Foundation was born."[3] These two concepts were formally stated in the "Mattachine Society Missions and Purposes which hold it possible and desirable that a highly ethical homosexual culture emerge, as a consequence of its work, paralleling the emerging culture of our fellow minorities – the Negro, Mexican and Jewish Peoples." This April, 1951, document also proposed "To push forward into the realm of political action to erase from our law books the discriminatory and oppressive legislation presently directed against the homosexual minority."[4]

In his article, "The Homosexual Culture,"[5] writing as David L. Freeman, Charles Rowland, Corresponding Secretary of the Mattachine Foundation and a Founder, strongly defended the proposition that homosexuals constitute a minority with a distinctive culture. Donald Webster Cory, not a Mattachine member at the time, in a speech he delivered in September, 1952, claimed that "It is today generally recognized that

---

[1] See Chap.2, p.34.

[2] *TDY* p.33.

[3] Ibid., p.35.

[4] Ibid., pp.13-4.

[5] David L. Freeman (pseud. of Charles Rowland), "The Homosexual Culture," *MAG* I:5 (May, 1953), pp.8-11.

homosexuals constitute a sociological minority."[6]

Controversy recurred almost unremittingly. During the stormy sessions of the April 11, 1953, Mattachine Constitutional Convention, and its continuation a month later, the words *minority* and *culture* triggered major disputes on several occasions during the proceedings.

As interested observers at all those sessions, ONE members could not help noting that for the most part, arguments were loosely stated. Non-sequiturs abounded. As temperatures rose, it was plain that many of the adversaries had a very confused grasp of the issues being debated so hotly. It seemed that Sociology might provide some welcome clarifications. Sociology had been one of the nine major fields making up the content of Homophile Studies during the initial Fall 1956 presentation.

Prior to the opening of the first full course on the subject, the article, "A Sociologist Looks at Homosexuality: A Criticism of a Current Sociological Text,"[7] discussed the failure of sociological theory to give due attention to the role of homosexuality in American society. The following excerpts point this out.

> The first criticism of the book lies in the definition of deviation from social and cultural norms in almost exclusively negative terms: crime, broken families, unhappy old people, unjust treatment of minorities, etc. That, strictly speaking, deviation refers to *any variation* from the norm, positive as well as negative, is not considered. For example, one might cite the fact that highly gifted people are deviants quite as definitely as those with criminal tendencies, and many have problems quite as serious for society. It has at

---

[6] D.W. Cory (pseud. of Edward Sagarin), "Address to the International Committee for Sexual Equality: University of Frankfurt, Germany," *MAG* I:2 (February, 1953), p.2.

[7] See Chap.2, p.35 above. Dr. M. M. (pseud. Merritt Thompson), "A Sociologist Looks at Homosexuality: A Criticism of a Current Sociological Text," review of Marshall B. Clinard, *Sociology of Deviant Behavior* (New York: Rhinehart & Co., 1957), *QTLY* I:2 (Summer 1958), pp.48-9, 64. Many years later Laud Humphreys devoted a full page to a critique of similar sociological shortcomings then prevalent in his *Out of the Closets: The Sociology of Homosexual Liberation* (Englewood Cliffs: Prentice-Hall, 1972), p.44.

times been very difficult or even impossible for the genius type in art, literature, and music to make a living in the United States. The life mission of Mrs. Edward MacDowell brought out this point so vividly. Educators have not yet learned what to do with gifted students in order to make available their talents in positions of leadership so much needed in our society. Then the prejudice of sociologists quite generally toward the recognition of innate qualities of persons leads the author to make only one reference to subnormality: the fact that no correlation has been discovered between level of intelligence and criminality including prostitution. As a matter of fact the treatment of subnormals, those upon whom no known technique has had very much effect, is one of the serious problems of society today. And finally there is no suggestion with reference to the situation wherein the social and cultural norms of a given society are repudiated by an intellectual minority and/or the larger community. (p.48)

Having made these criticisms of the term "sexual offender," the author still lists homosexuality under this heading without clearly indicating just what is meant by the concept, and just how homosexuality comes under it. Likewise, the author gives no hint of the constructive side of homosexuality or bisexuality, the deeper insight which might enrich such activities in counseling and teaching, but of course this oversight may be intentional and in harmony with the general policy of dealing only with the negative or problematic side of all the areas. Also, there is no reference to the great contributions of artists, writers, musicians, political figures, and others who were and are homosexuals. The periodicals mentioned have been opening up whole reaches of history that had been ignored by professional historians and not dreamed of by scholars hitherto. (p.64)

An exploration of "Homosexual Culture"[8] by faculty member Julian Underwood is another early look at this standard academic topic from the viewpoint of Homophile Studies. The excerpts which follow include the *Quarterly's* introduction.

Continuing one of the most critical discussions in the field of Homophile theory, Mr. Crowther, who has previously written for *ONE Magazine* and for the *Mattachine Review*, analyzes a problem that has bedeviled many in the Homophile movement. (p.176)

---

[8] R. H. Crowther (pseud. of Julian Underwood), "Homosexual Culture," *QTLY* III:2 (Spring 1960), pp.176-82.

If a minority culture, based clearly upon the homosexual temperament, does in fact exist as a definable quality or to a known extent, the homosexual would like to know it. Such a fact could be of great aid in individual and group orientation, in presenting a "case" for the homosexual, and in bringing about an increasingly satisfactory adjustment between the minority and the parent culture. What is proposed in this essay is a more or less specific analysis of the terms "culture," "minority culture," and "homosexual temperament," and an effort to find out whether these three terms can be interrelated in such a way as to prove that the term "homosexual culture" has a real meaning. (p.176)

Once we have isolated the elements which compose a specific culture, according to the general areas outlined above, we may think we have an adequate picture. But these elements must also be considered in time – "longitudinally" as they say in psychology – as they are in a constant state of flux, each modifying the others pro-foundly. For example, changes in the economic or political sphere may require whole new bodies of legislation, or significant changes in existing legislation; advancements in the arts and sciences may profoundly modify language; changes in religious belief often bring about pronounced alterations in the patterns of social behaviour – and so on and on. (p.177)

Whether we are talking about Feminism, the NAACP, ONE, Inc., or any other evidence of minority expression, all have one thing in common – the effort to educate the members of the parent or dominant culture concerning the special problems and social values experienced by the particular minority in question. Thus, certain special aspects of education do have a distinctive place in the dynamics of modern cultures, and will be referred to again at a later point. (p.177)

Homosexuals can claim to be a distinct cultural minority only as it can be proven that they make a group contribution to the dominant culture which is the specific outcome of the homosexual temperament. Otherwise, no matter how gifted they may be, no matter how wide their talents, they and the world must conclude that these gifts and talents arise independently of sexual orientation – that sexual orientation may temper or color them, but without possessing to any degree the attribute of cause. (p.178)

Prejudices and false assumptions concerning the psycho-sexual qualities of male and female greatly complicate the problem of describing the homosexual temperament. Is there such an entity as the homosexual temperament? We think so, and that it is important to attempt a description at once, before considering any culture that may be produced from it. The key to it is suggested as the basic autoeroticism common to all individuals, and which (in the homosexual's case, and for Freudian or other reasons) persists into adulthood and produces the phenomenon of homosexuality. The intellectual and emotional *temperament* consistent with autoeroticism is characterized by a high degree of introspection, imagination, abstraction, subjectivity generally, preoccupation with mood and fantasy, and a number of other qualities which spring logically from the basic condition in which the means of individual satisfaction and expression are sought within the self. With this definition in mind as a provisional and working hypothesis, we will proceed to examine the homosexual's contribution or relation to general culture, and the extent to which the homosexual temperament, as defined, has an active relation to one or more cultural areas.

There is no doubt but what the homosexual has developed a group language of sorts, mainly by grafting special meanings upon words already in the general language. (p.179)

The public seldom, if ever, hears about homosexual mechanics, clerks, inventors, teachers, technicians, etc., yet there is nothing in the homosexual temperament, *per se*, to exclude the homosexual from such pursuits. Sociological research on this subject is as yet almost non-existent, and broad statistics cannot be stated. Yet anyone familiar with the homosexual minority knows that the homosexual's place in the economy includes as wide a variety of occupations as that of the heterosexual. (p.180)

Temperamentally, the homosexual would much prefer to live life in harmony with himself and society, to be allowed freedom to impress his own particular set of esthetic, ethical and other values upon the main stream of culture, and to make whatever contribution he is capable of to the welfare of the parent society, whatever it may be. However, the sexual expression of the homosexual temperament is, unfortunately, the only aspect of that temperament now considered socially definitive, and, as everyone knows, the nature of this definition is such as to cast the worst possible light upon the temperament as a whole. Thus the struggle of the modern homosexual, whose primary object in assuming the status of an organized cultural minority group is to secure the revision of the public's attitude on this phase of morals, and ultimately to bring about a legal redefinition and reclassification of homosexual behaviour. Until this is done, other aspects of the homosexual temperament, of infinitely greater value and significance to society at large and to the dominant culture, can never be assessed in the proper light.

Even though the homosexual minority fails to show at present the earmarks which could plainly establish it as a cultural minority group, the current trends within the minority point clearly in this direction. It is impossible to predict the outcome, because it is impossible to know with certainty what the homosexual temperament, properly aware of itself, properly recognized by the general culture, and properly led and educated by the efforts of its own leaders, can eventually produce for the social benefit.

Educational effort, adequately carried out in each direction, must eventually place the homosexual temperament into an entirely different social position, in which it can realize its best social possibilities and avoid the mental and emotional pitfalls, which have so often stifled or misdirected it in the past. (p.182)

A preliminary syllabus, "Homosexuals in American Society,"[9] was issued when the sociology class began its sessions and evolved soon thereafter to include a "Table of Contents" for a projected Textbook on the subject. This became in effect the outline for the classes as they were presented. Also included were the "Point of View" outlining basic theoretical positions and "Sources of Information" challenging then current data deficiencies.

The section on Sources of Information in particular emphasized the objective, following the injunction, "Sociology begins with observation, data gathering and systematizing: investigation before theories."

ONE Institute faculty and students were already surfeited with theories. Books by psychologists, psychiatrists, criminologists, clergy and others rolled off the presses seemingly without end because they sold. A bibliography of sociology books was consulted. The partial list included here[10] does not cite pages or chapters because, as mentioned earlier, there was almost total unawareness that such a thing as a Homophile population existed. Better, it was thought, to scan the texts, but follow none, at least initially. Their record at that time did not seem reassuring.

Excerpts from published chapters from "a proposed textbook" on sociology by this editor have been included, which present a critique of generally accepted sociological theory as viewed from the standpoint of Homophile Studies. As reprinted here, the excerpts are drawn from

---

[9] *QTLY* I:1 (Spring 1958), p.22,23.

[10] See Appendix, 6-1: Sociology Bibliography.

preliminary notes, as well as the Introduction and Chapters I-III of *The Sociology of Homosexuality*.

The Sociology of Homosexuality[11]

It is generally acknowledged that the number of homosexual men and women in the United States must total several million. The exact figures are much in dispute for a variety of reasons, but few would argue that they do not add up to a very substantial total.

This being the case, one would expect to be able to consult an extensive sociological literature on homosexuality. Actually such a literature does not exist. Few sociologists find the subject warranting more than brief notice; most do not even mention it.

How [do we] explain this? Are social scientists actually unaware of phenomena that are common knowledge to every street urchin? Do these scholars suffer from some sort of in-group myopia? Whatever the explanation, it would seem clear that one is long overdue.

A clue may be had from the sociological classification of homosexual behavior under the heading of social deviation, along with drug addiction, alcoholism, crime and other forms of delinquent behavior. Such a formulation reflects many generations of medical and psychological theory. (p.60)

With such premises as a starting point, it is hardly surprising that social scientists regard homosexuality as something apart from their main interests and as having no particular bearing upon the development of their general theory.

The hypothesis that homosexuals are a special type of minority group, forming a subculture in societies all over the world but specifically in the United States, will be examined in this present study.

In exploring this concept it will be necessary to subject to the closest scrutiny a frame of reference implicit in all sociological theory,

---

[11] W. Dorr Legg, The Sociology of Homosexuality. "Introduction," "Chapter I. - Boundaries of the Field," and "Chapter II. - Some Fundamentals of Human Behavior," *QTLY* V:2-4 (Spring, Summer, Fall 1962), pp.60-71, and "Chapter III. - Group Behavior Among Baboons," *QTLY* VI:3-4 (Summer, Fall 1963), pp.58-64.

to which might be given the name, "the heterosexual assumption."
In general terms, this assumption supposes that any society, all
societies, arise out of the interplay of environmental and historical
factors upon the basic drives thought to be held substantially in
common by all humans. (p.61)

It is the point of view here that neither the theory of social
deviance in its current forms or "the heterosexual assumption" are
sufficiently precise for an objective study of society. It also is
proposed that new formulations will be required before valid analyses
can be made, either of the homosexual population or of the larger
society. Existing formulations seem to be quite inadequate for
understanding those millions of persons who, century after century,
massively resist participation in the procreational situation, or decline
to share in large segments of the values assumed to be applicable to
men and women generally; who in opposition to the most extreme
forms of social sanctions, even the death penalty, stubbornly exhibit
certain social patterns which are uniquely their own.

In view of the persistence of honest doubts concerning the
reliability of any of the texts now in print, the time does not seem
appropriate for listing any selected reference materials just yet. A
period of further winnowing is still required before recommendations
can safely be made. (p.63)

A view enjoying considerable currency among behavioral
scientists is that terms such as "a homosexual" or "the homosexual,"
are inadmissible. There is no such entity as a "tall man" or a "short
one," it is said; no such thing as "fair hair" or "high intelligence."
Such descriptive terms are meaningless in scientific study and should
be replaced by the concept of a continuum of imperceptible gradations.
Rigid lines of differentiation are then replaced by the concept of
clusters of focal nodes representative of "areas" or "tendencies."
(pp.65-6)

Man is an animal, higher on the evolutionary scale than others,
but sharing with them all certain fundamental needs and drives. He
must eat, drink, sleep, and eliminate in order to stay alive. From these
and other similar facts, a good many early sociologists constructed
theories of conflict, aggression, dominance and submission which have
not always stood the test of verification. (p.67)

In discussing the social behavior of animals and their sexual
aspects, so great a confusion of terms and of thinking has surrounded
the whole question that it is sometimes proposed that the word sex
be restricted entirely to use in connection with reproductive processes.
If this were done, it is possible that much confusion could be
eliminated.

We might, for instance, find it reasonable to continue the use of the word "heterosexual" in connection with male-female acts intended for and resulting in reproduction, but the word "homosexual" would become meaningless. As reproduction was neither intended nor possible through such acts, they would clearly be designated as of a different order. Instead, reference would be made to concepts such as: stimulus, response, affectional needs, affiliative drives, etc., in no way "sexual." (p.69)

A most important part of our study must be to discover the varied types of role identification found among homosexuals and the ways in which individuals having such attitudes strive for certain kinds of status while rejecting others. A great deal of the conflict between the homosexual and the majority population must be understood in terms of value in role-identification.

[The] sociological handling of homosexual behavior under such headings as social disorganization and deviant behavior, as these terms are generally understood, is admissible in the light of modern knowledge available to social scientists.

We have arrived at this conclusion by a number of routes, including a very brief review of arguments for and against the interpretation of homosexuality as possibly having a hereditary, or innate, basis and having noted the central importance of this question to our study. (p.71)

The previous chapter briefly discussed man, the animal; man, the social being; his quest for role identification; some aspects of theories of heredity; arguments as to the possibility that homosexuality is in part inborn; contemporary attitudes concerning this; some social implications of such recent views.

PRIMATE BEHAVIOR

We now turn specifically to sociological aspects of primate behavior, using by way of illustration an important paper, here referred to as "Baboons" by two anthropologists of the University of California, Drs. S. L. Washburn and Irwin DeVore.[12] The importance of this paper for our present purposes lies in its suggestive presentation of the earliest beginnings of what later in man have become more complex social patterns. (p.58)

The authors' insistence on the key role played in biological evolution by social behavior authorizes us to speak of man's social

---

[12] S. L. Washburn and Irwin DeVore, "The Social Life of Baboons," *Scientific American* (June, 1961).

heredity, as well as of his genetic heredity. While there is nothing essentially new in this, the authors' emphasis encourages us to inquire if it might be possible that there are factors present in the evolution of primates which, generation after generation, have perpetuated homosexual behavior.

The authors have held, contrary to much opinion, that baboon sexual behavior cannot claim a position of any such importance. If true, this is a revolutionary finding, quite at variance with a great deal of psychological thinking. (pp.58-9)

If any society, using the term broadly, is unable or unwilling to formulate ways of accommodating the needs of its members, that society will inevitably face internal tensions. These will continue to abrade that society from within until finally a solution of the conflict is imposed upon it, possibly by force.

The essential point to be noted here is that neither the larger society nor the homosexually-oriented population can avoid the losses and penalties automatically imposed upon them both by their refusal to evaluate the situation realistically, instead of in terms of moralistic ideology. (p.60)

What did the baboon observers learn about the structuring of the troops they studied? They soon observed that around the dominant males there gathered interest groups, held there apparently neither by the sexual reasons adduced by some other investigators, nor by the "brute force" so dear to cynical philosophers of the late Romantic period in European thinking. Instead, there was a focusing of clusters of both males and females around central males, in a polarity not dependent upon any particular overt expression, so far as could be seen.

If this interpretation is correct, the roots of social behavior may call for considerable reexamination and be looked for elsewhere than in the male-female relationships so familiar in classic anthropological writings. Also in question would be a number of the commonly accepted theories about dominance, submissiveness, leadership, and related topics.

What relevance would all this have to the study of homosexuality? Plainly, if the whole male-female relationship and its centrality in the development of social groups needs to be reexamined, so also does the apparently natural existence, speaking in evolutionary terms, of the male-centered interest groupings described above. (p.60)

Has the male-female relationship been as fundamental to social development as has been believed, or does evidence from baboons give reason for some skepticism in this regard? Do the baboons give reasons for our supposing that the male-centered social group is even more "fundamental" and more "natural" in primate history than the female-centered groupings with which we are more familiar? (pp.60-1)

As a step toward such understanding, much can be gained from a look at baboon behavior toward infants. From this it may be possible to believe that solicitude toward infants is innate primate behavior and occurs more uniformly than among the lower animals. If this be so, the violent reactions expressed in our own society concerning attacks upon children can be better understood. (p.61)

Hence it can be argued that the whole question of the propriety and the "normality" of sexual contact with the young, whether the contacts be homosexual or heterosexual, hinges upon social definitions among differing cultures of the word "child."

Training by adults is minimal among the baboons, at least until the very threshold of maturity is reached. (p.62) Maternal solicitude, which is extended over many years as practiced in some parts of our society, is [by no means] functionally successful.

The question must be asked if such measures do not inevitably maladjust many juveniles and doom them to serious difficulty in later life, encumbering them with built-in neuroses. A staple of psychoanalytic thinking is that the roots of much, if not all, homosexuality are to be sought in the mother-child relationship. While this overstates the case badly, there appears to be good reason for suspecting that much modern child-raising flies in the face of fundamentals of primate inheritance and violates biologically natural tendencies.

The baboon data indicate that the gang phenomenon is largely male, at least in those age groups older than the immediate post-infant level. It is in the gangs that the male leadership phenomenon has its inception, with the dominant-male clusters of baboon adulthood as an outgrowth.

"Baboons" did not find that sexual relationships were important to the welfare of the baboon groups, as we have earlier noted. This is contrary to the claim of many other observers who have emphasized the centrality of sex. It is from this latter data that much sociological theory about rudimentary social structures has been derived.

If "Baboons" is correct, revisions are called for. Sex itself would not be found as having a crucial role in the social organization of rudimentary society, whereas care for and interest in infants does have an important role. The welfare of the group is carefully and elaborately organized around nonsexual concerns, principally those involving the safety of the group and its access to food and water. (p.62)

It would seem undeniable that the baboons make no evaluations concerning either homosexuality or heterosexuality. Their activities in either direction appear to be a matter of indifference to them. Behavior that is strictly sexual is regulated by hormonal activity, specifically the period of estrus in the females, but foreplay occurs the year around, to some extent.

"Baboons" reports no semblance of family life as we know it, nor of monogamy, and the same situation is reported as existing among other apes and monkeys. Although speculation is easy on such points, there is little evidence to suppose early man to have been very much different in his attitudes. (p.63)

To what sources can aversion to homosexuality then be traced? Perhaps to that point in time and in social development when man discovered the scientific connection between sexual acts and the appearing of the infants whom he so highly prized. Could this have been "the apple of knowledge" whose eating brought on so much discord?

Once this discovery in primitive science was made, the relationships of male to male, female to female, and male to female underwent radical changes. Acts and the relationships of acts could then be assigned into hierarchies of values hitherto unsuspected or even wished for. The roles of males and females began to acquire mystical overtones which had immense power over men's imaginations.

It is held here that radical reconstructions of general sociological theory are mandatory. The "Baboons" study fortunately has provided the insights needed to commence such a program of reconstruction and reevaluation of existing sociological theory.

Sociological Study
That Just Happened

The Midwinter Institute in 1961 has been given mention earlier.[13] Notable in so many ways, its unexpected side effect was to greatly expand sociological studies at ONE Institute. This started with the circulation of a Questionnaire[14] which was widely distributed in the hope of getting responses from the 5,000 (mailing list then available) around the country who would not be expected to attend and participate

---

[13] See Chap.2, p.38 above.

[14] See Appendix, 6-2: Questionnaire.

in the meetings in Los Angeles. Responses poured in from near and far, beyond all expectations.

What to do with this volume of information? It was far too large and unwieldy to be used during the Sessions. The solution was to hold a series of four semester-long Sociology Seminars to see what information this large volume of materials might reveal.[15]

Heading the project was John Burnside, a scientifically trained professional (physics) and ONE Institute student. After a tally of the many Questionnaires received from all over the world, the number was close to 1,000. Accompanying the Questionnaires were uncounted essay-style personal communications ranging from handwritten little notes to typewritten manuscripts 100 pages long.

To start organizing these materials, Seminar participants were referred to a list of textbooks dealing with social survey research methods. They then began to sort the jumble. First to be eliminated were all overseas replies as inapplicable to U.S. social conditions. Then, Canadian and Mexican respondents also had to be removed as not qualified to respond to questions about the U.S. Constitution. Women's replies could not be used because their number was too small to make a separate category. The disqualifications brought the number down to around 700.

Next came the one-by-one inspections. Those incomplete, however interesting, had to go. Next went the illegible, or partly so, bringing the total down still more. Finally, a close reading found some frivolous replies and others which did not specifically answer the questions. By the time all of those were rejected, the final number came to just below 400.

Remember, the study group was from varied educational backgrounds and met not more than four hours per week for a fourteen-week semester. The questionnaires had not been specifically intended as a social science survey at all. Consequently, much of the class time was necessarily devoted to reinterpreting the questions into categories usable in survey terms, and rightly so. This entailed much valuable direct sociological teaching.

The essay-type replies were excluded entirely and have not been effectively utilized even yet. When tabulations had been carried as far as the Seminars were able to accomplish, the data were turned over to

---

[15] See Appendix, 6-3: ONE INSTITUTE, 1967-1968, HS-222, Sociology Seminar.

a team: Loma Linda University Professor of Psychiatry Ray Evans and ONE Institute Psychology Instructor Julian M. Underwood, to prepare the final report.[16]

On February 1, 1969, Julian Underwood presented the following paper at an afternoon session of the 1969 ONE Midwinter Institute held in Los Angeles. Following his reading of the paper, a panel consisting of psychiatrists Richard Green, M.D., Director of Gender Identity Clinic at UCLA, Richard Parlour, M.D., in private practice, and Barry M. Dank, Assistant Professor of Sociology, California State College at Long Beach, discussed the paper and answered questions from the audience.

Copies of the data referred to in the paper as "Basic Percentage Tables" were supplied to members of the audience to enable them to follow the discussion.[17]

A STUDY OF 388
NORTH AMERICAN HOMOSEXUAL MALES

THE BASIC PERCENTAGE TABLES

For this presentation, time will permit review only of the more salient statistics from these tables, together with brief explanations of how the raw data from the questionnaires were evaluated and tabulated into the categories used.

Because of the kinds of information requested, the resulting data fell inevitably into two major classes, one objective in nature, the other non-objective. Data of the former sort were characterized by some objective attribute, such as income, or career interest, or age. On the other hand, the non-objective data, such as state of health, gender identification, etc., depended entirely on subjective criteria applied by the individual respondent.

In organizing the Basic Percentage Tables, it was found desirable to subdivide them according to these two major classes of data because

---

[16] Institute for the Study of Human Resources Publications, V:2, 21pp.

[17] See Appendix, 6-4: Basic Percentage Tables.

of the basic distinction between the criteria applying to them. For objective data, these criteria were easily and clearly defined. Moreover, this sort of data could be readily compared with similar data from the general adult male population, thereby clarifying its significance for ONE's sample. These descriptions, of course, could not be applied to the non-objective data, interpretation of which, from responses given, might have differed appreciably among different analysts, besides lacking comparable data from the population as a whole.

It will be observed that a few of the data areas shown on the Questionnaire are not included in the Basic Percentage Tables or in this evaluation. Data in these areas were rejected for one or more of the following reasons: (1) It was universal for sample, such as "sex of respondent;" (2) It was not considered materially relevant to the statistical profile sought, such as "how long divorced;" (3) There were insufficient responses to qualify the sample, such as "how long at former address;" or (4) [The question was] too ambiguous or general for satisfactory reply, such as "how do others regard you," or "is sex a problem to you."

A. THE OBJECTIVE DATA. – These take in most of the sociological information, and consist of the following specific categories: *age, education, career, income, home ownership, marriages* (homosexual and heterosexual), *psychiatric histories, symptoms of alcoholism, social conflict data* (arrests, etc.), and *sex frequencies*.

Age. The range was from 21 to 71 years, with the median at 34.8 and the mode at 30 years, with 24 individuals at the mode.

Education. Median length of schooling stood at 15.1 years, compared with 10.6 years for the general male population (GMP). Of the respondents, 53.2% were college graduates (8% for the general male population). Of the 206 college graduates, 43.6% (90) reported post-graduate studies leading to 13.1% Masters' degrees (51) and 7.7% Doctorates (30), whereas projected figures for the general male population (GMP) covering the age span represented in ONE's sample indicate not more than 2.5% with Masters' degrees and 0.5% with Doctorates.

Career. These data were finally grouped, for the Basic Percentage Tables, in a manner consistent with U.S. Bureau of Labor categories, though our detail was by no means fine enough to make precise or full use of these groupings. In ONE's sample, 208, or 58.3%, were in the higher career brackets (professional, technical, management, fine arts, etc.), compared with 29.2% for the GMP. Clerical and sales careers were indicated for 128 (34.2%) in ONE's sample, compared with 15.6% in the GMP, whereas trades, crafts, skilled labor, etc., comprised only 7.5% of ONE's sample but 55.2% of the GMP. The "fine arts" (defined for present purposes as the performing, graphic, and literary arts) are not singled out in the basic government categories, but were specially tabulated for ONE's sample. They showed an unexpectedly low representation, there being only 42 individuals (11.5%) in such careers, the smallest sub-group of all the upper career categories.

Income. The data here were predictably in accord with those for education and career. The per capita yearly income for ONE's sample, based on 345 earners, was $6,588/year, compared with approximately $4,500/year from a comparable bracket in the GMP. The above three fundamental categories of sociological data show ONE's sample to be on a markedly higher level than the general male population. To what extent it may also differ from the general *Homophile* population remains to be determined. However, we consider it justifiable to assume that ONE's sample represents a substantially larger population than itself, whose full dimensions and character in relation to the total Homophile population may become known only through continued surveys.

Home Ownership. This was reported affirmatively by 142, or 36.6%, of ONE's sample. The percentage of the total adult population of both sexes occupying their own homes for the comparable period was 30.8%. Although this favorable comparison may be accounted for partly by the career and financial data, we believe it to be primarily indicative of a level of social stability and adjustment not ordinarily associated with the male homosexual.

Homosexual and Heterosexual Marriage. Since a "homosexual marriage" lacks legal definition, it was necessary to establish an arbitrary criterion whereby to classify the responses in this area. Most respondents seem to assume much of the same definition for the liaison, i.e., the sharing of domestic accommodations with another male in a homoerotic attachment. It thus remained only to decide on a duration sufficient to demonstrate for such an arrangement the stability expected of a "marriage." One year was adopted as the minimum length for this purpose.

On that basis, 161 respondents (41.5%) reported 278 individual homosexual marriages, 97 of these exceeding five years, 11 exceeding 15 years, and five exceeding 25 years, with a median length of 3.8 years. At the time of returning the questionnaires, 113 homosexual marriages were in current standing, with a median length of 4.9 years.

By contrast, only 73 respondents (18.7%) reported heterosexual marriages, of whatever duration, each of which was tabulated regardless of length. Fifty-four of these marriages exceeded five years,

22 exceeded 15 years, and three exceeded 25 years, with 10.1 years as the median length. At the time of returning the questionnaires, 40 of these heterosexual marriages had current standing, with a median length of 14.2 years.

For heterosexual marriages ending in divorce, ONE's sample showed a ratio of about one in three, with a median length of 6.5 years. This compares with a ratio of about one in four for the general population, with a median length of 7.1 years. A somewhat high rate of separation appears among the homosexual marriages in ONE's sample, the ratio being about three in five, with a median length of 3.1 years. Nevertheless, this ratio was unexpectedly low in view of the social pressures against such partnerships and their lack of legal recognition or standing.

Forty-seven heterosexual marriages in ONE's sample were child-bearing, but 22 were nevertheless broken. About the same ratio of childless heterosexual marriages (14/29) were also broken, so the presence of children does not seem to have acted as a special pre-servative. The strongest binding force among the 40 current hetero-sexual marriages may well have been the presence of upper-level career status (Chi-square in excess of 11), reflecting the long and frequently observed practice of male Homophiles entering heterosexual marriage as a concession to (or perhaps means toward) the satisfaction of specific career ambitions.

Psychiatric History Data. Only 69 of ONE's sample reported three months or more of psychiatric treatments, and only an additional 30 reported psychiatric treatments of shorter term. Two-hundred eighty-nine respondents (75%) had never undergone psychiatric treatment. This large proportion of relatively self-regulated, non-anxious homosexuals formed the basis for critical comparisons with the 69 psychiatric cases, as will be described in Part 2.

Symptoms of Alcoholism. Such data were reported by only 26 respondents (6.7%). These were tabulated from responses indicating typical intensity of involvement, such as blacking-out periods, inability to restrain consumption, loss of jobs, friends, etc. This percentage appears to stand in favorable contrast to many public health estimates, which place incidence of actual and incipient alcoholism in the general adult population as high as eight to ten percent. Smokers were not included in the Basic Percentage Tables; however, there were only 232, or about 60% of the sample.

Social Conflict Data. (Arrests, robbings, beatings, blackmail-ings.) One hundred eighty-five, or 47.8% of ONE's sample, were involved in at least one incident of the above types, of which 304 incidents altogether were tabulated. In order of frequency, there were 130 robbings, 78 arrests, 64 beatings, and 32 blackmailings.

Sex Frequencies. ONE's data could be readily tabulated in terms of a weekly rate, and was thus conveniently comparable to Kinsey's data on the same subject, as reported in *Sexual Behavior in the Human Male*. Initial tabulation, and the association tables later established, made use also of three broad frequency ranges, low, medium, and high, taking the medium frequency range as between 2X/month and 6X/week. For the Basic Percentage Tables, the separate weekly rates were tabulated. Although included in the low frequency range for establishing association tables, the "seldom" or "never" responses were excluded from the weekly rates in the Basic Percentage Tables for lack of an actual frequency figure.

Comparison with Kinsey's figures should be made, bearing in mind that the latter were based on general sampling of many thousands of heterosexual and homosexual males, and a count of all forms of sex outlet, including autoeroticism, petting, etc. The Kinsey sample, moreover, included the adolescent ages of 15-20 years, in which he found the highest sex frequencies to lie. None of these conditions are true of ONE's sample, however, which included no adolescents, and which, to all intents and purposes, consisted exclusively of homosexual males.

In spite of all this, ONE's sample definitely contradicted the Kinsey conclusion that homosexual acts, even among practicing homosexuals, have markedly lower frequency than the general average for all forms of sex outlet. Indeed, after adjusting the Kinsey median and mean sex frequencies to eliminate the adolescent group, these measures fall appreciably below, rather than above, the corresponding figures from ONE's sample. The latter yields a median frequency of 2.04/week, and a mean of 2.64/week, compared with Kinsey's 1.35 and 1.95. Clearly this disagreement raises some fundamental questions concerning sampling techniques and/or the methods of obtaining the raw data in such sexological surveys.

B. THE NON-OBJECTIVE DATA. This comprises all of the psychosexual information called for in the questionnaire, along with certain other types of subjective data. These are made up of the specific categories of: *sex role preference, gender identification, health, physique photo interest, pen pal interest, religious attitudes, civic and social interests, hobby and recreational interests*, and *sports interest*.

Sex Role Preference. The question allowed complete latitude for the respondent in labeling his own preferences. The strength of the habit, or tradition, by which we categorize sex activities as "male" and others as "female" showed its force in the data here, since most respondents adopted these, or cognate terms, to describe their sex role preferences as male, female, or both. Male sex role preference was indicated by 148 (45.2%), female by 56 (17.1%), and both by 124 (37.7%).

Gender Identification. Most responses to this question were in terms paralleling those used in the "sex role" question. They showed almost twice as many identifying themselves with masculine gender as with male sex role preference, whereas of those who claimed the dual, or male-female, sex role preference, only about half accepted this duality as a personality, or gender, factor. This sharp disagreement between self-estimates of sex role and self-estimates of gender could be regarded as having very important psychological and social implications, our full understanding of which will need much more extensive surveys.

If "gender role" reflects one's actual (or coveted) social appearance or behavior as a person of one sex or the other, then "sex role" must reflect in some way the individual's actual (or coveted) psychosexual identification. That the two are distinct has long been noted in psychoanalytic studies and is clearly borne out in ONE's sample. That the psychosexual identification has some reality independent of either biological or social factors is suggested by the transsexual who suffers from identifying with one sex mentally or emotionally while being the opposite sex physically.

A tentative but, we believe, sound explanation for the great excess of masculine gender identify over male sex role preference is to be found in the structure of our socio-sexual mores in which "masculine" and "feminine" have become either-or categories, with all variants being placed under criteria defining one or the other, no matter what their physical sexual preference may be, and no matter what their artificial conformity may cost them in dissatisfactions and anxieties.

The contrasts and conflicts between gender and sex roles are well known to play an important part in psychiatric problems. The way in which ONE's sample bears this out will be discussed in a later section.

Health. These evaluations showed self-estimates of good-to-excellent health in over 90% of the respondents, suggesting that Homophiles are not generally victims of neurasthenia, as frequently supposed.

Physique Photo Interest was positively indicated by 267, or 69% of ONE's sample.

Pen Pal Interest was positive for only 219, or 56.4%. Data on this and physique photo interest were requested as a means of estimating the extent to which these interests were pursued as substitutes for actual social and sexual contact.

Religious Attitudes were determined by weighing the responses to the three relevant questions. Where religious beliefs and/or church activities appeared to exercise a regulating or otherwise beneficial or stabilizing influence in the life of the respondent, a positive value was assigned. There were 150 such responses (or 38.9%), which was unexpectedly high in view of the violent and historic antihomosexualism of the churches. Only an antagonistic attitude, or an attitude of calculated rejection, was assigned a negative value, which categorized no more than 16 respondents. The remainder (56.8%) were categorized as indifferent.

Civic and Social Interests, that is, interest in general community affairs and administration, was shown as positive for 154 respondents, or 40.3%. There was no means of gauging degrees of interest, each indication being tabulated simply as positive.

Hobby and Recreational Interests were tabulated as "extensive," "average," or "negligible," depending on the scope and/or degree of interest expressed in responses to the numerous questions in this bracket. Two hundred sixty-six respondents (or 68.7%) were tabulated as "average," 68 (or 17.5%) as "extensive," and the remainder as "negligible."

Sports Interest was shown as affirmative for 172 respondents, or 44.3%, again with no means of estimating degree of interest. We see no reason to suppose that this figure varies widely from the average popular interest. Since the special category of sports did not specify any particular type, it is assumed that respondents construed the term "sports" to mean the competitive spectator sports which occupy the largest share of public attention. In none of the last three categories of so-called "outside" interests does ONE's sample seem to stand out as exceptional to the general population.

The final value of all of this non-objective data cannot properly be ascertained except against the background of much larger surveys which include the general population. Its present value may be summed up under three headings: (1) as an aid in determining profitable areas for future investigation, (2) as an aid in correcting the misimpression that Homophiles are, psychosexually, some kind of homogeneous group, having "typical" sex role preferences and self-estimates and "typical" habits of living, and (3) as an aid in correcting another misimpression that male Homophiles are, in their social interests, very different from the general population.

SPECIAL TABULATIONS AND ASSOCIATIONS

In addition to providing a general profile of a sample group, which may then be compared with known or hypothetical characteristics of related, or perhaps very different, populations, the data from a sample as large as ONE's may be used to serve an equally important purpose – that of indicating possible associations between different kinds of data. Is any special relation indicated, for example, between mental or emotional disturbances and alcoholic symptoms; or joblessness; or between a male sex role preference and sex frequency; or heterosexual marriage? Such areas of association are sought through special tables which are set up to indicate apparent differences of contingency among selected types of data, as well as the relative levels of these contingents. A strong contingency indicator points to the possible existence of a real association, or dependency, of one kind of observed conditions upon another. This, in turn, may be made the basis of special investigation.

The information from ONE's sample considered to be deserving of the closest study was that related to psychologically disturbed respondents, specifically, the 69 who reported undergoing psychiatric treatments of three months or longer duration.

Of course this group corresponds to the groups which in the past have almost always been singled out for study by psychiatrists, in consonance with the traditional thesis that homosexuality was a form of psychopathology. Where a statistical approach was used (as in the case of Bieber's *Homosexuality*), heterosexual males have been included as a control group. Presumably the latter group was supposed to supply the normative psychosexual data, in contrast to which the homosexuals were viewed as contributing the "abnormal," "deviant," or pathological data. In any case, the use of psychiatric patients exclusively for the Homophile group ensured that all data from the relatively undisturbed, self-accepting homosexuals were also excluded; and this, combined with use of heterosexual controls, established a set of preconditions which could not be adopted in more general data studies because of risk of falling into serious errors about the contingencies in the group being studied. This risk is magnified by attaching concepts of "normative" and "deviant" to the respective groups, for in our culture this would necessarily imply a rather awesome, universal judgment that one form of sexual inclination had some absolute value, or propriety, lacking in the other.

In analyzing ONE's sample, it has seemed for all of these reasons entirely proper to try to avoid these pitfalls; and it has also seemed equally possible to do so, since 75% of ONE's sample is reported free of any severe psychiatric disturbances, and may be used as a basis of comparison or control for the 69 who have such disturbances. At any rate, this is the comparison which has been made, and it has been made free of any assumptions about whether homosexuality is or is not a pathological condition.

For the purposes of this report, we will now compare observations of attributes in the psychiatric group with those in the non-psychiatric group only where the probability (P) is 10% or less that the same proportions of observations could occur between each pair of attributes if the latter were independent. The smaller this probability, the greater is the possibility that there exists some association, or contingency, between the two attributes. The 10% probability is referred to in statistical studies as the "0.10 or 10% level of significance," which is considered by many statisticians as marking the upper limit beyond which no association should be inferred. These levels of significance are based on the chi-square value, which, at 10%, equals 2.706, increasing to 10.827 as the probability decreases to .001.

Income. The no-income group, that is, the jobless, hold the spotlight among the psychiatric cases, with the level of significance below .001, suggesting a high degree of association between unemployment and psychiatric disturbance. Other income levels show no outstanding significance indicators, though the "low" level shows a trend toward association.

Home Ownership. This is negatively associated for the psychiatric cases (that is, non-ownership is positive) with the significance level within .01, or 1% probability. This is quite in accord with expectation for this group.

Other positive associations, within the 10% level of significance, are indicated for the following attributes: *Absence of Homosexual Marriage*, at the 10% level; *Symptoms of Alcoholism*, at the 2% level; *Extremes of Sex Frequency*, low or high, at the .001 or 0.1% level; *Inferior Health Estimate* (fair to poor) at the 1% level; extremes of *Hobby and Recreational Interest* (extensive or negligible) at the 2% level. Not all of these were in accord with expectation, and may be noteworthy for panel discussion. All, however, seem to be related in some manner to mental or emotional instability.

The question now arises as to whether to consider levels of significance exceeding 0.10. It seems to us unwise, if not impossible, to completely ignore these cases, for in many cases the association, however indecisive, confirms many years of practical observation and experience, and thus adds valuable support to the validity of ONE's data generally.

In the social conflict area, for example, the psychiatric cases show positive association indicated at a significance level only slightly escaping 0.10. This is quite within expectation, and can scarcely be disregarded, inasmuch as among self-accepting, socially-adapted homosexuals, social conflict incidents are absent or rare. An examination of the attributes whose significance levels are as borderline as 30% suggests that at least some of these should be further investigated, through other and perhaps more comprehensive surveys. Among the psychiatric cases, such promising areas may be noted in connection with male sex role preference, non-masculine gender identification, absence of heterosexual marriage, physique photo and pen pal interests, and indifferent or negative religious attitudes.

In addition to the psychiatric cases, ONE's sample was investigated for associations by Sex Role Preference (SRP). This highlighted the male-female or dual sex role preference group as having by far the most balanced position among the attributes surveyed – that is, the fewest special associations, or extremes of frequency. Only four categories of data registered within the 0.30 level of significance; others indicated frequencies at or close to the independence values. These four categories themselves tended to suggest a special stability for this group. Uppermost levels of education were strongly indicated for association, with a .02 level of significance, and absence of alcoholic symptoms were also associated at about the same level. Non-feminine gender identification showed potential association at the .05 significance level, whereas the dual, masculine-feminine gender identification was positively associated at the 0.10 level. Superior health estimates (good to excellent) were also associated at close to this level.

In contrast to the above, the Male Sex Role Preference (MSRP) group and also the Female, each showed many special idiosyncrasies, which in several instances paired off to suggest contrary trends.

The MSRP group showed an association with top careers at slightly above the 0.20 level, whereas the FSRP group was negative in this category at the 0.10 level. Under technical careers, this relation was reversed, with MSRP's negatively associated, FSRP's positively.

The MSRP group was strongly associated with the medium range of sex frequencies, at the .02 level of significance, but the FSRP group was negatively associated for this range. Its data showed potential association primarily with the low frequencies, near the .01 level.

Gender identification was overwhelmingly masculine for the MSRP group, but even more overwhelmingly feminine for the FSRP group.

Physique photo and pen pal interests were negative for the MSRP group, at about the 0.20 level; however, physique photo interest was strongly positive for the FSRP group, at the .001 level.

All civic, recreational, and other outside interests show as moderately associated with Male Sex Role Preference, with levels of significance between 0.30 and 0.10, but as negatively associated for the FSRP group at considerably stronger levels.

These statistics tend to show the FSRP group as relatively withdrawn from participation in economic and social affairs, and as relatively non-aggressive and/or inactive sexually, perhaps closely related to the Kinsey sampling.

The MSRP group stands out by itself for an association with heterosexual marriage, at close to the 0.10 level, while the FSRP group is markedly positive for symptoms of alcoholism. None of the three sex role preferences stands out as associated with psychiatric problems, though a positive trend in this direction is suggested by the MSRP's, and a negative trend by the dual, or Male-Female SRP's.

One final area of data was explored for associations – namely, the heterosexually- and homosexually-married. These were studies in groups of 130 respondents homosexually-married only, one of 31 respondents heterosexually- *and* homosexually-married, and one of 42 respondents heterosexually-married only. These groups were tabulated for the following selected categories: Gender Identification, Sex Role Preference, Sex Frequency, Psychiatric Histories (three months or more), Physique Photo Interest, Home Ownership, and Presence of Top Career.

The three groups, taken together, showed a striking resemblance to the Sex Role Preference groups, in that the 31 having duality of interest (i.e. in both heterosexual and homosexual relations) showed, like the male-female sex role preferences, the fewest areas of possible association. The strongest positive association was with high sex frequency, at the .05 level, and there was a more moderate association, at the 0.20 level, with ownership of residence. The one negative association was with masculine-feminine gender identification, indicating to us a psychosexual uncertainty which could not be resolved or reconciled subjectively, leading to experimentation with both male and female connections.

For male sex role preference, the homosexually-married group showed positive association at the 0.10 level, while the heterosexually-married group was negatively associated at about the same level. This, with other data, tends to suggest that many male Homophiles may try to over identify with the "male-masculine" stereotype so widely advertised.

The homosexually-marrieds were strongly identified with medium sex frequencies, the heterosexually-married with low sex frequencies. The homosexually-marrieds indicated strong negative association with physique photo interest (at the .01 level) while the heterosexually-married group showed an equally strong positive association. The homosexually-married were negatively associated with both ownership of residence and top careers, while the heterosexually-married showed positive association in both. No married category showed special association with psychiatric disturbance.

CONCLUSION

The above report covers only the highlights of the statistics obtained from ONE's sample. Time does not permit us to review the mass of secondary information, or to discuss the many inferences which may be drawn.

The study of the 69 psychiatric cases pinpoints the need for investigations which are not limited to mentally or emotionally disturbed homosexuals, or by methods which involve comparison with heterosexual controls. We believe that such preconditions, and the assumptions prompting them, must inevitably lead to distorted conclusions. The associations derived from these 69 respondents also suggest a general observation, namely, that ONE's data do not pinpoint the *causes* for psychiatric disturbance in the homosexual, though it strongly suggests that a conflict between sex role preference and gender identification may be involved. Obviously, homosexuality *per se* is not the cause; otherwise ONE's entire sample would be similarly affected, not merely a small fraction of it. Thus, we believe that the true causes for psychopathology must indeed lie somewhere in dimensions of experience not reached in ONE's survey, even while considerably worked over by others, specifically, in the psychosexual and sociosexual histories of individuals.

The associations studied under sex role preference and marriage data suggest most important conclusions of a different sort. These are that "male" and "female," "masculine" and "feminine," do seem indeed to have some kind of real duality, or polarity, in our experience. The patterns of association in this area shown by ONE's sample would seem impossible to explain, unless this were so. Are such distinctions entirely cultural, merely the product of a certain set of sociosexual traditions imposed on each individual from infancy; or is there some natural, biological, constitutional basis; or must we deal with both kinds of elements in order to understand the complexities of human sexuality?

Only comprehensive studies such as this pioneering effort by ONE, which integrates both the psychological and sociological aspects of experience, are likely to lead toward the answers so badly needed if we are to create a more favorable social climate for the rational and complete fulfillment of man's sexual instincts. It is to be hoped that future studies will continue these comprehensive approaches and thus help to resolve further the many important questions raised by this survey.

ONE Institute did not have recording equipment at the time the foregoing paper was given, so that comments and criticisms made during the discussion period following its presentation have not been preserved. However, two years later, one of the participants, Howard E. Fradkin, Associate Professor of Sociology, California State University, Long Beach, gave a lecture (October 3, 1971) in which he commented upon the data in some detail in order to give emphasis to those conclusions he felt were of enduring importance. A report of his lecture by James L. Kepner, Jr., a former ONE Institute faculty member, follows.[18] Because the lecture presented a discerning and judicious critique of the study, the report is reprinted here in full.

A 1960 Questionnaire, initially conceived as drawing information for a proposed homosexual "Bill of Rights" to be written at the 1961 Midwinter Institute, drew relatively few answers which could be tabulated regarding those rights which homosexuals felt were being denied them; however, the proposal data on the 388 usable questionnaires were found to be of considerable interest. Though copies of the questionnaire had been sent out not only to ONE's mailing list, but to the Mattachine and Daughters of Bilitis lists as well, there were not sufficient answers by women to be statistically significant. Answers coming from Europe and elsewhere outside North America were excluded for much the same reason, as also were those where the answers seemed unclear or not serious enough to appear reliable.

Before his death in early 1970, Julian Underwood, and other members of ONE Institute as well, had spent many hours analyzing and tabulating (no small job) these questionnaire results and reported preliminary findings in a highly technical paper delivered at the January, 1969 Midwinter Institute.

Dr. Fradkin, in the 162nd Lecture of ONE Institute's Lecture Series, discussed his own examination of the data and of Woody's analysis of those data compared to statistics derived from the U.S. population as a whole, for example, Labor Department statistics regarding population percentages at specified career and income levels.

---

[18] *LTR* XVI:10 (October, 1971), pp.3-5.

Fifty-eight percent of ONE's sample were in the "higher" career brackets (professional, technical, managerial, fine arts, etc.) compared with 29.2% in the general male population. Likewise, the per-capita annual income, based on the 345 who replied to that question in ONE's sample, was $6,588, as compared to $4,500 a year (1960 level) for a comparable sample in the general male population. Also, 53.2% of ONE's sample were college graduates, as opposed to only eight percent in the general population.

Fradkin warned that we ought not assume from this that homosexuals in general are better educated and have better economic and social positions than is the average for the general population – but we were aware from the beginning that ONE's readers, as well as [those on] the partly overlapping Mattachine and DOB mailing lists, are a select lot. It would go without saying that the readership of any magazine would be more likely to be more literate, and therefore better educated, than the average population. It might further be observed that persons with better than average education might be somewhat more likely to voluntarily fill out and return such questionnaires. At any rate, 43.6% of ONE's sample reported some postgraduate work and 7.7% of them (30 persons) had doctorates.

Even if ONE's sample was not entirely typical of homosexuals generally, the facts that 36.6%, or 142, owned their own homes, and that 41.5% of the respondents reported at least 278 home-sharing homosexual relationships lasting a year or longer (97 homosexual marriages lasting over five years) strongly belie the popular image of homosexuals as unstable, rootless dropouts. In addition, 18% of ONE's sample were or had been involved in heterosexual marriages of 10.1 years median duration, and 47 of them had children. It was noted that the percentage of heterosexual marriages that had broken up was about the same for those having and those not having children.

Dr. Fradkin found great probable significance in certain correlates regarding the 69 persons in ONE's sample who had undergone three months or more of psychiatric treatment (75% had never undergone such treatment) with questions relating to the individual's assessment of sex role preference. How significantly attitudes on a question of this sort have changed in the last decade remains to be seen – one report by Dr. Evelyn Hooker indicates a radical change away from exclusively feminine role and identity – but at least a decade ago, a great many homosexuals would describe their sex-role preference in terms such as "male, female, or both," and it was most widely assumed that "female" was a synonym for "passive."

A curious factor in the responses to the question "What role do you prefer?" as compared to "Do you consider yourself effeminate (males)?" was that almost twice as many report masculine gender identification as those reporting male sex-role preferences. Only half as many accepted male-female sex identity as those reporting either sex role preference. Part of the problem here is that a new terminology and new ways of thinking about these factors have evolved since this questionnaire was composed and circulated. One cannot be certain how many of the respondents interpreted and answered those questions in sharply differing ways. What is female sex role preference in homosexual relationships? taking a passive position for sodomy? which way for fellatio? Playing the girl in bed as to manner, use of pronouns, giggling, etc., acting the coquette, or the whore, or the housewife, regardless of sexual positions? One might assume that most respondents meant some combination of these factors.

What Dr. Fradkin found most significant was the fact that the percentage of those expressing a male sex role preference was significantly higher (7%) among those who had undergone psychiatric treatment than among those who had not. Those preferring female sex roles were fractionally less frequent among the therapy set, and those who classed themselves as AC-DC [amenable to both roles] were 6.2% less common in the group which had experienced therapy.

Since this would tend to suggest that those who expressed male sex role preference were the most likely to seek therapy, and those who had neither male nor female preference the least likely, most of the audience questioning centered on the postulate that butch-type gays suffered greater psychological strain identifying with their homosexuality. However, the statistics were reversed, though with less contrast, when it came to gender identity. Of those males who considered themselves masculine, 5.5% fewer had experienced therapy than those who had not, as against 2.3% more for those considering themselves in the middle. This would suggest that preference for "male" sex roles is more likely to lead to the psychiatrist's couch, but that a masculine self image is less likely to do so. There may be some deeply significant truth hidden in these figures, but this writer feels the original ambiguous question needs to be broken down into several more precise questions before it can become clear what these figures may signify.

Dr. Fradkin also noted the very high percent of the respondents who had been the victims of arrest (25.8%), robbings (42.8%), beatings (20.8%), and blackmail (10.6%). While some respondents checked off more than one category, there was no figure on multiple arrests, etc., per respondent. Fradkin noted, with surprise, that only 6.7% of the sample indicated symptoms of alcoholism, somewhat below the national average, and particularly significant in light of the fact that, in 1960, most public avenues of gay social life involved drinking.

The following report describes an unprecedented course, "The Sociology of Sexual Behavior," given jointly by ONE Institute of Homophile Studies and California State University, Long Beach. This course was first offered in Fall, 1971, and repeated in Spring, 1972; it was repeated in the Fall, 1972, and the Spring, 1973, semesters.

Other sociology classes have been offered at ONE Institute on a regular basis since then; see, for example, the course description of "Theoretical Concepts" as taught in Spring, 1982, by Laud Humphries, Ph.D. and Brian Miller, Ph.D., also other class offerings.[19]

REPORT TO THE ERICKSON EDUCATIONAL FOUNDATION

PROJECT

The Erickson Educational Foundation Training and Research Fellowship program at California State University, Long Beach.

PURPOSE

As its goal, the project attempted to train a small number of carefully selected students in *The Sociology of Sexual Behavior*. Students were initially screened by instructors Howard Fradkin and Dorr Legg with the assistance of Evelyn Hooker of the UCLA faculty. The intention of the above named faculty in initiating this course was to go beyond the conventional boundaries of the usual college course in order to provide student trainees with an emotional or cathartic experience in knowing, listening to, and interacting with, persons of variant sexual backgrounds. Students were encouraged to explore library resources and to conduct individual research projects in order to examine the parameters of subjects in which they had special interests. The quality and intensity of the work carried on by the student group during the Spring Semester (1972) would not have been possible without the financial assistance of the EEF grant.

---

[19] See Chap.4, p.76 above.

ACADEMIC AND EXPERIENTIAL ACTIVITIES

The classes met two evenings a week for a period of two hours each evening. On Tuesday evenings theoretical discussions were held on the CSULB campus, while on Wednesday evenings the class met at ONE, Incorporated in downtown Los Angeles. In addition, students were required to attend six field trips, usually on alternate Friday and Saturday evenings throughout the semester. Field trips (most students participated in more than the six required trips) encompass the following:

1. Neighborhood gay bars.
2. Prestige gay restaurants.
3. Nude male dancing bars.
4. Cruising bars.
5. Lesbian bars.
6. Gay liberation, male and female, facilities (voluntary); gay church services.
7. A French film on incest: "Murmurs of the Heart."
8. Meetings of the Family Synergy Association, and expanded family association.
9. Gay young people dance bars.
10. A visit with a verbal "swinging" couple telling of their experiences in the swinging scene.
11. A visit to Sandstone, an institution catering to the needs of swingers (voluntary).
12. A performance by Charles Pierce, a renowned female impersonator.
13. Visits to gay student groups at the University of California, Irvine, and at California State University, Long Beach (voluntary).
14. The monthly meeting of a large transvestite group in Los Angeles.
15. A visit with a Guyon Society representative.
16. A visit to the Center for Marital and Sexual Studies conducted by Dr. William Hartman.
17. A visit to the Gay Academy Awards Presentations in Hollywood sponsored by SPREE (Society of Pat Rocco Enlightened Enthusiasts), a drama and cinema group.

This semester our carefully screened student group began with nine but ended with seven participants. Two individuals were dropped from the group for non-attendance due to conflicting interests. Of the seven final participants one held a Ph.D. degree, one an M.A. degree, two were graduate students working on master's degrees in psychology, and three were undergraduates of whom two were sociology majors and one a criminology major.

This was a highly motivated student group, a group that put in many extra hours of time and energy in the pursuit of their special interests and in the conduct of their research projects.

RESEARCH

Worthy of special note were the following research papers (copies filed at the Sociology Department, CSULB).

(1)   Prock, Bernie, *Male Prostitution*
(2)   --------------, *Gay Sado-Masochism*
(3)   Boyd, Maureen *et al*, *Incest*
(4)   Symonds, Carolyn, *Swingers*
(5)   Mayers, Kathleen, *The Male Transsexual as a Child*
(6)   Tadema, Pearl, *Group Marriage*

The Boyd paper on incest was totally unique in that the students placed an advertisement in the *Los Angeles Free Press* soliciting interviews about incestuous experiences. More then one hundred usable interviews (mostly by telephone) were conducted – interviewees responded from as far away as Minnesota and Louisiana. After quantifying and tabulating the results with the assistance of Dr. Fradkin, a totally new (and as yet unique to the existing literature on the subject) picture of the middle- and upper-class person engaged in incestuous behavior emerged. Almost all prior research findings were based on lower class samples. Those generalizations applicable in the lower classes proved to be erroneous when looked at from the perspective of a fairly large sample (N=84) of middle-class incestors. The most interesting generalizations found was that participation in middle-class incest did not harm the individual psychologically, nor did it alter the family role structure in any significant way. Far from being harmed, individuals reported feeling closer to their respective families.

While the incest study was limited in scope, further research (particularly if concordant with the present findings) should dramatically alter the thinking of psychologists and psychiatrists on the subject of the effects of incestuous behavior on young people.

OVERALL EVALUATION

Verbal feedback from the student group was very favorable; several students reported that the course had a tremendous emotional impact on their lives. One of the students recommended the course for all psychiatric and psychology interns at Orange County General Hospital where she was employed as a psychologist.

Dorr Legg (co-instructor) and I believe that the course might be tailored to the needs of the professional community, i.e. MD's, psychologists, social workers, educators, and ministers. If the course broadens horizons and opens-up new avenues of insight to professionals, we believe that it would make a significant contribution to the overall community.

CRITIQUE AND FUTURE PLANS

(1) In future semesters we will plan our tours and visiting lecturers well in advance. Our advance planning this semester suffered somewhat from our lack of information on worthwhile tours and significant speakers. To a great extent this semester was highly "experimental," but we now have a fund of information and experience from which to draw.

(2) There was some difficulty in articulating with an on-going ONE, Incorporated Institute Class during the semester. We merged student bodies, so to speak, on Wednesday evenings, but there was a great difference in preparation and background between student groups and the combined group was not as cohesive a body academically or psychologically. In the future it appears desirable to plan to have specific lectures tailored to the needs of the college class. These lectures would be prepared in advance and all lecturers would receive a standard compensation.

(3) Dorr Legg and I agree that the fellowship program for student participants is no longer necessary. Our student body this past year served as our experimental group and demonstrated to us that maximum student participation can be actualized by providing financial support for creative projects rather than being used as a blanket subsidy. In any future grant we would plan to use funds to support field trip events and creative research, e.g. in the incest study, two of our students had phone bills of fifty to one-hundred dollars per

month for three consecutive months. Such reasonable expenses should be born by the project.

(4) Our experience this past semester suggests that approximately half of the student group will be interested in creative research, while the other half will probably confine their activities to term papers using standard library facilities. In future grant programs we would like to provide a research subsidy to approximately half of the student body.

(5) During the past semester we (the faculty) probably over-worked our students. Not only did we require up to eight hours of class or field work activities, but we encouraged individual projects, often of a substantial nature, e.g. our incest study had students answering phones at all hours of the day and night – up to 20 and 30 hours per week. In the future we have decided to offer the course one evening per week for three hours and that Friday evening be se-lected, since most field activity events can take place on that weekend type evening.

(6) Not enough time was allowed or allocated this semester to help students integrate their experiences. The course content is highly emotionally charged and field visits, particularly face-to-face contacts, can and often are threatening in a psychological sense. Very often we found students asking the question, "Who Am I?" Two of our students came to the decision that they were bi-sexual – it was not easy for them to verbalize this. Both had never really understood themselves and their feelings before taking the course, and I suspect they were freed of much guilt through their knowledge and under-standing of the full range of human sexual behavior. In the future, more time should be set aside for free expression of feelings: bull sessions, encounter groups, and other integrating techniques should be part of the structure of the course.

(7) In general, both faculty members were pleased with the course and its impact on the student body. Both faculty members confess that the course was a rich learning experience for them personally.

Prepared by:

Howard E. Fradkin Ph.D., Professor of Sociology, California State University, Long Beach.

W. Dorr Legg, Associate Professor of Sociology, Extension Division, California State University, Long Beach.

Further Reading

Boyfrank, Monwell "Augmented Families," *MAG* VIII (February, 1960), pp.6-9. The article calls attention to challenges homosexuality makes to conventional sociological views of the family.

Kepner, James L.   "The Campaign That Deviated," *MAG* VII (November, 1959), pp.512. Report on the outcome of a San Francisco mayoral campaign during which homosexuality and the Mattachine Society provoked a public revulsion and defeat of the mud-slinging politician.

Prosin, Susanne   "The Homosexual Minority: A Sociologist's Viewpoint," *MAG* X (June, 1962), pp.9-10.

Smith, A. E. "Coming Out," *MAG* X (June, 1962), pp.6-8.

ONE Institute Extension Lectures:
Sociological Topics

Extension Division Lectures which have supplemented courses on Sociology began with a panel discussion of "The Homosexual in the Community" on January 30, 1960, as one of the main features of ONE's Midwinter Institute that year.

Other Lectures on Sociology are listed below in order of the dates on which they were given.

January 30, 1960 (#34) A panel discussion of "The Homosexual in the Community" as one of the main features of ONE's Midwinter Institute that year.

January 30, 1960 (#36) "Normative Factors and Cultural Determinants in the Dynamics of Homosexual Pairing" by W. Dorr Legg.

January 30, 1960 (#37) "Value Conflicts and Value Congruence of a Homosexual Group in Heterosexual Society," by Evelyn Hooker, Ph.D.

October 14, 1964 (#90) "Homophile Opinions and Attitudes," a panel discussion chaired by Institute faculty member John Burnside. Students enrolled in evaluating and tabulating the 1961 Survey Questionnaires discussed both what they were learning about social science surveys and the many new insights they were gaining on the wide range of behavior and attitudes found among Homophile males.

January 29, 1966 (#102) "Goals of the Homophile Movement" A panel gave a comprehensive cross section of social attitudes among a dozen of the active Movement organizations, from the East Coast across the U.S., representing both men and women. This was perhaps the most broadly representative opinion exchange ever presented to that date.

October 1, 1967 (#123) "A Sociological Approach to Homosexuality," by Sociology Professor Marion F. Steele, California State College, Long Beach. His views, stimulating and unconventional for the time, earned him wide media publicity and eventual dismissal from his university post. ONE Institute felt privileged to have been able to hear his views.

December 1, 1968 (#136) "Innovations in the Poverty Program," by Don Lucas, Executive Director of the San Francisco Central Multi-Service Center, who gave a very street-level presentation of social problems as they existed in San Francisco at the time.

February 1, 1969 (#138) "Study of 388 North American Homosexual Males," by a panel of psychiatrists and others commenting upon ONE Institute's project of that name.

March 7, 1971 (#160) California State College, Long Beach Sociology Professor Barry M. Dank spoke of "Coming Out in the Gay World" based upon his doctoral dissertation presented at the University of Wisconsin where he had done work under Professor Climard previously mentioned. Professor Dank was also one of the panelists on the following program.

October 2, 1971 (#164) California State University Professor of Sociology, Howard E. Fradkin gave a detailed examination of "Sociological Implications of ONE's Study of 388 North American Homosexual Males." It should be noted here that California State, Long Beach, had for several years been remarkably open in the number of its departments scheduling speakers from ONE Institute; in addition to Sociology – Psychology, Public Health, Criminology and History.

November 5, 1972 (#179) "The New Politics of Homosexuality" given by Laud Humphreys, Professor of Sociology, Pitzer College, Claremont, California, already a famous sociologist for his 1970 study, *Tearoom Trade.* A copy of his second book, *Out of the Closets, the Sociology of Homosexual Liberation*, 1972, bears a written inscription to this editor inside the cover for his "great assistance in this research."

May 6, 1973 (#185) A panel of Long Beach students offered a lively lecture, "Sociology and Sexual Behavior," at ONE Institute. Unfortunately, reactionary forces began to stir on the Long Beach campus not long afterward, setting up a series of repressive actions, including the dismissal of a qualified women instructor who taught a course on women's sexuality.

June 8, 1974 (#198) "Incest: Some Recent Data," Howard G. Fradkin's discussion of controversial findings made by Maureen Boyd.

June 8, 1974 (#203) "Sources of Hostility Toward Sex Variants," by Vern Bullough, Professor of History, California State University, Northridge.

November 6, 1977 (#234) "Emerging Gay Culture and its Impact on Identity Formation," by Laud Humphreys.

January 20, 1980 (#258) "Our Goals as Citizens in Society," a panel discussion, Robert Earl, moderator.

January 2, 1986 (#314) "Redefining Youth," by members of the Community Youth Education Project.

June 1, 1986 (#319) "Growing Up and Coming Out in the 1930s and '40s," by Martin Block, a Founder of ONE, 1952; first editor, *ONE Magazine.*

May 3, 1987 (#327) "Cosexual Politics," by Sue Moore, Director of Connexus, women's' organization.

April 10, 1988 (#334) "The Radical Religious Right," by Betty Brooks, Ph.D., discharged faculty member, California State University, Long Beach.

May 6, 1990 (#363) "Act Up Speaks," by Bruce Mirken and Helene Shpak.

June 2, 1991 (#363) "A Family Retrospective," by Dr. Dwain E. Houser, former ONE Institute Chancellor.

October 6, 1991 (#364) "Gay Oriented Media: Past, Present and Future," by Paul Lerner, USC School of Communication.

In addition to the excerpts from faculty and student papers cited in this chapter, several video cassettes, each of them an hour or more in length and containing valuable sociological material, are located in the Audiovisual Collection of ONE's Baker Memorial Library.

#279   "The New Politics of Homosexuality" given by Laud Humphreys.

#301   "Accent on Youth," a panel discussion by several, under-twenty-five, young men and women.

#343   "Two Lives Remembered," presented by a lesbian couple in their nineties who recount some of their experiences in military life and elsewhere.

#364   "Gay Oriented Media," given by Paul Lerner, a graduate student in the USC School of Communication.

CHAPTER 7

PSYCHOLOGY

T he January, 1953, first issue of *ONE Magazine* brought enthusiastic praise, some criticism and, unexpectedly, many requests for counsel and advice. ONE's Articles of Incorporation included two "Primary Purposes" for the new organization, one of which was "to aid... the sexual variant."[1] Early demands for counseling were so important that ONE soon found itself operating a veritable Community Services Center almost as soon as the little corporation came into existence.

The earliest published corporation report contains the following: "ONE Incorporated has received hundreds of letters, telephone calls and personal requests for advice and assistance. Between the sharply conflicting demands of a heterosexual society (itself often schizoid) and his own innermost needs, the homosexual finds himself in a morally and socially untenable position where he desperately needs advice."[2] Excerpts from the following case history vividly indicate the human dimensions of the many problems into which ONE's ad hoc "Community Services Center" found itself plunged.

It was in the fall of 1953 that a tiny man wearing a jockey cap walked into ONE's barren office. He was small enough to have been a jockey. Anyhow, he was wearing the cap. It was a good many interviews later before that cap ever came off, to reveal the baldness of which he was at that time ashamed.

This was little John. He had found *ONE Magazine* on a newsstand, bought it one minute, and got on the bus the next, to come to ONE's new office as the earliest applicant for ONE's Social Service Division. John stuttered rather badly; gradually, he managed to get his story out.

It had a good many of the familiar outlines: a rather stormy boyhood and adolescence in a small town in the Middle West; a good deal of boisterous slamming around with the gang; a good deal of show at making passes at the girls and at trying to deceive relatives and friends about himself; a good deal of trying to deceive himself about himself; a good deal of drifting from job to job. He hadn't gone very far in

---

[1] See Appendix, 1-1: ONE, Incorporated. Articles of Incorporation & By-Laws, 1953, Art II A.

[2] Charles Rowland, 1954 Annual Report, *MAG* III:2 (February, 1955), p.7.

school. The speech difficulty took care of that. It was pretty hard to say he was trained for anything in particular.

By a series of fortuitous circumstances, John finally found a pretty good niche as an orderly in a large Veterans Hospital in Los Angeles. This gave his long–evaded homosexuality some congenial and useful expression. No task was too distasteful for him, nothing too unpleasant or menial, so long as he could feel he was being of service to those men in need.

John cheerfully helped the nurses and usually ran, not walked, for John liked his work. Besides, there were many working side-by-side with him – doctors, nurses, administrative assistants, orderlies – who shared his own emotional orientation. Life was always interesting.

All went along well for a few years until Senator McCarthy's demonic career began to send homosexual tremors throughout the entire structure of federal employment in the United States.

In due time a Gestapo-like task force got around to the hospital where John worked. The wily ferrets who made it up soon discerned that little John was just their boy.

There is little need to describe the methods of the vice-squad kind of mentality which will do anything in the name of virtue, so long as it is well paid. John told all; all about himself; all about everyone else... After John and many other "undesirables" were fired, the task force could proudly report a real "purified" hospital. The veterans were safe once more.

There stood John in ONE's office shaking as he told it all. Sometimes he cried, abysmally ashamed of himself, utterly debased at the thought of the disasters he had brought down upon so many others. At the same time he was choking with rage and contempt at those who had taken advantage of his honesty to entrap him, and with loathing for the Senator who was the apparent cause of it all.

His beloved job was gone, the only job he had ever really liked and given himself wholly to. Gone were all the happy associations he'd enjoyed at work, and gone was the opportunity to serve the sick whom he wanted to serve and who needed the help. It was a bitter, bitter pill.

Down to ONE's office John came nearly every day to volunteer his work. The floors were swept and mopped. Boxes were lifted. Errands run. Work was his therapy, work and talk, for he had to talk it all out.

Today, John can face himself and others quite unabashed. In fact he tells people, at work or elsewhere, just exactly what he is. They can take it or leave it, so far as he is concerned. On his job they like him and give him the responsibilities his honesty so completely warrants.[3]

Thirty five years later John still stutters. He now has other infirmities but has maintained himself throughout the years and has done the best he could with such resources as he had. Tears and talks of suicide have long since stopped.

Confused, fearful, and unhappy men and women brought their problems to ONE. Where would they go to get medical help? Did the staff know of a sympathetic psychologist? Should they, or could they, try to change? Would marriage be a solution?

Those who had been arrested, and they were many, faced court, sentencing, and probation. Did ONE know of a good lawyer, one that would not demand large amounts of money? Requests came in one by one, and ONE's staff members tried to do whatever they could.

Psychology and psychotherapy in the 1950s generated a veritable quagmire of books full of "answers about homosexuality." The "big" books were heavy with ideas derived from late 19th century German sexology. Some of the books threw in a spice of Freudian theory whether in approval or in opposition. Echoes still lingered from the days when Pinel began to observe the "criminally insane" in Paris prisons, thus launching the field of professional psychology.

There were Bergler, Caprio, Albert Ellis and a host of semi-charlatans. Newspapers of the day carried accounts of electric shock treatment, lobotomy, and experiments with castration for "sex offenders" in Denmark.

The scores who called ONE or came to the office repeated over and over the failure of various therapies to help them. Some of these people had spent time in public institutions and spoke of their encounters with public psychiatrists and the drugs that were administered.

By default *ONE Magazine*'s writers and editors found themselves cast as counselors practicing peer counseling, a phrase not widely in use at the time.

For a time there were discussions of expanding the counseling services at ONE to meet this need. A prospectus was prepared outlining

---

[3] *MAG IX*:8 (August, 1961), pp.19-21.

a project to be called "The Walt Whitman Guidance Center." This dream of a facility which would provide counseling, employment assistance, legal referrals and access to medical and psychiatric assistance, was envisioned by Charles Rowland, first director of ONE's Social Services Division, described here as follows:[4]

> At this time a year ago we in the Social Service Division were starry-eyed with some rather grandiose plans for aiding certain homosexuals, estimating that there arrive in Los Angeles and vicinity, each month, about 250 homosexuals.
>
> The prospect of these lost battalions (hundreds of teenagers among them) descending upon Los Angeles with its police raids, degenerate vice squaders and dirty minded do-gooders was to us an appalling spectacle. Literally thousands of these people are without jobs, without funds, without friends, without adequate job training or education. Where do they go? What do they do? What happens to them?
>
> From these questions emerged our dream of a social services center affording vocational guidance, employment services, legal advice, medical and psychiatric treatment, altogether a many splendored facility! None of us has changed his mind about the desirability of these things, their actual social necessity, but we have had to fit our dreams to reality.
>
> In the past year we have actually placed four people in suitable jobs. All have fine positions with excellent working conditions. Directly or indirectly we have assisted 32 more in finding jobs, and we have given vocational counseling to an estimated 50 persons.
>
> We have given our time, our hearts and such skill as we have in the solution of problems of social acceptance, problems of getting along with other homosexuals, problems of housing, problems of cultural orientation, including the special problems of immigrants from foreign countries.

Another milestone was reached the day we were approached for assistance by a young man most desirous of having psychiatric therapy. It happened that the year's bounties had just made available to us the services of a highly skilled psychologist. He was able to provide the young man with the most advanced therapy and on the highest professional level at an extremely modest fee.

---

[4] *TDY* p.81, pars. 1-5, 11, 12.

Those who heard Dr. Baker at the 1955 Midwinter Institute remember that she said the problems of homosexuals could not all be solved by the professionals, that actually only a tiny fraction could be resolved by the experts. She warned that most homosexuals would have to seek solutions to those special problems themselves.

Reality, however, soon showed that an organization which became involved in trying to do too many things for too many people could easily find itself helping no one. The concept of peer counseling had been born and been found effective.

There were those who found such efforts to be wildly irresponsible, claiming that such work should be performed only by "professional therapists." This despite the fact that peer counseling had helped many men and women to keep functioning, to be less dependent on alcohol, drugs and helped many to live with some measure of stable adjustment. Today, peer counseling is taken for granted by many who are entirely unaware of ONE's pioneer work in the field.

Such was the setting in which ONE's staff members first became acquainted with Professor of Clinical Psychology at the University of California, Los Angeles, Dr. Evelyn Hooker. Dr. Hooker had made known her wish to make a psychological study of male homosexuals and had been invited to appear before members of the Mattachine Society and ONE to explain her intentions. She was asked many pointed, often hostile questions. For example, "What do you mean by scientific methods for studying homosexuality?"

Dr. Hooker's frank and open replies gradually began to win grudging respect and an agreement to cooperate with her for a tryout. So began ONE's long friendship and association with Dr. Evelyn Hooker.

Very different but in no way less remarkable was psychiatrist, Blanche M. Baker, M.D., Ph.D., whose coming into ONE's orbit has been described earlier.[5]

Through several appearances at ONE's Midwinter Sessions, and generously frequent consultations with ONE's peer counselors, Dr. Baker had become the *de facto* professional consultant for ONE's social service peer counseling efforts. Cases of special difficulty were often discussed with Dr. Baker. In relatively rare instances individuals were referred directly to her.

Dr. Hooker in psychology, and Dr. Baker in psychiatry and

---

[5] See Chap.1, p.18ff above.

psychotherapy, so profoundly influenced the attitudes of ONE's staff members toward those professional fields and their role within Homophile Studies that some further explanation is appropriate.

Why did Dr. Hooker's research into the male bisexual community have so great an impact? Mention has already been made of the general level of psychological theory regarding homosexuality, unproven at that time, which was so full of contradictions and elaborate Freudian speculations. Reactions by the Homophile Community ranged from cynical contempt to outrage and in some instances fears that resulted in discouragement, depression, alcoholism and even suicide.

Dr. Hooker's public discussions of the nature and scope of her research brought an entirely new tone into attitudes toward psychology by her listeners. From the very beginning of her project, the realization was growing that while by no means ready yet to give answers, Dr. Hooker was in effect challenging many fundamental assumptions of her own profession, challenging her colleagues' methods which was what many in the Homophile Community had been arguing against.

Staff members of ONE first met Dr. Evelyn Hooker of the University of California at Los Angeles Department of Psychology in 1953 when she contacted the Mattachine Society to find subjects for her projected testing of psychological differences between overt male homosexuals and heterosexuals. Intense personal bias had colored most previous studies of homosexuality, studies which assumed basic personality differences which had not been proven. We have since followed Dr. Hooker's work with interest and admiration.

She formally initiated her study in 1954, supported by a research grant, Grant M-839, from the National Institute of Mental Health of the National Institutes of Health, Public Health Service. Selecting thirty exclusive homosexuals screened from a much larger group, none of whom were undergoing therapy, she matched them with thirty exclusive heterosexuals of comparable ages, I.Q.'s, and educational levels, and administered such tests as the Rorschach, the TAT and MAPS, in addition to lengthy life history interviews.

When Dr. Hooker's initial reports were first published,[6] it was as if a new order had come about. (1) Outmoded psychological

---

[6] "The Adjustment of the Male Overt Homosexual," *Journal of Projective Techniques* (1957), pp.18-31; "Male Homosexuality in the Rorschach," ibid. (1958), pp.22, 33-54.

methodology had suffered a withering defeat. (2) Never again would psychologists be taken seriously by the Homophile Community without first proving their claims. Such has been the view held in Homophile Studies ever since.

In ONE's continuing association with Dr. Evelyn Hooker, between May, 1959, and December, 1983, she gave twelve ONE Institute Extension Lectures to large and appreciative audiences. Dr. Hooker has also attended numerous other ONE Institute events as an interested observer.

ONE Institute's role in publishing the "Final Report of the NIMH Task Force on Homosexuality," which was chaired by Dr. Hooker, should be given special notice. After completion of the work, the National Institute of Mental Health unconscionably delayed publication. ONE Institute thereupon published the "Report" before it was given official publication in Washington.[7]

Readers of the *Quarterly* could thus study this important policy paper during the period it was being withheld from publication by bureaucratic wrangling and timidity.

In a recent summary of Dr. Hooker's career[8] it is stated that "One of Dr. Hooker's contributions to the research community has been to legitimize homosexuality as a field of study."

The following introductory biographical comment and interview of Dr. Hooker by a ONE Institute faculty member, Laud Humphreys, is reprinted here, not only for its intrinsic value and interest but for its fascinating interplay between two unique and brilliant personalities: Laud, administrator and ONE Institute faculty member, and Evelyn Hooker, long time friend and formidable social scientist.

An Interview With
Evelyn Hooker

From The Laud Humphreys Papers in the Baker Memorial Library and Archives.

---

[7] *QTLY* VIII, 5-12, (1970).

[8] *LA Times Magazine* (June 10, 1990).

In August of 1956, a paper read by Evelyn Hooker at meetings in Chicago of the American Psychological Association marked a turning point in the course of social scientific research on homosexuality. The Kinsey research had already provided the western world with a fresh, empirical approach to the study of human sexuality in general; however, in spite of data presented by Kinsey and his associates, the study of "sexual inversion" (one of the less prejudicial phrases in style at that time) continued to be dominated by analysts, psychiatrists, and others committed to a clinical model. As Dr. Hooker pointed out in that crucial paper, "The Adjustment of the Male Overt Homosexual:"

> From a survey of the literature it seemed highly probable that few clinicians have ever had the opportunity to examine homosexual subjects who neither came for psychological help nor were found in mental hospitals, disciplinary barracks in the Armed Services, or in prison populations. It therefore seemed important, when I set out to investigate the adjustment of the homosexual, to obtain a sample of overt homosexuals who did not come from these sources.

What she did, just over twenty years ago, now seems obvious: the pairing of thirty homosexuals who "seemed to have an average adjustment" with the same number of like heterosexual subjects, for all of whom she and a panel of experts analyzed a battery of projective techniques and attitude scales. What is not so obvious is that Hooker did not assume pathology on the part of her research subjects, an important difference from nearly all predecessors in the field.

The conclusions of her study were also extraordinary. Among other points, she found that: "Homosexuality as a clinical entity does not exist. Its forms are as varied as are those of heterosexuality. Homosexuality may be a deviation in sexual pattern which is within the normal range, psychologically... The role of particular forms of sexual desire and expression in personality structure and development may be less important than has frequently been assumed." (Hooker, pp.29-30)

Research in homosexual behavior and orientation has not been the same since that study. A few individuals, chiefly centered around a group of New York psychoanalysts, have continued to ignore Hooker's findings, but most others picked up on the new, non-pathological paradigm. In a tentative paper delivered a year earlier, Hooker noted that "many homosexuals are beginning to think of themselves as a minority group, sharing many of the problems of other minority groups and having to struggle for their 'rights' against the prejudices of a dominant heterosexual majority." Published in a relatively obscure journal, however, that prophetic paper escaped notice until portions of it were rephrased in a chapter written for Judd Marmor's volume, *Sexual Inversion*, (New York, 1965), pp. 103-105.

Over the next three years, she published a series of papers that expanded upon the methodology employed in her paradigmatic research. Throughout the 1960s, she contributed a half dozen more papers to the literature, focused primarily around the male homosexual community. This phase of her work culminated in the "Hooker Report," the "Final Report of the Task Force on Homosexuality," which she chaired for the National Institute of Mental Health. The appearance of that quasi-official study in 1969 coincided with the Christopher Street Riots and the launching of a new movement for gay liberation.

By that time, nourished by the cultural relativism of the anthropological study, *Patterns of Sexual Behavior* by Ford and Beach (1951), along with the Kinsey heritage passed down by Gebhard, Pomeroy, and others from the Institute of Sex Research, a generation of primarily sociological researchers were producing empirical data and developing a body of theory that corresponded with the non-pathological paradigm of Hooker.

The American Psychiatric Association's action, at the end of 1973, to remove homosexuality from its official *Diagnostic and Statistical Manual of Mental Disorders* was due, in no small part, to years of persistence and careful social science practiced by Evelyn Hooker. No less a testimonial to her work, however, resides in the fact that a "third generation" of researchers in homosexuality look to her as a leading pioneer and mentor. Still a Clinical Professor at the Neuropsychiatric Institute of the University of California, Los Angeles, Dr. Hooker maintains a private practice in therapy and serves as consultant for many research projects in human sexuality. She is currently engaged in a follow-up study on her original group of thirty respondents.

Beginnings:
"Your Scientific Duty To Study Us"

(Laud Humphreys, author of *Tearoom Trade: Impersonal Sex in Public Places* and *Out of the Closets: The Sociology of Homosexual Liberation* is Professor of Sociology at Pitzer College in Claremont, California.)

Laud Humphreys: According to my files, your first paper dealing with homosexuality was "A Preliminary Analysis of Group Behavior of Homosexuals," appearing in the *Journal of Psychology* in 1956. (That is a remarkably prophetic paper, incidentally, in which you predict a number of themes involved in the growth of gay liberation.) Are there earlier works I have missed?

Evelyn Hooker: No, that's the very first one, Laud.

L: When did you actually begin gathering data on homosexual subjects?

E: That involves telling you the story about how I got into this research to begin with. During the War, in 1943 or '44, I had a student, Sammy From, who was an extraordinary individual. He was an absolutely brilliant person, who was working as a liaison between the Air Force and the aircraft industry and decided to take a course in introductory psychology from me at U.C.L.A. He had lived with his lover (whom he introduced as his cousin George) for ten years; and, very soon after finishing my course, he called one evening and invited me to dinner.

At that time, I knew absolutely nothing about homosexuality, except what was in the sex books (and you can imagine what that was like!). Oh, I had read *The Well of Loneliness* when it was smuggled in, but I knew nothing about the subject.

Sam was very eager to have his friends meet me, and they were anxious to gain my approval. Everybody was very formal that first night and didn't let down their hair at all... Anyway, from that night on, my first husband and I had a great deal of social life with Sammy and George and a group of gay men and two gay women who lived in an old, ramshackle house on Benton Way. The core members of this group had met in college, came to California as a group, and lived together. A number of prominent, creative homosexuals stayed at Benton Way when visiting Los Angeles; I remember meeting Paul Goodman and many others. My husband and I often went to parties there. We saw a whole cross section of gay society in that house...

There was no moment at which they said: "Well, we're gay and what do you think about it?" But they gradually began to see that nothing they did would offend or disturb me. It must have been about a year after that first dinner party that we four decided to take a Thanksgiving holiday trip to San Francisco. We stayed at the Fairmont and Sammy took us to Finocchio's. I had never been to a gay bar. My mouth was open ten feet wide – thought it was absolutely fantastic!... We came back to the Fairmont and were going to have a snack before we went to bed; and Sammy turned to me and said: "Evelyn, we have let you see us as we are. We have hidden nothing from you. You probably know more about people like us (meaning people who function in society and don't go to see psychiatrists because they don't need to) than any psychiatrist or psychologist in the country. Now, it is your scientific duty to study us."

Well, I was teaching about eighteen hours a week – and I was doing some experimental work with neurotic rats – and I said: "First of all, I'm not interested; and second, all of you are my friends. I simply couldn't be objective about you!" But he persisted. We came back home, and he would not let me go. He kept saying: "You've got to do this!"

Finally, he was so persistent that I went to Bruno Klopfer, the famous Rorschach man, with whom I shared an office (Bruno used to say, "Evelyn and I cubiculate together."). He practically leaped out of his chair and said: "Evelyn, you must do it! He's absolutely right! We don't know anything – all we know about are the sick ones." And so I began with this group – this is around 1945 – and I collected Rorschachs, I collected a little bit of life history material, but not too much... Well, then, my life changed: I went through a painful divorce, spent a year teaching at Bryn Mawr, and, in 1951, was married to Edward Hooker; meanwhile, I remained in contact with Sammy and his friends.

Of course, I had all this material – I was absolutely haunted by this material! It was absolutely unique; and I was working, trying to make sense of it. In 1953, I finally said to myself: "I'm going to apply for a six months grant from NIMH. I want to get a new group: sixes on the Kinsey scale, if possible, and zero on the Kinsey scale for a control group – no one I know in either group." And that is when the study began. None of the people who taught me what I knew of the gay life were in that study.

What apparently sold NIMH on the project was not that I was going to study the individuals but that I was going to study them in their social setting. They said, "Now, Evelyn, we're prepared to give you this grant but (this was 1953, at the height of the McCarthy era) you will be investigated; and, if you don't get it, you won't even know why. But you're mad if you think you can do this in six months. Take a year." The real groundwork for my being able to write the proposal was knowing this group for ten years. That is important because, when I started, I was able to say to the people whom I knew: "Help me find subjects." Actually, while some of the gay men were members of Mattachine or ONE (early Homophile organizations), the majority of them were not members of either organization. (Please put that in, Laud, because I didn't make that clear in the paper.)

L: So you began your systematic data gathering in the Spring of 1954? Then, in 1957, the paper on "The Adjustment of the Male

Overt Homosexual" came out – and that has been a major milestone. How would you describe its reception? What was the reaction to that paper?

E: Well, the reaction at the meeting of the A.P.A., where I read that paper, was very mixed. On the one hand, it was a reaction of, "This is extraordinary! We knew it all the time but we needed empirical proof." Or, on the other hand, "It can't be true. It absolutely cannot be true! You must have had to search and search and search to find those guys." Then all the literature that has followed since, as you know, has debated that issue. The response that I got from a number of colleagues in very different fields – from gay people as well as professional people – was, "My God, for the first time, somebody has empirical data!"

Changes:
"Gay Researchers...Examining The Setting"

L: In the twenty years since that paper appeared, what do you think have been the principal changes in the study of homosexuals? We know what the history was before that time. There was a major change with the appearance of the Kinsey studies; but that paper was a turning-point. That was the first time we began to see that we are not dealing with an illness, *per se*.

E: That original assumption which I put to an empirical test has continued in the literature and with more sophisticated designs, with more rigorous methodology; but let me turn to some of the areas that were neglected at that time. Now, we have to come to my community paper (1961), because that's a part of the sequence. At the time I wrote that paper (as you know, it was an invited address at the International Congress of Psychology in Copenhagen), there was only one paper on the gay community and that was the Canadian, the Leznoff & Westley (1956) study. Simultaneously, there began to appear sociological and anthropological studies.

I think that major changes which have occurred are not in the area of personality dynamics or of the adjustment of individuals but in the questions which concern gay people in their social setting. I was convinced at the very outset, and said so in that preliminary paper, that the interplay between the two sets of variables – those of personality dynamics and social variables – is essential. So that if one wants to understand the behavior of gay men, for instance, one has not only to understand individual dynamics, one has also to understand the milieu in which they live. What delights me in what has happened since I gave that paper, in 1961, is that the most significant research, your own, for instance, has been done by examining the setting along with the individuals who operate in that setting.

The second major change is the advent of gay researchers. That '57 paper gave a large number of professional people who happen to be gay, who were in the social sciences, courage to do research. You can imagine, from my standpoint, believing what I believe about the importance of participant observation, that the most significant change in these past twenty years is: whereas, before that, professional people might be gay but they wouldn't dare let people know that they were – they had to have all kinds of elaborate covers – now the research is being done by professional people who are openly gay. There is, of course, a danger of homosexual bias entering in, which a gay person has to watch just as thoroughly as a straight person has to watch his or her bias.

In the old days, when I would talk to ONE, I would say, "I think I have been every place that gay men go, except for gay baths and tearooms. Somebody else has got to do those places." The social aspects of gay lifestyle, the most crucial material, can now be researched by gay psychologists, sociologists, anthropologists, and so forth. So we can now get material which somebody who is straight could never get!

Continuity:
"A Passion For Social Justice"

L: What I see happening here is that you have gone through a tremendous personal change in your own professional life as a result of this study. You start as a "rat psychologist," a real experimental psychologist, and are changed through this research into a social psychologist – carrying with you the other backgrounds, of course – to the point that sociologists look on you as the primary sociologist in the field.

E: Yes, you're right. In fact, they write about me as a sociologist. You said, "you were an experimental psychologist, you were a rat psychologist." When I was in college, I was bitten by the scientific bug and I've never lost it. I read *Arrowsmith;* and Karl Muenzinger, who was the most careful scientist, directed my graduate work at the University of Colorado. In a way there is no break in my professional development, although it is true I was not working in social psychology; nevertheless, my whole scientific training and my whole scientific outlook has not changed. It's true the subject matter has changed, but the essential methodology has not.

Now I want to mention one more thing. All of us have to examine our past, I think, if we are to be as conscious of our motivations as possible (and, if we don't do it, I think we are in a bad way.) I have often been asked questions and have thought a great deal about how it should happen that I would end up spending half of my professional life working on sexuality and especially homosexuality. I have never thought about it in these terms, however, until you asked these questions.

My father was a tenant farmer. There were nine children, and we grew up in a sod house. He did not own any land of his own until he moved us, when I was about seven or eight years old, lock, stock and barrel to an unbroken section of land in eastern Colorado (there was nothing on it but rattlesnakes and weeds); and we lived (all eleven of us) in a two-room tar paper shack. We lived well, that is to say we had lots of good food, fresh air, a marvelous time, but we were dirt poor. My father was a marvelous man, very strong but very gentle. My mother had a driving, consuming ambition – my mother came in a covered wagon, at the age of four, from Michigan City to Nebraska and that's where she and my father met. She was married at the age of sixteen and she had a child every other year for eighteen years! She would say, "Get an education and they can never take it from you." My mother was a practical nurse, and she went out and took care of neighbors during the flu epidemic in 1918. Always in her mind was, "I'm going to move to the next town so the children can have a better school." When my sister and I were ready for high school, my mother just put her foot down. Nothing would do but that we would move to Sterling, which was the County Seat, because they had a better high school.

My mother was head housekeeper in the only hotel that Sterling, Colorado, had. And my sister and I worked in that hotel as chambermaids every summer. We all worked – everybody worked: my two brothers, when they were seven years old, were messenger boys for Western Union. Very early on, I was keenly aware that we were from the wrong side of the tracks (but we were never allowed to believe that by our mother). But I knew poverty and, very early, while I was at Boulder (this was in 1927, at the time of the Colorado Fuel and Iron strike), we had a magnificent Dean of Women who went out and got up on that platform for the strikers; and I was strongly influenced by her. I was also strongly influenced by Karl, who had a passion for social justice and the oppressed. What I am saying is that the methodology fits in with my training as a scientist; but the fact that I should end up studying an oppressed, a deprived people comes from my own experiences, in part, of being stigmatized. We were keenly aware of the fact that we didn't have the right clothes – if we had shoes to wear, we were damned lucky and my high school teacher used to give me her clothes! When I went to Europe in 1937 and 1938 to study at the Institute of Psychotherapy in Berlin and, secondarily, could see what was going on under Fascism, and then went to Russia, I debated long and hard whether I was going to join the Communist Party – was that the way to social justice? I couldn't bring myself to do it – could not accept a totalitarian government. My becoming a social psychologist comes out of my whole life experience, then.

The Cutting Edge:
"Issues Of Civil Liberties"

L: What do you think has become the cutting edge of research, now that we're into the third generation of the new, much more sociological paradigm?

E: Well, I think that we have to tie in the gay liberation movement because of the tremendous impact that it has had. It's remarkable to me that the same year the Task Force report was published the Stonewall Riot occurred. Now, gay people are no longer willing to be treated in the way in which they had been treated. Remember the policy section of the Task Force Report, in which we urged that studies be made of discrimination against gay people and attitudes towards gay people. I think that now the cutting edge is really in terms of the socially relevant issues as gay people confront them every day, that is, issues of civil liberties. What is extraordinary, absolutely phenomenal, is that we should have John DeCecco (1977) now, instead of having the gay activists marching up and down and saying, "You can't discriminate, we're going to sit on your doorstep until you let us do this." Here's John DeCecco quietly gathering data on what brings discrimination, who discriminates, what is the effect on the person who is discriminated against, what is the effect on the person who does the discriminating, what are the clues that they give you?

This brings in what I think is one of the most important issues that I have been talking about for twenty-five years – we will never understand homosexuality until we understand heterosexuality – never, never, never! And our first recommendation in the Task Force Report, which I fought for bitterly (I wrote that whole agenda anyway, except for the section on prevention, which I didn't want in there), that there should be established at NIMH a center for the study of sexuality, human sexuality. I did not want a center for homosexuality. It seems to me that what is happening increasingly is that we're going to understand much more about sexual stereotypes; we're going to understand that it's not only the gay guy who suffers, it's also the straight man who does not conform to masculine stereotypes.

L: Not to mention the suffering of women...

E: Absolutely! In 1967, there was nothing on lesbianism, nothing! And the Task Force insisted that we have studies of lesbians. That is absolutely crucial to our understanding – not just of how lesbian women live, and how their identities are formed, and what the social milieu is in which they live – but from those studies we're going to discover, I am sure, that a lot of women who have had long heterosexual histories are moving into homosexual relations. For example, some years ago I supervised the therapy of a terribly bright woman. She was, at that time, as straight as is possible. She had never had a homosexual experience, she had children, etc. She is now a practicing therapist; and, about a year ago, she called me and said, "We must get together. I have so much to tell you about what is going on, including the fact that I've just had my first lesbian relationship." She went on to say, "You know, Evelyn, what I am discovering is an increasingly frequent phenomenon, namely, heterosexual women are discovering that what is most deeply satisfying to them is the love of another woman."

Lesbians:
"Developmental Processes"

E: When I make a speech, women will come up and say, plead-ingly, "Why don't you do for us what you did for the men?" And I always say, "Well, if I live long enough; besides, I don't need to do it now because other people have done for lesbians what I did for gay men." Now, I have always believed that these are qualitatively different phenomena, no doubt about it.

L: The lesbian and gay male experiences...

E: Yes, because a woman is more influenced by the fact that she is a woman in the way she lives and what she does than by the fact that she is a lesbian.

L: I think that's very true.

E: Although we have some good studies, that is one of the more neglected areas, and I think that is one of the prime areas for future research. I'd like to take a group of those women to see what gratification they are finding, what the problems are, because they would be a much more interesting group, in terms of the variability of what has gone into the change, than those who have always been this way. By studying those women who have moved from lengthy heterosexual identities into satisfying lesbian relationships – and, perhaps, lesbian identity – in studying them, we would not necessarily be studying homosexual behavior.

L: What we would be looking at is what Brian Miller calls "adult sexual re-socialization" in his gay father study; and that is the phenomenon that would tell us something about heterosexuality! Now, we've established two cutting edges: first, in the area of civil rights and with the nature of homophobia; second, in the sexual re-socialization of adult women and men. In addition to these, where are the major gaps in our knowledge of the subject today? What should researchers be doing that they are not? What are the dead ends in research on homosexuality? What are the major needs?

E: I think that the question of etiology is a lost cause. That does not mean only that we do not want to understand the process of development instead of talking about causation; but also, since we know that we are not dealing with a unitary phenomenon, we simply must abandon the medical model. We are dealing with a very complex set of phenomena. There is no group that we can call "homosexuals." What that means is that to talk about even eight or ten variables as causal is false conceptualization! We well know that we are looking at an infinite variety of patterns of behavior and personality structure and function. I prefer to talk and think in terms, not of etiology, but in terms of developmental processes, which is a very different way of conceptualizing. How does it develop? What are the variables which play into its development? Bieber takes it for granted that there is a biological drive towards heterosexual behavior – nonsense, as we all know! What are the variables which, from the moment of conception on, play into that developmental process: biological variables, hormonal variables, neural organization variables, socialization processes, relations with peers? What are these developmental processes which lead to a gay identity or to a straight identity or to a bisexual identity, and to all gradations in between? Now that seems to be not only legitimate, but I would give that topic high priority. To understand sexual differentiation, sexual orientation, how all of these develop seems to me to be absolutely essential if we are going to understand anything about homosexuality or heterosexuality or sex roles or sexual orientation.

Needs:
"A Superb Agenda"

L: I like that way you put that, because it points up the unity in your thinking since the first paper you published on the subject. You've been building to that point all along. Twelve years ago, in "Male Homosexuals and Their Worlds," you insisted that we can't take the simple answer because it is not a simple phenomenon. Your work has developed logically and consistently along that pattern from the beginning.

E: And now we have, as one of the newer developments in developmental psychology, life-span psychology; so we don't stop at age 21, but we look at adult re-socialization, which is a never-ending process. Along that line, then, I would repeat that one of the greatest needs is for further study of gay men and lesbians who have been heterosexually married – or, at least, have had extensive heterosexual experience and experience as parents. I think of all those trials on custody of children with gay parents, just crying for empirical data!

If we could add that priority to the list of needs that Stephen Morin provides in a recent paper in the *American Psychologist,* we'd have a superb agenda for future research. Having just finished reading it, may I conclude with a paragraph from that excellent paper?

> Research on lesbians and gay men should give higher priority to questions relevant to the wide variety of homosexual life-styles. Specifically, research is needed on the dynamics of gay relationships; the development of positive gay identity; the positive and negative variables associated with self-disclosure to significant others including families, relatives, friends, and co-workers; the advantages and disadvantages of varying degrees of gay identity and commitment; specific problems of gay children and adolescents; aspects of aging in the gay subculture; and conflict involving gay civil liberties.

L: I think that gives us a good summary of your chief points, Evelyn. Thank you very much.

E: If you'll let me move back, once more, to my passion for social justice (originating, perhaps, in the poverty of my childhood in eastern Colorado) I must read one more sentence from Morin's paper:

Finally, research on the nature and meaning of attitudes toward homosexuality and on methods by which pejorative attitudes can be changed should continue and should be geared toward social action.

Further Reading

Ford, C. S. and F. A. Beach. *Patterns of Sexual Behavior.* (New York: Harper and Row, 1951).

Hooker, E. "The Adjustment of the Male Overt Homosexual," *Journal of Projective Techniques,* 21 (1957) pp. 18-31.

_____ "The Homosexual Community," *Proceedings of the XIVth International Congress of Applied Psychology, Personality Research* (Copenhagen: Munksgaard, 1961) Vol 2., pp. 40-59.

_____ "Male Homosexuals and their "Worlds'," in J. Marmor (ed.) *Sexual Inversion.* (New York: Basic Books, 1965) pp. 83-107.

Morin, S. F. "Heterosexual Bias in Psychological Research on Lesbianism and Male Homosexuality," *American Psychologist* (August, 1977), pp. 629-637.

Peer Counseling and Dr. Baker.

Dr. Baker used her training as a psychologist Ph.D. and psychiatrist M.D. to greatly encourage ONE's peer counselors. She was in frequent consultation with them during her visits to Los Angeles, also by letter and by telephone. Those who heard her speak or learned of her work made so many demands for advice that the Editors of *ONE Magazine* asked her to conduct what became the earliest column ever published which directly addressed homosexuals and their problems. For a title she chose "Toward Understanding." It appeared in *ONE Magazine* during 1959-60. The columns were later republished in *ONE Institute Quarterly* with such headings as "Causes of Homosexuality;" "Problems of Adjustment and Loneliness;" "Latent Homosexuality and Fetishism;"

"Homosexual Marriage;" "Homosexuals in the Armed Forces."[9] No
attempt will be made here to summarize her views on so wide a range
of topics.

What should be emphasized, however, is that this dedicated and
very busy psychiatrist managed to find so much time to encourage
ONE's peer counselors, supporting them as colleagues working
alongside her in a field where the needs were so great.

Collaborating with her and also encouraging ONE's staff was Harry
Benjamin, M.D, German-trained physician and gerontologist, special-
izing in the medical adjustment problems of older men from his offices
in New York and San Francisco. His Lecture for ONE, September 18,
1966, "Endocrine Research and Gerontology," made a great impression.
In it, he made mention of his work with Christine Jorgensen and others
as described in his well-known book *The Transsexual Phenomenon*.
This Lecture was given at a beautiful home in Los Angeles' Laurel
Canyon whose owner had designated it as "ONE's Social Service
Center."[10] A considerable number of transsexuals and transvestites
came to ONE's offices for counseling over the years.

By the time of Dr. Baker's death in 1960, ONE's peer counselors
had dealt with nearly 7,000 applicants for counseling assistance, both
men and women, young and old.[11]

Soon afterward a very different type of column began appearing
in *ONE Institute Quarterly*. Edited by clinical psychologist Ray Evans,
Ph.D., The "Abstracts Department" provided critical and professional
evaluation of the work of highly regarded psychologists then prominent
such as Rado, D. G. Brown, Clara Thompson, Doidge, T. Lang, Gresey,
Brenda Dickey, Hampson, Perloff, Coretta Bender, Bakevin, B. H.
Glover, and others. All of them were given Dr. Evans' coolly objective
inspection.[12]

---

[9] *QTLY* VII; 3,4 (1967), pp.6-19.

[10] Annual Report, 1966, p.17 (ONE's Baker Memorial Library & Archives)

[11] Report of Committee on Counseling of the Council on Religion and
the Homophile, August 28, 1967 (ONE's Baker Memorial Library & Archives)

[12] Abstracts Department, Ray Evans, Ph.D.: *QTLY* IV;1 (Winter 1961),
pp.7-14; IV:3 (Summer 1961), pp.94-101; IV:4 (Fall 1961), pp.121-2; VI:1,2
(Winter, Spring 1963), pp.31-35.

From 1966 he served as Director of Research for the Institute for the Study of Human Resources, a foundation affiliated with ONE "To promote, assist, encourage and foster scientific research and investigation of male and female homosexuality and other types of human behavior." The following "1968 Research Plan" is an example of Dr. Evans' work.

**Research Plan for Multi-faceted Assessment
and Therapy of Homosexual Male Minors
Ray Evans, Ph.D.**

Introduction: Homosexuality has been a subject of serious study for many years, with inquiries generally becoming increasingly scientific in nature during the greater part of the present century. Nevertheless, there is remarkably little about this phenomenon that is generally accepted as established fact; instead, almost everything relating to the subject remains a matter of opinion, interpretation, or speculation. One point of agreement probably is that a single, direct, causal factor is unlikely, and perhaps one reason for the general lack of agreement is that most investigations have proceeded from a single point of view. The absence of consensus applies to treatment or modification of homosexuality in addition to etiological factors. There is general concurrence, however, that for any behavioral problem, the earlier the intervention the greater the likelihood of modifying the pattern. Adolescence would therefore appear to be the optimum time to study remedial or causal factors in homosexuality.

Aims: It is assumed that an approach to the problem which considers several of the possibly relevant etiological factors should have a greater opportunity for positive and meaningful findings. There are two aims in the proposed investigation: (1) To assess young homosexual males with a view to causative, contributing, or enabling factors, using techniques from psychology, physiology, endocrinology, neurology, and psychiatry; (2) to alleviate the intra- and inter-personal strain associated with being homosexual by promoting adaptation or reversing the pattern where indicated, if possible.

Methods: Subjects for study will be males under the age of 21 with a homosexual problem, referred through the resources of ONE, Inc., an organization concerned with aiding homosexuals, and by juvenile authorities. Appropriate non-homosexual males to be studied for comparative purposes will be obtained from patients without known endocrine or neurological disorders who are attending outpatient clinics at the White Memorial Hospital [Los Angeles], and/or from private schools in the area. It is difficult to estimate how many subjects would be available for study, but it should be possible to obtain at least 75 homosexual and 75 non-homosexual subjects. With the relatively intensive methods of study planned, even a smaller number of subjects could provide significant information. Each subject will be studied from a number of points of view.

(a) Psychological: Extensive psychological testing will be done in an attempt to discover basic personality characteristics or pattern, if there are any, in these young men. Included will be self-rating inventories (such as the 16 Personality Factor Questionnaire and the Adjective Check List) and projective testing (such as the Holtzman Inkblot Technique, which has several advantages over the traditional Rorschach technique, at least for research purposes).

(b) Endocrinological: A 48-hour urine specimen will be collected from each subject and a spectrum of urinary hormone metabolites will be determined, including 17-ketosteroid fractions, estrogen fraction, and adrenal corticoids.

(c) Physiological: Height and weight will be measured, and in addition somatotyping will be done using the Parnell method, which is considerably more objective and thus yields more reliable results than the well-known Sheldon method. Parnell's method includes measuring the subcutaneous fat in three sites of the body, measuring certain bones and muscles of the arms and legs, and dividing height by the cube root of weight. Some measure of muscular strength will also be made, such as by means of hand dynamometer.

(d) Neurological: Electroencephalograms will be done in an effort to determine whether the patterns differ for the two groups (or differ from usual EEG patterns). If possible, some measure of autonomic functioning will also be included.

(e) Psychiatric: Developmental history will be explored in detail, including age of the mother at the subject's birth, together with a complete inquiry into the dynamics of the family constellation. Particular attention will be given to investigating the extent to which the child's temperament affected the early relationships and attitudes. It is commonly believed that parents mold the child's personality, and undoubtedly that is true within limits, but too often it is overlooked that children are born with differing temperaments which to some degree determine how they will be treated by parents and others.

The second major goal, to alleviate the intra- and inter-personal difficulties associated with the homosexual problem, will be approached with traditional psychotherapeutic methods. However, unusual flexibility will be maintained in order to provide the greatest possible help for any individual, and also to discover any clues as to what methods might generally prove most useful in dealing with the problem of homosexuality and its ramifications. Wherever the parents are willing, counseling will also be undertaken with them in an effort to promote better understanding between them and their sons.

An important and expanding activity also conducted under Dr. Evans' chairmanship for the next several years is described below.[13]

Aspects of the Institute's Research Program which take up considerable staff time include aiding graduate and doctoral students in designing and developing their theses, dissertations and projects; consulting with professional research bodies and teams concerning their investigations; evaluating projects submitted to this Institute for grants: applications made to other foundations for grants; counseling undergraduate professional students concerning their study programs and research projects. A whole field of such activities falls to the Institute staff because of the shortage of facilities elsewhere for obtaining such assistance. While it is admittedly important that the Institute serve in this capacity, it is again necessary to point out that such functions are offered without cost to those applying; that financial support to pay for the time and expertise involved must therefore be obtained if such services are to continue.

As indicated above, research grants of extremely modest size can occasionally be made by the Institute. The first of such were in 1971 to students affiliated with the Community Psychology Clinic, Long Beach, California.

A somewhat different educational service dating virtually from ONE's beginnings has been that of informational contacts with the media: newspapers, magazines, radio and television.

One such early television contact included several days of filming of a documentary series for the Canadian Broadcasting System. A portion of the ONE Institute segment featured Dr. Evans in an exposition of psychological theory dealing with homosexuality.

At one point the interviewer said, "Dr. Evans, what about the Oedipus complex?" Evans' response, "I have never seen one," which

[13] 1972 ISHR Report. (ONE's Baker Memorial Library & Archives)

threw the television interviewer into confusion. "But, Dr. Evans, Freud says..." the interviewer began. Dr. Evans' response was that there undoubtedly were therapists who found Freud's hypothesis helpful in understanding some of their cases but that, scientifically speaking, the "Oedipus complex" was without empirical verification and so remained just a hypothesis.

An Important Forum.

The June 7-9, 1974, "Forum on Variant Sex Behavior," was one of the largest events ONE Institute had organized by that time. Held in Los Angeles' Century Plaza Hotel with funding assistance from the Erickson Educational Foundation, it brought together professionals and other registrants from all over the country, including New York City. Among those attending were several physicians who were engaged in transsexual surgery and the psychological aspects involved.

The highlight of the three days of sessions for many was the large and impressive banquet featuring famed author Christopher Isherwood; he gave a deeply dramatic introduction of his close friend, Dr. Evelyn Hooker, who was by then one of the commanding figures in clinical psychology in the United States. The entire program can be found reprinted in the Appendix.[14]

Peer counseling by ONE staff members continued as usual. One aspect of this activity during 1968-70 was "The Counseling Center," staffed jointly by clergy from several church denominations and counselors from ONE's staff.

An article, "Some Facts About Lesbians,"[15] should be noted here. It was based upon the dissertation by Virginia Armon, Ph.D.[16] ONE Institute's connection with her project consisted, on several occasions,

---

[14] See Appendix, 2-14: Institute for the Study of Human Resources, Forum on Variant Sex Behavior, June 7-9, 1974.

[15] *QTLY* 11:4 (Fall 1959), pp.111-123.

[16] Armon, Virginia. "Some Personality Variables in Overt Female Homosexuality" (Ph.D. Dissertation. USC, 1958).

of delivering her subjects for their appointments. Dr. Armon's lecture on her research for the ONE Institute Extension Series was in March, 1959 (#28).

One Institute Extension Lectures:
Psychology

January 28, 1955 (#1) "The California Sex Psychopath Program," by Howard Russell.

January 28, 1955 (#3) "A Psychiatric View of Homosexuality: Causative Factors, and Therapeutic Suggestions," by Blanche M. Baker, M.D., Ph.D.

January 31, 1959 (#25) "Mental Health and Homosexuality," by a panel including Dr. Baker; Trent E. Bessent, psychologist; Vita S. Sommers, Ph.D., clinical psychologist.

March 22, 1959 (#28) "A Comparative Review of Lesbian and Heterosexual Women," by Virginia Armon, Ph.D.

November 5, 1961 (#53) "Keeping the Homosexual Marriage Going," by Leonard Olinger, Ph.D.

November 4, 1962 (#68) "Recent Developments in the Clinical Theory of Homosexuality," by Richard E. Timmer, Ph.D.

May 5, 1963 (#78) "Some Plain Talk About Homosexuality," by Edward E. Robbins, M.D.

November 3, 1963 (#82) "Mirror, Mirror on the Wall: Fairy Tale or Fact?" by Leonard B. Olinger.

December 6, 1964 (#92) "Intimacy and Trust," by Fred J. Goldstein, Ph.D.

May 2, 1965 (#97) "Every Tenth Man," by Ray Evans, Ph.D.

October 3, 1965 (#99) "Emerging Trends in Research," by Evelyn Hooker.

September 18, 1966 (#113) "Endocrine Research and Gerontology," by Harry Benjamin, M.D.

May 7, 1967 (#121) "The Homophile Movement: Its Impact and Implications," by Richard R. Parlour, M.D.

February 1, 1969 (#137) "Transsexualism, Transvestism and Homosexuality," by Richard Green, M.D.

February 2, 1969 (#140) "Studies in Personality Characteristics of Homosexual Males," by a panel of psychologists and psychiatrists.

March 1, 1970 (#151) "The Hooker Report," by a panel.

November 1, 1970 (#157) "Is There a Continuum: Homosexual to Heterosexual," by Peter Bentler, Ph.D.

February 7, 1971 (#159) "The Task Force on Homosexuality," by Evelyn Hooker.

January 29, 1972 (#168) "The Seattle Counseling Center for Homosexuality," by Robert Deisher, M.D. and panel.

January 29, 1972 (#170) "Implications of Some Current Research," by Peter Bentler and panel.

May 7, 1972 (#176) "A Young Psychologist Lays It On The Line," by David Mitchell, Ph.D.

June 8, 1974 (#206) "Reminiscence and Forecast," by Evelyn Hooker.

March 9, 1975 (#113) "Sex, Role and Gender," by Christine Jorgensen.

March 7, 1976 (#222) "Gender, Identity and its Implications," by H. Lindauer, M.D.

April 2, 1978 (#243) "Recent Trends in Research," by Evelyn Hooker.

January 6, 1980 (#257) "The APA Diagnostic Manual," by Vern Bullough, Ph.D.

December 4, 1983 (#292) "Homosexuals in the 1950s," by Evelyn Hooker.

January 2, 1986 (#314) "Redefining Youth," by the Community Youth Education Project, panel.

October 2, 1988 (#337) "Homosexual Panic and Other Psychological Oddities," by Paul A. Walker, Ph.D.

January 8, 1989, (#340) "Psychiatry and the Law," by Richard Green.

April 1, 1990 (#352) "Child Photographs of Gay Men," by Edward Grellert, Ph.D.

April 5, 1991 (#371) "Homosexual Panic and Other Psychological Oddities," by Paul A. Walker, Ph.D. (See #337)

In addition to the excerpts from faculty and student papers cited in this chapter, several video cassettes, each of them an hour or more in length, containing valuable psychological material, are located in the Audiovisual Collection of ONE's Baker Memorial Library: lecture nos. 290, 309, 316, 337, 340, and 352.

CHAPTER 8

LAW

L aw occupies an important place in Homophile Studies as one of the methods by which societies have enforced obedience to their own particular systems of belief. Although ONE Institute's curriculum has at no time provided for training individuals in the practice of law, neither has law been viewed as a philosophical abstraction. ONE Institute has been primarily focused on the examination and analysis of how laws have evolved at different times in various cultures, and specifically, on how law has affected the lives of Homophile men and women.

In the early 1950s the massively destructive effects of law and its enforcement in Southern California and across the United States raised an almost unanimous outcry from the newly emerging Homophile Movement for changing the laws and curbing the police. Harassments, beatings, random arrests, loss of jobs and of civil rights were so commonplace at the time as to be considered perfectly normal and, in fact, a service to society. Many felt there was only one problem: laws and the police. Given this perception, it was believed that curbing the police and reforming laws would solve all problems. Many were so convinced of this that they were unable or unwilling to listen to any other arguments.

The unchallenged power and dimensions of the entire legal system then in force were so great that it seemed absurd, even frivolous, to raise other questions. How could anyone seriously argue that law was not the problem and the only problem, when two men could be charged with indecent behavior and arrested for putting arms around each other's shoulders in public; that if either were a school teacher, he could never teach in a public school and his record would follow him to every state in the union? Or, that, if convicted, he could never vote again? He could be denied a license or permit to work in a pet store? There were countless comparable cases.

Such classic weapons of social protest as political action, appeals for support from friends in high places, could hardly be said to be available when, as one Los Angeles Police Chief stated, "I will never meet with or confer with criminals." This was the majority judgment on Homophiles at the time. In trying to deal with such attitudes, it is easily understandable that the fledgling Homophile groups which were trying to cope with the existing situations were in almost continual internal conflict and debates over tactics, strategy and policies.

There is no need to further detail social conditions and attitudes at that time other than to indicate how the educational policies of ONE, Incorporated were evolving and being influenced by such conditions. In January, 1953, the first issue of *ONE Magazine* included an article on "The Law of Entrapment." Its writer had professional legal training but his career had been terminated by an unfortunate encounter with the so-called "sex laws," then in force.

Earliest of ONE's legal skirmishes bearing upon the yet-to-be-born ONE Institute came in August, 1953 when that issue of *ONE Magazine*'s cover bore a bold and artistic design with the words, "HOMO-SEXUAL MARRIAGE." Notification came shortly that the Postmaster of Los Angeles was withholding the issue from the mails. At that time the little ONE organization did not even have an attorney. Eric Julber, a brilliant recent UCLA law graduate, agreed to represent ONE without fee. He soon obtained release for mailing of the August, 1953 *ONE Magazine*, then stayed on to review manuscripts and advise the editors as to what was and what was not safe to publish. So began ONE's first lessons in the law.

In October, 1953 the *Magazine* cover proclaimed in large letters "ONE IS NOT GRATEFUL" to "have been found suitable for mailing," and added, "Never before has a governmental agency of this size admitted that homosexuals not only have legal rights but might have respectable motives as well." By January, 1954, *ONE Magazine* had a new page size, better articles, more art work, and contained a page carefully detailing "Your Rights in Case of Arrest."

ONE's growth was at times a bit more than the budget could handle. There was a gap of two months after the July issue, but the October issue more than made up for the interval. Talented Art Director Eve Elloree had created a cover boldly warning "You Can't Print It." The lead article by ONE's counsel Eric Julber was a scholarly review of "The Law of Mailable Material." This was followed by a long satirical and slightly ribald poem about some current events in England. A story, "Sappho Remembered," by James Barr, a writer well-known at the time, writing as Jane Darr, completed what the government alleged to be a "lewd, obscene, lascivious and filthy" publication.

Once again came notification that the *Magazine* was being held by the Post Office but now there were several thousand subscribers. ONE's legal education had moved into quite a different learning experience, one that would go on for the next four years. ONE's first response was to file suit, as a corporation, in Federal District Court, seeking to enjoin Otto K. Oleson, Postmaster of Los Angeles, from withholding the October, 1954 *ONE Magazine* from the mails. This made ONE the plaintiff and the postmaster of a major city the defendant.

On March 1, 1956, U.S. District Court Judge, Thurmond Clark, found that the satirical poem was "filthy and obscene." "Sappho Remembered" was "obviously calculated to stimulate the lust of the homosexual reader." Most absurd of all his judgments was "the suggestion advanced that homosexuals should be recognized as a segment of the populace is rejected." A fuller account of this episode can be found in a contemporary issue of *ONE Magazine*.[1] ONE's response to all this was to file an appeal to United States Court of Appeals for the Ninth Circuit.

After taking this fateful step, attorney Julber commissioned the magazine's editors and others interested to conduct legal researches of an unconventional sort: to search for published literary sources referring in some way to homosexual behavior, male and female. Many of the group had extensive professional and amateur backgrounds in American and English literature. The remarkable pages of references they were able to bring together ranged from Melville down to mid-twentieth century writers, providing remarkably frank and explicit references to support the Julber contention that *ONE Magazine's* writers were in no way exceeding well-established literary standards.

From this exercise those who undertook the searches could begin to see that law and literature were but two aspects of an inter-related field embracing several disciplines.

The appellate case was finally heard November 2, 1956. The court's decision was made on March 1, 1957. Their judgment in upholding Judge Clarke's earlier decision was, while more lengthy, extremely preposterous and worth reading in its entirety.[2]

---

[1] *MAG* V:3 (March, 1957), pp.5-15.

[2] Ibid., pp.16-19.

"POST-OFFICE CASE"
BYPRODUCT

The March, 1957 issue of *ONE Magazine* carries the full and up-to-today story of the Corporation's "Post Office Case." On the following pages you can now read one of the interesting byproducts which have resulted from all this legal hassle.

It came about this way: At a Corporation meeting the names were mentioned of some foundations and other groups who might conceivably be enlisted in helping ONE with this case. It was felt we should leave no stone unturned, faced as we are with anything so big as this.

A member of the Corporation chanced to be able to arrange direct access for us to an official of a [major] foundation. We were courteously received and our story heard with interest. It was pointed out, however, that the foundation was not set up to undertake legal defenses of any nature, its work being mainly educational.

At the word "education" our ears pricked up. The official being interviewed suggested that if we had some educational project in mind dealing with legal questions concerning homosexuals that this might come within the scope of the foundation's interests.

This was all that was needed to set us off on round-the-clock activity. Fortunately, ONE's interest in legal questions had, by necessity, never been perfunctory. From the very first issue of *ONE Magazine* in January, 1953, with an article on "Entrapment," down to our first two semesters of class work in ONE Institute, we had been collecting material and developing our thinking in the general area of homosexuals and the law. So we were not entirely unprepared for the hurry-up task of framing an outline for a thorough investigation of the entire question of the civil rights of American homosexuals. Still, it called for plenty of work, much debating of specific points, methods of approach, and so on.

A brief interim outline was first prepared and presented to the official of the foundation, again in more than a two-hour session. The reception was generally favorable, though there were specific objections to a few points, and doubt raised as to whether an organization such as ONE might be considered objective enough to undertake a study of this nature.

It was suggested that the whole project might be agreed to be of prime importance, but that another group should make the study, or that ONE might possibly assist in the undertaking.

By this time we had become so convinced of the value of the whole thing that we felt quite willing to work with others on it, or even to see others do the entire job, all for the sake of having it done and the results put before the public. Incidentally, the foundation in question had ample funds for undertaking just about whatever it might choose.

So back to work we went. The finished outline of the study we proposed as being one that someone must make some day. It is not likely that the foundation in question will sponsor the inquiry, for when we went back with the finished outline, fears and objections had mounted, while enthusiasm had correspondingly cooled.

We were courteously referred to a higher-up, who just as courteously offered to see us if we thought it "worth the time." In short, bravery faded and moral courage melted away when it came to the showdown. This great foundation just could not bring itself to face the moral issues concerning the lives and welfare of millions of American men and women, though agreeing heartily with us that the study should be made.

The "Study of the Civil Rights Status of Homosexuals Under the Existing Laws of the Several States" was prepared jointly by ONE Institute faculty members and the editors of *ONE Magazine*, several of whom served in both capacities. The "study" was a large and ambitious proposal detailed in fifteen sections:

I.	The Need for Definitions.
II.	Statistics and Problems of Interpretation.
III.	Concepts About the Homosexual Explicit or Implicit in Law.
IV.	Can These Concepts be Factually Validated? Have they Been?
V.	Laws Applicable to Homosexual Acts and Persons.
VI.	Application of the Law.
VII.	Legal Precedents and their Antecedents.
VIII.	Preliminary Analysis of Sex Laws and Civil Rights.
IX.	The Concept of Civil Rights.
X.	Civil Liberty Infringements.
XI.	Present Extent of Studies and Information in This Area.
XII.	Related Issues (Juvenile Delinquency, Obscenity Laws, etc.).
XIII.	Conclusions.
XIV.	Recommendations.
XV.	Appendix and Bibliography

The full text as submitted to the Center for the Study of Democratic

Institutions is included in the Appendix.[3]

In March, 1957, however, even before the "study" was submitted, ONE had taken the unprecedented and historic step of deciding to appeal its case to the United States Supreme Court.

A year later, on January 13, 1958, the Supreme Court reversed the rulings of the two lower courts *per curiam.*[*] This ruling became at once a landmark in the freedom to publish. *For the first time in American history the right to publish serious literature about homosexuality and to disseminate it through the mails had attained legal status in the United States.*

The far-reaching implications of this pioneering court action aroused immediate interest among attorneys and in law schools across the country. Eric Julber became an instant celebrity. *ONE Magazine* began receiving more mail and visitors that ever before. The full text of the succinct and successful Julber brief submitted to the Court on ONE's behalf is reprinted in *ONE Institute Quarterly.*[4]

As mentioned above, ONE Institute has not offered training for professional legal practice. However, courses have been offered in "Law and Law Reform," "Sexual Minorities and the Law," and "Use of Legal Materials as Research Sources." Articles on legal topics have been published in *ONE Magazine, ONE Confidential, ONE Institute Quarterly*, and *ONE Letter.*

An extensive list of some of these articles on legal topics will be found at the end of this chapter. The *ONE Magazine* news column "Tangents" also included items on police behavior and related topics. A list of Extension Lectures given by attorneys and others will also be found at the end of this chapter. The total of all these references add up to a highly specialized legal education not available elsewhere.

Special mention must also be made of the 134-page issue of *ONE Institute Quarterly*, "The Right of Association."[5] In his introduction, then Editor James Kepner, Jr. called attention to the precedent-setting

---

[3] See Appendix, 8-1: A Study of the Civil Rights Status of Homosexuals under the Existing Laws of the Several States.

[*] A *per curiam* opinion is a brief, unsigned ruling where the holding is so obvious, based on applicable precedents, that no extensive opinion is needed.

[4] *QTLY* I:2 (Summer 1958), pp.60-64.

[5] *QTLY* III:1 (Winter 1960).

legal arguments made in it by San Francisco attorneys Morris and Juliet Lowenthal, and Karl D. Lyon with several *Amici Curiae*. Their argument that "homosexuals have a civil right to congregate in bars" was affirmed by the California Supreme Court in contrast to long-held police practices and court rulings.

The many legal citations and professional opinions from Kinsey, Karl Bowman, and others make this entire *Quarterly* issue a veritable textbook. Lowenthal himself reported discovering while on a visit to England that it was listed as recommended reading for university students studying for the bar in that country.

Civil rights were so frequently under discussion that a large scale examination of the topic was selected as the theme for the three day January, 1961, Midwinter Institute given mention earlier.[6]

The program was organized as follows, along lines developed by the 1960 Fall Semester class, "The Theory and Practice of Homophile Education."

SEVENTH MIDWINTER INSTITUTE

Thursday, January 26 - Sunday, January 29

Theme: "A Homosexual Bill of Rights"

A Group-Participation Project in Homophile Education

SCHEDULE OF EVENTS

January 27   Workshop Day

Morning
Discussion of the procedures to be used on following days in framing the "Bill of Rights;" tabulation of data from questionnaires submitted.

Afternoon
Continuation of data tabulation; briefing of committee chairmen, secretaries and other participants on their duties during Saturday and Sunday sessions.

---

[6] See Chap.2, p.38 above.

January 28   <u>Bill Of Rights Day</u>
    <u>Morning</u>
        Registration and Choose Your Chairman Period.
        Address of welcome, Ms. Sten Russell, Associate
        Editor, *ONE Magazine.*
        Study by the five Drafting Committees of typical
        questionnaires and proposals submitted by mail, as
        follows:

           <u>Drafting Committee I.</u> Preamble and Defini-
        tions; Chairman, Ron Longworth, Editor, *ONE Con-*
        fidential.

           <u>Drafting Committee II.</u> Social Rights; Chair-
        man, Ms. Helen Sanders, Charter Member, Daugh-
        ters of Bilitis.

           <u>Drafting Committee III.</u>   Religious Rights;
        Chairman, Professor Alan Hart, La Verne University.

           <u>Drafting Committee IV.</u> Scientific Questions
        and Overpopulation; Chairman, William F. Baker,
        San Francisco.

           <u>Drafting Committee V.</u> Legal Rights; Chair-
        man, Robert Gregory, Secretary, ONE Institute.

    <u>Afternoon</u>
        Compilation by each Drafting Committee of material
        found pertinent to its section of the Bill; no additions
        to be made after 3:30 Recess period.
        Preparation of the outlines for their respective portions of
        the Bill by each of the five Drafting Committees.
        During the work sessions Saturday and Sunday, members
        of HS-260 Seminar will be available to answer questions
        concerning areas of interest of the various Drafting Com-
        mittees, or other problems of Committee jurisdiction.

January 29   <u>Adoption Day</u>
    <u>Morning</u>
        Drafting of the five sections of the Bill for presentation
        at the Banquet; each Drafting Committee to prepare and
        adopt its own section (by Committee acclamation, or by
        majority vote, as preferred).[7]

---

[7] See Appendix, 8-2: General Instructions For All Drafting Committees.

There is no need to recount at length the Daughters of Bilitis' formal motion at the opening session to cancel the entire program, nor their grim, watchful non-participation during the entire three days, nor the DOB President's manifesto of disapproval read at the closing banquet. What was clearly evident was that questions of rights and law evoked much tension in the Homophile community.

The 1962 Tenth Anniversary Midwinter Institute has been described earlier.[8]

The January 25-27, 1963 Midwinter Institute, "New Frontiers in the Law," was less controversial than that of 1961, but memorable for including a taped greeting sent from his home by the much loved Dean, Merritt M. Thompson, his last public participation in a ONE Institute event.

Activist attorney Frank C. Wood's hard-biting, "The Right to be Free from Unreasonable Search and Seizure," was later published in *ONE Magazine*.[9] "The Double Standard Moral Code as an Instrument of Corruption," by San Francisco attorney Morris Lowenthal was very much in the same vein as his "The Right of Association."[10] A major contribution came from Chicago Father James G. Jones, whose "Man's Laws and God's Laws" brought a large banquet room to a complete standstill as the chefs and other workers stopped all work for over an hour to listen to this charismatic Episcopal priest saying things none of them had ever heard before.

A Chronological Selection Of Articles In
ONE Publications, 1953-90

Volk, Elwin "Common Law Notions of Decency," *MAG* I:3 (March, 1953), p. 14.
Julber, Eric "And the Law," *MAG* II:1 (January, 1954), p. 13.

---

[8] See Chap.2, p.40 above.

[9] *MAG* XI:4,5-9 (April 1, 1963), pp.5,21.

[10] See p.186 above.

_____ "The Law of Entrapment," *MAG* II:4 (March, 1954), p. 7.

_____ "The Law of Mailable Material," *MAG* II:8 (October, 1954), pp. 4-16.

_____ "A Change in America's Sex Laws," *MAG* III:7 (July, 1955), p. 4.

Staff "The Post Office Case," *CONFI* I:1 (March, 1956), pp. 12-19 [Judge Clarke Opinion].

_____ "The Post Office Case Again," *CONFI* I:2 (August, 1956), pp. 8-11 [9th Circuit Court].

_____ "Query," *CONFI* I:2 (August, 1956), p. 5. [FBI Confrontation].

_____ "You and the Law," *CONFI* II:2 (April, 1957), p. 5. [Military Case, etc.].

_____ "The Post Office Case," *CONFI* I:3 (November, 1956), p. 4.

_____ "Legal Report," *CONFI* III:1A (Winter 1958), pp. 7-9.

Catholic Committee, "Homosexuality, Prostitution and the Law," *QTLY* I:5 (Spring 1958), pp. 17-21.

Julber, Eric "ONE, Inc. vs. Otto R. Oleson," *QTLY* I:2 (Summer 1958) pp. 60-64 [*Writ of Certiorari*].

_____ "Kelly vs. San Francisco," *QTLY* I:3 (Fall, 1958), p. 84-88.

Fleishman, Stanley "Sexual Unorthodoxy and the Law," *QTLY* II:2 (Spring 1959), pp. 52-58.

Kempner, Jim "Court Upholds Gay Bars," *MAG* VII:3 (March, 1959), pp. 6-9.

Fleishman, Stanley "N.Y. Court Clarifies Obscenity Citing ONE, Inc.," *QTLY* II:4 (Fall 1959), pp. 133-144.

_____ "Homosexuality and the Law in England," *QTLY* III:3 (Summer 1960), pp. 221-235.

Underwood, J. M. "Postal Censorship," *MAG* IX:8 (August, 1961), pp. 5-18.

Legg, W. Dorr "The 1961 Midwinter Institute," *MAG* IX:9 (April, 1961), pp. 5-9.

Staff "The Bielecki Case," *CONFI* VII:6 (June, 1962), pp. 1.2 [Restroom Arrests].

Merritt, Thomas (Merritt M. Thompson) "Law and Psychiatry," *QTLY* VI:3,4 (Summer/Fall 1963), pp. 43-45.

Staff "Obedience to What?" *MAG* IX:5 (May, 1964), pp. 3-5.

Hansen, Joseph "The Right to Read," *MAG* XIIII:4 (April, 1965), pp. 5-7.

Crowther, R. H. (J. M. Underwood) "Press Control and Tyranny," *MAG* XIV:3 (March, 1966), pp. 6-9.

Bullough, Vern "ACLU Statement of Policy," *MAG* XIV:1 (January, 1966), pp. 6-8.

Staff "Black Cat Raid," *CONFI* XII:4 (April 1, 1967), pp. 5-10.

_____ "U.S. vs. Spinar & Germain," *CONFI* XII:7 (July, 1967), pp. 4-11.

_____ "A Military Case," *LTR* XIII:9 (September, 1968), pp. 5-8.

_____ "Court on Teacher's Credentials," *LTR* XIV:11 (November, 1969), pp.6-8.

_____ "288d Voided; Raid," *LTR* XVII:8 (August, 1972), pp. 1-4.

Gordon, Albert "Gay Couples and the Laws," *LTR* XIX:4 (April, 1974) pp.1-6.

Staff "You and the Law," *LTR* XIX:5 (May, 1974) pp. 3-6.

Levie, J. G. "Vice, Victim and Entrapment," *LTR* XX:1 (January, 1975), pp.4-7.

Staff "The Sexual Law Reporter," *LTR* XXI:7 (July, 1976), pp. 1-9.

Staff "Rights and Voting," *LTR* XXIII:II (November, 1978), pp. 1-6.

"Governor's Employment Order," *LTR* XXIV:4, (April, 1979}.

"Chicago Attorney Goldman," *LTR* XXV:3 (March, 1980), p. 4, 5.

"Constitutionality of Loitering Statute," *LTR* XXV:12 (December, 1980), pp.4-6.

"Trial of Canadian Magazine," *LTR* XXVII:6 (June, 1982), p. 5.

Coleman, Thomas F. "The Hardwick Case," *LTR* XXXI:5 (May, 1981), p.1.

Staff "Family Life and New Laws," *LTR* XXXII:5 (May, 1988), p. 1.

Green, Richard "Psychiatry and the Law," *LTR* XXXIV:, (January, 1989), p.3.

Staff/Superior Court "ONE, Inc. vs. Erickson Foundation," *LTR* XXXV:1 (January, 1990), p. 1-7.

One Institute Extension Lectures:
Law

January 20, 1957 (#7) "Censorship and Civil Liberties," by J. B. Tietz, Treasurer, Southern California Chapter, ACLU. [Earliest ACLU speaker for ONE] Text published, *MAG* V:4, (April, 1957), pp. 5-10, 17.

February 1, 1958 (#15) "ONE's U.S. Supreme Court Case," by Eric Julber, Attorney. [ONE's successful challenge of U.S. Post Office.]

January 30, 1960 (#30) "Community Standards and ONE Magazine's Editorial Policies," by Eric Julber.

January 30, 1960 (#38) "Civil Liberties and a Free Society," by Eason Monroe, Executive Director, Southern California Chapter, ACLU.

February 29, 1961 (#47) "A Homosexual Bill of Rights." Panel discussion, including Herbert Selwyn, Esq.

March 5, 1961 (#49) "Homophile Rights." [Tapes of discussions at February meetings.]

June 3, 1962 (#66) "The Bielecki Case," by W. E. Mohler, Jr., Assistant to Frank Wood, especially in victory in Long Beach restroom surveillance case. See also *CONFI* VII:6 (June, 1962) pp. 1, 2.

January 26, 1963 (#70) "New Frontiers in the Law," a panel discussion.

January 26, 1963 (#72) "The Right to be Free from Unreasonable Searches," by Frank Wood, Esq. [Published, *MAG* XI:4 (April, 1963), pp. 5-9.]

January 26, 1963 (#73) "Public vs. Private Rights," by Abraham Gorenfeld, ACLU attorney and panel.

January 26, 1963 (#74) "The Double Standard Moral Code as an Instrument of Corruption, Persecution and Abuse of Power," by Morris Lowenthal, Esq., San Francisco.

June 6, 1963 (#80) "Obscenity and the Law," by Harriet Pilpel, New York ACLU attorney with years of experience defending the Kinsey Institute against attempts to censor its research and library material.

December 1, 1963 (#83) "Private Lives: The Concern of One or the Many," by Phyllis Deutsch, Los Angeles attorney.

January 3, 1965 (#93) "Bruce Scott vs. John W. Macy," by Bruce Scott. [A several hour long presentation of records in his case against the U.S. Civil Service Commission.]

March 7, 1965 (#95) "California's Sex Laws: The Prospect for Reform," by Stuart A. Simke. [Gives special emphasis to the use of "Administrative Law" in denying employment and firing employees.]

December 5, 1965 (#101) "Homosexuality and Civil Rights," by Vern Bullough, ACLU Board Member and CSNU History Professor.

January 29, 1966 (#106) "Illinois Changed Its Laws: So Can Your State," by Paul Goldman, Chicago attorney long active with ONE in Chicago.

March 6, 1966 (#109) "Fink or Fact; An Expose of the LAPD," by Herbert Porter, Esq.

May 1, 1966 (#111) "Homosexuals and the Draft," by attorney Frank G. Wood and panel.

November 6, 1966 (#115) "A Defense Lawyer Looks at the CLEAN Amendment," by Burton Marks.

March 9, 1967 (#119) "The Case of the Black Cat Bar Raid," by a panel reporting conspicuous cases of LAPD brutality.

November 5, 1967 (#124) "Homosexual Law Reform in Britain," by Antony Grey, London. [Repeated in month-long cross-country U.S. Tour sponsored by ONE Institute.]

January 7, 1968 (#126) "American Civil Liberties and the Outmoded Sex Laws," by attorney Joan Martin.

October 6, 1968 (#133) "The Police, the Public and You," by Michael Hannon who was running for L. A. District Attorney.

January 31, 1970 (#150) "My Special Investigations of the Los Angeles Police Department," by controversial investigative reporter Paul Jacobs.

May 3, 1970 (#153) "The Challenge and Progress of Homosexual Law Reform," by University of New Mexico Law Professor Walter Barnett whose *Sexual Freedom and the Constitution* (U. of New Mexico, 1973) is an important reference work on the topic.

April 4, 1971 (#161) "Recent Legal Implications of Fair Employment for Homosexuals," by Professor Irving Kovarsky, University of Iowa.

June 6, 1971 (#163) "The President's Commission on Obscenity and Pornography," by Professor Michael Goldstein, UCLA, Department of Psychology.

January 30, 1972 (#172) "Some Rights and Many Wrongs," by attorney Herbert Selwyn and panel.

June 4, 1972 (#177) "The Prospect for Civil Rights in the 1970s," by Eason Monroe, retiring Executive Director, Southern California Chapter, ACLU.

April 1, 1973 (#184) "Gays and the Law," by a panel of political activists.

November 4, 1973 (#188) "New Legal and Social Service Thrusts," by ACLU panel and others.

March 3, 1973 (#192) "Gay Couples and the Laws," Albert Gordon, Esq. [Reported in *LTR* XIX:4 (April, 1974), pp. 1,2,6. Also, *Los Angeles Times*, March 25, 1974.]

June 8, 1974 (#201) "Sex Variants and the Double Standards of Law Enforcement," by Albert Gordon.

January 5, 1975 (#210) "Vice, Victim and Entrapment," by Attorney Gerald J. Levie, who later became L.A. County Superior Court Judge.

June 1, 1975 (#216) "Helping the Civil Rights Bill to Become Law in California," by George Ray, Sacramento lobbyist.

June 1, 1980 (#226) "Need for the Repeal of 647a and 647d Laws," by Albert Gordon.

March 1, 1981 (#271) "Liaison: Gay Community and LAPD," a panel discussion.

October 2, 1983 (#290) "Origins of Homophobia and the Law," by Paul Hardman, San Francisco, ONE Institute Ph.D., 1986.

April 1, 1984 (#295) "Big Brother in the Bedroom," by Thomas F. Coleman, Esq.

December 2, 1984 (#303) "FBI Surveillance, Freedom of Information Records," by Dan Siminoski, Investigator.

May 5, 1985 (#308) "A Long Beach Sex Scandal in Grandfather's Day" by David Cameron, Attorney at Law. A report on 30 men arrested in an early example of gay resistance (court acquittals of two). The report also includes an analysis of the history of criminal law on lewd vagrancy.

May 9, 1986 (#318) "The Hardwick Case: U.S. Supreme Court," by Thomas F. Coleman.

February 7, 1988 (#332) "Police Relations: The Political Response," by Frank Richiazzi, Republican activist.

January 8, 1989 (#340) "Psychiatry and the Law," by Richard Green, M.D., J.D. Forensic Psychiatrist, UCLA.

March 5, 1989 (#342) "Former LAPD Sergeant, an Insider's View," by Mitch
    Grobeson.
March 1, 1992 (#370) "Legal Records as a Source of Homophile History,"
    by David Cameron, Attorney at Law and ONE Institute Dean of
    Extension & Special Programs.

In addition to the excerpts from faculty and student papers cited
in this chapter, several video cassettes, each of them an hour or more
in length, are located in the Audiovisual Collection of ONE's Baker
Memorial Library: lecture nos. 290, 296, 303, 340, 342, and 370.

CHAPTER 9

RELIGION

R eligion has a place in Homophile Studies second to none in importance. Law, history, and sociology: each of them bears the
unmistakable imprint of religion's influence. Classes at ONE Institute
have spent little time in examining contemporary religions. They
became interested, instead, in studying religion's formative years, giving
particular attention to such evidences referring to homosexuality as could
be found. A review of studies on religion from any special period or
from any doctrinal point of view has not been the concern of ONE
Institute classes. Exploration of the record of comparative religion and
how each happened to go in its particular direction were found to be
of greater value for Homophile studies.

Proceeding in this vein, the classes observed that "in the beginning"
there was no such thing as religion or, if preferred, everything was
religion. As early man struggled for survival, it was urgent to first learn
the skills of survival. At the same time these humans were acutely
aware that there were uncounted phenomena which they both feared
and could not understand. Their innate primate curiosity and their urge
to discover causation led them to keep searching for explanations.
Theories and hypotheses proliferated in luxuriant variety as attested by
the arts they have left. Those hypotheses which could be verified
became what we today call science. This category embraced their
technology and impressive skills of survival. Against these were arrayed
the unknowns, the mysteries, the fears and thoughts which began taking
on that special tone we now call religion.

Throughout the very lengthy Paleolithic period, change seems to
have come relatively slowly. Technologies required for survival within
a given environment and under particular climatic conditions did not
occasion changes of decision making or the development of flights of
speculation during that early period. A point very relevant to
Homophile Studies is the fact, however, as mythology and other
evidence indicate, that during a long and relatively static period, the
scientific fact of how impregnation takes place was not yet known.
Science moves more slowly than does speculative thought. The
significance of this upon taboo and mythologies about male – female
interaction can hardly be overestimated. Entire value systems we tend
to think of as primordial had no existence at the time because they were
without any support in cause and effect observations. While sexual

behavior might at the time have derived in general from their acute observations of animal behavior, early man had no way of knowing about hormonal differences affecting such behavior. Not yet having developed the hypotheses and elaborate rationalizations which humans would later apply to sexual interactions, whether between males and males or females, or between females and females, their value systems had an entirely different frame of reference from what are now believed to be the given norms of human behavior.

As a result of the ice age, changes began to occur in various parts of the world. These led to profound modifications of all sorts. Most important of all these was the ongoing series of innovations which has been called "the Neolithic revolution," a wide-ranging alteration of much of what had gone before. Whether it was the immense ideological upheaval brought about by the development of agriculture or the scientific discovery of how pregnancy occurred is of less importance than the fact that now a whole new way of looking at gender was evolving. Females no longer were just another, albeit different, part of the group. Agricultural technology began to bring with it the new concept of women as being surrogate deputies for the Earth and its fertility. Earth goddesses and the forces over which they presided were thought to have delegated unseen powers to women as their visible proxies in the community. Powers, rights, and obligations never before given thought were being assigned and accorded mystical values with force and authority which could best be understood by means of symbols and metaphor. Gender and sex differences were becoming subjects for endless concepts and hypotheses. What some feminist theoreticians have today viewed as being basic and natural became instead a perverse arena for the proliferation of the very rigidities of theory now imputed to patriarchy. Roles, duties, and "cosmic rights" were being assigned to both men and women which began to provide the foundations from which sprang a whole range of religions. Unfortunately, the homophobia often blamed on the Old Testament or on Christianity was already becoming a highly developed ideology centuries before either Christianity or Judaism came into existence.

This is the context within which excerpts from faculty and student papers are presented on the following pages. The usual precautions need to be observed: These are not to be seen as complete papers. Neither are they intended as abstracts of any writer's general argument. Rather, they are illustrations from faculty and student reactions to the subjects under study, which specifically illustrate their relevance to Homophile Studies.

Religion, Real and Counterfeit
By Julian M. Underwood
Writing as R. M. Crowther[1]

Throughout human history, so much has been said and done in the name of religion that it is often difficult to distinguish the real, potent factors of religion which determine character and conduct and present a forceful picture of the spiritual goals of man's destiny, from the many questionable notions and activities which often masquerade under religious trappings. Those [people] who have been close to ONE during recent months have witnessed a rather bizarre outbreak of fanaticism which appears to fall in the latter category. Religion has so often been used as a name for dogma, superstitions, hysteria, theatrical display, intellectual and social tyranny, and other negative or vicious elements in human experience, that we cannot be over-careful about how we use the word, and about how we ally ourselves with activities which seem to carry religious associations. (p.36)

The word "religion" has lost a good deal of its meaning for most of us. We tend to apply it to anything which purports to deal with God and with a tradition and a literature regarded as sacred. We presume, meanwhile, that we know God, and that we also have infallible means of distinguishing sacred from profane things. Since either presumption is rash, any group desiring to find for the first time a community of religious ideas and ideals would do well to consider seriously, at the beginning, what religion should be to the individual and to society. Religious thought and language, like many other branches of thought and language in this complex civilization, have become compartmentalized. We fail to connect it clearly even with other closely related fields, such as philosophy, sociology, esthetics, and science, and we usually do not connect it at all with the so-called "secular" affairs of life. Yet if religion has an intellectual and emotional content supposed to be centered around a God, a unitary Creator of all experienced things, it is difficult to see how religion could fail to have a close bearing upon all other aspects of our thought

---

[1] *MAG* IV:4 (April/May, 1956), pp.36-40.

and being. (p.37)

Stereotypes of language, symbol, or ceremonial spell failure for any effort to approach religious values in a progressive, original manner. In religion, the idea of God is the sole constant; all else, including our own personalities, is His creativeness and growth, and the endless changes of relationship which creation and growth entail. Stereotypes in religion are, in fact, a flat denial of the very principle supposed to be operative in religious ideals and practices. No type of thought should be so free from stereotypes as religious thought. Every new sect or cult reflects the instinctive effort of persons to shake loose from traditional stereotypes in the religious field. However, the ones who spurn old stereotypes most vehemently are usually those busiest inventing new ones. Few, if any, modern religious groups seem to have succeeded in eliminating the stifling atmosphere of formalism. The tendency of the human mind to seek solace in fixed images or patterns of thought is a formidable one. In its proper place among the worldly institutions necessary to society, this tendency is desirable and useful. But in the religious sphere it must be avoided at all costs as the primary barrier to spiritual and intellectual freedom, and therefore to true worship. (p.39)

In religious matters, we are still very weak on the thinking end of the scale. As a start to correcting this situation, there are many questions which should be asked, and answered, and the answers understood. What are the basic assumptions of our most advanced religious thought? How is the individual, in the various phases of his life, related to these assumptions? How far can we trust our present records of the world's religious leadership in reflecting the true meaning and essence of this leadership? What could be done to clarify these records and to bring them, and modern derived knowledge, into the necessary harmony of thought? How do religious truths bear upon individual thought and conduct, and how may they best be reflected in the social laws and processes of justice which regulate this conduct? Finally, how may these same truths be translated fully into terms of the practical activities of modern society, so that we may obtain their full benefits in our social life? (p.40)

World Religions
and the Homophile
By James Kepner, Jr.[2]

The tormenting difficulties which many Homophiles endure in trying to find satisfying expression for both their sexual and their spiritual desires, in the face of popular conviction that religious faith and homosexual[*] activity are incompatible, endow the present topic with wide practical urgency.[3] It is hardly necessary to add that, in both conservative and liberal denominations today, homosexual individuals as well as acts are generally viewed with an alarm and distaste surpassing the usual reactions reserved for such orthodox sins as murder and mayhem.

It is our general aim in this survey course to attempt to put Homophile questions into some sort of world context, and to define the "place" of the individual homosexual. In considering what relationship homosexuality and other variant sex patterns may be found to have to "the general scheme of things," we have in previous sections of this study asked whether homosexuality is indeed "against nature," as is often presumed, or whether it is a functional, understandable, and necessary part of nature. We have tried to comprehend and see past all the clashing theories and claims about causes and cures, to ascertain the ways in which Homophiles have related themselves to varied pre-literate cultures, and the ways in which they actually live in our contemporary society, the accommodations and the dislocations they experience.[4]

---

[2] *QTLY* II:4 (Fall 1959), pp.124-132.

[*] While we sometimes use the words "homosexual" and "homophile" interchangeably, by the latter we generally intend a distinct preference for company or friendship of one's own sex, without necessary sexual connotations. The former term intends specifically sexual acts, relationships or desires, and persons having same.

[3] *MAG* II:6 (June, 1954) p.21-24.

[4] Further sections of this study to appear here in future issues. For earlier portions, see "An Introduction to the Sociology of Homophilia," *QTLY* I:1 (Spring 1958) p.22: "An Introduction to Homosexuality and the Biological

Our approach to this study will be historical in form, concerned with tracing the origins, the evolution, and the variant side paths of religious sexual morality. As in other sections of our study, we will see that homosexual questions do not exist in isolation, but are always related intimately to concepts of the family, the state, individual responsibilities, sexual norms, etc. So we study homosexual questions within a broad context of morals and social structure. We shall, however, keep in mind the religious context of homosexuals in American life today, and shall therefore constantly be concerned with the following practical questions of direct importance to those homosexuals who are, consciously or unconsciously, seeking the means of social reconciliation within that religious context.

We shall consider scattered congregations, denominations, and unusual sects in which homosexuals, individually or collectively, openly or secretly, have found some place, and at the same time, we shall discuss the current faltering movement toward tolerance, understanding or acceptance, most forthrightly expressed in England by the recommendations which the Church of England,[5] the Roman Catholic Advisory Committee, and the Methodists made to the Wolfenden Committee.[6]

We shall sift the evidence from various peoples and different historic eras regarding religious movements which have approved of homosexual activity or inclinations, sometimes in ritual contexts, or accommodated themselves to it. Tracing back anthropologically toward the sources of early religions, we shall attempt to evaluate the widespread homosexual aspects of Shamanism, the apparent ritual homosexuality of classical religions, as well as some Hindu, Moslem, or Buddhist groups or trends.

Evidence," *QTLY* I:3 (Fall 1958) p.89: and "Homosexuality in History," and "Philosophy for the Homophile," *QTLY* II:3 (Summer 1959) p.77 and 93.

[5] *Sexual Offenders and Social Punishment* (London, 1956).

[6] A Departmental Committee was appointed by Her Majesty's Government in 1954 under the able chairmanship of Sir John Wolfenden, Vice Chancellor of Reading University, and commissioned to study and report on the effects of current English laws regarding homosexuality and prostitution, and to recommend such changes in the law as seemed necessary. In 1957, the Committee submitted to the government its now famed recommendation that homosexual acts in private between consenting adults cease to be a concern of the law. The government has thus far sidestepped action on the homosexual aspects of the report [1959].

We shall examine at length the degree to which other religions of the world, particularly in regard to their moral and sexual ideals and taboos, have influenced or infiltrated those religions that make up our Western environment. From fertility and Mother Goddess cults, to the sophisticated cults of Egypt, to the long Zoroastrian-Gnostic-Manichean-Catharist chain overlapping the Christian communion, from Pythagorean, Stoic, Neo-Platonic and other religio-philosophies, from Buddhism and Shivism to those oriental currents of Theosophy, Vedanta and Zen today, the Judaeo-Christian stream has been fed and often diverted by other currents. (p.127)

As with the orthodox Fathers of the early Church, so today, a good deal of Christian energy goes into the attempt to fit the *Old* and *New Testaments* into a congruent pattern. Today, though many Christians recognize certain contrasts between what they consider to be the two parts of one book, it is considered heretical in most denominations to suggest that the two do not form a unity. It was not always so in the Church, and at any rate, the study of the *Old Testament* involves a quite different set of problems from those facing *New Testament* scholars, aside from the facts that they were written by different peoples, for different purposes, in different languages, and centuries apart.

In sifting the textual vagaries of the *Old Testament*, to discover how the ancient Hebrews looked at sexual matters, we run into the confusing oscillations between what scholars have labeled the J, E, P, S and L sources, of which the present text is supposed to be composed. We shall attempt to see what Judaism had in common with its neighbor religions, what it borrowed from them, and at what period and in what ways it actually came to be set apart. We shall examine such elements as: Adam's original hermaphroditism;[7] the fumbling evolution of marriage customs traced in the Old Testament;[8] the Sodom story[9] and the strange Gibeah account of *Judges* 17-19, and the failure of later Biblical and Talmudic references to the fate

---

[7] Inferred from questions regarding the proper translation of *Gen.* 1:26-27; 2:21-24; 5:2; by Maimonaides and others.

[8] For example, *Gen.* 2:24; 3:16-20; 12:10-20; 16:1-6; 25:1-6; 29; 30; 34; *Ex.* 20:12, 14; 22:16-24; *Lev.* 12:2-8; 18-21; *Deut.* 21-24; *Ruth*; also accounts of the wide matrimonial experiences of David and Solomon: *Song of Solomon*; etc.

[9] *Gen.* 13, 14, 18, 19.

of the city and its inhabitants to note any homosexual implication;[10] the apocryphal story of the Watchers;[11]   the curious mystery of Cain's wife[12] and the marriages of the Sons of God to the daughters of men;[13]   the offense of Ham;[14]   Jacob's wrestlings with the angel;[15]   the offense of Onan;[16]   the serpent in the wilderness;[17] Ruth and Naomi; David and Jonathan; the nature of the Baalim;[18] varied references to the Qadhesh or Kadeshim, or temple prostitutes,[19] often mistranslated into English as either sodomites or dogs; the Greek and Syrian ascetic influences and dualism which stand out in the pre-Christian Judaism of the *Apocrypha* and Dead Sea manuscripts; and many other elements suggesting a story less simple than heretofore supposed, that possibly homosexuality once had a part in Hebrew religious ritual, and that anti-homosexual feelings developed rather late among the Jews.

We shall give close attention to the question of possible homoerotic tendencies underlying the Christian or other religions.

---

[10] *Deut.* 29:23; *Isaiah* 1:9; 13:19; *Jer.* 23:14; 49:18; 50:40; *Lament.* 4:6; *Ezek,* 16:50; *Amos* 4:11; *Zeph.* 2:9; *Matt.* 10:15; 11:23-24; *Luke* 10:12; *II Pet.* 2:6-8; *Jude* 7; *Rev.* 11:8. *Koran* 26:165-166, six centuries later, gives the homosexual interpretation of the Sodom story.

[11] *Enoch* 6-10; *Jub.* 7:21; 10:5; *Test. Reub* 5:6-7.

[12] *Gen.* 4:16-17.

[13] *Ibid.* 6:1-2

[14] *Ibid.* 9:20-27, sometimes interpreted as homosexual incest.

[15] *Ibid.* 32:24-32.

[16] *Ibid.* 38:9.

[17] *Num.* 21:8-9.

[18] Supreme male Canaanite deity, probably phallic, long worshipped by Israelites. *Num.* 22:41; 25:3-18; *Deut.* 4:3; and numerous references in books of *Kings.* Perhaps synonymous with Bel, Beelzebub.

[19] *Deut.* 23:17-18; *I Kings* 14:22-24; 15:12; 22:46; *II Kings* 23:7. The Kadeshim were male temple prostitutes who according to some writers serviced feminine worshippers. Others say they sexually initiated young boys, as is still the custom with some primitive tribes. A regular feature of the Jerusalem Temple till at least 600 B.C., such temple prostitutes, both male and female, continued in some parts of the Middle East till the last century.

It has been suggested that the heterosexual impulse binds men together only in small family groups, while it requires broader, homophilic feelings of fraternity, of what Whitman called *adhesiveness*,[*] to provide the necessary impulse toward universal fellowship. In an earlier and superficial article,[20] we maintained that Christianity was in essence heavily homoerotic. We shall see.

The central aim of this study will be to find possible means to reconcile the Homophile and religious positions. We have no personal commitment to this task. We are not looking to pave the road to religion for ourselves, but for those who seem to need it.

A Moral Imperative
By W. Dorr Legg[21]

THE FAILURE OF THE CHURCH

Thousands of homosexuals have told us or have written what this means to them. It means that, broadly speaking, their churches have refused to accept them into religious communion as homosexuals. Many of them find themselves entirely unable to square the thought of pretending to be other than what they are, or of dissembling, with the ethical standards their religions profess. Yet, if they tell the truth, the doors of the churches are closed in their faces.

Homosexual acts, they are told by clergyman, priest, and rabbi, are sins so vile in the sight of God as scarcely to bear discussion. The revulsion of most churchmen at the mere mention of homosexuality is so intense that the hapless subject is quite unlikely to avoid feeling condemned both of God and of man. In desperation, many homosexuals sincerely strive to conform to a pattern of living which they are told is The Divine Plan, but the attempt seldom is a success. Their failure then sinks them deeper into feelings of guilt, self-condemnation, and despair, according to the degree of their own

---

[*] Borrowing a term from the phrenologists, then enjoying such a vogue as psychoanalysts enjoy today [1959].

[20] "Thorn in the Spirit," *MAG* II:6 (June, 1954), p.21.

[21] *MAG* XI:12 (December, 1963), pp.7-13.

integrity and sensitivity to ethical problems.

Some homosexuals seek escape through the use of alcohol or drugs, so many of them in fact that some observers believe repressed homosexuality to be the prime cause of alcoholism and drug addiction. Others turn for help to psychiatrists, or else struggle weakly on until some mental hospital is the only way out.

The stronger ones are apt to rebel and become reckless outcasts of the gutter or prison fodder. It sometimes happens that in prison for the first time in their lives they discover their homosexuality to be just what it is, simply another aspect of the human condition, neither good nor bad of itself. In such cases, blessed are they who lose all, for thereby do they find themselves – an ironic beatitude wrung from the dregs of disaster.

Only slightly less trying than ecclesiastical condemnation and rejection are the indifference and temporizing so often encountered. Many clergymen to whom homosexuals appeal for aid are so immersed in the delights of theological speculation or plans for some new stained glass window as to find little time for less pleasant pursuits.

Upon being pressed, this sort will ooze a synthetic charitableness, saying, "Come into the church by all means, but please soft-pedal your homosexuality. You have a fine choir voice and so long as there is no stir, I certainly won't condemn you. After all, the old Sodom story is in considerable textual disrepute these days anyway, and the mission of the church is to save sinners. I don't see why this would exclude you, my son."

So runs the thinking of the under-carpet sweepers, but large numbers of homosexuals want higher standards of honesty than this. They charge the churches with harboring far too many scribes and Pharisees and expect the church to face the whole homosexual question squarely and fairly.

To innumerable homosexuals the failure of the churches is of two sorts: a failure of commission, instanced in countless inhumanities vented upon countless homosexual men and women; a failure of omission, shown in an unreadiness and unwillingness to wrestle with the knotty question of the acceptance of the homosexual in the order of things. (p.7)

TOWARD A HIGHER MORALITY

Many homosexuals charge that it is the duty of the world's religions to become aware of the inadequacy of their moral standards respecting homosexual men and women. It is their contention that the churches uphold one standard of morals for heterosexuals and another for homosexuals.

Historically speaking, the association between morality and religion is comparatively a recent one, and so varied have been the religious interpretations of moral questions over the centuries as to arouse considerable skepticism regarding the reliability of their statements.

For example, homosexuals are told that marriage is a sacred institution and part of God's plan for humans. Why, then, it is asked, did priests not perform marriages until fairly late medieval times, and why was marriage considered too profane to be performed anywhere within proximity to a church?

In Imperial Rome, Christians were fed to the lions as having violated the moral codes of the Roman religion. Moslems executed "the Christian dogs," because their conduct violated the moral codes of the Koran. Subscribing to a different moral code, Christians enthusiastically slaughtered Moslems during the Crusades, when they were not slaughtering each other for "heresies."

The Inquisition under Church approval executed a code of morals featuring refinements of physical torture undreamed even by Hitler's experts. The story of the Portuguese and Spanish conquerors of North and South America as well as the more recent British, French and Dutch records in Africa, India, and Indonesia again throw a clear light upon the flexibility in practice of what religions claim are immutable moral laws.

Many homosexuals mean exactly what they say when they announce that they are placing religion and the churches on trial. They refuse any longer to accept as valid a moral code based on ancient Jewish records appropriate to other days and other ways. Nor do they find themselves persuaded as to the authoritative value of every single phrase ascribed to Saul of Tarsus. Especially suspect do they find his statements concerning homosexuality in view of his own well-known instability and some circumstantial evidence that he himself was a repressed, hence fearful, homosexual.

A moral imperative of compelling urgency faces the churches today, say homosexuals. For if religion is unable to produce men who are humane and decent, then the moral codes of the churches are ineffective. "By their fruits shall ye know them." The old excuse that one should not judge Christianity by Christians no longer seems persuasive in a pragmatic age such as our own.

The churches will continue to lose the respect and the allegiance of those homosexual men and women who refuse to settle for an ethical standard that has two faces. Either religion makes provision for the inborn goodness and dignity of man – all men – or religion is found wanting.

The moral imperative has now been so defined. The churches must come humbly and willingly before the judgment seat of the religious demands of all humanity. If their self-righteous obduracy should stiffen instead and if old shibboleths persist, then, like dinosaurs covered by ice, the overriding strata of higher ethical levels will cover the churches from sight. The religions of today will become footnotes of history, alongside Mithraism, Isis or Adonis worship, and all the myriad others which have vanished with the dust of the ages. (p.10)

The following excerpts from an article by Monwell Boyfrank, ONE Institute lecturer and member of the Board of Directors for many years, exemplify his independent line of thought and quirky originality. Of Native American ancestry, he was born in the Oklahoma Territory on an uncertain date in the 19th century.

Lot, Sodom, Onan And Paul
By Monwell Boyfrank
Writing as J. P. Starr[22]

Several attitudes toward sex are traceable among Christianity's originators. You may take the esoteric approach, practice man-love secretly and live at peace with your neighbors as the Essenes did; you may try the evangelical approach, telling the whole world androphily's glad news and get hanged for your pains as Jesus did; you may try the ignorant-idealist tactic of resolving to go without sexual exercise and carry on an endless war with yourself as many have done and do; you may adopt the ruthless, reckless and cruelly selfish policy of staying celibate and fucking other men's wives as millions of priests have done; or you might retreat into a mystical fog in which nobody can tell for sure what your policy is and you can't either. It was the last-named attitude that Paul took.

Paul or Saul was a Christian – or better say a Pauline – preacher, about the loudest, most persistent, and most ingenious of his time. He is supposed to have lived from about 3 to 68 A.D. His contemporaries have left no word of him; and the only evidence about

---

22 *MAG* XVI:7 (July/August, 1972), pp.10-15.

him is afforded by "The *Acts of the Apostles*" and the epistles or letters of the *New Testament*. The *Acts* were written anywhere from ten to a hundred years after the supposed date of Paul's death; and the letters also seem to have originated toward the end of his life if, indeed, they were not written by other men after he was dead. All of those documents bear evidence of revision at the hands of men, friendly to Paul, who could have fabricated the early part of his autobiography wherever they chose to; and that part on which his churchly authority is based is the very part that sounds fishiest. The latter and better substantiated part sounds like the diary of a modern circuit-riding Methodist.

Paul said he was born at Tarsus, then a 900-year-old city that had been for sixty years under the Roman rule. Tarsus lies on a river ten miles from the Mediterranean, where that sea is enclosed in a square corner by Asia Minor on the north and Syria on the east. Paul, a Roman citizen, seems to have belonged to the propertied class, which participated in government.

Born a Jew and later professing Christianity, Paul had an incentive to dramatize his conversation and give other Jews to understand that they should follow his example. So he represented himself as a Jew of Jews who had "seen the light." That pose would call for at least one trip to Jerusalem, training in a rabbinical school, and perhaps membership in the Sanhedrin. That he should get thunderstruck with a vision of the messiah whose gospel he was to preach was part of the preparation for his racket, as was the report of his having meditated in Arabia. Tradition, superstition, and the intellectual climate called for that sort of thing.

It is guessable that a man who carried on a humdrum trade in Tarsus and did a little political conniving on the side decided, at about the age of forty, that making tents is too hard work and that agitating a new religion is more fun. In religion, Paul was a great shopper-arounder – if he did not make up his religion as he went along; and he was always a leading exponent of his faith of the moment, making up in vehemence whatever he lacked in constancy. Saul's contact with any survivors of that band which once palled around with Jesus, if any such contact (or, for that matter, any such group) ever existed, was, by Paul's own report, uncordial. We might concede his own trip to Jerusalem, but that may have been invention or a mere going through of the motions.

Paul charged "that which is unseemly" against some men whom he disliked, along with a long list of other misdeeds, great and small. We find here a tirade, neither clear nor important, not in the gospels nor in the *Acts of the Apostles* but in the epistle, one of many letters of which several are conceded by Christian scholars to be spurious

(and of course to Jewish scholars they are all heretical) appended at
the *New Testament's* latter end and purported to have been written
by Paul to a congregation of Romans.

Before Saul became Paul and muscled into the apostle business,
the Jesuine church was composed chiefly of Hellenized Jews –
Essenes, Adventists, and miscellaneous. With the death of their
central figure or, if he be only imaginary, his failure to make an
appearance, they would naturally fall apart. Those who remained
strong in their particular conviction or who were active in proselytiz-
ing would, if they lived among the Jews, accommodate their religion
to that of their relatives and friends, would form a sect of reformist
Jews. Such evidence as we have supports this view.

But Paul was Hellenized in a greater degree than were the
companions of Jesus, and he was to a still greater degree Romanized.
As did the Romans, he disapproved of circumcision and the limitation
of offspring; and as were they, he was inclined to accept practical
expedients rather than cling, as Jews do, to a family or tribal
observance. (pp. 13,14)

Saul-Paul never saw Jesus, and his religion usually differed from
that of his pretended master. A highly emotional man, Saul had
persecuted the murdered religious agitator's followers. Paul said that
he changed his mind as the result of a fit or seizure that he suffered,
in which, he said, he saw the then-dead Jesus. That Paul was epileptic
is no reproach to him, but it is consistent with the instability that he
showed throughout his career. He apparently couldn't hold any
attitude for long at a time. He is not to be blamed for changing his
mind as he grew older and acquired knowledge and experience; but
an inconsistency which may be only a sign of honesty and growth
in an ordinary man is devastating to the pretensions of a messenger
from God. Changing his religion was one of the things Paul did best;
he revised his opinions from the first we hear of him to the last.

Paul's letter to the Romans is regarded by scholars as relatively
genuine, if any epistle can be so regarded, but its peculiarities indicate
garbling. It looks to be two letters matched together. Be it discourse
classified as indicative, interrogative, imperative, and exclamatory,
Paul's epistle to the Romans is one of the longest exclamations in
our language. (p.14)

Sometimes Paul made converts and sometimes he ran into
opposition. In Jerusalem and Rome he got arrested and in Athens
he met with indifference or contempt. Now and then he encountered
insuperable resistance or was expelled from a community, as in each
such case he cloaked the indignity under a divine mandate to go
elsewhere. He wandered up the Aegean's eastern coast as far as Troy
and crossed over into Macedonia, whence he ambulated down through

Hellas to Corinth. (p.15)

Upon his arrival at Corinth and his attaining something like his fiftieth year, he wrote two letters that are considered his earliest, those to the congregations at Thessalonica or Salonica, which lies 150 miles north of Corinth and supposedly upon Paul's line of march.

As contributions to the historic record of some messiah or other, these earliest of Christian documents are worthless. The supposition was that the messiah had been crucified about fifteen years before, and that a few years after the crucifixion, Paul had seen Jesus in a fit. In these letters, Paul exhorts his followers to believe in the doctrines that he has told them in person, doctrines which he does not here recapitulate. He is quite sold on the saviorhood of Jesus; but for all we can tell from these letters, that messiah may be Paul's own invention.

Corinth was something of a headquarters of Paulines; and when Paul was a long time away from there, he wrote letters to the Corinthians to resolve schisms, suppress bickerings, and maintain his predominance. In First Corinthians he indicates that a man had best find his sexual gratification in other men, but he permits marriage where a man can't content himself without a woman. Much of Paul's counsel is practical, conciliatory, and in accord with the customs and thought of the time and place. He asserts in an offhand way that he has seen Jesus Christ and that he is a brother of Peter; apparently, we are to take these statements as made in a spiritual sense.

In First Corinthians' 15th chapter, Paul gets around to stating his doctrine of Christ's death, burial, resurrection, and appearance to Peter, to the other apostles, to 500 men "and last of all he was seen of me also, as of one born out of due time." He states Christianity's elements and gives instructions for taking up the collection. Church management and a defense of his religious authority are the themes of his other letters.

Paul tells how he went to Jerusalem, entered into the Jewish temple, and there got into a brawl of even greater severity than his others. Only thus lately does he declare himself a pupil of the famed Gamaliel and a once-scrupulous Jew. Carried in arrest by the Romans to Caesarea, Paul was held there two years and then sent to Rome, where he dwelt two years. These two-year periods sound more like a mannerism than history, each coming at the end of a chapter with an abrupt change in the narrative's pace.

Christian historians seem disposed to get Paul out of the way by 65 A.D.; some of the time-killing expedients introduced seem designed to make his conversion and ministry begin curiously early. Thus he is seen as Gamaliel's disciple at the early age of fifteen; he spends three years in Arabia doing nothing immediately after experiencing the most exciting event of his life, the event that is supposed to have prompted his becoming the most active of the apostles; he is held two years by Felix and Festus with strangely little motivation; he is sent, on little or no provocation, on a leisurely voyage to Rome, where he is held in oddly liberal confinement by a government that customarily disposed of capital cases promptly; and thereafter it is indicated that he made trips to Spain and to the Levant, finally to return to Rome and get himself killed. (p.15)

God's wrath, says Paul, "is revealed from heaven against all ungodliness and unrighteousness of men, who hinder the truth... knowing God, they glorified him not as God," and took to the worship of images. Wherefore, Paul argues, God gave them up to the lusts of their hearts unto uncleanness, that their bodies should be dishonored among themselves..."

Saul-Paul's indictment does not run against us here. We men who love men do not worship lifeless images; and as for dishonoring men's bodies, it is we who love those bodies. Mortification of the body is a Christian practice. We see in the seed-bearing, male human body a veritable temple of goodness, truth and beauty.

"For this cause," Paul goes on, "God gave them up unto vile passions; for their women changed the natural use into that which is against nature; and likewise also the men, leaving the natural use of the woman, burned in their lust one toward another, men with men working unseemliness, and receiving in themselves that recompense of their error which was due."

Paul accused those who disbelieved him of many other things: "all unrighteousness, wickedness, covetise, malice, full of envy, murder, strife, deceit, malignity; whisperers, backbiters, hateful to God, insolent, haughty, boastful, inventors of evil things, disobedient to parents, without understanding, covenant-breakers, without natural affection, unmerciful," and so on, verbosely and incoherently. That fellow certainly had a mad-on. He follows this blistering judgment with an exhortation against judging, "for wherein thou judgest another, thou condemnest thyself." The upshot of the whole tirade is Paul's emphatic dissatisfaction with people who heard him preach and were unimpressed. (p.15)

A Move Toward Reform[23]

A remarkable movement aimed at bridging the gap which has long lain between homosexuals and most churches was started on the West Coast about two years ago and is now spreading elsewhere. How did so unlikely an association come about?

The answer is that such great changes in traditional religious attitudes toward many topics have been taking place of late years that even something previously so taboo as homosexuality has come in for a reevaluation. Their participation in the civil rights movement has convinced many conscientious clergymen that not only ethnic minorities have been victims of social discrimination. Those who have been working with juveniles and with problems of the central areas in our large cities have found they needed to know more about homosexuality, and so it was that some San Francisco ministers approached leaders of the Homophile organizations in that city to see what they had learned about the problem.

After some months of discussions by these clergymen, they felt the time had come to take some definite action, and in May, 1964, issued invitations to a meeting to be devoted to the topic of religion and the homosexual. Representatives came from the National Council of Churches (New York), Methodist Board of Social Concerns (Washington), Urban Training Center (Chicago), and Methodist Board of Education (Nashville). San Francisco clergymen attending were Lutheran, Episcopal, United Church of Christ, and Methodist. Members of the city's Homophile community from the Daughters of Bilitis, Mattachine Society, League for Civil Education, and others participated.

The three day retreat was chaired by Methodist minister, the Rev. Theodore McIlvenna, and resulted in the formation of "The Council on Religion and the Homosexual" of San Francisco, one of whose stated purposes was "to promote a continuing dialogue between the church and the homosexual." For the next twelve months The Council engaged itself in a vigorous series of public confrontations, including one with the San Francisco Police Department which is still pending in the courts. Council speakers addressed many church and other groups. A rousing "Brief of Injustices" was published, setting forth

---

[23] *MAG* XIII:10 (October, 1965), p.6-17.

some of the situations which confront homosexuals.

In June, 1965, several members of the Council traveled to Los Angeles, giving a report concerning their activities in San Francisco to the clergymen and representatives of Southern California Homophile organizations who had assembled to hear them. The outcome of this meeting was the formation of "The Southern California Council on Religion and the Homophile."

Its activities have included sending numerous speakers to address Roman Catholic, Methodist, Episcopal, Southern California School of Religion, and other audiences. Counsel has been given to many persons troubled about their homosexuality. At a three-day "Consultation" held last January, Episcopal, United Church of Christ, Methodist, and Presbyterian ministers met with representatives of the Los Angeles Homophile community, including representatives from ONE, Incorporated, Daughters of Bilitis, PURSUIT, and others.

Both in San Francisco and Los Angeles there has been general agreement that, by sharing and learning from each other, both "sides" have been greatly benefited. Many of the ministers and Homophile men and women have told how their mutual association has brought them awareness of a broader feeling of human problems and enlarged sympathies, which has been a deeply felt emotional experience.

There has now been formed "The Washington, D.C. Area Council on Religion and the Homosexual," and there have been reports of similar steps being taken elsewhere. The goal of bringing about a better understanding and accommodation between two groups, which for so long stood in opposition to each other, offers horizons and challenges of almost unlimited scope. The Councils on Religion and the Homosexual have dedicated themselves to furtherance of this ideal.

CONCERN[24]

On June 1, 1965, at the invitation of the Council on Religion and the Homosexual (CRH) of San Francisco, twenty persons met in the Los Angeles suburban Westchester YMCA for an all-day session, as reported above.

Approximately half were from San Francisco and half from Los Angeles, the number of clergymen and representatives of Homophile organizations also being in the same proportion.

---

[24] *Concern* 1 (July, 1966), pp.2-3.

During the morning, the Rev. Ted McIlvenna of San Francisco discussed the broad social changes now affecting all levels of American Society, pointing out that in consequence, a "sexual revolution" was forcing the churches to reexamine their traditional attitudes toward all sexual matters, including male and female homosexuality. The churches, he said, were now coming to see that a new ethic was needed to answer the problems of the ever-increasing number of city dwellers, and particularly the large proportion of single men and women who virtually become lost in our large cities. The CRH was set up in the Bay Area to start grappling with the complex questions facing this sector of the population, and it was through an interdenominational conference held there on the problems of "Young Adults in Metropolis" that most of the Los Angeles ministers had been introduced to the homosexual question.

After lunch, Donald Lucas of the Mattachine Society of San Francisco described the origin of the Council there and its operation. Los Angeles Attorney Herbert Selwyn discussed the California laws applicable to homosexual acts, after which the San Franciscans told the Los Angeles group that they were on their own if they wished to establish a similar Council in Southern California. They did so wish, and an ad hoc committee, composed of the Revs. Alex Smith and Ron Ohlson, as well as Sten Russell of the Daughters of Bilitis and W. Dorr Legg of ONE, Inc., was chosen to arrange for the next meeting.

Over twenty meetings have been held since that date, in members' homes, in ONE's offices, and in the First Methodist Churches of Glendale and Los Angeles, as well as an inspiring weekend Retreat attended by thirty ministers and Homophiles at the Presbyterian Camp Grounds in Pacific Palisades. Most of these meetings have been devoted to careful efforts to lay a sound organizational basis, and to acquaint ministers and Homophiles with one another's problems and ways of thinking.

Ministerial representation on the Council has so far been largely limited to United Church of Christ, Methodist, Episcopal, and Presbyterian clergymen, but not from any intention to so limit participation. For awhile, members of ONE, Inc., carried most of the Homophile side, but participation has now expanded to members of eight local organizations and publications.

The first ten months were on a provisional, "organizing committee" basis. In April, 1966, the newly named Southern California Council on Religion and the Homophile was "christened" at Attorney Selwyn's office when the five original Directors (the Revs. Alex Smith, Kenneth Wahrenbrock, and Hargie Likins, along with W. Dorr Legg of ONE and James Kepner of *Pursuit* magazine) signed the

Articles of Incorporation. A set of by-laws was adopted by the Board in May and ratified (with several minor changes proposed) at the first official membership meeting, held at Glendale First Methodist Church, June 8, 1966, one year and a week after the first Los Angeles gathering.

It had been an exciting year – a year of exploration, of defining the problem areas, of getting acquainted, and, on both sides, of shedding preconceptions. Homophiles who came to the group thinking of all clergymen as Puritanic thunderers, or as oozing piety, had their eyes opened, just as did ministers who had stereotyped and unflattering notions about homosexuals. It was a year of spiritual growth for all concerned, and a year in which Council representatives began to present the concerns of the Council to other organizations, both Homophile and religious.

ONE Institute continued to take an active part in "The Council on Religion and the Homophile" as an interested supporter. Faculty members spoke for many church groups and participated in retreats and interdenominational conferences on religion as a social institution. During the early 1970s the growth of Metropolitan Community Church branches of Dignity, Integrity, the Jewish Temples, and other denominational groupings gradually superseded "The Council." With the opening of the ONE Institute Graduate School in 1981, several courses on "Religion and Sexual Minorities," "Morality and the Homophile Lifestyle," and others were included in the curriculum.

ONE Institute Extension Lectures: Religion

February 2, 1958 (#17) "Religion and the Homophile," by Julian M. Underwood and panel.

January 31, 1959 (#23) "Must Christians Live With Guilt?" by Rt. Rev. Thomas Martin and Rt. Rev. Bernard Newman, American Eastern Orthodox Church, Las Vegas, NV.

May 8, 1960 (#42) "Christ and the Homosexual," book by Rev. Robert Wood, reviewed by James Kepner Jr. and panel.

January 28, 1962 (#61) "The Homosexual seeks a Religious Focus," by Sten Russell and panel.

April 1, 1962 (#64) "Anti-Homosexuality in Religions," by W. Dorr

Legg.

January 26, 1963 (#71) "Man's Laws and God's Laws," by Fr. James G. Jones, Director, St. Leonard's House, Chicago, Episcopal.

May 7, 1963 (#77) "The Path of Truth," by Fr. Bernard Newman (see above).

June 7, 1964 (#89) "Contrasts in Morality: U.S. and Abroad," by Dr. Dean Franklin.

January 29, 1966 (#103) "What Can We Do to Help Those in Trouble?" by Rev. Alex Smith, Downtown Methodist Service Center.

June 5, 1966 (#112) "The Church and the Homosexual, a Re-evaluation," by Rev. Morton T. Kelsey, Episcopal theologian.

October 2, 1966 (#114) "The Homosexuals Experience of the Church," by Don Lucas, Mattachine Society, San Francisco.

April 2, 1967 (#120) "New Trends in the Church," by Rev. Dr. Hargie Likins, United Church of Christ.

June 2, 1968 (#131) "The Churches Look at Homosexuality Today," by Fr. Derek Lang, O.S.M. and panel.

October 5, 1969 (#146) "Why a Homophile Church?" by the Rev. Troy D. Perry, Metropolitan Community Churches.

July 8, 1970 (#155) "Homosexuality and Roman Catholic Theology" by the Rev. Dr. Herman Van de Spyker, Theologian, Amsterdam, Holland.

January 28, 1972 (#167) "The Gay Challenge to Religion and the Churches," by the Rev. Troy Perry and panel of clergy.

March 4, 1973 (#183) "Dignity: A National Program for Gay Catholics," by Joseph Killian, a Dignity founder, and panel.

May 7, 1974 (#193) "Sex, Gay Love and the Bible," a panel discussion.

January 4, 1976 (#220) "How Judaism Came Out," by Jarow Rogovin and panel.

March 3, 1977 (#229) "Lives of Quiet Desperation," by the Rev. Dwain Hauser and panel.

June 5, 1983 (#289) "The Triangle Project for the Young," by the Rev. Albert Ogle, Episcopalian.

March 4, 1984 (#294) "Beth Chayim Chaddshim," by Rabbi Janet Marder, Los Angeles.

May 10, 1988 (#334) "The Radical Religious Right and American Education," by Betty Brooks, Ph.D., formerly, California State University, Long Beach.

The Audiovisual Collection of ONE's Baker Memorial Library includes a video of lecture no. 334.

CHAPTER 10

BIOLOGY

With its opening class, October 22, 1956, ONE Institute bravely tackled Biology as its first and leading introduction into the uncharted field of Homophile Studies. There was every expectation that so serious and scientific a discipline would provide solid documentation for irrefutable basic principles upon which could be founded a scientific understanding of homosexual behavior and of those who so behaved.

Such expectations were rudely dashed when it was discovered that, so far as most textbooks on Biology recorded, there was no such topic. How could this be? Had not biologists long been making observations of human behavior?

Institute students soon realized that although biology claims that it "treats of living organisms," it does so in very narrowly–constrained ways. With this in mind, students found themselves embarked on a Socratic inquiry as to what in fact Biology does investigate and what it has actually discovered. They began to thread their ways through endless masses of information about taxonomy, genotypes, and a host of other information which, however useful in some connections, had little applicability to Homophile Studies. The crucial questions students asked focused on the cell, its chromosomes, and what biologists could tell about cell development from the initial point of insemination through successive stages up to the mature human organism. Was there some kind of "road map," the inquirers asked? The answer, never quite clearly stated, was that, yes, human cells by elaborate processes, not well understood as yet, do go through a series of developmental phases, juvenile, pubertal, and mature by which a human organism becomes capable of replicating itself. But was it true that *all* human organisms followed an inexorable process of maturation *impelling* them to replication?

This seemed roughly what biologists had assumed as true. Did this mean that *all* human bodies contained identifiable, deterministic structures in their cells which would lead to such a result? Not exactly. The best that could be said was that in a *statistically large number* of instances this formula seemed true. The Socratic method seemed to be finding a gap in the scientific regimen of biology. ONE Institute students quickly named this gap "The Heterosexual Assumption," an assumption which claimed to describe a *universal* norm. Yet Kinsey had already designated any sexual behavior the human body was capable of doing as natural.[1]

Biology begs the question by affirming that such questions fall outside its legitimate subject matter. The following extracts from faculty papers pose questions for which biology does not appear to have answers.

Socratic inquiries continued at some length and with considerable insistence. For instance, would biology maintain that reproduction is an inborn human drive? Would biology claim that the millions of men and women the world over and throughout history who have chosen not to reproduce are in some way defective? If so, biologists seem to align themselves with the theologians rather than scientists.

Again, has biology demonstrated that there is this innate tropism by which *all* human males at a certain stage in their development find themselves irresistibly attracted toward looking at and touching the female body? What of the massive evidence that this is not always true, that *some* males *never* regard the female body as attractive; that *some* females *never* find themselves drawn toward looking at and touching the male body?

Or, stating the question from the opposite perspective, has biology scientifically demonstrated that *all* males find all parts of another male's body, including his sex organs, without attraction or interest? Is there biological proof that *some* males do not find the bodies of other males, including their sex organs, highly pleasurable to touch intimately; that *some* females do not find intimate physical bodily contact with the bodies of other females highly pleasurable? What scientific evidence is there that the allegedly "natural" repugnance against intimate male/male and intimate female/female bodily contacts is not a socially induced and irrational taboo?

In an article "It Just Isn't Natural," then faculty member, Jim Kepner, lists a number of the salient questions asked of Biology.

---

[1] Alfred C. Kinsey "Concepts of Normality and Abnormality in Sexual Behavior," in *Psychosexual Development in Health and Disease*. (New York: Grume and Straton, 1949) pp.11-32.

It Just Isn't Natural
By Jim Kepner[2]

One of the most common charges against homosexuality, and one that the critic seems to feel is devastating and unanswerable, is that homosexuality is unnatural, or, as phrased in many laws, a crime against nature. To the homosexual, it may seem hard to understand how such harmless acts can be considered crimes at all – particularly against Nature. Yet even the otherwise tolerant person will come up with that old canard, "But really, it just isn't natural." (p.8)

What is natural to man? What is not? This depends in very large part on what man's nature is. Without becoming sidetracked into theological quibbles, we can generally agree that whether or not man has a spirit, he surely has flesh, and that is, to say the least, rather fundamental to his nature; his nature is at bottom biological, like the birds and the bees and the flowers.

Our object here is to get to the root of this notion of natural and unnatural acts. Even the most other-worldly must concede these terms do refer to the world of Nature, to the plant and animal kingdoms and their environs. A thing commonly found in Nature is, *per se*, natural. Even if some may still want to judge it immoral, they can't logically call it unnatural.

Our liberal critic doesn't want to concede so easily. He admits it's a shame homosexuals are mistreated, but is disturbed about the alleged purposes of nature. "Homosexuality," he says, "is unnatural because it is against the purposes of nature." This concept is most popular with those who have the least real acquaintance with Nature. If our critic would open his eyes and investigate the birds and the bees and the flowers before generalizing about them, he might be a bit more cautious.

One philosopher may say, for example, that Self-Preservation is the heir of these purposes operating in nature and inherent in every creature. An experienced biologist could dispense quickly with this argument. Self-preservation is of course extremely important to many creatures, and all-important to a few, but extreme self-sacrifice is about as common in Nature. In hundreds of species, it is natural for an individual to destroy itself to produce the next generation.

---

[2] *MAG* V:8 (August\September, 1957), pp.8-12.

"But, ah, the next generation," our critic will say. "That's just what I meant in the first place. Homosexuality is unnatural exactly because the chief purpose of Nature is the preservation of the species. We're right back to the birds and the bees and the flowers."

Actually, our critic has a bit to learn about the birds and the bees and the flowers, though it's hard to imagine he can be so ill-informed about the bees, at least. Preservation, or reproduction of the species, simply does not require that every individual must procreate, or even try to. Every schoolboy knows that in a hive swarming with thousands of bees, only the queen and a few short lived drones (of no further use to the community) are even capable of sex and repro- duction. The rest have other allotted tasks. Like man, the social insects have learned the advantages of division of labor, and each job, including reproduction, is left to specialists (though in the start of an ant colony, as in early human societies, the reproducer must be a jill-of-all-trades until the colony is large enough to permit division of labor; then she becomes a mere egg-laying machine). This should be emphasized. (p.8)

According to the storybooks, the monogamous family seemed well established throughout nature, carrying with it the same sex roles our society considers proper, the male as a good provider and protector of the family and the female having all the maternal instinct, and blessed fidelity. Actually, examples of this idyllic picture are somewhat rare – a few birds and such disreputable animals as the wolf, the fox, and the weasel.

Paternal instincts are so far from being universal as to be quite the exception. Mother love is more common, but not universal. Among ostriches, seahorses, and others, the father serves the "natural" maternal role and females have nothing to do with hatching, nursing, or child care.

As for homosexuality, we find it cropping up throughout nature, not perhaps in every species, but certainly in every other one, and very pronounced in many (as our Biological Survey Course at ONE Institute illustrates). The fact that a heavy incidence of homosexuality is reported among almost every sort of domesticated animal could indicate that closer observation would turn up even more evidence in the wild breeds. Gide noted, in *Corydon* (an excellent, though somewhat dated essay on this subject) that every breeder seemed quite astonished to discover homosexuality among his animals, few sus- pecting that the story is similar whether one raises ducks or pigeons, goats, or cows.

Male frogs in heat often embrace other males, but observers suppose this is because bullfrogs aren't very adept at recognizing the sex of a prospective partner. With fireflies it's more definite, and quite a sight since the males have all the fire, and sometimes gather by the thousands in glittering, orgiastic stag parties.

It could be argued that homosexuality preceded heterosexuality in evolution, since the Copromonas and other one-celled Paramecia which alternate sexual reproduction with simple cell division form a union of like individuals. (In other Paramecia, apparently a later development, sex differentiation occurs, and the individuals who unite sexually are distinctly different, comparable to the sperm and ova of higher creatures.) Nor is sex change or hermaphroditism at all rare among animals.

What we discover in the long run, and the evidence is overwhelming, is that nature is infinitely more varied, more "tolerant" than those moralists who so glibly use the terms natural and unnatural.

Ford and Beach, in their *Patterns Of Sexual Behavior* (ref. p.171), maintain that, "When it is realized that 100 per cent of the males in certain societies engage in homosexual as well as heterosexual alliances, and when it is understood that many men and women in our own society are equally capable of relations with partners of the same or opposite sex, and finally, when it is recognized that this same situation obtains in many species of subhuman primates, then it should be clear that one cannot classify homosexual and heterosexual tendencies as being mutually exclusive or even opposed to each other." Also, "The cross-cultural and cross-species comparisons... combine to suggest that a biological tendency for inversion of sexual behavior is inherent in most if not all mammals, including the human species."

Finding homosexuality (and other variant sex patterns) so widespread in nature, we need no longer permit it to be labeled unnatural. Homosexuality is a distinct part (if perhaps minor) of the natural pattern of things. (p.10)

Sex is a very complicated matter, as Freudians say. Nature frequently produces curious by-products, and throughout Nature, sexual energies are commonly diverted to non-procreative uses. So if we can discover that homosexuals are sometimes useful to society, we needn't be unduly apologetic about the waste of a certain amount of sperm or ova. Nature produces both in fantastic abundance and most of it goes to waste under the best of conditions.

Our critic is persistent: "But homosexuality uses the organs for purposes they weren't designed for." Well, we haven't seen the blueprints, but putting things to new uses is only human. Everything civilized about man is functionally unnatural. Education is a process of reshaping or distorting the "natural clay." We weren't designed to fly. Our hands weren't designed for typewriters or paint brushes. Who worries? We buried Rousseau's "Noble Savage" a generation ago. It is man's nature to change his nature. It is natural for man to be unnatural.

Our critic may interject at this point that homosexuality attempts to foil the universal law of Nature that opposites attract and likes repel. This may be a universal law of electromagnetism, but it is far from being true in Biology. If it were so, we would expect to find lions trying to mate with mice. It is almost always erroneous to take a law derived from one science and arbitrarily try to superimpose it on another science. In many species, male and female are so alike that a male in rut apparently can't tell another male from a female except by smell. Many recent psychological studies have shown that among humans at least, like attracts like in the great majority of cases. And again, a reference to those Copromonas where sexual congress takes place between sexually undifferentiated identical twins.

"But," our critic comes back, on a different tack, "Heterosexuality is wholesome and beautiful, while homosexuality is degenerate, sickly and vulgar."

Another old argument. But, pray tell, what was degenerate or vulgar about Johnathan's love for David, described in the Bible as "surpassing the love of woman." If perhaps the proportion of degeneracy among homosexuals in our present society seems high, it is because society forces most homosexuals into the role. The names of Ruth and Naomi, Plato, Sappho, Erasmus, Michelangelo, Tennyson, Florence Nightingale, Carpenter, and Gide are testimonials to the fact that homosexuality is not synonymous with degeneracy. Nor do homosexuals monopolize degeneracy. Any newspaper is daily witness to the degeneracy, vulgarity, and sickness of much of contemporary heterosexuality. And that idealized picture of happy heterosexual life is a bit more common in story books than in real life.

One last word from our critic, "But everyone has a duty to reproduce himself."

Whatever for?

The population of the United States and the world is increasing at an alarming rate. Not a single state in the U.S. is prepared for the deluge of children entering already overcrowded, understaffed schools. We need a lower, not a higher, birthrate. One would think that a handful of people who shirked this duty would be congratulated. And in some countries suffering from fantastic population explosions, giving birth to more children is socially immoral.

Society needs to face the fact that not everyone is fit to be a parent. Many homosexuals certainly would not make good parents (most heterosexuals are bad enough). Why force the creation of families that are only too likely to be maladjusted?

Instead, why not use homosexuals in those functions of modern society where a family is a drawback? Many scientific jobs run the serious risk of genetic damage. Why not reserve those jobs for men and women whose habits insure against the tragedy of monstrous offspring? Many jobs require a nomadic existence. Why wreck or strain families by putting heterosexuals in such jobs? There are many other occupations for which homosexuals show talent. Instead of trying to fit round pegs in square holes, society would benefit by learning to make full and tolerant use of the talents possessed by homosexuals. Ancient Greece found rich dividends in such policy. It could pay off again today.

If only our society would learn to accept Nature at face value (and not only in regard to homosexuality) and lay off the counterfeit... for this must be clear: the sex mores of our society are counterfeit. They are unnatural, against Nature. And every day we read in the papers the shocking price our society must pay for its rigid and unnatural attitudes.

Dr. Ray Evans' article, "Biological Factors in Sexual Behavior," contains many valuable and challenging paragraphs. His role as lecturer and faculty member has been referred to in Chapter 6.

Biological Factors in
Sexual Behavior
By Ray Evans, Ph.D.[3]

In mammals low on the evolutionary scale, sexual behavior occurs only when fertilization can take place, and is thus closely tied to reproduction, but that is less true of higher animals such as apes, and still less of humans. (p.113)

This progressive reduction in control over sexual behavior by the sex hormones is related to changes in the structure of the brain as the evolutionary scale is ascended. The most recently evolved and the most complex part of the brain, the cerebral cortex, constitutes less than one quarter of the brain in the lowest mammals. In apes it is proportionately much larger and more complex, and in adult humans, a cortex of an extremely complex nature forms ninety per cent of the brain. As the cerebral cortex increases in size and complexity, its control over sexual behavior increases, while the

---

[3] *QTLY* IV:4 (Fall 1961), pp.113-120.

influence of sex hormones decreases. (p.113)

To summarize the mammalian sex pattern: As the evolutionary scale is ascended, there is decreased control over sexual behavior by sex hormones and increased influence of the cerebral cortex. Also increased with advancement on the scale are variety in sexual behavior, dependence upon practice for efficient performance, and selectiveness in sex partners. The mammalian pattern is further characterized by common physiological reflexive elements, sexual behavior before puberty, self stimulation, stimulation of the partner prior to intercourse, occasional relations between species, homosexual behavior, and a predominance of heterosexual coitus. (p.114)

Theoretically most important is the greater modification of sexual behavior through experience in the male than in the female, which suggests that the cerebral cortex may play a larger role in the male. The part of the brain known as the hypothalamus is essential in organizing the mating responses of female animals, but there is no evidence that it contributes to sexual behavior in males. On the other hand, if the cerebral cortex is surgically removed, female animals continue to display mating behavior and may even become pregnant, whereas males deprived of the cortex immediately become totally unresponsive to sexual stimulation. (p.114)

In humans the kinds of stimulation and the types of situations that become capable of producing sexual excitement are determined largely by learning, and the actual behavior through which this excitement is expressed depends heavily upon the individual's previous experience. Perhaps most crucial of all is that man, with his highly developed cerebral cortex, is capable of thinking about himself, and his sexual behavior is thus highly influenced by fantasy and imagination. That can foster richer, more varied, or more intense sexual experience, but it may also prolong the disrupting effects of negative attitudes and feelings on sexual performance and satisfaction.

People's sexual attitudes and behavior are learned essentially from other humans, and are largely governed by the social structure of their group. Every society accumulates codes of acceptable sexual behavior which are passed from one generation to the next. Despite group pressure to behave in the traditional manner, however, there are always individuals who disregard the code. Heterosexual intercourse is the predominant form of sexual behavior for the majority of adults in all known human societies, although it is never the only form, and all cultures are strongly biased in that direction. (p.115)

Tendencies leading to relations with individuals of the same sex are perhaps not as strong as those toward the opposite sex, but they do exist in a large majority of people, even though they may not be recognized or acted upon. People who are totally lacking in any conscious homosexual leanings are as much a product of cultural conditioning as are the exclusive homosexuals, both extremes representing movement away from the original intermediate condition of capacity for both forms of sexual expression. (p.117)

Further, if it is acknowledged that the relative strengths of dispositions toward the same and the opposite sex may vary, then it must also be admitted that for certain individuals the inclination toward the same sex may be stronger. The fact that homosexual behavior at times is essentially a matter of environmental influence does not mean it is always or exclusively a result of learning. Nor does the fact that in certain cultures it is customary for all males to engage in homosexual behavior signify that all homosexuality is determined by experience. Even in those groups there is undoubtedly individual variation in behavior, feelings, and preferences regarding homosexuality. There is no doubt that sexual behavior is more variable in man than in other animals, that his cerebral cortex is relatively larger, and that he is more capable of learning. It does not necessarily follow, however, that all human sexual behavior is therefore a direct result of learning, although man's complex nervous system does predispose him to the widest range of stimulation and response. Finally, the very fact that throughout the mammalian scale, a great many more males than females engage in homosexual behavior is in itself suggestive of a constitutional factor.

Attempts to account for homosexuality solely on the basis of learning as a result of experience leave other questions open. For instance, countless people are exposed to homosexuality or actually experiment with it, but for only certain ones does it seemingly become the only possible way of life. Such differences occur among siblings, even in families lacking such usual "explanatory" circumstances as treating the boy as a girl, absence or inadequacy of the father, or presence of a seductive mother. Among animals also, homosexual behavior is manifested only by some of them, and that is true even in groups of laboratory animals whose experiences presumably are reasonably similar. Within isolated groups such as prisons or the armed services, only certain individuals engage in homosexual practices, perhaps because of prior experiences, or conceivably because of a different innate disposition. Despite innumerable case histories and expansive psychoanalytic "explanations," there is no incontrovertible evidence as to how homosexuality is acquired through life experiences. There is no known set of conditions which invariably leads to its development. For any individual, only after-the-fact speculation is possible, which by its very nature can never be verified by that person.

Homosexuality is only one of a great many phenomena which

have been subjected to protracted controversy regarding the relative importance of hereditary and environmental factors, and obviously no final answer is yet possible. (p.118)

There is no denying the very important role of experience in the development of sex patterns, though the limits are fixed constitutionally, but it is still necessary to understand explicitly the nature of forces promoting homosexuality in those in whom that is made possible through the inheritance of factor X. The life experiences of some individuals with that factor in their genes are probably such that they may be the ones who temporarily engage in homosexual behavior only under special circumstances, such as isolation from women. When virtually all pressures and attitudes of parents and society tend to teach and enforce heterosexual behavior, it is perplexing how anyone learns to be homosexual. There is no reliable information as to precisely how that comes about, but there are clues for exploration. (p.119)

Review:
Biological Factors
in Male Homosexuality
By Ray Evans Ph.D.[4]

The journal, *Medical Aspects Of Human Sexuality,* (July, 1973) contains an important article, "Biological Factors In Male Homosexuality," by Ray B. Evans, Ph.D. Dr. Evans is an Associate Professor of Psychiatry, Loma Linda University School of Medicine, Loma Linda, California, and has since 1965 been a Trustee of the National Advisory Board of the Institute for the Study of Human Resources. He has had numerous other articles published in scientific journals.

The current Evans research findings include highly pertinent data obtained from homosexual volunteers supplied to him by ONE, Incorporated, as he states in his article. These findings begin to supply a much-needed corrective to the psychiatric and psychological extremists who would have us believe that homosexuality can be explained only in terms of the developmental experiences of children, particularly those imposed by mother, father, and, to a lesser degree, siblings. In opposition to such theories, Dr. Evans writes, "Recent reports have restored the likelihood that such (biological) factors are

---

[4] *LTR* XVIII:7 (July, 1973), pp.3,6.

important, if not crucial." Whereas the psychoanalysts consider parental influences crucial, particularly the mother's, Dr. Evans suggests quite otherwise, basing his conclusions upon a carefully developed line of reasoning developed from the data his research has revealed.

The importance to child-rearing practices and public attitudes toward homosexuality to be derived from such findings can hardly be overestimated. Clearly, if the upbringing of children is what is at fault, then change the upbringing and homosexuality would be expected to vanish. Parents who refused to conform to supposedly "correct methods" would be judged to be culpable. Those who have suffered from such faulty training would be required to seek immediate psychotherapy, mend their ways, and turn from what some psychotherapists have long called the "disease" of homosexuality.

Because "experts" told them to do so, countless thousands of men and women have spent large sums of money trying to rid themselves of this "disease." The mental suffering to themselves and their families can never be calculated, nor can the moral responsibility for imposing such views upon them ever be forgiven in the day of judgment. Innumerable courts have in their blind and culpable ignorance imposed probationary sentences of expensive psychotherapy upon countless thousands of hapless men and women. Worst of all, in violation of all tenable ethical and legal standards, those refused probation and remanded to jails and prisons have been subjected to experimental chemical and surgical tampering by hack therapists who have blandly preyed upon their subject's helplessness as full justification for taking the opportunity to indulge in damaging so-called "research."

Now, thanks to Dr. Evans, and, it must not be overlooked, thanks to the fact that ONE has for so long struggled to exist so as to be ready and available to assist in corrective scientific work of this sort, changes are beginning to come about. The role of the Institute for the Study of Human Resources should not be overlooked in this context either, for without its steady, consistent backing of ONE's Research programs, ONE would be right back where it was many years ago, i.e., having ambitious research hopes and plans but no funds with which to do anything about them.

There isn't space here to give a detailed description of what Dr. Evans' findings have shown. The full article should be read and studied. What can be done is to draw some conclusions as to their significance for the welfare and future status of the literally millions of persons to whom such findings apply. If, as he writes, "The results indicate that biological factors in at least some homosexuals cannot be ignored," then research, public policy and social attitudes are going to be faced with the need for doing a right-about face so drastic that a lot of overblown reputations will be damaged, and many vested financial interests are going to find their dollar flows dwindling down to mere trickles. Police and prison practices will require overhauling, and the courts will be forced to face the ethically painful possibility that merely because some statute says so does not necessarily mean that such legislative perversions are "law," or that a judge can be excused from evaluating this question.

To regard homosexuality "in at least some homosexuals" as having "a biological factor" is to announce the start of an entirely new ball game. For neither therapy nor the courts can be permitted to have any jurisdiction over classes of natural persons: short, tall, brown-haired, blue-eyed, or whatever. Likewise, homosexuals. "But it is behavior that we deplore, not persons," some will say. Unfortunately for such protesters, they are going to have to learn the lesson that society is inherently pluralistic, always has been and always will be, as Nature's stern laws have decreed. Nature neither deplores nor approves. Nature merely presents realities. Of such realities, none are imposed more imperatively than "biological factors." We had better start learning what this means, or we shall find Nature's punishments equally impartial and drastic and just.

Sections from articles by a British/American author, widely published and writing in ONE's publications as D.B. Vest, follow. Both as ONE Institute lecturer and instructor in a series of two invitational seminars for faculty only, Vest's influence on the study of biology at ONE Institute has been provocative and highly influential.

The Isophyl
as a Biological Variant
By D. B. Vest[5]

From the Kinsey school to the average sociologist, we are told "the homosexual," to quote the latest study in the British Medical Journal, "is the victim of his own emotional problem and environmental factors, not a victim of hormonal imbalance, alcoholism, or

---

[5] *QTLY* I:2 (Summer 1958), p.43-47.

genius." As one of our most self-assured weeklies rendered the report, this person is neither more "hippy" nor highbrow than the rest. This doctrine certainly is agreeable to all conservatives, for it contains for them the comforting, though disproved, doctrine that they alone are natural and all the other patterns of Eros are unnatural. Here theologian and scientist could find a common platform for excommunicating the variant. (p.43)

Even Humanist Progressives are tempted to approve the verdict "it's all acquired." For they can read it in the light of their own desire. For this ridiculous peccadillo is no genetic danger. It will not put any obstacle in the way of breeding nor is there any risk that, should these social aberrants breed, they could pass on their quirk. For it is not a racial factor. It's simply a childish prank. (p.44)

The artist type has, however, too long been known for the classification to be dismissed as fictitious on such statistically shallow grounds as such reports (e.g., this last from Britain) are built. The jester type, too, has been well marked in history. Such characters as Rahere, the powerful licensed wit at Henry the Angevin's court and the founder of St. Bartholomew's Hospital, illustrate the isophylic energy when given leave to express itself, while the specific costume chosen, the variegated multicolored dress, the cap and bells headgear, and the ithyphallic rod of office show the exuberant displayfulness. (p.44)

The person of inborn inversion, whose psychophysical binary nature has never been in doubt to himself, early learns like the intelligent and harmless animals to keep out of the way of the raptors who treat him as their natural prey and to employ protective coloration and movement. (p.44)

Erotic energy that would have gone, in the male, into siring children by a swarm of mates now goes into building up a way of life much more complex, extensive, and commanding than that of the family. This new structure is the society with its three-fold combination of crafts and arts, laws and ideals, and those devices of mutual personal expression such as liveries, vestments, taboos, and annulations, ordeals, and displays which give rise to carnivals, dances, dramas, and mysteries. This is what is rightly called social heredity. Its power appears already among subhuman species.

All man's many cultures from the primal group rites of identity which he integrated psycho-socially, every economic invention (fire, instruments, costume), every aspect of civilization has its origin and fount in the inventiveness, the designingness, the decorativeness of those who could stem the erotic drive from short circuiting away at immediate physiological level in repetitive unconscious breeding, the blind persistence of animal breeding, and raise it to the conscious development of man's specific heredity-of-knowledge, social heredity. In the Paleolithic, we now know, the extraordinary art of early stone age men which inspire the small gang armed only with flints and sticks to attack mammoths, rhinoceros, and cave bear, this magical spell-faith was exercised for the group by a small caste of traveling artists.

From that time onwards through the small castes of the metal workers (as Gordon Childe has pointed out), from the slenderly-built Pictish bronze workers, to the traveling fraternities of the tinker smiths in the Iron Age, it was these pre-Masonic brotherhoods practicing their mystery that are the growing edge of the arts and crafts, and who keep blended the delight in the chanted rhythm of the workmanship with the utilitarian value, the weapon or the utensil, as it is finally fashioned and ready for employment. Hence their work was considered not only as outwardly efficient but also as charged with meaning and manna, e.g., the sacred cup, spear and sword. (p.45)

Certain it is that the original maker of the social heredity is not at the start the Lawgiver such as Moses or Solon. He is the seer, the priest, the vates. It is quite clear that when we trace back this type as far as we can (e.g., in that extraordinarily retentive social pattern as we see it in the proto Chinese culture), we find that the source of the seer is a boy; they were called Shi in early Chinese. These lads were thrown into trance (the method is still used in India and among the Bantu tribes in South Africa) by their trainer and so used as a medium or metagnome. If he retained the gift after puberty, he then became a seer in his own right. Such was the primal and greatest of all the Greek seers, Teiresias, who was also claimed to be fully hermaphrodite. (p.46)

The Isophyl is therefore panaesthetic and so neither committed to fertilization nor conception, but employs the undifferentiated libido to retain a mind of full compass (e.g., with the originality of creativity), an emotional life of the *civis* rather than the *domus*, and a freedom of fashion that exhibits the symptoms of continual experimentation.

As to the future, the value of this experiment of Nature looks as though it must rise rapidly. For not only does mankind, involved in an increasingly complex civilization increasingly require original thinkers rather than repetitive breeders, but, literally, the breeders are bankrupting civilization. As Arthur Clarke, the mathematically-minded writer of science forecasts, has pointed out in his "Standing Room Only" article in the April number of *Harpers*, not only is the deluge of new births threatening us with starvation (all population experts have been pointing this out for the last 50 years), but Clarke has had the courage to say that Nature probably knew what she did when she made man sexually polymorphous. For only if Nature makes an unbreeding way of life influential can mankind be saved from its own fatal fecundity. (p.47)

Editorial Comments[6]

The lead article in this issue, by D. B. Vest, is the sixth which he has written for ONE's publications. In "Evolution's Next Step" (ONE, November, 1953), he described our society as one inherently self-destructive, due to the failure to develop socially and emotionally in pace with our intellectual and technological advances.

He rejected the popular emphases upon moral, social, and educational short-comings, viewing the problem in biological and evolutionary terms. A main cause of the difficulty lay, he said, in the over-development of the fore-brain, with its "disbalanced activity." He urged our society to consciously encourage those intergrades lying between "the wholly specialized male and female."

It is these intergrades, he felt, which could furnish the greatly needed cohesion so lacking in our society, riven as it automatically is by its own stubborn insistence on male-female polarity and the tottering family structures erected precariously upon that foundation.

"What is Religion?" (ONE, June, 1954) introduced his own distinctive term, the Isophyl, derived from the Greek, "iso" (equal, the same) and "philos" (loving). In "A Future for the Isophyl" (March, 1955) he considerably expanded his theory of the intergrade, pointing out our need in this age for new social types to meet the social situations now confronting us. He drew particular attention to the careful distinction to be made between "panaesthetic response," which is "purely erotic rather than specifically sexual," and the term "sexual" as used in its biological connotation, i.e., concerned with reproduction.

Again in "The Isophyl as a Biological Variant" (*Quarterly*, Summer, 1958), he continued his discussion of isophylia as a phenomenon, genetically triggered and indicative of "the binary nature" of the intergrade. He contrasted the Freudian theory that each adult passes through an isophyllic phase with his own view that the paedomorph is a type retaining in maturity "the binary unspecialized

---

[6] W. D. Legg, "Editorial," *QTLY* III:4 (Fall 1960).

nature of the boy."

He saw the Isophyl, by virtue of the sexually polymorphous capacity humans possess, as employing "the undifferentiated libido to retain a mind of full compass" throughout maturity. Thus, in consciously controlling and balancing the activities of the thalamus and the cortex, the civilic, or social, contribution of the Isophyl is made.

"Swish or Swim" (ONE, January, 1959) entered a protest against repressing "the profound need for expression" felt by the isophyl, and warned that such repression is "very often the root cause of a deep neurosis." In conclusion he counseled the isophyllic minority not to turn against its own minorities and to bear in mind that Nature would appear, "as Carl Jung has long asserted, aimed at producing... what he calls the great hermaphrodite."

The Isophyl in Society

In his current article, printed herein, Vest further extends his theory of paedomorphy in such a way as to describe a sub-genus, which he terms *homo crescens*. He urges the view that, if man remains content to be merely sapient, he will be unable to cope with the rising crescendo of the problems of our times. The alternate way and the solution lies, he feels, in conscious employment of neoteny as a tool for the attainment of social goals. *Homo crescens* would then be defined as man ever-maturing and producing, by not reproducing, just as the horticulturist learns to extend his flowering seasons by the prevention of seed formation.

During the years since his first articles have appeared in ONE's publications, Vest's theories have come in for considerable discussion at ONE Institute. Although they have occasioned much controversy and will continue to do so, it is hoped, there is general agreement that his insistence is entirely sound that homophilia, or isophylia, must be viewed broadly from the standpoint of many scholarly disciplines.

It is writers like Vest who have sounded the death-knell of the old notions that human variations and deviations necessarily involve neurosis, psychosis, endocrine imbalance, the Oedipus complex, or such hypotheses. ONE considers itself privileged in having been able to publish so distinguished and provocative a series of papers.

The Phylogeny of Homo Crescens
By D. B. Vest[7]

Not so long ago the sciences believed that the one sure way to knowledge and power lay in an ever narrowing focus. The rise of ecology and the concepts of gestalt have made a quiet and yet profound revolution in this respect. We now know it is far more realistic to view "the world as an organic whole" (in Nicolai Lossky's famous phrase) than to believe it must be in its ultimate structure and meaning a jumble of incoherent particles and unconnected drives. The significance of form has reasserted itself against the mistaken "realism of matter," and intelligence has now been defined, not as the mental force to break things down, but the power to recognize correlations till now unperceived.

This deep shift in basic concept has given us a stronger fulcrum for leverage on all the anomalous problems which the scientific process has exposed and the academic specialists have shunned. Therefore, it should help us to get under the isophylic anomaly. Indeed we might hope that, as "hypothesis" means an insight that penetrates below appearances down to common roots, we could come upon some such basic correlation.

Let us then assume, and it is a moderate and more than moderately secure, assumption, that the isophylic shoot stems out from a root-complex of urges, drives, potentialities, and explorations that age generated in the deep, unfinished, still-to-be-developed resources of human vitality. We should then be able to throw light on this particular behavior-pattern by recognizing parallel developments.

To start then with our earliest knowledge of that intense and rapid divergence, self-named, prematurely auto-labeled, *homo sapiens*, better called *homo crescens*, "man the still-growing." As Leakey (the now famous finder of maybe the first certain tool-maker, zinjanthropus) has said, this fossil confirms what all other "hominid" (mannish but not quite manly) skeletons show, i.e., the tremendous pace (in comparison with natural change in any other animal) at which dimorphism (the radical difference between male and female) began to disappear, as "trial men" became not "true men" or "full men" (we

---

[7] D. B. Vest, "The Phylogeny of Homo Crescens," *QTLY* III:4 (Fall 1960), pp.252-57.

have yet no idea what that creature will be) but men able to direct their fate, to shape their society and to think, experiment, and explore themselves.

That is point one. There is an inherent drive in man's make-up which is rapidly modifying extreme masculinity-femininity into an intergrade type. The extreme dimorphism was valuable as long as a parent-and-sib pack, a hunting family, was the maximum efficient group. With the rise of crafts, arts, and rudiment sciences (e.g. agriculture), the settlement and its imprint and precipitation, the townlet, appears, and with the townlet's craftsmen (seers as much as sowers, and weavers of words equally with weavers of wools) the blended bimorphic (instead of the disparate dimorphic) typing becomes of value. Social heredity and those who produce its patterns become as important as (and increasingly more important than) those who produce, by physical reproduction, the next generation of body-minds whose frame of mind and impress of behaviour-pattern will be given them by the social heredity, the volume of ideas, comprehensions, perspectives, and goals.

Point two stresses even more the role of the intergrade, the bimorphic, the ambinatured. We now know that "man is the foetalization of the ape" (L. Bolk) as "the dog is the foetalization of the wolf." All mammals owe their supremacy over the once-dominant order of animals, the reptiles, because they care for their young so that by feeding the newborn with the parent's own milk, the young can exist in a womb-state outside the parent's body, a womb-state that permits further brain growth than would have been possible in the womb itself.

But to this invaluable stage of infancy (that infancy which permits the big, victorious brain of the mammals and has given this the last great order of animals its predominance), man, on the top of this plinth, has added a further shaft. For on the top of infancy and its uncommitted openness (and so ability to grow in understanding), man has developed his specific extension of growth, childhood, or to give this phase its technical name, paedomorphy. Man in addition to his increase of brain growth made possible by infancy (an infancy all mammals to some extent profit by) has his own prolongation, childhood, a span of further mind-growth through independence of (or leave of absence from) the reproductive obligation, obsession, and absorption. (p.252)

Cope's law of the survival of the unspecialized shows that the open mind, not the expert specialized technician, "inherits the earth." As noted above, intelligence lies in the width of the span of correlation. In studying creativity, ("integral thought," "the extension of the span of correlation") we have, however, found that this open mind that delights with unstinted curiosity in the anomalous, the odd, and the strange, is so kept open, elastic, responsive, and exploratory, by its matrix being the open heart. The hopelessly ambiguous word "love" can best be rendered with any approach to semantic accuracy as Interest-Affection. In this term we can state the essential reciprocity between thought and feeling. For real interest (and so insight) is, as Konrad Lorenz points out, made possible by "empathy," that sense of kinship without which the basic conviction of comprehensibility is impossible.

It is here we therefore come to the subtlest point of our problem, the enigma of man's future. If (1) as now seems clear, "Nature's next step" must be the production of a highly generalized type to carry on human social heredity, a neotenic type that thus retains a capacity for elastic comprehension permitting profoundly original correlations, (2) if this type is so effective because it retains through most of its life (and maybe through the whole) potentiality rather than actuality, because it spends most of its life (perhaps all of it) on the rising side of the growth curve and not (as do most of our lives) on the downgrade: then this being must have its own particular psychophysical emotive life. What would that be? (p.254)

The radical mistake in Freudianism is to be found, as we should expect, in his initial assumptions and misdiagnosis of the infant. There he sought, rightly enough, for the stem (if not the roots) of the individual's after-conduct and adult desires. But owing to his mistaken and prejudiced assumption as to what he must find, he misinterpreted his data. To be brief, he described the behaviour of the infant as being that of "a polymorphic pervert." For the infant indicates a vivid psychophysical interest in every part of its body. Freud, obsessed with specific sexuality (his emotional reaction as a Viennese Jew against the ascetic core of the established Roman Catholic Church) and with a semantically crude vocabulary, labeled this infantic conduct as sexually perverted behaviour because the child plays with bodily pleasure with areas and organs not specifically involved in the reproductive cycle. Quite obviously to any unprejudiced observer, the child is incapable of specific sexuality. As clearly can we see, semantic accuracy compels us to avoid the emotional vagueness of Freudianism and to use the word *sex* only for those functions in which the mature organs of reproduction are being employed to bring about fertilization and conception. (p.254)

The young of all mammals, and therefore the young of the latest mammal, are panaesthetic transits. That is to say, because they are, with their big brains, psychophysiques, they cannot develop simply by being physically fed. (p.255)

The type that our civilization must produce must, we see, be a type that retains the staunchless capacity for original associations, insights, and ideas that is so soon lost by the normal man. The type that must carry on and develop our social heredity must be one whose neotenic endowment of creativity is sustained throughout the rising curve of development, and that curve must be extended far up into the life span. This is why Haldane and Berrill, both brilliant researchers in biology, have forecast that if man is to continue his evolution and sustain the coordination of his proliferating knowledge, he must extend infancy from its present 2½ years up to 6 and 7 years old, childhood well into the teens, adolescence into the twenties or thirties. And that is why, as an actual fact of observation, it is now found that the profoundest, most original, most creative insights in our present master science, Physics, are already made by men in their adolescent years and often with a strong isophylic quotient. (p.255)

In short, then, as man, as we now know him, neoanthropic man, man-with-the-big-forebrain (still largely unused) is "the foetalization of the ape," so man as he must now emerge (as the family is over, the community is now the unit and the community can only coalesce into a comprehensive civilization if the social heredity can be carried on by original minds free of taboos), this new necessary scanner, seer and goal-indicator must be the foetalization of present man. (p.255)

The answer to this interrogation lies in our latest information as to the psychological history of mankind, which can be called in the widest sense, the history of religion.

This we now know has been in five phases. The first and much the longest was co-conscious.

(1) (a) During the Paleolithic, rites of identity, group performances, gave the required sense of solidarity to the constituents. (b) These identifications became more specific with intensifying consciousness and resulted (i) in the matriarchy and (ii) in the gypnocracy (a society held together by a fourfold organic structure, the seers of which were astrologers).

(2) This collapsed in the chaos of the Heroic Age which also seems to have brought in (instead of the sacraments of water, milk, and semen) the blood and flesh sacrifice of a tortured and unwilling victim.

(3) In turn this led to the great ascetic, life-rejecting religions of celibacy and mortification to win a non-physical after-life.

(4) This collapsed with the rise of the Humanic phase (totally self-conscious, individualized man).

(5) And now this modern man has himself collapsed as we, the first generation of self-conscious men to be conscious of the nonselfconscious, confront afresh the problem of the mind-body and

the converse problem of the individual and the race. (p.256)

In closing this chapter, ONE Institute Dean, Merritt M. Thompson, writing as T. M. Merritt, calls for continuing sex research and breaking through ancient taboos and open rational discussion.[8]

> For anyone who reads or listens to the radio or television extensively in the field of current affairs, the term most descriptive of the world situation today would probably be "chaotic." One hears extremists from every point of view shouting their contentions until the cacophony leads him to wonder whether there is anything that could be called truth in the current world. And, when any one position has behind it a long history of prejudice, bias, and distortion, the difficulties of arriving at reliable conclusions are compounded. There is, however, a way out. Since the Renaissance from the fourteenth century on, Francis Bacon and others have formulated a method for seeking truth which may be characterized broadly as *rationality*, that is, correct thinking in the derivation of conclusions from observed facts. That this technique is reliable is abundantly proved by the enormous advance and success man has had in the mastery of the natural world of his environment, especially during recent years. At present there seems to be almost no limit to his achievement.
>
> Perhaps the strangest aspect of the whole scientific movement, as it may be called, is man's unwillingness to apply the techniques of discovery and application to his human relationships, which are so far behind his control of the natural world that his very existence on earth is now being threatened. It is perhaps not so difficult to analyze the reasons for this "culture lag" as it is to suggest remedies. The facts and conditions of the world of chemistry and physics, while in fact of the utmost importance in bearing upon man's welfare and happiness, are not so obvious in their relation to man's self-interest. Furthermore, the social principle, that is, the interrelatedness of the concerns of all men, while known to the master minds of history, has been quite unrealized by the great mass of mankind. Self-centered concern has dominated man's thinking and activities to the exclusion of consideration for ultimate outcomes and effects on mankind in its larger extension. Every evil known to man has been profitable, materially if not spiritually, to individuals and groups somewhere. The participation of munitions-makers in fomenting the great world wars is now sufficiently documented. When man makes a living by

---

[8] *QTLY* V:1 (Winter 1962), p.4-5.

teaching a certain doctrine, he becomes a strong protagonist for that doctrine and doubtless comes to believe in its infallibility. The strong hold which the profit motive as an incentive to man's greatest exertion has upon business men in spite of the large number of teachers, scientific research workers, and others who are not moved by expectation of profit proves the power of self-orientation as opposed to the larger point of view.

No aspect of human concern has been subject to more vagaries than sex with its countless involvements in joy and sorrow. As ONE can abundantly testify, homosexuality has had no small part in these human vicissitudes. It has now been pointed out that the original taboos against sex variation among the ancient Israelites may have had some point, but with succeeding years, irrational connotations have clung to the subject, both generally and in specific areas, until they resemble barnacles so heavily encrusted on its hull that they threaten to sink the ship. The chief task, then, of those who wish to make a constructive contribution to the field is to further the acquisition of truthful solutions to its problems.

Thus in harmony with the best thought of our times, research is the applied form of rational thinking and becomes central to all other activities. In the last number of the *Quarterly*, the library of ONE was described with its already extensive collection of materials, which are the raw stuff of research. A beginning has also been made toward a recognition of these materials as a source for university research. Some people have questioned the advisability of the study of homosexuality by groups which were themselves homosexual, but the fact is that much of the best work to date has been done by just such groups. Of course, collaboration with heterosexual psychologists, sociologists, psychiatrists, and others is most valuable, but nothing takes the place of first hand experience. While ancient taboos, misrepresentations, and quite unjustifiable vilification of workers in the field occur from time to time, progress is being made toward a truer conception, and open rational discussion is increasing in amount and is occurring in places which would have been impossible not so long ago. Doubtless, much of the advance is due to sympathetic collaboration.

ONE Institute Extension Lectures:
Biology

May 8, 1958 (#20) "Magnus Hirschfeld in Germany" by Rudolph Burckhardt, Zurich.

November 11, 1961 (#54) "Biological Patterns in Sexual Behavior," by Ray Evans, Ph.D.

April 4, 1965 (#96) "A Triple Revolution," by D.B. Vest (Gerald Heard).

September 18, 1966 (#113) "Endocrine Research and Gerontology," by Harry Benjamin, M.D., New York.

February 1, 1969 (#137) "Transsexualism, Transvestism and Homosexuality," by Richard Green, M.D.

November 1, 1970 (#157) "Is there a continuum: Homosexual to Heterosexual?" by Peter Bentler, Ph.D.

November 3, 1985 (#312) "Scientific Briefing on Aids," by Victor Burner, M.D.

June 5, 1988 (#336) "An Inquiry Into the Origins of the Aids Epidemic," by Alan Cantwell Jr., M.D.

December 2, 1990 (#351) "The HIV Challenge," by Victor Burner, M.D.

Video cassettes of Lecture nos. 309, 312, and 351 are included in the Audiovisual Collection of ONE's Baker Memorial Library.

CHAPTER 11

ANTHROPOLOGY

W hen ONE's Third Midwinter Institute sessions opened on January 26, 1957, only a single semester of classes had been completed. The faculty's first effort had explored the nine fields of scholarly discipline which had been selected as being most likely to provide approaches for the study of homosexuality.

No one at that 1957 meeting was quite prepared for the two hour salvo on anthropology, "The Homophile in Search of an Historical Context and Cultural Contiguity," given by Mattachine movement theoretician Harry Hay. ONE Institute had been put on notice in no uncertain terms that Anthropology was a topic to be taken very seriously indeed.

The following excerpts from the Hay paper have been chosen without any attempt at offering a comprehensive overview of his arguments. They are merely provocative glimpses intended to illustrate the general tone and flavor of his presentation. The full text has not been published other than in ONE's *Confidential Newsletter* from which these selections have been made.

**The Homophile in Search of an
Historical Context and Cultural Contiguity
By Harry Hay[1]**

In recent years, scientific anthropology has gone to some pains to demonstrate some physiological validity for this small minority. Notable among these efforts is the thesis *Patterns of Sexual Behavior* by Drs. Ford and Beach which, through a comparative analysis of infra-human and sub-human primates with homosapienate behavior, has delivered a creditable warrant for the validity of some measure of homoerotic behavior as a "specie-universal," with the expectable concentration of behavior into the overt impulses of basic-drives on the part of a few. By their findings, impartially organized, Drs. Ford and Beach validate many of the earlier phenomenological

---

[1] *CONFI* II (August, 1957), pp.1-10.

inventories, smothered in bias and chauvinist sensationalism, of such scholars as Karsch, Ploss-Bartels, Baumann, Tarnowsky, Westermarck, and Havelock Ellis.

Dr. Ruth Benedict in *Patterns of Culture* initiates the second great step forward in excoriating not only the methodology and eschatological conclusions of such cataloguers as illustrated by those few listed just above, but also the formulations and conclusions of such men as Sir J. G. Frazier. (p.4)

In discussing the usual topical approaches to studies of marriage, ritual, religion, and the like, Dr. Benedict aptly underlines the pervasive tendency to presume 20th century European standards upon a diversity of anciently-evolved cultures. Westermarck explains marriage as a situation of sex preference, and the usual interpretation of initiation procedures is that they are the result of puberty upheavals. Therefore all their *thousand modifications* (my emphasis, HH) are facts in a single series, and only ring the changes upon some one impulse or necessity that is implicit in the generic situation. [Now] very few cultures handle their great occasions in any such simple fashion. These occasions, whether of marriage or death or the invocation of the supernatural, are situations that each society seizes upon to express its characteristic purposes. The motivations that dominate it do not come into existence in the particular selected situations, but are impressed upon it by the general character of the culture.

The significant sociological unit, from this point of view, therefore, is not the institution but the cultural configuration. Based upon such premises, Dr. Benedict proceeds to discuss within the context of the Pueblo Indian configuration the permissive Homophilic households, or Berdache, not in its usual dross as an unnatural bestial vice out of any reasonable context (more usually encountered in chauvinist works as demonstrating the chronic irresponsibility of inferior cultures), but as a dignified and socially useful function integral to the community in which it appears. (p.4)

Thus Bancroft's observations, taken anthropologically, can introduce us only to the recognition of the need to study mankind's evolution into and through the Neolithic stage of history. If what the Pacific Indians exhibited is endemic to the Neolithic consciousness, then perhaps paralleling institutions (implicitly exhibiting characteristics of social Homophilic employments) may be postulated as possible specie-universals within Neolithic expectations... but universal as socially derived and recognized contributors to collective permanence and continuity... and not merely as oft repeated bits and patches of isolated novelty scattered widespread throughout the seven seas.

The recorded instance that people have accepted Homophilia at various points of observable history does not, in itself, constitute either social or historical justification – even as the observed instance of cannibalism does not justify any derogatory judgment of primitive savagery upon the society so practicing. (Indeed, a sizable plurality of the Western World does homage to an interestingly persistent survival of the Semitic Sacrament of Cannibalism every Sunday of their lives, "Eat ye – for this is my body; drink ye – for this is my blood.") (p.5)

The term "berdache" enters social anthropology by way of the several journals of New France contributed by such men as Fathers Marquette, Hennepin, de Lahontan, and by such explorers as de La Salle and Perrin du Lac. The term was employed to represent the diversity of social employment of the Homophilic phenomena by varying social levels of Amerindian cultures. "Berdache," "bardaccho" and "bardascia" in the Italian, from the Arabian, "baradaj," appears in the recording-class levels of literate society as meaning slave or captive, as distinct from "catamite" (from the old Latin epithet for Ganymedes... Catamitus) implying a social utility or a cultural condition for berdache in contrast to an antithetical, personal opportunism impugned to catamite. But it is historically apparent that the institution of *berdache* does not belong to the accoutrements developed by the chronicling class (or estate) or itself. Rather it seems to underlie and historically precede, as part of the vast sub-stratal acculturation of the mass, or folk pattern, which provides the imperturbable foundation of all social and political complexes until astonishingly recent days. In deprecating folk ritual-magic, the alien or disparaging ruling-class elements tended to equate the fold-Berdache (metaphysically inducing "first-causes") as captives or slaves ... in the sense of the Sumerian and Semitic *kedeschim*, the "devoted" assignees of the holy precincts of all human societies, who had evolved a recognition of the potency of imitative or invocative magic. Their Berdache were captives... and in a sense slaves; but these Berdache were captives of the Spirit World, and/or slaves to the service of the Gods, in that their tenures were absolute and permanent. Berdache, then, was a cultural institution in the service of social necessity; whereas Catamite remains, in all etiologies and etymologies, an individual condition presumably opportunistic. (p.6)

By the turn of the 20th century, the Berdache Minorities of Europe and America had been isolated sufficiently enough and long enough, had been falsified enough through scholastic chauvinism and deliberate distortion, that the whole society including the Minority itself could be persuaded that the Homophile (a curious freak, a sport really belonging in a bottle, a spiritual blight not to be mentioned in decent society) was from all eternity rootless and unrootable, rudderless and incapable of social objectivity, and – as a stereotype – unusable and incapable of social or political integration. (p.8)

At present there is a host of disjointed cultural artifacts... both material and philological... which bear serious and impartial re-examination in the light of the Berdache, when postulated as an integral social factor, emerging as a dimension within the embryonic social complex of the gynarchic semi-sedentary village. The several evidences in the Mesolithic (the upper stages of savagery) of magic-makers who were not full-time specialists may prove to be cases in point; the Paleolithic (or lower savagery) paintings of the masked-men of Trois Frères in Ariège; the Fourneau du Diable in the Dordogne; the ceremonial dance of women around a single nude man (with a pregnant animal apparently conjured up) at Congul in north-eastern Spain; the Mesolithic fertility figurines whose sexing is unclear; the two men of the Beaker Folk, of the early Bronze Stages, buried together who would have been presumed to prove slavery except that both men are of the same stock and of apparently the same social level; the Champaign burial vault presided over by a graven female effigy; the early Neolithic funerary configurations which testify to mysterious prestige males who were *not* chiefs – [these] are but random samplings of the host of archaeological curiosae which presently lie uncoated, and socially unrelated, in the archaeological grab-bag. Topping all, we have the famous "matriarchal" or "gynarchic" evidences of the Grimaldi Cave burial of two youths and an older matron, and, well within our own time, the Latin word for farmer – still germane in 14th century French legal documents, AGRICOLA, AGRICOLAE, feminine.

Regardless of the overt disinclination of Dr. V. Gordon Childe, admittedly the foremost archaeological scholar of our times, and others, to adduce a matriarchal or gynarchic culture as a formative stage in the evolution of European society, we will rely on much of his magnificently lucid and solidly-rooted summarizations to reconstruct the emergence of the Berdache phenomenon as a constructive social institution. (p.9)

Anthropology continued to be included as a topic forming part of the "Introduction to Homophile Studies" during following semesters. Why it did not stimulate faculty and student papers in large numbers is not clear. This editor's "The Berdache" gave some notice to reports on this phenomenon by early travelers. Excerpts follow.

The Berdache and
Theories of Sexual Inversion
By W. Dorr Legg[2]

The classic theory of sexual inversion is posited on the assumption that homosexual behavior arises from a reversal of the natural sex roles of the male and the female, the male adopting the sexual attitudes of the female, the female those of the male. The natural roles of each are defined, in this view, as those to which a statistical norm adheres.

Unfortunately, account is seldom taken in such discussions of those many societies in which the natural sex roles of the male and female do not conform to those commonly found in late western cultures. Theories of sexual inversion assume that there is a pattern of sexual behavior natural to both the male and the female the world over, without bothering to discover what that might actually be. (p.59)

A specialized aspect of the theory of sexual inversion, possessed of curious yet instructive value to the student, is that of the *Berdache*. According to some American lexicons, there are two similar terms which are assumed to be related: *Berdache*, from the Spanish, *bardaje* or *bardaja*, meaning "a kept boy," and defined as "in American Indian tribes, a male prostitute" and *bardash*, from French, *bardache*, Italian, *bardascia*, Arabian, *bardaj*, a slave, Persian, *bardah*, a catamite.

The most learned French and English lexicons appear not to carry these forms at all but refer only to *burdash*, of unknown derivation, an article of men's clothing, variously described as an effeminate sash, worn around the waist, and a lace collar or tie.

The term as commonly found in anthropological literature describes the social institution reported by explorers as existing, in some form, in nearly every Indian society in North America, from the extreme south to the Arctic. By extension the term has later been applied to similar institutions occurring elsewhere in the world, especially in Siberia and other parts of Asia. Some writers have also applied it to various historical phenomena such as the transvestite medieval mummers, the male temple prostitutes of India, Sumeria and elsewhere. These cultural forms appear, however, to include elements so diverse as hardly to conform comfortably to the North

---

[2] *QTLY* II:2 (Spring 1959), pp.59-63.

American tradition.

Several passages from early writers are cited herewith to illustrate some aspects of the North American Berdache which undoubtedly have hitherto strongly reinforced the general theory of sex inversion. The first of these is taken from the writings of Pietro Martire D'Anghiera (1455-1526), also known as Peter Martyr, whose *De Orbe Novo*, in Latin, is one of the most fascinating sources covering Spanish explorations in America at the opening of the sixteenth century.

During one of the expeditions of Vasco Nunez de Balboa, or Vaschus, the Latin version of his name, while crossing the Isthmus of Panama in 1513, the following incident took place:

"Therefore ere ever he came to the tops of the high mountains, he entered into a Region called Quarequa, and met with the king thereof called by the same name, with a great band of men armed after their manner, as with bows and arrows, long and broad two handed swords made of wood, long staves hardened at the ends with fire, darts also and slings. He came proudly and cruelly against our men, and sent messengers to them to bid them stand and proceed no further: demanding whither they went and what they had to do there. Herewith he came forth and showed himself being appareled with all his nobility: but the other were all naked. Then approaching toward our men, he threatened them with a lion's countenance to depart from thence except they would be slain every mothers son. When our men denied that they would go back, he assailed them fiercely. But the battle was soon finished. For as soon as they heard the noise of the arquebusses, they believed that our men carried thunder and lightening about with them. Many also being slain and sore wounded with quarrels of crossbows, they turned their backs and fled. Our men following them in the chase, hewed them in pieces as the butchers do flesh in the shamwelles, from one an arm, from another a leg, from him a buttock, from an other a shoulder, and from some the neck from the body at one stroke. Thus, six hundred of them with their king, were slain like brute beasts. Vaschus found the house of this king infected with most abominable and unnatural lechery. For he found the king's brother and many other young men in women's apparel, smooth and effeminately decked, which by the report of such as dwelt about him, he abused with preposterous venous. Of these about the number of forty, he commanded to be given for a prey to his dogs. For (as we have said) the

Spaniards use the help of dogs in their wars against the naked people whom they invade as fiercely and ravenly as if they were wild boars or harts. In so much that our Spaniards have found their dogs no less faithful to them in all dangers and enterprises, than did the Colophonians or Castbalenses which instituted whole armies of dogs made to serve in the wars, that being accustomed to place them in the fore front of the battles, they never shrank or gave back. When the people had heard of the severe punishment which our men had executed upon that filthy kind of men, they resorted to them as it had been to Hercules for refuge, by violence bringing with them all such as they knew to be infected with that pestilence, spitting in their faces and crying out to our men to take revenge of them and rid them out of the world from among men as contagious beasts. This stinking abomination had not yet entered among the people, but was exercised only by the noble men and gentlemen. But the people lifting up their hands and eyes toward heaven, gave tokens that god was grievously offended with such vile deeds. Affirming this to be the cause of their so many thunderings, lightning, and tempests wherewith they are so often troubled: And of the overflowing of waters which drown their sets and fruits, whereof famine and divers diseases ensue, as they simply and faithfully believe, although they know none other god than the sun, whom only they honor, thinking that it doth both give and take away as it is pleased or offended." [3]

David Thompson (1770-1857), born in London, was apprenticed to the Hudson's Bay Company as a young boy and spent the rest of his long life in exploration, trading, and cartography, becoming renowned as one of the great geographers of the period. In company with Alexander Henry he made a trip through western Canada. The following extract from the journal of Alexander Henry the Younger, written on January 2, 1801, at his fort on the Red River in Manitoba, details an incident from one of their trips. (p.60)

"Berdash, a son of Sucrie, arrived from the Assiniboine, where he had been with a young man to carry tobacco

[3] Peter Martyr (Pietro Martire), "The Decades of the New Worlde or West India etc.," 1516, in the first *Three English Books on America*, ed. Edward Arber (Birmingham, England, 1885), p.138.

concerning the war. This person is a curious compound between a man and a woman. He is a man both as to members and courage, but pretends to be womanish, and dresses as such. His walk and mode of sitting, his manners, occupations, and language are those of a woman. His father, who is a great chief amongst the Saulteurs, cannot persuade him to act like a man. About a month ago, in a drinking match, he got into a quarrel and had one of his eyes knocked out with a club. He is very troublesome when drunk. He is very fleet, and a few years ago was reckoned the best runner among the Saulteurs. Both his speed and his courage were tested some years ago on the Schian river, when Monsieur Réaume attempted to make peace between the two nations, and Berdash accompanied a party of Saulteurs to the Sioux camp. They at first appeared reconciled to each other through the intercession of the whites, but on the return of the Saulteurs, the Sioux pursued them. Both parties were on foot, and the Sioux have the name of being extraordinarily swift. The Saulteurs imprudently dispersed in the plains, and several were killed; but the party with Berdash escaped without any accident, in the following manner: One of them had got from the Sioux a bow, but only a few arrows. On starting and finding themselves pursued, they ran a considerable distance, until they perceived the Sioux were gaining fast upon them, when Berdash took the bow and arrows from his comrades, and told them to run as fast as possible, without minding him, as he feared no danger. He then faced the enemy, and began to let fly his arrows. This checked their course, and they returned the compliment with interest, but it was so far off that only a chance arrow could have hurt him, as they had nearly spent their strength when they fell near him. His own arrows were soon expended, but he lost no time in gathering up those that fell near him, and thus he had a continual supply. Seeing his friends some distance ahead, and the Sioux moving to surround him, he turned and ran full speed to join his comrades, the Sioux after him. When the latter approached too near, Berdash again stopped and faced them with his bow and arrows, and kept them at bay. Thus did he continue to maneuver until they reached a spot of strong wood which the Sioux dared not enter. Some of the Saulteurs who were present have often recounted the affair to me" [4]

Another description of Indian life was made by John Tanner (1780-1847) who was captured by the Indians as a boy and spent thirty years of his life among them. His account is detailed and throws considerable light on the social attitudes toward the Berdache institution existing in the particular tribe he describes. Notice should be taken of the fact that marriage of the Berdache to another man was perfectly acceptable here, as in many other tribes, so much so that the chief himself, Wa-ge-to-tah, polygamously married Yellow Head, adding "her" to his harem, with "less uneasiness and quarreling than would have been the bringing in of a new wife of the female sex." His account follows.

> "Some time in the course of this winter, there came to our lodge one of the sons of the celebrated Ojibbeway chief, called Wesh-ko-bug, (the sweet,) who lived at Leech Lake. This man was one of those who make themselves women, and are called women by the Indians. There are several of this sort among most, if not all the Indian tribes: they are commonly called A-go-kwa, a word which is expressive of their condition. This creature, called Ozaw-wen-dib (the yellow head) was now near fifty years old, and had lived with many husbands. I do not know whether she had seen me, or only heard of me, but she soon let me know she had come a long distance to see me, and with the hope of living with me. She often offered herself to me, but not being discouraged with one refusal, she repeated her disgusting advances until I was almost driven from the lodge. Old Net-no-kwa was perfectly well acquainted with her character and only laughed at the embarrassment and shame which I evinced whenever she addressed me."

The famous painter George Catlin (1796-1872) devoted a large part of his life to the faithful detailing of every aspect of American Indian cultures. Between 1829 and 1838 he painted six hundred portraits of Indians of both sexes and of all ages from a wide range of tribes. Later, from 1852 to 1870 he painted six hundred and three detailed scenes of Indian life, including some portraits. His published

---

[4] Elliott Coues, "New Light on the Early History of the Greater Northwest," *The Manuscipt Journals of Alexander Henry and of David Thompson, 1799-1814* (New York, 1897) 3v., pp.163-165.

Letters add to the richness of this record by commenting on particular paintings and the plates reproduced from them.

From his travel among the Sacs and the Foxes living along the Mississippi River six hundred miles below the Falls of St. Anthony, the following extract gives a clear account, with its accompanying painting, of the Berdache institutionalized even more explicitly than in any of the preceding examples. Here are also included, apparently, those who have had sexual relations with the Berdache, as disclosed in a ritual public proclamation. Catlin notes this and calls it a "society... of odd fellows." His complete account follows.

"Dance to the Berdashe, is a very funny and amusing scene, which happens once a year or oftener, as they choose, when a feast is given to the 'Berdashe,' as he is called in French (or I-coo-coo-a, in their own language), who is a man dressed in woman's clothes, as he is known to [sic] be all his life, and for extraordinary privileges which he is known to possess, he is driven to the most servile and degrading duties, which he is not allowed to escape; and he being the only one of the tribe submitting to this disgraceful degradation, is looked upon as medicine and sacred, and a feast is given to him annually; and initiatory to it, a dance by those few young men of the tribe who can, as in the sketch, dance forward and publicly make their boast (without denial of the Berdashe), that Ahg-whi-ee-choos-cum-me hi-anh-dwax cummeke on-daig-nun-chow ixt. Che-ne-a'hkt ah-pex-ian I-coo-coo-a wi-an-gurotst whow-itcht-ne-axt-ar-rah, ne-axt-gun-he h'dow-k's dow-on-daig-o-ewhicht nun-go-was-see.

"Such, and such only, are allowed to enter the dance and partake of the feast, and as there are but a precious few in the tribe who have legitimately gained this singular privilege, or willing to make a public confession of it, it will be seen that the society consists of quite a limited number of 'odd fellows.'

"This is one of the most unaccountable and disgusting customs, that I have ever met in the Indian country, and so far as I have been able to learn, belongs only to the Sioux and Sacs and Foxes – perhaps it is practiced by other tribes, but I did not meet with it; and for further account of it I am constrained to refer the reader to the country where it is practiced, and where I should wish that it might be extin guished before it be more fully recorded." [5] (p.62)

Little attention has been given in the literature so far to the theory that homosexual behavior is in no way related to or connected with "masculinity" or "femininity" in either men or women, or that sexual attraction involves factors quite apart from the biological structure of the partners, or their masculinity or femininity as defined in terms of a particular culture. Discussions of homosexual behavior have hitherto been so ineradicably intertwined with theories of sex as a reproductive measure that clear distinctions have proven difficult to establish. (p.63)

Sex Habits Among the Zapotecas, Mixtecas and Chatinos of Mexico By Paul D. Hardman[6]

Despite the sparse references to the sex habits of Native Americans, there is enough information extant to draw the conclusion that they enjoyed sex, including homosexual expression, with unabashed pleasure. Although I intend to focus on those modern Indians who live on the tropical coast of southern Oaxaca, Mexico, it is important to begin with a brief overview of Native Americans as they begin to appear in written history.

Thanks to the research of Dr. Walter Williams and others like him, we know that homosexual conduct among Native Americans was accepted within those societies and often used as the basis of respect and high honors. Homosexual Indians, singled out for special attention, were sometimes referred to by French explorers as Berdache in the late seventeenth century around the Great Lakes region.

---

[5] George Catlin, *Letters and Notes on the Manners, Customs, and Conditions of the North American Indians* (London, 1844) 2v., pp.214-215.

[6] Paul D. Hardman, "Sex Habits Among the Zapotecas, Mixtecas, and Chatinos of Mexico." Paper given at the 40th Anniversary Celebration of ONE, Incorporated, Los Angeles, January 26, 1992. (ONE's Baker Memorial Library & Archives)

Father Marquette described the Berdaches among the Illinois and Nadowessie Indians. He observed that they dressed as women. "There is some mystery in this for they never marry and glory in demeaning themselves to do everything the women do. They go to war, however, but can use only clubs and bows and arrows which are weapons proper to men. They are present at juggleries and at solemn dances in honor of the Calumet; at these they sing, but must not dance. They are summoned to the councils, and nothing can be decided without their advice. Finally, through their preference of leading an extraordinary life, they pass for Manitous, that is to say, for Spirits, or persons of consequence."

So that there is no misunderstanding regarding the sexual orientation of Berdaches, the etymology of the word should be understood. Originally, the word was Persian. It found its way into Arabic and was then adapted by the French to describe the transvestite Indians. As used by the Persians, it described a boy slave, particularly, one kept for sexual pleasures.

In the year 1564, before the French were in the Great Lakes region, in a book describing French adventures among the Indians of Florida, the word hermaphrodite, in Latin, was used to refer to homosexuals. The word Berdache was not then used. That book was published in London under the title, *The Whole and True Discovery of Terra Firma, (Englished and Flourishing Land), Containing as well the Wonderful Strange Manners of the People, and Marvelous Commodities and Treasures of the Country: as also the Pleasant Portes, Havens, and Wayes there unto never founde out before the last year 1562.*

In the section of the book describing the functions of hermaphrodites, it was written, "In this country there are numerous hermaphrodites, a mixture of both sexes." At this point the author indicates his own prejudice by declaring, "They are considered odious by the Indians," then goes on to admire them, "but as they are robust and strong, they are used to carry loads instead of beasts of burden. When the king is set out to war, it is the hermaphrodites who transport the supplies."

The author goes on to notice that it was the Berdaches who tended to the wounded, sick, or dying warriors, ministered to their needs, and tended to their burial: "...they take belts of leather, about three or four fingers wide and fix them at both ends of the poles and put them on their heads, which are very hard; then they carry their dead to the place of burial. Persons with infectious diseases are carried to places reserved for them on the shoulders of the hermaphrodites who supply them with food until they are well again."

At one point the European author could not resist observing that the hermaphrodites were handsome with long curly hair! In the same breath he would note that they "were much addicted to this abominable vice." While he might have been appalled, at the same time, he admitted that they were held in high esteem. These ambivalent reactions are common among European observers.

John Heckewelder, an eighteenth century observer, affirmed that when an Indian believed he had reason to suspect another man of evil designs against his friend (lover), he had only to say emphatically, "This is my friend, and if anyone tries to hurt him, I will do to him what is on my mind." In other words, it was explained, he would defend his friend with his life! Jean Bossu, another eighteenth century observer, noted that the Choctaw Indians, "...have, besides, very bad morals, *most of them*, being addicted to sodomy..."

To bring this all into contemporary focus for Mexican Indians, I have personally observed similar behavior among the Zapotecas, Mixtecas and Chatinos of southern Mexico over a period of many years.

Some of the earliest observations of Mexican Indians are found in the writings of Bernal Dias, who first visited the mainland in 1517 and was with Cortes during the conquest which started in 1519. During his first visit, he observed a village which had three masonry houses that were being used as temples for local gods. They contained, "... many idols of baked clay, some with demons' faces, some were women's, and others equally ugly which seemed to represent Indians committing sodomy with one another." His writings have many such observations.

There are strange tales to be found in the written observations of monks who accompanied Juan Bautista de Anza overland from Mexico City to the San Francisco Bay area in 1776. Fray Font, for example, became upset when he noticed that the Quechan (Yuma) men exposed "...their most indecent parts." He was even more upset with them when they would fondle themselves and have erections while he was talking to them.

Fray Font relates an incident which must have been something to behold when it happened. It seems that only women and effeminates among the Yuma Indians covered their genitalia. Never having seen white men before, the Chief of the Yuma, Palma, asked permission of de Anza to permit his warriors to inspect the trousers of the Spaniards to assure themselves that the Spaniards were actually men.

As in any culture, there are effeminate men and there are "macho" men. Among those Indians I observed, most were married, even the effeminate men. The social pressure to marry has more to do with having a family than sexual preference. That pressure is not Christian, for it predates the conquest. Marriage provides security and a form of social bonding necessary for tribal life which guarantees the support of old folks and relatives. It also frees the men to engage in things expected of men in that culture and precludes their having to do "women's" work like cooking and housekeeping. The men dominate the social structure of village life. However, these observations are being restricted to the people who live in the area around Puerto Escondido, Oaxaca, and the mountains nearby. Just below this region, related people appear to have a strong matriarchal attitude, and differ in customs and dress. Still further down and high in the mountains of Chiapas are the Mayas. They are more distinctive. Their sex habits may differ and should be studied separately.

When dealing with the Zapotecas, Mixtecas, and the Chatinos near Puerto Escondido, confusion may arise regarding requests for gifts or money by an Indian lad when sex is offered. [These boys] are not necessarily hustlers, especially in the villages. They may well be when they are in the big cities, but that is a different phenomenon. The whole question of asking for things along with sex requires more study to determine if the phenomenon is based on ancient culture, as it appears to be, or merely an adaptation to meet modern needs.

My own observations indicate that relationships may start by mutual attraction and develop to a point where requests for things, or money for things, is made. Those with more may be expected to be generous with their friends. The requests are usually quite modest. Such things as a pair of sneakers, a shirt, or "loan" of ten dollars (in pesos) to cover some pressing need may be requested. An oyster diver, for example, might suggest you buy a "pearl" from him. The local pearls are tiny and really quite worthless.

Apparently, it is the avoidance of simply selling oneself for sex that seems to be the face-saving issue involved [in such requests]. Lads who are "better off" do not usually ask for anything; however, the face-saving mechanism may still be at work. A macho lad may feel justified in engaging in male-to-male sex if he can satisfy himself that the act was "only for the money" for which he believes he has a need.

The proper response seems to be to go along with the face-saving ritual and avoid being overly generous, thus creating more problems and embarrassment. Keeping in mind that most of the lads are relatively poor, it is considered proper to offer a gift as a courtesy. This ritual is appropriate with regular relationships, other than actual lovers, of course.

There is a tendency to be involved with the same young men in the local area. This is important to save face and avoid being indiscreet. While there is no opprobrium apparent, there is always custom and proper deportment [that should be observed]; indeed, respect is engendered by discretion. But do not be fooled, there are few secrets among the local lads.

In closing, I should call attention to an observation made by Spaniards during the conquest: the Indians are very clean in their hygiene. They bathe often, a fact that bothered the early Spanish fathers; it was pampering the flesh. That is still an obvious characteristic of the Mexican Indian. I make this observation being fully aware that certain Indian tribes in North and South America were not careful regarding their hygiene. Those who were lax appear to have been less advanced groups living at a mere subsistence level. The Jesuit scholar, Father Bernabe Cobo, observed the ordinary natives of Peru during the first half of the sixteenth century and lived among them. He found them to be filthy.

A ONE Institute student paper, "Elmer Gage: American Indian," is reprinted in its entirety as an account of berdache-like customs.

Elmer Gage:
American Indian
By Bob Waltrip[7]

For unknown numbers of years the Mohave Indians have lived along the lower part of the Colorado River, farming the rich bottom lands and managing to make a living from the river itself. Presently, their reservation lies along the river from Needles, California, south to Yuma, Arizona. The U.S. Bureau of Indian Affairs helps them in managing their lives, granting them land allotments which they can either farm or lease to the number of large produce companies that raise lettuce and melons along the river. Most of the Mohaves choose to lease out their land and attempt to live on the income this offers.

Elmer Gage is such an Indian. He lives on the Colorado River Indian Reservation along with his 83 year old aunt, whom he calls his grandmother. Both he and his aunt lease their land and are able to live, not comfortably, perhaps, in a two room house, secluded in a maze of brush and trees. In his small town, Elmer is almost

---

[7] *MAG* XIII:3 (March, 1965), pp.6-10.

universally known as a homosexual. The white towns people consider him something of a village idiot. The Indian boys tease each other about sleeping with him, yet their teasing is somehow not ridicule of him. Among the Indians he is accepted with equanimity, and their laughter is as much at themselves as at him. His fellow tribesmen treat him as if he were an unattractive woman. They often talk about making love to him (in a crowd which includes him), yet it is understood that they don't really mean it. Men being men, however, more than a few of them do share his bed when they're sure none of the others will catch them at it.

Elmer supplements his land-lease income by making Indian artifacts which he sells to tourists through local variety stores and through the Tribal Council, an organization of Indians who work together for their mutual benefit. In an era when most Indian art pieces have a "made in Japan" stamp on the back, Elmer is faced with bitter competition. It takes him hours to make a beaded belt, which he must sell at a ridiculously low price in order to sell it at all. Since he works slowly and with extreme care, it would be safe to assume that he is paid not more than fifty cents an hour for his labor. The injustice of this is immediately apparent when one considers that Elmer is recognized as being one of the last remaining makers of genuine Mohave Indian artifacts.

Mr. Gage is a thirty-five year old man, standing about six feet tall, with a happy, well-fed air about him. Though delicate of bearing, he has prodigious physical strength, the fruit of long hours of hard farm labor. He has the evenness of temper and the quick wit that is peculiar to Mohaves.

He and a few others are Bird Dancers. Bird dancing (a charming dance with one man and three or four women which imitates the actions of birds) is a social dance that is performed for celebrations and various other gatherings. He has danced before statesmen, movie stars, and foreign dignitaries, yet his success has been relatively small. In plain, unpleasant truth, no one cares anymore.

Elmer's "grandmother" is a magnificent old woman who wears the ceremonial tattoo of the Mohaves, which has been abandoned for many years. This tattoo consists of five thin, blue, parallel lines running from the lower lip to the bottom of the chin. Her face is arresting in its unique beauty. Her hands move with a fascinating grace as she performs such mundane tasks as cooking and sewing. While talking, her elegant, expressive hands are continually in motion, punctuating phrases and adding a singular symmetry to her speech. Although her eyes are growing dim, she can still weave and sew, and is one of the very few Mohaves remaining who knows the reason behind many of the tribal ceremonies and stories.

The following interview was recorded the day after Christmas, 1964. We three sat around the table in the Gage home while a half-coyote puppy frisked on the floor and "Constantine and the Cross" raged across the television screen. We ate pinal, which is a sort of stone-ground wheat cereal made by the Maricopa Indians, close relatives of the Mohaves.

Q:	Elmer, how long have you been making art objects for sale to tourists, and what kind of things do you make?

E:	Gee, I started a long time ago during school. About 1947. Selling things to the tribe. I make necklaces, bola ties (Maybe I'll make you one for Christmas), beaded belts, complete cradle boards, Mohave ceremonial dolls. Also pottery. I make ceremonial costumes, like for the Bird Dancers. My own costumes. Beaded earrings. Headdresses. All kinds of stuff.

Q:	You mentioned ceremonial dolls. What exactly are they?

E:	The Mohaves have a ceremony where they try to bring the dead back. They make a doll and dress him in the dead man's clothes. They have a ceremony where they dance these dolls. Of course the dolls I make for tourists are just little ones, copies. But I can also make the real ones. The life-sized ones.

Q:	Where did you learn to make all these things?

Grandma:	I taught him how to do these things when he was young. He was interested. Like the cradle boards for babies. You have to know they're different. For boys we have a narrow board to put them on, and for the girls it's a little more wider, like this [motioning with her hands]. They always are happier when a boy baby's born. [Laughing.] I don't know why. But Elmer learned all these things, how to make things. And when something's going on he goes there and watches. That's how he learns.

Q:	Can any of the other Mohaves make the things Elmer makes?

Grandma: Um-hum. Some of them could if they wanted to.

Q:	Do they?

E:	No. It seems like I'm the only one that's keeping these traditions alive.

Q:	And after you're gone these things will just die?

E:	Yes.

Q: Doesn't anybody care? Any of the Mohaves?

E: No. Young people don't take any interest in these things. They just stand around the Oasis. [A local tavern.]

Q: It seems a shame that they don't take more interest.

E: [shrugging] They're just getting modern. What can you do?

Q: Grandma, how did you get your tattoo, and what does it mean?

Grandma: [laughing] The Mohaves... which is pronounced Hahm-ah-kah-va in Indian language... say that you can't go to the happy hunting ground unless you have this tattoo. If you're not wearing one when you die, they say you'll go into a kangaroo rat's hole and he'll lock you up there and you'll just stay there. There was a man in Needles, California, when I was twenty-five and he wanted to tattoo me. He kept on pestering me and finally I let him, though I didn't want to. It hurt. That was in 1906, when I was young. I was already a baptized Episcopalian, but I thought it wouldn't hurt to make sure. [a pause] Oh, they just say that about the rat's hole and everything. They don't know. Just like heaven and hell. They don't really know.

(We ate some more pinal for awhile, and then Grandma retired, leaving Elmer and myself alone.)

Q: Does your grandmother know you're gay?

E: I don't know. She still talks about me getting married. But I tell her I have to stay with her and take care of her. I went into the service, the army, in 1951, and left her by herself. But she couldn't take care of herself so I had to get a discharge and come back here to take care of her. She's so old. I hate to think of when she'll die.

Q: Do you think being gay has proven a disadvantage in any way?

E: I guess so. I can't say. We all have bad things in our life. I can't say if it's a disadvantage being gay, because I've been this way so long. Who knows? It's a disadvantage being a lot of things. It's a disadvantage not having money... a lot of things.

Q: Do you ever feel inferior because of your homosexuality?

E: All of us feel inferior for one reason or another.

Q: How do you feel about the people here? They seem to treat you rather cavalierly. How do you react to this kind of treatment?

E: You mean, how do I like being made fun of? I don't like it much. When they start to talk about me, I just go along with it. I'm not crazy about it. But, for the most part, we all get along. They don't mean any harm by it.

Q: How did you learn about sex?

E: From other boys my age. Of course, it took me awhile to get it all straight in my mind. But we played around a lot and I enjoyed it. Now most of these kids are married and have children of their own.

Q: Do you regret not having children?

E: I don't know. I don't think so. They're kind of frightening, the little ones. They're always falling on their heads and everything. I probably wouldn't know how to raise a kid if I had one. I'd probably be a nervous wreck.

Q: What was the extent of your education?

E: Up to the tenth grade, then I got out.

Q: Why?

E: They said I was old enough to get out and work. I wanted to go on, but the social worker wouldn't help me. Grandma had a stroke and couldn't work in the cotton any more, so I quit school and took care of her.

Q: Tell me something about your private life, if you would. Do you have a steady lover?

E: No. I never have had. But I've been in love.

Q: With a straight guy?

E: Yes.

Q: It's pretty awful, isn't it?

E: Yes, it's pretty awful.

Q: Do you find it a hindrance to be living in a small town rather than a city?

E: Yes, as far as having fun goes. But I feel kind of obligated here. I feel like I'm kind of responsible for it in some way. It's as if I were needed here, not only by Grandma, but by other people too. I would feel kind of guilty leaving it, but at the same time I want to get away and have a life of my own. I want to go to California, maybe L.A., but I can't because of Grandma. This is her house, and her hospital is nearby. So we have to stay here.

Q: Do you think you'll eventually find a steady lover and "settle down," as the saying goes?

E: Well, I'm pretty well settled down already. Only without the lover. I hope I'll find somebody. I want to find somebody. But I'm not really sure that I will. I'm not sure of anything. They say the most adventuresome hunt in the world is the hunt for a lover. I'll admit that it's taking a damn long time to bring him to bay. But I still hope.

It's hard to find anyone here because everyone knows everyone else's business. But some of the boys run around with me. We have a good time. Oh, I don't mean like sex all the time. I mean we have a good time like friends, singing Mohave songs and dancing Bird and stuff like that.

But it gets lonely living here with only Grandma. And I'm not getting younger. I get depressed sometimes, thinking that life is passing me by. I wish there was something I could do to kind of break out of the rut. But I don't know what it is.

Q: Then you don't have any plans for the future?

E: I have dreams for the future. But it doesn't do much good to actually plan. I found that out a long time ago. I could plan to inherit a million dollars and marry a handsome movie star. But it wouldn't do much good, that kind of planning. The only things I plan are things like fixing the leak in the roof and making myself a new shirt. I guess everybody else is pretty much the same way.

Q: I guess they are at that. Do you consider yourself an average American?

E: Of course. There's nothing special about me. Oh, deep down inside we all think we're special, but we're not, actually. You know, most people don't know what Indians are like. They've seen so many television westerns they think we all still ride horses and run around half naked with headdresses and everything. The only time I dress in the traditional dress is for things like state fairs and lecture tours and things like that. It's all like a show. This picture of me is just a kind of publicity picture. The Bird Dancers go on tours once in awhile, dancing for audiences, and everyone thinks all Mohaves dress in bright costumes and hop around like birds. I was at a gas station in town one day and this guy from Pennsylvania pulled in and we started talking. He asked if this was really an Indian reservation, and I told him it was. Then he asked me if there were any wild Indians around. He didn't even know I was an Indian. I told him that all the Indians around here were tame as kittens.

Q: Do you regret it when people don't recognize you as an Indian?

E: Yes. I hate to see the Indian pass from the scene. Most Easterners mistake me for a Mexican. One time, when I was on a visit to Disneyland, this tourist came up to me and started speaking Spanish. Now I speak English and I speak the Mohave language, but I can't understand Spanish, so I told him I wasn't a Mexican but a Mohave. He said, "What's that?" The Indian is gradually being absorbed into the white culture. Mixed marriages and things like that. Before too long there will be no more pure-blooded Indians left.

Q: I guess that's true. Well, you've told us a lot about yourself, but I'm running out of questions. Do you have any closing words for our readers?

E: God no. I don't know anything. Except that I would like to say that the American Indian is pretty much like the American anyone else. Indians dress like everyone else. They live in the same kinds of houses and work at the same jobs and drive the same kinds of cars. As for me, being gay has its disadvantages. But I don't think I would like to change. I guess I'm just on my own personal little warpath, not against whites but against heterosexuals who think everyone should be like them. I'm not always happy, but I'm always me. And they can like it or lump it. Life's too short to spend your time being something you don't want to be. Like the old saying, "To thine own self be true." I'm true to myself and my own nature. I think that's all anyone has a right to ask of me.

Excerpts from the introduction and commentary by Harry Hay on "The Hammond Report," a 1978 publication giving observations by

Dr. Hammond of certain Pueblo Indian customs, follow:[8]

> One of the most spectacular examples of the Conspiracy of Silence on the American anthropological scene is the burial by omission of the once-famous "Hammond Report," the observations by a Dr. Wm. A. Hammond, physician and surgeon attached to the United States Army, which were made between 1850 and 1852, of certain deviant phenomena observed of the Indian Pueblos of Laguna and Acoma in the New Mexico Territory. (p.6)
> For it happens that during the very turn-of-century decades, which witnessed the international and wholesale "appreciation" of Hammond's findings as mentioned above, the eminent American anthropologists, Alfred Kroeber, J. W. Fewkes, Frank Cushing, J. P. Harrington, and Mathilda Stevenson already had begun to undertake perhaps the most exhaustive anthropological analysis of a subscribed region of "unchanged" village life ever to be tackled. Of the literally thousands of reports, journals, monographs, and surveys made (between 1885 and 1950) of this region, not one of them ever presented a jot of evidence which in any way evoked the Hammond report, and not one of the scholars ever so much as acknowledged he'd ever heard of Hammond or his findings. (p.6)

His commentary concludes with several detailed pages of technical problems with translating and interpreting reports recorded in various languages with particular reference to the Pueblo Indian.

> It is true that, in the light of exhaustive 20th century studies of Pueblo sociology, many of Hammond's opinions concerning what he was are quite impermissible. However, in the very negating of some of his misinterpretations of his own observations, questions shall be raised which call into doubt some of the now commonly-held scholarly assumptions. This may even exemplify what can happen when observers distort a complex of social patterns to evade contemplation of a phenomenon which may be, to such observers, inclinationally distasteful or at variance with the overall picture which the funding institution might wish to have revealed by a particular study. (p.13)
> It is patent that the Latin-trained-and-or-conditioned 19th century anthropologists disdainfully isolated, when they couldn't ignore

---

[8] Harry Hay "The Hammond Report," *QTLY* VI:1-2 (Winter\Spring 1963), pp.6-21.

outright evidences of culturally-employed Homosexuality, as extraneous and overt acts, devoid of any possible or conceivably acceptable motivations by Victorian or Biedermeier standards. In the same way, Hammond, like unto such others as Frazer, Crawley, Carpenter, Westermarck, Bancroft, Bloch, etc., picked at, fussed with, and stridently belabored the socially established Berdache institutions, of pre-mercantile communes, as indicating simply men unaccountably dressing and behaving as women... "partaking of those menial tasks and alliances to which the inferior sex was condemned by Barbarism," i.e., the typical 19th century chauvinist appraisal of the sexual divisions of social labor under Matriarchy, Matrilochy, and Matriliny. (p.14)

University of Southern California Professor of Anthropology, Walter L. Williams, has published extensively on the berdache institution in various cultures, and has given several ONE Institute Extension Lectures on such topics. Video cassettes of Lecture nos. 321, 339, and 365 are included in the Audiovisual Collection of ONE's Baker Memorial Library.

One Institute Extension Lectures: Anthropology

January 26, 1957 (#8) "Anthropology Looks of the Homophile," by Harry Hay.

February 2, 1964 (#85) "Folklore of American and European Heritage," by Richard Chase.

January 20, 1967 (#117) "Famous American Comfort Stations in History," by Harry Otis.

February 5, 1967 (#118) "Experiences in Europe and North Africa," by Raphael Wirth.

July 19, 1968 (#132) "The Varieties of Homosexual Expression," by Hal Call, film.

February 1, 1969 (#139) Same as above.

October 7, 1973 (#187) "ONE's Tour of the Orient," by W. Dorr Legg.

January 28, 1978 (#240) "Gay Life in Mexico," by David Lennox.

December 5, 1982 (#284) "Homosexuality Among American Indians," by Walter Williams, Ph.D.

March 3, 1985 (#306) "Homosexuality in Traditional Hawaiian Culture," by Walter Williams.

December 4, 1988 (#339) "Homosexuality in Indonesia," by Walter Williams.

November 3, 1991 (#365) "Life in Java Today," by Walter Williams, USC Professor of Anthropology.

CHAPTER 12

LITERATURE AND THE ARTS

S ame-sex relationships have found a place in the works of artists and writers since earliest times. Long before writing was invented, the theme was given notice in the oral tradition of mythologies around the world. Later, these traditions were given written form. Earliest of these still remaining is the famous "Gilgamesh Epic," dating from around three thousand years before our era. When ONE's attorney gave *ONE Magazine* the green light for printing fiction, the pent up interest and urges for the magazine's readers yielded a veritable flood of stories, poetry and literary criticism. Although some of it was little more of an outlet for long suppressed emotions, some of these writings had considerable merit. Under his own name, Norman Mailer wrote an article, "The Homosexual Villain," for the January, 1955 *ONE Magazine* at the request of a friend of ONE in New York. Since then, Mailer has thriftily reprinted it under different titles and circumstances.

Readers of the *Magazine* had broadly eclectic tastes and had done a great deal of reading. Their book reviews and critical articles cover an astonishing range of literatures from various periods and languages. For response to a review of "Last of the Wine," see Mary Renault's letter.[1]

No survey of Homophile tastes is either intended or needed here, but anyone interested might consult the Indexes of *ONE Magazine*, *ONE Institute Quarterly*, and the two Newsletters, *ONE Confidential* and *ONE Letter*, its successor. They could find many items of literary esoterica. Drama and cinema have both been given attention at ONE. Some experimental films have been made (see listings under the heading Extension Lectures at the end of this chapter). Several fully staged art exhibits are listed under the same heading. Drama has had a more structured history at ONE; see the following:[2]

---

[1] See Appendix, 12: Letter from Mary Renault to Donald J. Leiffer, dated 23rd May '58.

[2] *LTR* XXXII:6 (June, 1987), pp.1-3.

Many newcomers to ONE Institute's educational programs may not be aware of what a long tradition of theater and drama there has been at ONE, beginning as far back as 1957. Following is a listing of information about these programs.

Previous One Institute Dramatic Presentations

1. Scenes from "Mama Doll", a play by James Barr. Director: Samson, January 27, 1957.
2. "The Patterns of Sparta", a dramatic reading by Rachel Rosenthal of scenes from *The Corn King and the Spring Queen* by Naomi Mitchison, February 2, 1958.
3. Two original one act plays by Doyle Eugene Livingston; Spanish Dancer, Antonio Reyes; readings by Rachel Rosenthal and Morgan Farley, February 1, 1959.
4. Poetry readings by Morgan Farley and gay folk songs by Lisa Ben, April 19, 1959.
5. "Game of Fools", a play by James Barr. Director: Chuck Taylor, January 31, 1960.
6. "Marionettes In Camp", a marionette show by Hank [Rabey]; Spanish Dancer, Antonio Reyes, January 28, 1961.
7. "An Afternoon in the Theater", readings, songs and dances. Director: Antonio Reyes, January 28, 1962.
8. "Cavafy, His Personality and Poetry", an impersonation by R. H. Stuart, May 6, 1962.

THE FIRST PRODUCTION DURING
THE 1963-64 SEASON

"The Eternal Quest," October 6, 1963
Solo and concert readings of
classical and modern
Homophile love poetry
by the Drama Group

THE SECOND PRODUCTION DURING
THE 1963-64 SEASON

Sunday, May 3, 1964, at 3 P.M.

The ONE Institute Players group was formed for the purpose of providing diverse Homophile entertainment and a mode of self-expression.

Plans are currently underway to establish a permanent Department for the Performing Arts of ONE Institute. Anyone wishing to participate please contact any of the group members. Persons acquainted with any phase of production such as actors, writers, dancers, musicians, make-up, etc. are especially invited to confer with the staff after the performance.

CURRENT REPERTORY MEMBERS

John Brunside
Jerry Dealey
Keith Dyer
Harry Hay
Thelma Varga

"HOMOPHILE KALEIDOSCOPE"

A Mixed Media Production in Color and Sound
Produced by John Burnside and Harry Hay

INTERMISSION
(ten minutes only)

II

"HOUSE OF ROSES"

Adapted From Tennessee Williams
Cornelia........................Thelma Varga
Grace...........................Kay Farber [Keith Dyer]
Scene: Breakfast room of Cornelia's Edgewater Drive Mansion in a city of the deep south. The time is mid-morning.

Directed by.....................Keith Dyer
Costumes by.....................T. Varga
Hair styles and make-up by......Tintore

The ONE Institute Players and their productions were the outgrowth of the ONE Institute Drama Workshop which met for two semesters in 1962 and 1963 as conducted by noted actor of the New York and London stage, Morgan Farley, who had retired and come to LA to live. Plans at the time "to establish a permanent self-sustaining repertory company within a Department for the Performing Arts, in conjunction with ONE Institute" did not, for a number of reasons, come into being at that time. One problem was the lack of a truly suitable space for performances with adequate dressing rooms and space for storage of scenery and costumes, to say nothing of stage lighting. Audience seating was fairly good but the stage was movable; there was no proscenium or a reasonably workable curtain arrangement. Despite these difficulties, the ONE Institute Players did some very commendable productions. Although there are several theaters around Los Angeles which produce Gay plays, there undoubtedly are audiences for more productions and much talent in the vast metropolitan area of this city. There is certainly solid precedent for having a theater company in conjunction with a college level school such as ONE Institute.

Turning to papers on two famous Homophile literary figures and one composer, excerpts from papers by productive ONE Institute student Merritt A. McNeil, who wrote as A. E. Smith for his literary and biographical papers, are reprinted here. His fiction in ONE Magazine under the pseudonym of K. O. Neal was highly popular as also was his QUEERZLE, the earliest Homophile crossword puzzle series.

"The Curious Controversy Over Whitman's Sexuality" well illustrates Smith's scornful dismissal of much of academia's so-called scholarship in print at that time, and has relevance to the viewpoints of Homophile Studies.

The Curious Controversy
Over Whitman's Sexuality
By A. E. Smith[3]

No man in all history has had the question of his heterosexuality or homosexuality so publicly, hotly, and continuously fought over as Whitman. It is a unique distinction. It has seemed to this researcher that this unique and curious controversy should be chronicled.

The literature on Whitman is truly extensive. The following does not cover everything in the field, but was selected as representative and significant. (p.6)

In "Studies In The Psychology of Sex," Dr. Havelock Ellis devotes six pages to a discussion of Whitman, by far the most space given to one man. Whitman is a "great personality of recent times" who "has aroused discussion by his sympathetic attitude toward passionate friendship, or 'manly love,' as he calls it." (p.7)

Dr. Ellis' opinion is that at the very least "we can scarcely fail to recognize the presence of a homosexual tendency." However, he believes that Whitman should be approached as the "prophet-poet of Democracy," and he protests against the tendency "to treat him merely as an invert, and to vilify him or glorify him accordingly." (p.7)

The English essayist, social reformist, and poet, Edward Carpenter, wrote on the subject of Whitman's sexuality in the February, 1902, issue of the magazine, *Reformer*. Carpenter, like Symonds, was homosexual.

In this article, his first publication on Whitman, Carpenter advances his theory which later he was to write so extensively on – that bisexuality "indicates a higher development of humanity," a type of human "so far above the ordinary man and woman that it looks upon both with equal eyes." (p.9)

Eduard Bertz, a German, in 1905, published his *Der Yankee-Heiland*, a violent attack on Whitman as a thinker or philosopher. Bertz plainly calls Whitman one of the "intermediate sex," or a Uranian, stating that no one familiar with modern psychology and sex-pathology could be doubtful of it. He insists, however, that Whitman is one of the major lyric poets of the world.

---

[3] *QTLY* II:1 (Winter 1959), pp.6-25.

Bertz's work is not translated and probably had little influence, but it is mentioned as perhaps the first publication to unequivocally call Whitman a homosexual. (p.10)

In 1919, in an introduction to a book of translations of Whitman poetry, the Danish poet and novelist, Johannes V. Jensen, discusses Whitman's homosexuality as if it were an accepted fact. Whitman's private life was restricted "to a sphere which is familiar ground to those who suffer from the same malady and is a closed world to others." Whitman's writings "reveal the dark secrets of feminine psychology." Whitman's nature is "pathological," and it is a "disease;" however, "the nature of his impulses need not diminish the artistic value of his work," and "he is a Prince of Words and a Gateway to America."

Mr. Jensen's critique was only a small introduction to a limited edition, and what little influence it might have had was probably limited to Scandinavian countries.

In 1920 appeared the first giant in the field of Whitman scholarship and research, the American, Emory Holloway. Mr. Holloway made his appearance via an article in the magazine, *The Dial*, and he called it, "Walt Whitman's Love Affairs." (p.11)

This article is still the most important milestone in Whitman research and scholarship. It was the first appearance of a thorough Whitman scholar and one who was primarily interested – at least in this scholarly magazine article – in facts, not surmises or romancing.

Not a single statement made by Mr. Holloway in this article has ever been even questioned, let alone disproved. However, though no one has even questioned the facts, many have done the nearest thing and ignored them. (p.12)

Edward Carpenter re-entered the field in 1924 when the British Society for the Study of Sex Psychology published in pamphlet form his speech before them, "Some Friends of Walt Whitman, A Study in Sex Psychology." (p.13)

He is now again using Whitman as a springboard for a pet theory. In 1902, it was the superiority of the third (bisexual) sex. This time it is to illustrate that the widespread existence of the "homo sexual" anomaly proves that the main purpose of love and sex is not continuation of the race, but that it is "the double life," which is "when two people love each other to that degree that they become in effect one person." (p.13)

In 1932 appeared the book, *Expression in America*, by the American critic and novelist, Ludwig Lewisohn, expressing in five pages most blunt opinions on Whitman's sexuality:

Walt Whitman – most strange and difficult figure in all our letters

and perhaps the greatest – it is time... to inquire why all or
nearly all commentary on Whitman is characterized by either
a faint sliminess or a furtive dullness, or by such downright
misinterpretations and little white, extenuating lies as Andre
Gide points out with bitter amusement in the amiable
biography of the poet by the late Leon Bazalgette... I
purpose, then, in regard to Walt Whitman, to sweep away
once and for all the miasma that clouds and dims all
discussion of him and his work. He was a homosexual of
the most pronounced and aggressive type. Nor has there ever
been any good reason to doubt it. Considering his place and
time, the *Calamus* poems are of an amazing outspokenness.
(p.15)

In 1934, *Walt Whitman in England* by the American, Harold
Blodgett, was published, a book limited to writing the history of that
amazing early burst of enthusiasm among the English intellectuals
for Whitman.

Blodgett is completely aware of the role homosexuals played in
this period, and while only naming as homosexuals Symonds and
Carpenter, he also covers the influence of "those who William James
called the tender-minded" – Dowden, O'Grady, Rhys, Roden Noel
(friend of Symonds), and the Bolton group.

Blodgett's minute research into this period yields many interesting
asides as, for instance, this footnote appended to remarks on Symonds:

See also the opinion of Gosse, written in a letter to Bliss
Perry, March 6, 1907: "The real psychology of W. W. would
be enormously interesting. I think the keynote to it would
be found to be a staggering ignorance, a perhaps willful non-
perception, of the real truth about him; (the innermost truth)
escapes from almost every page for those who can read."
(Charteris, *The Life And Letters Of Sir Edmund Gosse*, p.
300.)

Thus, twenty-six years later is revealed the author of this
extremely early and frank opinion that Whitman was homosexual,
which Bliss Perry mysteriously footnoted in 1908.

Blodgett's coverage of the relations and correspondence between
Whitman and Symonds is the most thorough anywhere. (p.17)

The American critic, poet, literary editor, and anthologist, Mark
Van Doren, published in 1935 in *American Mercury* his article, "Walt
Whitman, Stranger" (reprinted in his 1942 book, *The Private Reader*).
It is probably the most poetic and beautifully written article of

criticism on Whitman.

Whitman was an "inverted individual." *Calamus* was "the clearest indication" of it. It "had remained possible" that *Calamus* was a work of "dramatic imagination, as Shakespeare's sonnets are assumed to be," but to Van Doren that possibility has disappeared, because in the biographies "too many" details fit the hypothesis of inversion – the dressing for a certain effect, his being a nurse in the Civil War instead of a soldier, etc. – and, above all, the poetry.

For *Calamus* alone of the poetry "is convincing as love poetry." The man-and-woman poems are "athletic" with "full-bosomed, muscular matrons." But *Calamus* has "the right words, and the emotions are those secondary ones, shyness, longing, jealousy, which guarantee the authenticity of an attachment. We no longer hear of Man in the embrace of Woman; we stand where one man stands, lonely, unsure of himself, glancing side-wise at another man in the hope of an answering look." *Calamus* is "drenched with longing."

To Van Doren, homosexuality is the very key to the complexity, the sophistication, the difficult symbolism of Whitman's poetry, *Leaves of Grass* being "still one of the most difficult of modern masterpieces."

"To express himself," Whitman strained the resources of the language past "the breaking point" for the average reader because he had to "devise a series of symbols, the reference of which was to something he not only could not but would not discuss in plain terms." (p.17)

Another giant appeared in the field, in February, 1946, the American, G. W. Allen, with his first book on Whitman, the invaluable *Walt Whitman Handbook*.[4]

Allen's eloquent criticism of the *Calamus* poems is of the best. He believes they are homosexual love poetry, really, "Whitman's love poems," and that "the secret of Walt Whitman's poetic inspiration is recorded in the *Calamus* poems." Also:

The kind of love which these poems reveal will perhaps always be debated among Anglo-Saxon critics, who cannot enjoy the lyrics of Sappho without first assessing her morality.

Allen is the first scholar to discover that the men-and-women poems were merely written to counterbalance *Calamus*. This he deduces from, primarily, an entry found in a Whitman notebook:

---

[4] This researcher wishes to acknowledge his enormous debt to Dr. Allen, far above any other source, and to state that without his *Handbook* and later, *The Solitary Singer*, this article could not have been begun.

> A string of poems (short, etc.) embodying the amative love
> of woman – the same as *Live Oak Leaves*[5] do the passion
> of friendship of man.

Allen's deduction: "Evidently *Children of Adam* was written more
or less to balance *Calamus*." (p.19)

In the March 18 and April 8, 1946, issues of the magazine *New
Republic*, appeared the two articles by the American critic and poet,
Malcolm Cowley, entitled, "Walt Whitman: The Miracle," and, then,
"Walt Whitman: The Secret."

Cowley's essay is by far the most frank, comprehensive, and
trenchant opinion on Whitman's homosexuality ever published, or
likely to be. His general tone is that he has had enough of the
professors' genteel preference not to "offend" the reader. (Cowley
was the author of the *New York Times*' unenthusiastic review of
Allen's *Handbook* a few months previously, and one cannot help but
suspect a connection.)

Unlike the few predecessors who had also proclaimed Whitman
an active homosexual, Cowley backs his statement up and unabashedly
presents all the patent evidence.

Whitman was an active homosexual, and as to the alleged
heterosexuality, "the evidence fails to show that he was ever sexually
attracted to women." Whitman never had any romances "except with
young men like Peter Doyle."

As to the meaning of the *Calamus* poems, Cowley is pithy: (p.19)

> Whitman is sometimes vague and a little hard to follow in his
> metaphysical symbols, but his sexual symbols are as simply conceived
> as an African statue of Potency or Fertility.

The participants in the controversy fall into two schools, generally
speaking – those who believe Whitman was definitely and consciously
homosexual and, more or less, active, and then those who believe that
it was "unconscious," "half-conscious," but at least inactive.[6]

It is extremely interesting to compare the make-up of the two

---

[5] Whitman originally planned to call his homosexual poems "Live Oak
Leaves" instead of *Calamus*.

[6] This division into two schools disregards Binns, Perry, and Bowers, who
never bring up the matter and have no stand, Symonds and Ellis, who are
interpreted both ways, and Bazalgette, the day having long past when at least
unconscious homosexuality is flatly denied.

schools.

Believing Whitman was definitely and consciously homosexual are Carpenter, Gosse, Bertz, Jensen, Lewisohn, Mark Van Doren, Masters, and Cowley.[7]

Believing Whitman was "unconsciously" or at the most "half-consciously" homosexual are Holloway, Schyberg, Blodgett, Canby, Allen, and Oakes. (p.22)

With no exception, all have one thing in common – each is, or has been, a college professor.

And with but one exception, *Canby*, a novel, none has had published an original creative work of poetry or prose. (p.23)

There exists in the field of literary biographies on the indisputable all-time greats no literature even nearly so confused and unrealistic as that on Whitman. The basic source of the confusion is embarrassment or willful non-perception regarding the homosexuality. (p.25)

The poet who went daily as a young man to the public baths, who daily sent flowers to young Peter Doyle, who exchanged with another young man kisses half a minute long, who invited another to a "mild orgy," who went around at night to the "gay places" and wrote of "the gayest party of young men" – and above all, the poet who wrote some of the most searing lines drenched in love and longing in all homosexual literature – this man was no frustrated example of paternal, fraternal, or maternal sublimation; he was simply a homosexual. (p.25)

Smith's article "On Gertrude Stein" shows his great interest in and openness to the topic of lesbianism. It should be noted that this paper was written several years before lesbian feminism began gaining a widespread following.

On Gertrude Stein
By A. E. Smith[8]

The sharply divided critics called her a fad, a primitive, a hoax, a literary experimenter, a joke, an important innovator, and a few

---

[7] Jensen and Lewisohn had novels published, the others, books of poetry.

[8] *QTLY* II:3 (Summer 1959), pp.83-90.

called her a genius. One of the few things during her life she was not called in print was a homosexual or a lesbian. It is evident now that during her life, it was common literary gossip that she was homosexual.

She was a woman of many well-earned distinctions. Even if her masterpiece, *Three Lives*, hadn't been written, certainly in the homosexual world she would never be forgotten, because one of her little-known distinctions is that she was the first person in history to write a completely homosexual novel – her *Things As They Are*, written at the age of twenty-nine in 1903.

Before 1903, works of literature that were explicitly and wholly homosexual were confined to poetry, such as Sappho, Pindar, Whitman, and a few plays, such as the Earl of Rochester's *Sodom*. When homosexuality had appeared in a novel before 1903, it had always been incidental, episodic, or bisexual, as in Petronius or in Escal-Vigor, or in Colette, or heavily veiled, such as *The Girl with the Golden Eyes* or *The Picture of Dorian Gray*.

There is certainly nothing veiled or episodic about the homosexuality in *Things As They Are*. Amazingly, this novel, the first "gay novel," remains today the most completely homosexual novel ever written. Of what other novel can it be said that a heterosexual does not even appear? And only by a third-person recounting is a heterosexual even accorded a mention, a man who had dared flirt in a restaurant – and the lesbian lady doing the recounting is properly livid with outrage!

The gay novel in which the homosexuality is assumed just as heterosexuality is assumed in heterosexual novels, with no explanations, apologies, pleadings is, unfortunately, still all too rare. But in *Things As They Are* the reader is never told the characters are homosexual, it is simply a fact made a fact when one woman makes love to another. And if there is any fuzziness about it, they keep doing it right along. Nobody thinks of a man. Nobody wants to go out for a recess and have a baby. (p.84)

But Stein's style was too harsh, too unsweet, to call merely fresh or pristine. It was primitive. Stein's contribution to literature has been to bring the artistic style of primitiveness to literature.

Which brings us to Hemingway.[9]   For it is largely through

---

[9] The Stein-Hemingway feud, too long to detail here, was one of the bitchiest. Hemingway has always had a peculiar fascination-horror of sexual anomalies, and lesbians and queens are frequent targets. In print he has railed at Capote (Hemingway's blurb for *Man with the Golden Arm*: "Truman Capote

Hemingway that Stein's influence is widespread (though ill-recognized) among American writers today.

It has been said that Stein had nothing to say but had a superb style to say it with, and that Hemingway had very much to say but no style to say it with and so stole Stein's.

This isn't completely true, or course, but then again it isn't completely false. (p.86)

Fame did not come to Stein until publication (1933) of her *Autobiography of Alice B. Toklas*. Just why she dashed this best-seller out in six weeks is unexplained, but probably it was a bid for popular recognition and extra money, which it certainly did bring. *The Autobiography*, *Things As They Are*, and *Three Lives* are her only works not written in her "difficult" (or "non-sensical," as most called it) style. (p.86)

On reviewing the literature on Stein, one is struck by its paucity. Only one biography has been published on this important figure, Elizabeth Sprigge's *Gertrude Stein, Her Life And Work* (1957), an unsatisfactory work, mainly because of its guarded, pedestrian, and unimaginative style, which with a subject as magical as Stein is incongruous. The book performs the amazing feat of purportedly writing the complete life of Stein without once mentioning the word homosexual, lesbian, or even any synonym thereof, and the one hint of the subject, an emasculated abbreviation of Edmund Wilson's frank review of *Things As They Are*, is so veiled that only the pre-informed reader could catch it. (p.87)

Of supreme importance in criticism on Stein are, of course, the writings of the great American critic, Edmund Wilson, whose standing as a critic is one of the highest in the entire world. His many faceted brilliances also include, among others, history, sociology, psychology, and languages, all of which are brought into his main *forte*, literary criticism. This gives his writings an unequaled comprehensiveness and erudition with, however, a style clear and uncluttered with professorial scholarisms and a refreshing directness that calls a spade a spade. Mr. Wilson is plainly not particularly interested in the subject of homosexuality, for in all his voluminous writings only passing references to it are made when necessary, but on the other hand it is plain that he is not prejudiced, and in a critic of his stature, that is important.

---

fans grab your hats, if you have any, and go. This is a man writing."); at Proust, Radiguet and Cocteau, *Hound & Horn*, VI (Oct.-Dec. 1932), p.135; at Alexander Woollcott and Stark Young (letter quoted by Max Eastman in *Saturday Review*, Apr. 4, 1959).

Mr. Wilson's main evaluation of Stein is contained in the essay devoted to her in his *Axel's Castle* (1945), his study of the literary movement known as Symbolism. Therein he parses her artistic methods "of unmistakable originality and distinction" (explaining one of her so-called "nonsensical" pieces by comparing it to, of all things, a section from the U.S. Courts Martial Manual), and explaining the why and wherefore of her immense importance and influence in the world of art.

Of more particular interest to us is Mr. Wilson's unique review of *Things As They Are*, published in the *New Yorker*, Sept. 15, 1951, and reprinted in his *Shores Of Light* (1952).

To Mr. Wilson, *Things As They Are* is only "of some literary merit" but it is "of much psychological interest," and here is why:

> The reviewer had occasion some years ago to go through Miss Stein's work chronologically, and he came to the conclusion at that time that the vagueness that began to blur it from about 1910 on and the masking by unexplained metaphors that later made it seem opaque, though partly the result of an effort to emulate modern painting, were partly also due to a need imposed by the problem of writing about relationships between women of a kind that the standard of that era would not have allowed her to describe more explicitly. It seemed obvious that her queer little portraits and her mischievously baffling prose poems did often deal with subjects of this sort. Now the publication of *Things As They Are* comes to confirm this theory. It is a story of the tangled relations of three Lesbian American girls of the early nineteen-hundreds, told with complete candor and an astonishing lack of self-consciousness.

This review-essay is extremely important in the study of Homophile literature. In the first place, of course, it brings out in the open the subject of homosexuality in an unprejudiced manner in a publication that was widely read and by a writer who will be read and studied in the future, a rare occurrence. (p.87)

Perhaps no artist has been more vulnerable to prejudice than Stein: she was a woman, she was a Jew, she was moneyed, she was an artist, she was homosexual. And, as if that weren't enough, superimposed was her outrageous megalomania. Not only did she proclaim over and over that she was a genius of her times, she had the gall to say, and in print, that she was "in English literature the only one." And this in the times of Eliot, Joyce, Pound, *et al.*, whose relations with Stein were, to say the least, frosty. (p.89)

In his later paper on Tchaikovsky, "Mac" drew upon his own extensive contacts in the international musical world of renowned pianists, composers and musicologists frequenting their high-ceilinged music room in Los Angeles' suburban San Rafael Hills, where he and his partner often held forth as hosts. In his paper, "Mac" vigorously attacks the romanticized critical and biographical views of Tchaikovsky as a tragic and pathetic figure, presenting well-documented evidence that he was an active and vigorous creative personality as well-adjusted and happy as a homosexual could manage to be in 19th century Russia with its strict social and religious codes.

His paper opens with the following scene:[10]

> The three musicians were letting their hair down in an 1875-version private jam session with an impromptu composed, choreographed, and danced ballet dubbed "Pygmalion and Galatea."
>
> Gaily improvising at the piano was the famous Chief of the Moscow Conservatory of Music, Nicholas Rubinstein. Portraying the blushing, shy, statuesque female being dance-wooed into life was the witty and gay French composer, Charles Camille Saint-Saëns. And doing the whirling and eloquent dance-wooing was a laughing, high-spirited man, in ordinary hours the shy and serious young Professor of Composition at the Conservatory, but now, among gay convivial friends, merely a young bohemian joining in a high artistic camp, the Russian who was to eclipse them all: Peter Ilyich Tchaikovsky.
>
> This scene hardly tallies with the picture, both physical and mental, of Tchaikovsky that has come down to most of us. (p.21)
>
> The literature on Tchaikovsky is headed by one of the best biographies ever written on a homosexual: *Tchaikovsky* (New York, 1943), by the famous music critic and musicologist, Herbert Weinstock, to which book and author I owe the greatest of debts. Also invaluable is *The Diaries of Tchaikovsky* (New York, 1945), translated from the Russian, with notes, by Wladimir Lakond.
>
> Tchaikovsky is of special importance and interest in the field of Homophilia on several grounds.
>
> One is the fact that he is one of the very, very few of history's famous people about whose homosexuality there is no controversy. Nobody is going to shrilly scream that we are "claiming" Tchaikovsky. He is ours. And he is ours with all the facets of his personality

---

[10] "On Tchaikovsky," *QTLY* IV:1 (Winter 1961), pp.20-36.

whether we like them or not, and whether we like the fact that undoubtedly heterosexuals have, and will, take those facets as typical for homosexuals. (p.21)

Another ground making Tchaikovsky of special interest is the fact that he had a younger brother, Modest, who was also completely homosexual. Also, Modest had a twin, Anatol, who was not homosexual but knew all about it, was very sympathetic, and was their close confidante. Then, in addition, there was their nephew, Vladimir Davidov (called Bob), who was homosexual and with whom Peter was in love (and had sexual relations with in all probability). (p.21)

Homosexual brothers, sisters, nephews, and nieces are far from a rarity, as any homosexual with a large acquaintanceship knows. It is a situation extremely intriguing to scientists due to the genetic (or inheritance, hormonal, intersexual, imbalance, or biological) theory of homosexuality. For the history and present status of this theory, see "Twin and Sibship Study of Overt Male Homosexuality" in *The American Journal of Human Genetics* (June, 1952) by Franz J. Kallmann, part of a study aided by a grant from the Committee for Research in Problems of Sex of the National Research Council. (p.21)

His early musical training was but little and was at his own insistence. One governess, not musical, tried to keep the child away from the family piano and from hearing music, finding it made the boy even more ill, nervous and intractable than ordinary. His early piano teachers he always soon outdistanced. (p.23)

At the age of ten, Peter was placed in the School of Jurisprudence in St. Petersburg, where he stayed for nine years, getting his diploma (entitling him to the rank of Government Clerk) when he was nineteen. (p.23)

Freed from school, earning his own money, Peter entered a period unique in his life. He became a social butterfly and something of a fop. He had always before been a dresser more on the sloppy side, but now he dandied up in the latest fashions. He made the rounds of the opera, theaters, bars, and social gatherings where he was very popular because of his piano playing.

There is no indication from this period that Peter courted any girl and since he was, however, so meticulous in his appearance, it is most likely that this is when he "came out," to use that piquant expression we have for signifying discovery of the homosexual world, its magnitude, and the meeting of other homosexuals and possible lovers. (p.23)

Diaries and letters from a later period show that Peter had a guilt feeling about his homosexuality, and there is no indication to make us believe it came on only when Peter became mature. It was large and unremitting. To be sure, it was not too large; it was not large enough to keep him from indulging quite often. But after indulgence, the shame and remorse was enormous.

As to the cause or root of the guilt feeling, there are several indications. One is religion. Peter's deep religious feelings were completely channeled into orthodox Christianity. (p.24)

Be that as it may, guilt feeling or not, during his "fop period" in the ages of nineteen to twenty-one, Peter burned the candle at both ends. His clerical job was merely something to get through, then he dandied up and was off. He commenced a life-long love of drinking. The amounts he consumed would have made a drunkard out of an ordinary man, but all his life Peter maintained undiminished an extraordinary capacity for holding his liquor. It was the admiration of all his friends, and considering the fact that it was other Russians doing the admiring, his capacity must have been phenomenal indeed. Sober, Peter was tremendously shy and nervous, and he used liquor to conquer these traits. He used it also to temporarily quiet his tremendous feeling of sexual guilt. (p.24)

The big decision to quit his job and go full time to the newly founded St. Petersburg Conservatory was made when Peter was twenty-two. (p.25)

In 1886 Peter graduated from the St. Petersburg Conservatory. Anton Rubinstein's brother, Nicholas, had just established a twin conservatory in the other capital, Moscow. On Anton's recommendation, Nicholas offered Peter the position of teaching the theory of composition. Peter accepted the post he was to hold for twelve years.

Nicholas, unlike the austere Anton, was the epitome of vivacity, charm, and high living. Like Peter, he could, and did, drink like a fish and, on finding a twin capacity, took a great liking to the shy Peter, otherwise so unlike him, and promptly moved Peter into a room in his own bachelor establishment, where Peter remained for six years. It was one of the closest, warm, and satisfying friendships Peter ever had.

There is no direct evidence that Nicholas was bisexual or homosexual. Nicholas had an enormous reputation as a woman-chaser. (p.25)

However, we know that Nicholas was Peter's confidant in matters homosexual, and it is a rare occurrence (to say the least) for a homosexual to trust a heterosexual in such matters. (p.25)

At around the age of thirty-five to thirty-six, Peter's musical reputation was beginning to be considerable, as was also the money coming in from his works. By then he had completed many songs, piano solos, chamber music, four operas, the symphonic works through *Symphony No. 3*, and the *First Piano Concerto*. (p.27)

In 1876 there commenced the correspondence with Madame von

Meck, a Russian millionairess widow, who was to generously subsidize Peter for fourteen years. (p.28)

Her generosity commenced by commissioning modest transcriptions. It culminated in, besides many costly gifts and unrepaid "loans," an annual pension from her to Peter the equivalent of $3475.00, a very handsome sum in those days.

The two correspondents, by mutual wish and agreement, never met, except for accidentally seeing each other at a concert or on a walk. (p.28)

Many homosexuals, female and male, have been driven into marriage with the opposite sex. No statistics exist to prove the wisdom or folly of this. In this instance it resulted in Peter's only suicide attempt. The woman died in an insane asylum.

Antonina Milyukova in 1877 was a good looking woman of twenty-eight when she wrote a letter to Peter, stating that she was in love with him. Where she had first seen or met Peter is unknown. He had no recollection of her. He answered with a purely formal note, thanking her for her letter. But she kept writing him, begging him to come and call on her. Finally, Peter did make a formal call. (p.30)

They were married in church on July 18, 1877. Peter wrote in a letter to his brother Anatol that he had told Antonina he could offer her only companionship. He also wrote that she was not very bright. It is certain that Antonina either did not comprehend Peter's "frankness" and conditions or, as appears more likely, she felt sure her charms would suffice.

Within two weeks of living with her, Peter found himself impossibly nervous and nauseated by her mere physical presence. He was especially revolted by her habit of biting her nails severely and leaving tiny blood stains on everything she touched in their apartment.

Peter fled. He stayed with his sister for a month, then he returned, but after two more weeks living with his wife he seriously believed he was going insane. By his own later admission, one night during these two weeks he attempted suicide by wading in and standing in icy river water, feeling sure it would result in pneumonia. (He evidently either did not have the physical courage to immerse and drown himself or did not want to be listed as a suicide, the stigma of that being a very real thing in Catholic Russia.) He did not even catch cold. (p.30)

The first thing he did was to send Anatol to his wife demanding a divorce, saying he would be listed as the guilty adulterer in the action.

After delaying tactics, and after finally seeing that Peter was not going to return to her, Antonina replied that she would testify in court that Peter was not an adulterer, that that was impossible, and that she might even say why. This was, of course, homosexual blackmail. It worked completely. Peter never divorced his wife. (p.31)

Peter gave his wife a handsome allowance. Even later when he discovered that she was living with another man by whom she had children, he never dared discontinue her allowance. (p.31)

In October, 1890, Madame von Meck, for a reason which still nobody knows (or if they do, it has never been in print), abruptly cut off the pension and all communication with Peter. She did it in a particularly cruel manner, though whether that was due to design or accident is unknown. Out of the clear blue sky she wrote him the complete lie that she had to discontinue his pension because she had just been totally ruined financially and, with that given as the only reason, she bid him farewell and asked that he think of her sometimes.

The lie was completely blatant because she knew that Peter would find out in one or two days that it was a lie, the von Meck fortune being a matter of fame. But before Peter found it out, he dashed off a letter commiserating with her and stating it would make no difference in their friendship and that his income from his works was sufficient for him. This letter, and all future letters he attempted to send her, were returned.

Finally, after a short period of bewilderment, Peter realized that Madame von Meck had dismissed him exactly as a servant or as a plaything she had grown tired of. It belittled him in his own mind, he wrote friends bitterly, that the minute the money was cut off, so also was all communication, all of what he had always thought was a close friendship. (p.34)

Regarding Peter's love affair with his nephew Bob, there have as yet been no letters published, perhaps because of the incestuous angle being considered in bad taste to discuss. But that letters or other written proof exist showing a sexual relationship between the uncle and nephew there can be no doubt. (p.35)

Modest tells us that the last period of Peter's life was one of the happiest. Of course he doesn't say so, but undoubtedly the main reason for making it so was Peter's love affair with his nephew.

There were other reasons. Honors and money poured in from all directions. Few composers have been so appreciated in their own lifetime.

Toward the end Peter was especially elated by the progress of his *Sixth Symphony*, for in one of his frequent pessimistic periods he had felt sure he was written out, and now he knew he wasn't. He wrote Bob (to whom he dedicated it) that he considered it the best and particularly the most sincere of all his works, that "I love it as

I have never loved a single one of my offspring," and "You cannot imagine what happiness I experience at the conviction that my time is not yet over and that I may still accomplish a lot." (p.35)

Peter, the man, is dead, but the music he wrote has had, and still has, a phenomenal life. It happens to have a magic not of the kind that speaks intensely and personally only to an elite or a cult but to the masses. He is the world's most whistled composer. (p.35)

Because of this phenomenal popularity, Tchaikovsky will always as a person be of interest to many people and, of course, especially to Homophiles. What slot does he fit into in the Homophile world? What type was he, and for his type what kind of adjustment did he make? All sorts of interesting questions could be raised. What part did homosexuality play in his music? (p.36)

Some things we can say about him as a homosexual: He wasn't latent. He "came out" early. He could "pass." He was shy and retiring while in the public's eye, but not effeminate nor swish. He was promiscuous. His restlessness, his passion for change of scenery, carried over into his sex life.

He also was exclusively homosexual. But he disliked his sexuality; it was to him a blemish, a sin. He did not withdraw into celibacy.

Peter's life and personality contain much that many in the Homophile movement would not call admirable. Being in a Homophile movement, in fact, is where Peter and his type would never be found, for besides being ashamed of his homosexuality, probably because of his religion, he never is curious about it intellectually, let alone being what might be termed oriented or inclined intellectually as a homosexual. Though a great reader, we never find him reading or commenting upon one thing homosexual.

That he knew of the existence of homosexual literature is a certainty because of his closeness to his brother Modest, translator of Shakespeare's *Sonnets*. Our modern Homophile movement had its very beginning in Peter's own lifetime, and it is possible that Peter knew nothing of it. (p.36)

Peter's life wasn't ideal in many respects, but then there is no reason why it should have been. He was human, very human, very fallible, with both admirable and less admirable traits. He had his own particular problems and lived with them and solved them as best he could. He lived fifty-three years and six months, overloaded with neuroses, a complete homosexual living in a completely anti-homosexual society; yet in that time allotted to him he not only crowded an amount of living and loving, and homosexuality, far above the average, but by his own bootstraps, a late-comer to his chosen profession, by sheer hard work he made of himself a major composer. Tragedy? (p.36)

The Gospel According to Ludwig II
by Jim Wurth[11]

According to current scholarship, Ludwig II, Bavaria's last reigning monarch, is to be judged from four primary perspectives. First, he was Richard Wagner's patron; without Ludwig, Wagner would not have been the singular influence he became in the musical world, at least not in his lifetime. Second, he built three castles – Neuschwanstein, Linderhof and Herrenchiemsee. Third, if not insane by modern psychiatric definitions, he was outrageously eccentric. Fourth, he was a Homophile. Depending upon the historian, this facet of Ludwig is regarded either as a despicable curse stemming from a nonmaturing id, i.e. Ludwig as the eternal adolescent, or as part of his overall eccentricity and, as such, not to be dwelled upon seriously.

As viewed by academia, this, then, is Ludwig.

Can a dominant force, a theme – in music, appropriately, a motive – be hypothesized that would begin to explain the complexities of the King so many savants seem determined to enshrine as an enigma?

The purpose of this paper is to propose such a theme: it is that the librettos of Richard Wagner's operas were far more than just grist for a king's fantasy mill; they were religious tracts, the manna from which Ludwig constructed and controlled his public and private lives. His private life, including his sexuality and a few eccentricities, will be examined in the context of five operas – *Lohengrin, Tannhäuser, Tristan und Isolde, Siegfried,* and *Der Walküre* ; his public, including his kingship and castles, will be discussed in the context of two – *Das Rheingold* and *Götterdämmerung.* The writings of Wagner and Nietzsche will be alluded to in both areas. *Parsifal,* Wagner's last work, is a special case and will be examined independently.

Within a period of about five years – from the ages of thirteen to eighteen – Ludwig had read and memorized virtually all that Wagner had so far published: essays, treatises, and the librettos of *Tannhäuser, Lohengrin, Das Rheingold, Siegfried, Die Walküre* and *Götterdämmerung.* In his first letter to Wagner after their first meeting, the King wrote:

---

[11] A student paper. (ONE's Baker Memorial Library & Archives)

> Unconscious though you were of it, you have been the sole
> source of my happiness ever since I was a mere boy, my
> friend, who spoke to my heart as no other did, my best
> teacher and educator.[12]

The prior year (1866) had found him involved in a relationship with his favorite aide-de-camp, Prince Paul Thun und Taxis. Their friendship had been formed in 1865 and was undoubtedly encouraged by Paul's father, who was scheming to create a small kingdom for his son in the Westphalian Rhineland. It was Paul who, in late 1865, Ludwig had dressed as Lohengrin and drawn across the Alpsee by an artificial swan while an orchestra played appropriate passages from the opera. By May (Ludwig's favorite month and one of no small symbolism in Wagner's operas), the alliance appeared to have developed into something more than just playmates.

If their liaison had indeed been consummated – and it should be noted that almost all references to Paul, including letters received from Ludwig, were purged from family records by subsequent generations of Taxis – is it not reasonable to believe that a year later, when he wrote the "Heinrich" letters to Sophie, he was already beginning to experience the "nightmarish" torments of a Tannhäuser?

Through the remaining two decades of his life Ludwig was to have but a handful of lovers.

By the end of his life, Ludwig was living almost entirely at night, completely ignoring his duties as King. Some scholars have explained this by positing an eye disease that may have kept him from seeing clearly except by dim light. The answer is more likely to be found in the text of *Tristan und Isolde*, which he acquired from Wagner in 1864.

Ludwig, the child, had had an interest in building churches and monasteries; Ludwig, the King, preferred castles. For him, there was likely little difference.

His first was Neuschwanstein, begun in 1869 but never completed. In a letter to Wagner dated May (again!) 13, 1868, is found the castle's impetus:

> I propose to rebuild the ancient castle ruins commanding
> wonderful views over the mountains of the Tyrol, a worthy
> temple for the godlike Friend through whom alone can
> flower the salvation and true blessedness of the world. The

---

[12] Herbert Barth, Dietrich Mack, and Egon Voss, eds., *Wagner: A Documentary Study* (New York: Oxford University Press, 1976), p.200.

outraged gods will take their revenge and sojourn with us
on the steep summit, fanned by celestial breezes.[13]

The castle, then, was to be a sort of shrine, dedicated in part to
the "outraged gods" of the *Ring*, in part to *Tannhäuser* and *Lohengrin*
(it contains a minstrel's hall inspired by the former and a courtyard,
by the latter), and to Wagner, "the godlike Friend."

In a letter dated January 7, 1869 lies another clue to the castle.
Ludwig writes:

Oh, how necessary it is to create for oneself such poetic
places of refuge where one can forget a little while the
dreadful times in which we live.[14]

It took Ludwig some years to realize that a nineteenth-century
state was held together by forces other than those that made a
sixteenth-century monarch and his people a spiritual part of each other.
With a full understanding of this came an awareness of being utterly
alone – more so than the gods of the *Ring*, who at least had each other
in their decline.

Wagner had once written to the King that Wotan's true glory
was in willing an end to the gods, in negating the will to survive.
When the end came for Ludwig, when he walked with his doctor at
Schloss Berg along a path leading to the lake, did he have in his mind
these words of Wotan from *Die Walküre*?:

Farewell, then
glory and pomp,
divine splendour's
flaunting shame!
Let what I
erected crumble!
I relinquish my work,
one thing alone I still desire,
the end –
the end!

---

[13] Wilfred Blunt, *The Dream King: Ludwig II of Bavaria* (New York:
The Viking Press, 1970), p.138.

[14] Desmond Chapman-Huston, *Bavarian Fantasy: the Story of Ludwig
II* (New York: Library Publishers, 1956), p.147.

Wagner had for years toyed with the idea of composing an opera based on the relationship between Jesus and Mary Magdalene. The libretto never materialized, but instead was metamorphosed into *Parsifal*, which he wrote in the summer of 1865, one year after meeting the King. The score, not composed until nearly two decades later, is dedicated to Ludwig. The dedication is appropriate, because music historians have come to believe that Wagner's story of "the innocent fool, enlightened through compassion" was actually inspired by the young, handsome, idealistic monarch.

Year after year ONE Institute classes on literature enrolled interested students. The first Sunday of the month Extension Lectures offered a wide range of speakers on literature from popular lesbian novelist, Ann Baanon, to cowboy/socialite writer and raconteur, Harry Otis, folklorist Richard Chase, and above all, Christopher Isherwood, who became a working member of ONE's staff. Many a fledgling writer was getting a start in *ONE Magazine*; best known today of that group is Joseph Hanson who at the time wrote as James Colton. *ONE Institute Quarterly* was making its mark as the first English-language scholarly journal in the field. From 1964, ONE's new foundation, the Institute for the Study of Human Resources, drew increasingly widespread support.

Who would have expected the serpent to enter this literary Eden? But such was the case as a handful of rebel editors and writers took physical possession of ONE – all its belongings – and attempted to oust its legally constituted officers and directors. These events can be read in more detail elsewhere, but the impact on matters literary was debilitatingly harmful. *ONE Magazine* and *ONE Institute Quarterly* were discontinued by 1970 or shortly thereafter. For a time literary concerns were pushed aside. Regular class semesters continued in other aspects of Homophile Studies: Sociology, History, Ethics, and some others.

When literature had its reactivation, it took a somewhat unexpected form: the several years of work on the massive two-volume, *Annotated Bibliography of Homosexuality* (New York: Garland, 1976). This major enterprise engaged the interest and efforts of virtually the entire ONE Institute faculty and many of the students during month after month of intensive bibliographical research. Of all the many fields of study, none surpassed literature in sheer volume of entries recorded. More than 6,000 titles: fiction, drama, poetry, and critical studies can be found on the pages of the two volumes as they were finally published. It is not suggested that this statistical ranking gives any grounds for fanciful flights of interpretation. What can be safely noted, however, is that in the literatures of many periods and cultures, countless writers have given some attention to Homophilia, its actors, and presence in society.

Founding Dean of ONE Institute, Merritt Thompson, often commented that insights and intuitive approaches writers made to the topic of Homophilia often came closer to bringing understanding than did the ponderously elaborate methods of those who called themselves scientists. Literature has never been regarded as a lesser or not "serious" part of the curriculum at ONE Institute.

When the graduate school was added in 1981, this emphasis is shown in the syllabuses reprinted in full in the Appendix to illustrate three different areas of Homophile study.[15]

**ONE Institute Extension Lectures:
Literature And Arts**

January 27, 1957 (#12) Dramatic readings from "Mama Doll," by James Barr.

February 1, 1958 (#16) "The Patterns of Sparta," a dramatic scene by Rachel Rosenthal.

February 1, 1959 (#27) An Afternoon of Poetry and Short Plays.

April 19, 1959 (#29) Homophile Poetry and Ballads, by Morgan Farley.

January 31, 1960 (#41) "Game of Fools," a play by James Barr.

October 2, 1960 (#44) Readings from the "Satyricon," of Petronius.

November 6, 1960 (#45) "Some Secrets of the Gay Novel," by Ann Bannon.

May 6, 1962 (#62) "C. P. Cavafy" an impersonation by R. H. Stuart.

October 6 1983 (#81) "The Eternal Quest", a reading of Homophile poetry.

April 5, 1964 (#87) "Music of Homophile Composers," by Brian Jennings, concert pianist.

May 3, 1964 (#88) "Kaleidoscope," mixed media by Harry Hay and John Burnside. "House of Roses," a scene by Tennessee Williams.

---

[15] See Appendix, 12-1: Homophile Literature 500, Literature 501, and Homophile Literature 500.

February 7, 1965 (#93) Christopher Isherwood talks.

January 30, 1966 (#108) "An Evening of Instant Theater," by Rachel Rosenthal and her students.

July 19, 1968 (#132) "Male Homosexual Expression," by Hal Call.

February 1, 1969 (#139) A repeat of the above.

December 7, 1969 (#148) "Gay Film Making," by Pat Rocco.

January 4, 1970 (#149) "Silent Movies Organ Playing," by Gaylord Carter.

April 5, 1970 (#152) Experimental Film, Gordon Meyer, cinema student.

October 4, 1970 (#156) "Homotropel, An Essay in Images," by Seth.

May 6, 1971 (#162) Homophile Art Show.

December 3, 1972 (#180) Homophile Art and Fashions.

January 27, 1973 (#182) "ONE Adventure, Homophiles Overseas," a movie by Pat Rocco.

January 6, 1974 (#190) "A Writer's life," by Harry Otis.

June 8, 1974 (#205) "A Friend of Mine," by Christopher Isherwood.

November 3, 1974 (#208) "ONE Adventure," repeated.

December 1, 1974 (#209) Gay Art Show.

November 2, 1975 (#218) "Homophile Drama," by Gene Touchet, Ph.D.

June 4, 1978 (#245) Gay poet, Robert Peters, reads.

March 4, 1979 (#250) "Politics and Poetry," by Larry Reh.

June 3, 1979 (#253) Film makers on "How Far Can We Go?"

March 7, 1982 (#278) "The Keval and My Other Works," by Harry Otis.

May 2, 1982 (#280) "Gay Folk Songs," by Lisa Ben, folk singer.

March 6, 1983 (#286) "Feminism in Literature," by Richard Follett, D.A.

May 6, 1984 (#296) "Some Gay Poetry," a reading by Gene Touchet.

July 9, 1989 (#300) "Shelley on Homosexuality," by Lou Crompton, Ph.D.

February 3, 1985 (#305) "Three Thousand Years of Our Literature," by Richard Follett, D.A.

October 6, 1985 (#311) "Leaves of Grass," a concert by Bill Bryan, pianist.

December 1, 1985 (#313) "Larry Kramer Speaks."

April 6, 1986 (#317) "Celebration Theater," by Charles Rowland, Founder.

December 7, 1986 (#322) "Poetry and Drama About Ourselves," by Gene Touchet.

January 11, 1987 (#323) "Whitman: The Good Gay Poet," by Charles Shively, Ph.D.

June 7, 1987 (#328) "Surviving in the 1980s," by Michael Kearns,

Actor.

May 7, 1989 (#344) "Music Around the World from Hollywood to the Vatican," by Bob Mitchell, organist, choir director.

June 4 1989 (#345) "Gay Films Today," by David Ehrenstein, film critic.

January 7, 1990 (#349) "Whitman's California Connections," by Charles Shively.

February 4, 1990 (#350) Poet Robert Peters reads from his newest book.

March 4, 1990 (#351) "Two Films Disclaiming Homosexuality," by Gregg Daskalogrigoras.

January 6, 1991 (#358) "Homophile Composer Marc Blitzstein," by Eric Gordon, Ph.D., biographer.

Video cassettes of Lecture nos. 296, 311, 322, 338, 344, 349, 358, and 359 are included in the Audiovisual Collection of ONE's Baker Memorial Library.

CHAPTER 13

PHILOSOPHY

P hilosophy has been included as an *essential* component of Homophile Studies, not to launch some arcane new addition to an already complex subject. It is there because the analytical abilities of philosophical method have so often been in short supply. In other fields surveyed at ONE Institute, the challenging of assumptions held as articles of faith in many scholarly circles has been a primary task in Homophile Studies. However, to challenge without offering anything as an alternate is one of those bad habits long endemic in much of academia.

ONE Institute has been keenly aware of the need for remedial goals and methods, and has as a matter of policy turned to philosophy for assistance with the observed shortcomings. Having said this, a much less ambitious approach will be offered in these pages: a selection of excerpts from the writings of faculty members on philosophical themes.

Foremost have been the writings of founding Dean at ONE Institute, Merritt M. Thompson. His many years as a professional philosopher and educational theorist, studying directly under John Dewey, have left a substantial written legacy. Their mark on the development of ONE Institute has been unmistakable.[1] The selections from his writings will begin with his intimate and personal account of some aspects of his own background.

Reminiscence of a Friend of ONE[2]

In the earliest environment which I knew and which was intensely religious, evangelical Protestant, the very word *sex* was the epitome of all evil and was not to be mentioned in polite society. Immorality was almost exclusively concerned with the practice of sex activities, the use of alcohol and tobacco being minor variations of sinful behavior. In the educational world, G. Stanley Hall, the foremost

---

[1] See Chap.1, p.20ff above.

[2] *LTR* XIV:10 (October, 1969), pp.6-11.

educational psychologist of the period, was complaining of being slighted by Edward L. Thorndike, his successor in preeminence in educational research and psychology, and attributing the slight to his interest in research in the sexual field. On the third floor of his home he had a collection of research materials on sex that was probably unique at that time in this country. As far as the Homophile is concerned, this group, now known to be large, was practically unknown outside a small esoteric group which included Havelock Ellis and Edward Carpenter. It was against this background that I came to Los Angeles in a professional capacity.

I became familiar with the office center of ONE, Inc., the central organization in Southern California. It was located in an old Los Angeles business building between Hill and Spring Streets, north of Third Street. Although shabby and occupied largely by small, lower class industries, it was centrally located, not unduly expensive, and offered ONE on the third floor, an office, store room, and several class-council rooms. A surprising number of activities were carried on here, including classes. Many individuals came and went constantly with profit to themselves which could not be obtained elsewhere.

The changes in both knowledge of and attitudes toward homosexuality on the part of the public during the period of my experience have been extraordinary. At the beginning of the twentieth century, as I have already pointed out, homosexuality was practically unknown outside of the small, esoteric group. Today, current literature, moving pictures, television, the radio, and the theater have all removed the veil from every aspect of sex, including homosexuality.

Undoubtedly, the ONE movement has made a real contribution to the greater freedom and rationality of the whole field. A few of the points I have learned largely from ONE include the following. First, homosexuality is much more extensive than we have ever dreamed of. Probably half of all males are involved to a greater or lesser extent. We do not know so definitely about females, but it is doubtless extensive among them. Individual scientists and groups are now studying the subject seriously. They find that it goes far back into history and involves practically all peoples, including many leaders and creative geniuses of the periods.

I now discovered that there had been developing over the years an ideology which I was to find rational, consistent, and defensible. The great problem was to be educational, that is, to promulgate this ideology against the bitter, emotional biases and prejudices behind which social ignorance always seems to barricade itself. Some of the tenets of this ideology may be identified. First, homosexuality is not a crime, an illness, or a wild eccentricity; it is a variation such as characterizes all aspects of nature. Every plant and animal reproduces true to its type up to a certain point, but beyond that point is subject to infinite variation. No two individuals are identical. Heterosexuality is essential to perpetuation, but instinctive sex urges are so much stronger than the need for continuity that a worldwide problem of overpopulation is now recognized by all thinking people. Homosexuality is simply a variation in nature, harmless for the most part, and even useful to channel off superfluous sex impulses.

With all this ideological development taking place in the background, ONE, Inc. faced the problem of deciding what activities it should cultivate and carry on. As the program as worked out has been published many times, I need not repeat it here, except to point out that social need was always a guiding concept. As I came into the work, like the leader, I was impressed by the fact that the biases, prejudices, and social maladjustments in general were nearly always based upon ignorance. Thus, the leader conceived the idea that the most helpful activity to the movement would be an Institute, a kind of specialized graduate school of classes covering the relation of sex, particularly homosexuality, to the larger field of culture. This point was where I came in. I had long experience in education at many levels and was especially interested in philosophy, psychology, and sociology, all of which seemed appropriate to the development of the project which was now being formed in our minds.

An evening was given to each of the following areas: philosophy, psychology, and social anthropology, with history and literature brought in incidentally. I need not list the classes and subjects that actually grew out of the discussions, as they have been covered abundantly in the literature of ONE, but I am glad to report that the educational and intellectual approach was never lost sight of and, in my opinion, has been largely responsible for the growth and expansion of the influence of the ONE movement in this area.

I am highly gratified by the facts that the intellectual and educational character which we tried to give the Institute carried the creation of the public image of the ONE movement in a gradual widening of the area of its influence. In these days support and requests for lectures and information are coming increasingly from reputable physicians, clergymen, college classes, and others of recognized standing. No better proof of the social constructiveness of the ONE movement is needed.

One of the early Thompson formal writings for ONE Institute was

"The Projected Encyclopedic Dictionary: The Terminological Impasse."

"To define and limit the concept of any encyclopedic dictionary is no easy task," he wrote. So monumental a work was not achieved by ONE Institute in 1960 as hoped. What did appear finally was *The Annotated Bibliography of Homosexuality*, in two volumes published in 1976, of which previous mention has been made. It was not until twenty years still later that an *Encyclopedia of Homosexuality*, also in two volumes, was issued in New York under the editorship of Hunter College's Professor Wayne Dynes.

Continuing with the Thompson article, he raised many other problems and issues involved in such a much needed undertaking.

Homophile Studies:
The Projected Encyclopedic Dictionary
By Dr. Thomas M. Merritt[3]

To define and limit the content of an encyclopedic dictionary of homosexuality is no easy task. The first step, however, must probably be the clarification of vocabulary. For anyone doing research in the field of homosexuality, the first difficulty he encounters is the confusion in vocabulary of terms used to describe the various aspects of the sexual functions and relationships. For example, pederasty derivatively means the love of children, but one is more likely to find it used as synonymous with sodomy or anal intercourse. In reading an article within the field, one is never quite sure just what reference the author had in mind. This problem is not helped by the fact that some terms have acquired emotional connotations which obscure their rightful use. For example, such terms as inversion, homosexuality, perversion, degeneracy, deviation, corruption, etc., have borrowed emotional overtones from one another until a writer is never sure just what impression he is conveying to his readers, when as a matter of fact, exact definitions would give to each term a proper use that would enlighten rather than confuse the reader. This problem is not peculiar to the field under consideration. Since the so-called Scientific Revolution high-lighted in the Seventeenth Century, one field after

---

[3] *QTLY* I:2 (Summer, 1958), pp.40-44.

another has found it necessary to define its terms more precisely in order to keep up with the progress of the learned world. Consequently, at the present time there are available dictionaries, more or less encyclopedic, in such fields as philosophy, medicine, psychology, religion, education, and many others.

A major necessity in all cases will be the tedious sifting and presentation of the evidence. We must avoid the error of which Hirschfeld has been accused, that of merely sweeping together the greatest list of names that historical hearsay could gather, with little regard for the credibility of the evidence in each distinct case.

Aside from biographical entries, there are organizations, periodicals, and special groups to be mentioned: Hirschfeld's Institute of Sexual Science, the Mattachine Society, ICSE, ONE, Inc., the newly established Homosexual Law Reform Society of England, with its spectacular list of prominent sponsors: Der Kreis, of Zurich, Arcadie, of Paris, Vriendschap, of Amsterdam; societies and magazines not formerly found in various countries; special groups not necessarily homosexual as such, but which have somehow involved homosexuality in their history, aims, and influence, groups as various as, for example, the Nazis, the Bloomsbury Set, the Elizabethans, secret societies and fraternities, troubadours, fringe religious and political sects or groups suspected of sexual non-conformity, frontiersmen, sailors, hoboes, migratory workers, sex-segregated prisoners as described for instance in Fishman's *Sex in Prison*.

In addition to individuals and specific groups and publications, there are more general categories: attitudes and practices in different countries, historic epochs, such for example as the age of Louis XIV, "The Great Century" in France, which recent studies have shown to be a prolific source of information on the practice of homosexuality; ethnic groups and primitive peoples who have been studied in detail by anthropologists like Margaret Mead in her *Coming of Age in Samoa* and Bronislaw Malinowski in his *Sexual Life of Savages* and others; religions and churches which have appointed committees in recent years to study the question, sources like Derrick Sherwin Bailey's *Homosexuality and the Western Christian Tradition*, with its reinterpretation of Biblical and traditional religious references; political groups and parties, social reformers and revolutionaries; and, finally, statistical studies such as those of Hamilton, H. Ellis, Kinsey, and others.

One of the most complicated and controversial areas has been that of law, investigated recently with much fanfare in England in the famous *Wolfenden Report* made to Parliament and commented upon throughout Europe. Various countries have laws of historic importance attempting to regulate sexual conduct (as Paragraph 175 in Germany, or provisions under "Stalin's Constitution" in the Soviet Union, etc.) and also covering censorship of publications in the field. This area is so extensive that it can only be summarized in the work projected here.

It is obvious that legal questions lead at once into the definitions of concepts which are used in the law, religion, morals, and philosophy. To what extent have homosexuals, or anti-homosexuals, developed ethical concepts of their own which may or may not expect general acceptance?

The field of art is likewise an almost unlimited one. Articles would be needed on homosexuality in the films, the theater, the dance, design and decorating, fiction and, poetry. For poetry, Carpenter's anthology of masculine love, *Iolaus*, is quite illuminating. It was first published in 1902 but has been reprinted many times since. It sometimes seems that the dramatists and fiction writers have given more correct analyses of the psychology of homosexuality than the more scientifically minded. The bibliography recently published in Arcadie lists a large number of titles. In an *Encyclopedia of Homosexuality*, some of the more important books and authors, such as James Barr's *Quatrefoil* or Roger Peyrefitte's *Special Friendships*, may well be given in synopsis with brief biographies of the authors and something of the major characters in the novels. The same may be said of such plays as *Game of Fools* and Robert Anderson's *Tea and Sympathy*.

In his "Philosophy For The Homophile," Professor Thompson provides an overview and summary of various well-known philosophic schools and trends suggesting salient points of entry for the Homophile into general philosophic methods and concerns.

Philosophy For The Homophile[4]

The structure of a complete and defensible philosophy for the Homophile is one that can never be finished, but the work and study of many devoted students can and will render an immeasurable service to those whose lives have not been any too happy hitherto. It is here that ONE Incorporated and its many activities including its publica-

---

[4] *QTLY* II:3 (Summer 1959), pp.77-82.

tions looks toward the future.

The present study will attempt to indicate a method by which a Homophile may develop for himself a philosophy which utilizes historic development and at the same time demands respect from those familiar with those developments.

Man everywhere has manifested a desire to reach some understanding of and relation to the universe at large, the totality of things, the forces that operate upon him, offering resistances to the expression of his will at times and at others reinforcing it. Having no real knowledge of their nature during the earlier epochs of history, he interpreted them in terms of what he did know, in terms of himself and his companions, and thus personalized and mythicized the world peopling it with beings who opposed or assisted him in carrying on his life activities. The religions of the world arose from man's attempts to put himself into right relationships with these beings. Thus, the most primitive tribes have developed some form of religion or mythicized philosophy to satisfy this desire for a relationship with the unknown.

Some persons have deprecated the subject because of the lack of finality and agreement in the historic solutions, but there has been perhaps more agreement than many realize and, in any case, the object for the Homophile is not agreement with others but personal acceptance of himself and a calm inner life which comes only from a philosophy which is satisfying and convincing to one's self.

The difficulty with naive and uncriticized philosophies lies in their unrealized inconsistencies and imperfections which destroy their satisfying quality without the holder's knowing the reason. One could illustrate endlessly the false and distorted notions which beset the path of the Homophile, and which can only be pushed aside by careful and thorough philosophical examination and the substitution of defensible ideologies. One studies historic philosophies in order to bring his own to the surface, to make the implicit explicit for the purposes of criticism and elucidation. Many religious business men would be shocked to learn that their business philosophy is an exceedingly crude materialism. Many Homophiles condemn themselves and are unhappy because of popular notions and epithets which are completely indefensible when examined in the light of philosophical and scientific principles.

Philosophy, as it has emerged in history, has been defined in many ways, but essentially it covers some five major purposes which have underlain the different modes of expression. It is first the defining and clarifying of concepts; then it is the organization or structuralization of one's world; third, it is the building of one's interpretation of his world around the basic concept of reality or that of value or of both; fourth, it is the determination of the nature of thought as the process by which the meaning of reality is attained; and last, it is a way of life as indicated in behavior or conduct.

The problem of defining the basic terms used in discussions of sex or homosexuality is now well known and has been discussed at length with various persons and groups working on its solution. Doubtless with time an adequate glossary will emerge which will clarify thinking in the field greatly. In the meantime, the individual must fortify himself against epithets and terms which bear all sorts of emotional and unjust connotations, frequently holdovers from now outmoded points of view rejected by intelligent people.

Pragmatism has been left until last and probably comes nearest to being the characteristic American philosophy. Pragmatism, called also Experimentalism and Instrumentalism, was first developed by Charles S. Peirce, a New England professor, scholar, and scientist, during the second half of the nineteenth century. He was followed by William James and by John Dewey, who has given it world prominence. Peirce's concern was with the method of thinking, rather than with the truth of events. He sought for the intellectual control of behavior in ideas, meanings, concepts, and beliefs. He also developed the pragmatic principle of awareness of meanings through active response and testing of consequences. In short, he bridged the gap between exact measurement in the physical world and analytic thought in the psychological world. Dewey developed at length the relation of the individual to the social environment and the meaning of a democratic world, but perhaps his greatest contribution was his synthesis of all the techniques of thought, or epistemologies, we have found in the historic overview, into what we call simply problem solving, rationality as it comes into the daily life of everyone. Dewey avoided, even deprecated, metaphysics, but the naturalistic basis for his thinking is obvious, and his technique of thought easily supplements any metaphysical position that does not itself deny the validity of rational thinking.

Our discussion has brought us to the final topic of the normative sciences, standards or norms of behavior and conduct. If we accept as the ultimate reality the absolute value of the person, and recognize that his problems must all submit to rationality, the Homophile may find ethical and aesthetic ideals not so difficult to formulate. The one who ever seeks the beautiful as expressed in art, nature, and good taste and the highest welfare and happiness for his fellows and himself will have developed a philosophy that may prove surprising in its power to withstand the adverse blows of a hostile and uncomprehending society.

The Thompson examination of "Homophile Ethics" touches on so many aspects of this controversial topic that the article is reproduced here in full for the value, not only of its content, but as a record of ONE Institute's many decades of attention to the questions which the article raises for consideration.

A still earlier ONE Institute faculty treatment of this topic was faculty member Julian Underwood's "Some Observations on Sexual Ethics." [5]

Homophile Ethics
By Thomas M. Merritt[6]

Of all the problems which confront homosexuals, perhaps none is more widespread and penetrating in its effect on the welfare and happiness of the group than that of the rightness and wrongness of homosexual acts, that is, their ethical implications. In the current literature of the day one constantly finds references to homosexuality as perversion, one of the crimes of the period, a characteristic of abnormal and perverse people. Preachers have condemned it; judges have scorned those who practiced it; ridicule has been heaped upon it; and in fact it has been listed in company with the worst human aberrations. Thus, homosexuals have been subjected to the most intense feelings of guilt or have defied social standards and lived secret lives apart from and coldly separated from their fellow men, if not victimized by their enemies and classified and secluded as criminals in penal institutions. The voices raised against such inhuman treatment have been few and far between with no organized effort to remedy the situation until our own day when, for the first time, questions are being raised and discussed in groups of intelligent people.

The reasons for the strong feelings against homosexuality are not wholly clear, but there are some historic facts which throw light upon the subject. The ancient Hebrew people were a small group alienated from their ancestral lands over a long period of time and, when

---

[5] *MAG* IV:9 (December, 1956), pp.28,29.

[6] *QTLY* III:4 (Fall 1960), pp.262-267.

circumstances permitted them to return, they found them occupied by strange and hostile nationalities who must be conquered and driven out by warring activities. Consequently, potential warriors were at a premium and a high birth rate was desirable. Polygamy became a virtue and anything which hindered the increase of population would be looked down upon. Thus, a point of view was established against irregular sex activities which was later extended to all sex activities. The transition from the Hebrew to the Christian culture carried over the antagonistic attitude toward sex. The views of Paul, the organizer of the Christian Church, are well known. His influence went so far that celibacy became a rule for the priesthood of the growing institution, and morality became practically synonymous with abstinence from sex activities. There may have been a psychological basis in part at least for the identification of chastity and holiness. That nature has made the organs of sex those also of excretion is one of the anomalies which are found in the natural world and which offend the rational mind. Sex thus becomes "dirty" merely by association. A possibly more profound reason may lie in the rise of mysticism, an aspect of human culture which has defied all attempts to define it or set limiting boundaries to it, but which has exerted enormous influence and is clearly recognized in the history of religion. The relation of mystical states of mind and sexual ecstasy is indicated in the writings of mystics, such, for example, as those of Santa Theresa and others, as well as in practices wherein, for example, nuns are called "the brides of Christ." Thus, sex and religion are placed in the position of rivals for human allegiance and, to our own day, sin is more vividly portrayed in terms of sex by the teachers of "morality" than in any other area. It is thus natural that the denial of man's basic urges must be accompanied by a philosophy of life which exalts suffering and deprivation in this life, only to be assuaged in a life beyond the grave. A curious fact of our times is the enormous increase in the membership of the churches at the same time there is a very lively exercise of skepticism which feels itself justified in examining and criticizing the basic beliefs and doctrines bequeathed to us by tradition. Thus, the whole subject of sex in general and homosexuality in particular is subject to the search for a truer and more satisfying basis than ever before. Just what do right and wrong, then, mean for the Homophile? The present study is an attempt to develop briefly that aspect of a philosophy of life which is termed ethical or moral.

Ethics has to do with the inner aspects of life, mental and spiritual, and conduct. It studies purpose as determined by outer conditions, or outer conditions of individual behavior or institutions as determined by the inner purpose. To study choice and purpose is psychology; to study choice as affected by the rights of others and to judge it as right or wrong by such a standard is ethics. To study an institution may be economics, or sociology, or law, but to study its activities as resulting from the purposes of persons or as affecting the welfare of persons, and to judge its acts as good or bad from that point of view, is ethics. The place of value as related to standards will be taken up later.

Following somewhat the Freudian theory of personality, conduct or behavior may take place on three levels. Behavior on the first or lowest level is initiated by various biological, economic, or other non-moral impulses or needs of the organism, non-moral so long as their ends are merely accepted, but becoming moral when their ends are compared, evaluated, and chosen deliberately. This type of behavior is characteristic of animals, children, and persons who act ordinarily without reflection, instinctively and disregarding of consequences either to one's self or to others. The purpose of moral education is to transform this type of behavior to the higher forms, that is, from non-intelligent action to intelligent action.

The second type of behavior is that which is determined by the "folkways" and "mores" of the group to which one belongs, and is approved by it. The standards are accepted by the individual with little or no critical reflection and are handed down from one generation to the next. They may be termed group habits, and are likely to be quite independent of intelligence and flexibility, although they may have had some utility in a previous age. The history of many of the religious sects illustrates this point extensively. A distinguished leader or a set of circumstances may have pointed out a specific need which became embodied in an ethical code, rational at the time, but later a mere formality imposed by group inertia. Many years ago a non-Prussian minority in Germany resented the arrogance and domination of the Prussian military of whom a notable characteristic was the wearing of conspicuous uniforms with large brass buttons. These buttons became the symbol of the hated overlords, and gave rise to a distaste for all buttons. This minority migrated to the United States and settled in western Pennsylvania. Years afterward, when doubtless the origin of the distaste was wholly forgotten, the religious sect representing this minority considered the wearing of buttons "wicked" and do so to this day. The writer has seen these people in eastern Ohio with their buttonless garments cut to long outmoded styles but conforming to the rigid ethical code of the group.

The third type of conduct is that in which the individual thinks and judges for himself, considers whether a purpose is good and right, decides and chooses, and does not accept the standards of his group without reflection. Complete morality is reached only when the individual recognizes the right or chooses the good freely, devotes himself wholeheartedly to its fulfillment, and seeks a progressive social development which involves the sharing of every member of society. A rational method of setting up standards and forming values must be substituted for habitual, passive acceptance. Voluntary and personal choice and interest must be substituted for unconscious identification with group welfare or instinctive and habitual response to group needs. The ultimate purpose is individual development with the demand that all persons shall share in this development. The worth and happiness of the person and of every person are paramount. Thus, one passes from the realm of the instinctive and merely expedient to that of the rational.

A concept that has had great vogue in our time with reference to the nature of personality is that of integration, the hanging together, as it were, of the various aspects of the person. Perhaps this quality can best be seen in connection with its opposite. So-called insanity or mental disease can best be understood in terms of the disintegration of the personality. One is shocked by the conversation of the abnormal as it will contain the most glaring inconsistencies and disharmonies. And the so-called normal is not always as consistent as he thinks he is. Someone has said that the greatest invention of the nineteenth century was the ability to hold two ideas at the same time which cancel each other out. One thinks of the "Free World" and the attitude of many of its citizens towards Negroes. Conduct and character are strictly correlative concepts. Continuity, consistency throughout a series of acts, is the expression of the enduring unity of attitudes and habits. In fact, conduct may be defined as continuity of action. Deeds hang together because they proceed from a single and stable self. Customary morality tends to overlook the connection between character and action. The essence of reflective morals lies in its consciousness of the existence of a persistent self and the part it plays in what is externally done. Motive is the attitude and predisposition of this self toward ends which are embodied in action. Mere foresight moves to action only when it is accompanied by desire for those ends. A set and disposition of character leads to anticipation of certain kinds of consequences and to the neglect of others. There is no such thing as motive and will, apart from anticipation of consequences and from effort to bring them to pass.

The discussion of motive leads directly into the larger area of value, the supreme concept of philosophy and the starting point for all consideration of personality. Closely related to it is the concept of freedom. The fundamental task of intelligent living is that of examining the relative worth of varying and opposed values and of bringing about their most valuable combinations. They assume moral significance in so far as they contribute to human living its worth and reason for being. To live as a rational being, man must organize his life and thought about the attainment of goals, which express his ideals and ultimately his values. As a matter of fact, men do live the greater part of their lives amidst their ideals and experience their highest moments of enthusiasm when they are working and sacrificing more immediate goods for them. The problem of the moral or supreme form of living is that of selecting and organizing ideals. To be free to choose one's goals does not mean to be free from all determining factors in one's nature, but rather to be free to express in action the preference to which these factors give rise. Custom, tradition, emotion, imagination, all these play their part, but reason must ultimately dominate. Freedom is self-determination leading to self-realization, which is the equivalent of living rationally or intelligently, the realization of one's potentialities, the expression of one's natural impulses within the limits of one's ideals. The product of conscious effort is willed action, wherein the motive, which represents the attitude of the total conscious being, is held at a particular time and in a particular act of choosing. One is free in an action when it represents the self as a whole and is not the sporadic and momentary expression of some impulse.

As was suggested above, it is in theories of value that all ethics finds its starting point. The theorists of the subject are divided between those who hold that value is inherent in the cosmic order, objective and ultimate, and those who hold that it is an attribute of a deeper reality, a construction of the mind. G. D. Moore, Bertrand Russell, and John Laird hold value as undefinable. Laird claims that nature itself possesses value. This objective interpretation of value is termed the realistic theory of value and was the one held largely by the older religionists who, however, approached objective idealism and located values, and more particularly ethical values in the mind of a personal God. Thus, ethical behavior was reduced to a list of prohibitions. One might use the divided page, listing the "wicked" or "sinful" acts on one side and the permissible acts on the other. The great defect of this procedure lay in the fact that the "mind of God" was confused with social and cultural origins, which, as was illustrated above, were likely to be lost in a historical perspective. And the most trivial and inconsequential acts were forbidden (when the writer was nine years of age, his father gave him one of the worst scoldings of his life because he and a friend took a walk in the woods on a Sunday afternoon), while great, obvious evils such, for example, as graft and special privileges in business and government, adulteration of food and drugs, etc., were never mentioned. Even some of the so-called realists have not held consistently to the completely objective theory of values. For example, Russell holds that values are the creations of man, and R. B. Perry defines value in terms of interest, and anything may acquire value when it is desired. That act which secures in the largest degree the interests of all is morally right. S. Alexander finds that truth, goodness, and beauty involve an "appreciating mind" and involve a relationship between mind and its objects. When satisfactions are organized and made coherent within the individual and in the relation of individuals within the social group, they are morally good. If one holds that ethical values are objective and inherent in the universe, it would seem that he has the obligation to discover them and present them to us. Thus far, no one has been able to go beyond purely abstract concepts which turn out to be mere classifications or categories, such, for example, as truth, beauty, and goodness, which give very little help in the actual concerns of living, and arbitrary lists of forbidden acts which obviously do not escape their cultural relativity.

To this writer the philosophy known as personalistic or dynamic idealism seems to offer a more acceptable basis for ethics than realism, although it does not deny an objective world, but sees it in a proper perspective which, in its relation to persons, is an inference rather than a primary datum of experience. The world, or reality, in its ultimate structure is a system of conscious beings whose most profound nature may be expressed in the term *persons*. The total universe is a system of selves or persons, who may be regarded either as members of one all-inclusive person who individuates them by the diversity of his purposing (this view represents that of absolute idealism), or as a society of many selves related by common purpose (this view represents a pluralistic idealism and is the one held by this writer). The person or self is the process of conscious experience ever moving forward in a time sequence, and having a two-fold character, first, a reaction to the objective world, and, second, a regurgitation of past experience in memory for the purpose of examination, criticism, and the deepening of meaning, in a word, for the development of insight. This process may be called the consciousness of consciousness, an ever more profound understanding of one's own nature and experience. The physical world is within the world of experience which is the entire world of reality. Some have thought that this view denies the existence of an outer or objective world. (*Esse est percipi*, to be is to be perceived, has often been interpreted in this way.) It does not do so, but it recognizes that, without a perceiving mind, it lacks reality, that is, an object which no one perceives is merely an inference, or abstraction, by a mind. The most hard-boiled research scientist never escapes himself in the process of his work, and it is becoming better recognized that all scientific conclusions are inferences drawn by the minds of persons without whom there would be, as far as human beings are concerned, just nothing. Values originate in the self and exist only for the self. They are not substantive, things, but attributes of the on-going process which is the consciousness, the person. The inner feel of the person, that by which he knows that he is a person, may be called the intuition of the self, or more immediately, desire. Ordinary living consists of the rhythm of desire-satisfaction, repeated endlessly. And the remote goal may be termed self-realization, the fulfilling of the potentialities of the person, his ultimate welfare and happiness, always recognizing that such fulfillment takes place in a social setting of other persons who are entitled to the same privilege. Thus, ethical value, the Good, becomes that which contributes to the welfare and happiness of all members of the human race. The sacrifices of individuals are sometimes required for the common good, but such sacrifice comes to be a good in its own right. Welfare and happiness are not entirely satisfactory as definitions of the Good, which is easier to see in specific situations than in purely abstract terms. The next part of the discussion will attempt to bring the matter down to earth.

The idealistic interpretation of value and ethics remains on a level of abstract concepts perhaps to too great an extent. It has remained for the pragmatic and instrumentalist philosophies to bring the discussion to the level of everyday experience. For these views value is the supreme category. Like the idealists they find human experience to cover the sum-total of available data. Absolute standards are not discoverable. Values vary from situation to situation and with specific needs. Facts are those aspects of the stimulus-reaction situation which seem to hold a certain consistency and the reactions to them are as near as we can ever come to absolutes. All objects of value receive their value from the functions they perform in the situation where they occur or in situations related to them. Nothing taken in isolation can be said to possess value. In fact nothing exists in such isolation. And the personal idealist says that nothing has reality in isolation from the person. Thus, welfare and happiness must be defined in terms of the activities of actual persons in actual situations. For example, in most cases the life of a person is better when he is well-nourished than when he is starving, when he is healthy than when he is sick, etc., as anthropologists describe the activities of human beings everywhere. The fact that those activities are so similar gives rise to the error that the goods of life are absolutes. Moral values arise, not alone when the good of the individual is referred to, but also when the situation is social, that is, when the interests of other people are affected by the object of value. Moral standards and attitudes are accepted because they manifest values in the social situations. There are no absolute and permanent standards other than these. There are no eternal ideas of good and evil. Utility, then, becomes a concept of high place in the discussion. Value is interpreted in terms of control, mastery, use. One thus returns to intelligence or rationality. Some are disappointed that ethics cannot furnish the list referred to earlier, these acts are moral, and these are immoral. Each individual must exercise his intelligence to determine the quality of his own behavior. The moral person is the one who does so and is not moved by blind impulse or enslaved by a narrow and bigoted society. I suppose no one escapes the necessity of expediency when a society will destroy the individual who departs too conspicuously from the norms which it professes with no regard for origin or rationality. Each person, unless he has a yen for martyrdom, is likely to conform to the point at least of survival, but, from that point on, he would seem to have a moral obligation to do what he can to create more rational attitudes and norms in the society where he finds himself.

Thus far the discussion has dealt with ethics in a general way which applies to all the aspects of life, but now it would seem appropriate to look a little more closely at the ethics of the Homophile. It seems somewhat presumptuous, however, to suppose that one can add to what René Guyon has written in his *The Ethics of Sexual Acts*, probably the most complete and rational treatment of the subject now extant. While paying him full honor, this writer differs from him in two points. In the first place Guyon objects to a metaphysical interpretation as the basis of ethics. Like John Dewey, who made the same mistake, he assumes that one can build up a theory without presuppositions and then proceeds to state certain principles which are based upon assumptions. John Dewey's followers were somewhat embarrassed, but found it necessary to specify the unconscious assumptions underlying his work. As a matter of fact, there is no genuine thinking without some presuppositions. The most thorough research scientist must assume the uniformity of nature, the reliability of sense observation, the worth of his research, and others. Thus, we have attempted in this study to find a legitimate starting point for the elaboration of our ideas, and that point lies as always in the realm of metaphysics. Our second point of disagreement with Guyon refers to his separation of the acts of living into two spheres, one involving moral decisions and one quite removed from that sphere, such, for example, as eating, and other acts of physiology, psycho-physiology, hygiene, etc., which cannot be either moral or immoral, but rather amoral. Sexual acts come within this amoral sphere and should not be used as criteria of virtue, utility, or value, since they are incommensurable things. This writer cannot see any act of the human being which is outside the realm of the ethical unless one returns to the view of the older religionists with their division of behavior into the "sinful" and the "righteous." When one sees the world as a whole and a consistent whole, he must recognize that there is a right way and a wrong way to reach even the most ordinary and commonplace goals. In baking a cake, if one does not use the right proportion of baking power to flour, his cake will fail. To claim that such an activity is amoral in contrast to a personal relationship involving honesty or its opposite, seems to this writer to come close to assuming the bifurcation of the world into natural and supernatural, a view here rejected.

Thus, we come to our conclusion that sexual acts, the same as any other, are subject to rational examination and are accepted or rejected as to whether they operate constructively toward the building of the Good Life or its opposite. Now it happens in a given society and a given set of circumstances that a particular act so often operates destructively that it becomes expedient to enact its prohibition into law, but even here one has to be careful not to think of such restrictions as absolutes. For example, in our society and that of Europe it is rather well accepted that unethical sexual behavior includes: relations with underage persons, the use of force or violence, public display, and the conscious transmission of venereal disease. And yet that these prohibitions are not absolutes is proved by the fact that there are other societies which think very differently about them. In some countries of the world where minors are not protected by law, pre-adolescents are sometimes prostitutes and initiate sex behavior on their own account; the writer once lived in a primitive community where the birth of a child in the family was a festive occasion and all members of the family, old and young, were invited to witness the event. Privacy had little meaning here. There is a certain inertia in man which leads him to wish to avoid rational thinking and find the situations of life expressed in simple terms of black and white, yes and no, but life is just not built that way, and successful living requires a price to be paid; that price is seeking for constructive goals and the use of rational means in attaining them. There is no other way.

An occasional lecturer and long time ONE Director, Monwell

Boyfrank, with his highly individual and unexpected viewpoints in many directions, although of the same generation as Merritt Thompson, left his own and special mark upon the development of ONE Institute.

The following excerpts are from his article, "Nothing Especially New."

Nothing Especially New
By Monwell Boyfrank[7]

An expert who has a string of letters yea long after his name can come and lecture you learnedly. He'll be a better speaker than I am, a faster thinker and more enjoyable to listen to; but when he stops talking, you'll note that he does not know all of the answers either.

Fortunately, common sense and commonly possessed knowledge are of help in this field. One of the best things that any expert can do is tell you to rely upon your own observation, your own measurements, and your own reasoning. Beyond that there are too many questions to be gone into; and until ONE, Incorporated, got on the job it was against the law to ask those questions.

ONE Incorporated's historic legal victory against the forces of ignorance and malice, forces spearheaded by the postmaster of Los Angeles of the time, was a very near thing. We were hanging on the ropes when the issue came up for decision in the Supreme Court. If the litigation costs had come to one more dollar than we had put into the fight, we would have lost. We couldn't have raised another cent.

Believing as I do that irresponsible fatherhood is a grave crime, that it is as bad to beget a child and be unable or unwilling to support it as it is to commit murder, I am eager to say anything that I can to dissuade men from engaging in it.

It is the non-procreative man or the man prudently procreative who is the responsible man, the man of righteousness. In our compacted world we have a right to ask of any father, "What justification have you for gratifying your sexual desires thus to probable detriment of your neighbors?" He may have a good answer,

---

[7] *MAG* XIII:5 (May, 1965), pp.6-10.

but the question is bound to be raised.   Men have argued for thousands of years that the love of a man for a man is eminently practical as a means of limiting the surplus of human beings.

Any man who argues against homophily has shut himself off cruelly from the real world. It is hard to believe that mere ignorance can be blamed for some of the perversity exhibited by the advocates of wanton proliferation.

Whether or not you are a homosexual is a metaphysical question, and such questions can get abominably murky. Any question that touches upon "being," any sentence that has the word "is," "are," or "be" in it is metaphysical.

Much man-to-man attachment is, I think, of a sort scarcely to be called sexual. A human being likes to have other persons around, sometimes some certain person, and not always with any logic to his preference. People like to have young persons around, much as they like trees, green grass, shrubs, vines and flowers. You probably prefer young persons, yourselves: I do. I have been young, though you wouldn't guess it to look at me now, and I have been old; and I can bear personal testimony, younger is better.

In the army and navy, in both of which I served, formation of a partnership is highly desirable for mutual protection. In a precarious world you need one good, reliable friend.

My personal connection with the movement is incidental to my interest in the world as I find it and the mess that it is in. My main idea is that a remedy will be found only in a reconstruction of the family.

A return to the old-fashioned autocratic family is no solution. Shortcomings and abominations that led to that family's extinction make its restoration intolerable. Something better can be contrived.

This Editor's position has been so often stated in earlier chapters that a single Editorial will be excerpted. This documents that ONE Institute's disparaging view of the generality of academic scholarship has been of long standing. The practice of forever questioning received wisdom as taught by philosophy has been and continues to be a fundamental method in Homophile Studies.

The class, "Introduction to Homophile Studies," launched this policy of critical analysis in 1956 and continued doing so year after year. When the Graduate School was opened in 1981, the word "introduction" was ruled to be no longer appropriate. After many suggestions had been considered, the same course was continued as "Philosophy 500

/ Homophile Studies: An Analytic Method." [8]   Later the name was changed to "The Field of Homophile Studies;" it is given as a course required of all graduate school students.

Editorial[9]

It has often been said that the social assumptions which in any culture do not raise doubts or cause controversy are the truly dangerous ones. Tacit acceptance indicated that society, in those directions at least, is losing touch with itself. As a creeping paralysis will affect sensory communication from the extremities of the body, so any social "blind spot" can be symptomatic of cultural atrophy.

A particular social assumption which has rarely been questioned or seriously examined for centuries past is that homosexuality is a minor, or an incidental, factor in our culture. It may well prove that much contemporary social disquiet can be traced to this incorrect evaluation.

Let us examine some aspects of its incorrectness, for history, sociology, religion, psychology, and other studies have as their foundations certain assumed social relationships conceived almost as if they were Platonic Absolutes. History, for instance, tells us only a heavily censored version of what really happened. The place of the Homophile is almost without exception passed over in silence, or dismissed with a few sketchy paragraphs, in favor of a picture of societies with which the historians find themselves more comfortable. Sociology purports to study social organizations.

And so on with psychology and other fields in which "heterosexual assumptions" so permeate their whole approaches and techniques as to give them a curious aura of unreality, once one's eyes have been at all opened.

Curiously enough, the charge has often been leveled at homosexuals that they are too biased to be in a position to study themselves impartially. Yet these charges come from those astride

---

[8] See Appendix, 4-1: ONE Institute Graduate school of Homophile Studies. Philosophy 500 "Homophile Studies, an Analytic Method."

[9] W. Dorr Legg, "Editorial", *QTLY* II:1 (Winter 1959), pp.4,5.

mutually contradictory "heterosexual assumptions" and quite unaware of the untenability of their own positions.

It is clearly evident that we are dealing in the United States with a homosexual population comprising many millions of men and women of all ages and educational levels. Yet, in the face of this one simple fact, sociologists assure us they are scientifically studying our society, all the while giving this aspect of it almost no attention. In the face of these contemporary statistics, which give every evidence of being also applicable to other periods and other cultures, at least in part, historians expect us to take them seriously while they studiously avoid mention of the influence of a factor of such massive weight.

Here at ONE Institute we charge without any equivocation that history must be judged both shallow and perverse until it shall have been rewritten to accommodate its diverse homosexual components. Just as flatly we hold that there is as yet no scientific sociology, nor will there be until sociologists begin to describe societies as they actually are. Psychology will never arrive as a science until it frees itself of the tyranny of norms, median groups, and other such statistical constructs and starts doing that which the behaviorists have claimed they do: actually observing man.

Literary studies for the most part studiously ignore the immense currents of Homophile expression flooding through the literatures of the world, from the very invention of writing (and earlier) down to today. There are to be found virtually no criteria for beginning such studies. Students of literature have systematically averted their eyes even in the face of overwhelming evidence.

Should anyone believe that a study of the influence of homosexuality on literatures can well be covered by a few minor works of a few major writers, or even by a few hundred such works?

He would soon discover that he had previously been studying only certain artificially delimited portions of literature, and from very restricted standpoints. He would learn for instance that lyric poetry has come to us directly as the expression of homosexual love. Thus, he would find that he must view all such poetry through new eyes, shocking though he may find this demand.

In law, in philosophy, and in all other fields touching upon the relations of human beings to each other, the same realignments are required, the same necessity for re-evaluation of the old viewpoints. What, then, have we so far said? Simply that the homosexual comprises so considerable a part of any population quantitatively that he cannot be any longer ignored by scholars, and that, qualitatively, his influence on society is and has been so important that a completely distorted picture is produced unless this influence is carefully assessed.

The following transcript of a lecture given to a ONE Overseas Group in Rome in 1971 is included here because it touches upon one of the currently most explosive topics in American society, so-called "child abuse." Dr. Palmieri's article, "Leonardo the Forerunner," [10] frankly includes Leonardo's sexual orientation. Palmieri's lecture, "Classical Boy Love and Modern Civilization" (#26, January 31, 1959), spelled out his detailed philosophical commitment to the classic Greek pattern of pederasty as expounded by Plato and others, holding this to be the true form of "Platonic Love" which characterized Greek ideals at the high point.

It is not known if the Palmieri book *Plato and Platonic Love* which had been announced for publication was ever completed before his decease in the late 1970s.

Boy Love
a Lecture by Mario Palmieri
given at the
Hotel Majestic, Via Vaneto, Rome
11 August 1971

I first arrived in the United States from Italy in 1921 and returned there in 1961, and so I was for forty years in the United States. I left for Rome in 1961 and so for ten years, exactly, I have been living in Italy.

During those forty years in the United States, I had the good fortune (I think since 1939) of knowing our friend, Dorr Legg, and of course the warm organization of which he is animator. Since then I have been thinking a lot about our own condition, especially because of the fact that over the years I have seen a tremendous change of outlook over our own condition. Originally, when I first arrived in the U.S. in 1921, we were regarded as the pariahs of society, and now we are considered on a level with every other human being, as should be. This is the most heartening thing I could say, because you can not even guess how one felt fifty years ago, knowing that he was different, and finding out the hostility that greeted you if you revealed

---

[10] *QTLY* I:3 (Fall 1958), p.76-83.

that side of yourself to the world. So, in deference to this [fact] and to my profession, I married and so on without the world knowing at all, shall I say, the intimate personal aspects of my life. In that respect I have been successful. That secrecy is not now so important is partly due to the work and efforts of Dorr and other people like him, and partly to our now being out in the open and asserting ourselves.

Now, how did I come to discover myself? A few personal facts may be of interest. Well, I was left without a father when I was seven years old. After the death of my father, my mother, who had a diploma, decided to make use of it by starting a boy's school. When I reached the age of sixteen, she said to me, "You are sixteen now, you are a bright boy... and it's time you should collaborate with me in bearing some of the work of the family. Why don't you teach some of the boys as soon as you come back from school at one or two o'clock until they go back in the evening?" So, at the age of sixteen, after my own school hours, while teaching these boys, I discovered something that was very peculiar about myself.

I discovered that a certain boy, who until that day I had taught like every other boy, all of a sudden, from one day to the next, acquired a fine personality so far as I was concerned. I remember him as though it were now, although almost sixty years have past. His name was Frederick. He was thirteen. He was studying to prepare himself for one of the higher grades [as I was]. Like other boys of his age, he wore shorts and shirt and sat opposite to me. I had occasion to look at his legs, but until that moment I thought nothing of it. Suddenly, the personality of that boy acquired for me an altogether different meaning. I do not know why, by what alchemy or by what reason or for whatever purpose of God, [he] acquired for me an altogether different meaning. I saw those legs and personality in an altogether different light than I had seen the day before. Is it a miracle? Is it the work of the Devil? Is it something that blossoms out from the inside of a person? I do not know. Up to this day I do not know. I know this much. On that same afternoon I had to, I could not help but pick up that boy from his chair, deposit him on my lap, start to cuddle him, kiss him and so on, which led, of course, to more intimate things. And that was the beginning of the whole thing. This might be of interest to you, I do not know. I am just trying to put things in their own perspective.

So, from sixteen to twenty-two or twenty-three this [affair] went on in the school more or less unremarked. Until my mother found out by opening the door one day and finding other things. So, then she said to me, "Now is the time when you must quit my school and teaching and go forth to maintain the standards of the school." [Her point] was true, of course, since the school enjoyed a tremendous reputation. She was a woman of [strong] character so she said to me, "Mario, although you are my only son, I see now why you must leave; the whole thing is very clear to me. What I should do is to send you to stay with my sister in the United States. She will take care of you in the beginning till you become established there."

So, at the age of twenty-three I said good-bye to my mother and went to live with her sister in the United States. Here I found it like falling from the frying pan into the furnace. The sister had twin sons, each thirteen, which was the critical age as far as I was concerned, and I fell in love with one of them. In a way it was unbelievable. I remember how I came back from work and waited for him to come and greet me. In the evening we would go out walking together for hours. I remember, too, how I would take him away with me for trips to various places. Once, I took him with me on a visit to San Francisco. It was four years of bliss until once again the inevitable happened. By that time he was sixteen and a half. So, my aunt said to me, "Mario, I think you and Victor are getting too close." We were close enough but she thought we were getting *too* close. "Don't you think you should leave Victor alone for awhile and go to Chicago?" She had a brother living there.

On arrival in Chicago I started my real career as an engineer. [There] I secured a job as an engineer of bridges for the Pennsylvania Railroad and I was able to do some rather important works for the railroad. One of them was a huge bridge between 9th and 14th Avenues in Columbus, Ohio.

Also in Columbus there [was] a huge area where the State Fair is held. [There], the Pennsylvania Railroad [had] four tracks which they desired to super-elevate across the whole of the area and asked for competitive designs. My design was adopted and the bridge has been in successful operation since 1927. Since then, I have built various [other] bridges for the Pennsylvania Railroad.

I regarded my career as a side issue. The main issue was how to find an outlet for my terrific sexual urge with which I have been provided... [That outlet], I decided, could be partly provided for by marrying and having a family. This I did, and I have two fine boys, one of whom is one of the biggest men [in his field] in the United States and the other one also is a fine engineer.

This [life] did little to satisfy my sexual urge, so I organized things so I could always be in touch with youngsters. I became a scoutmaster and was a very successful scoutmaster. Since then, I have organized various activities for boys and... have been very happy to have both my own family and to also be with boys all the time.

Eventually, my wife heard of my attraction to boys and, unwilling to accept this [situation], she suggested that we should separate. Since our sons were now grown and independent, this [decision] affected only my wife and myself and we separated by common accord. We are still good friends. She came to Rome recently and spent a week here with me. We had a wonderful time together. She understands my nature but once she knew that she was not enough for me, the whole thing was over. Of course, she has nothing now because she has no husband. She is getting old and would probably like to marry again, but not [to] me.

I am now seventy-four and when I look at myself in the mirror, I say, can it be that I am still attractive? Seemingly, it is so. That is something personal, but more important for the group as a whole, in Rome I have many friends who know me. They respect me and think nothing adverse about me. One of them is a great musician. Another is a schools superintendent from California from years past. So, we have a small coterie of our own, not that my acquaintanceship is limited; it is much wider than that.

Question [from the audience]: I can understand [what] the official attitude [is toward you], but what about the more personal opinions [of you]?

I am glad you made that distinction. In Italy people say, "Live and let live." Mostly, their opinion of me is one of amusement. Our group includes many well-known names. I mentioned a musician. Then, there is Luchino Visconti who directed "Death in Venice." At one time these people tended to be in hiding but now they are open. I do not know if many of you have seen "Death in Venice," but this [film] is a masterpiece.

Question: What about boy lovers?

Boy lovers are not made. They are born. No amount of reading, no amount of cajoling, no amount of suggestion can change an individual homosexual into a boy lover. What appeals to the boy lover is not sex *per se*. It is the beauty which lasts only two or three years and then vanishes. Even the boy who played in "Death in Venice," who was marvelous even a few months before he started to shoot the film, afterwards, was of no interest to anyone.

Let me go back to my sixteenth year. [The allure] relies on a certain blossoming. At a certain point in his life, the boy Frederick blossomed out in a way which captured my senses, in a way that there was nothing I could do about it. What this relationship is, like all phenomena of nature, is hidden to us and I do not think you can [look at] a lover, analyze [him], and find out actually what [the attraction] is. The fact remains that it blossoms. The relationship starts, evolves, flourishes, becomes rapturous, and slowly starts to decay.

In my fifty years of relationships I have had so many that it is getting a little bit cumbersome, as I was saying to Dorr, even to remember them all. But they have all followed the same pattern. So, I have got to say that we boy lovers are unfortunate in this respect. You gentlemen can have relationships which can last for years and years and be always meaningful, whether it is full of grief or full of happiness, but in our case long relationships cannot be.

I had a boy that I took in hand when I was with a shipyard in Los Angeles. He was then fourteen and is now one of the great engineers of America. At the time the boy was just becoming an engineer. I became so wrapped up in the personality of this boy that he transformed me into becoming a poet. I wrote sheaves of poems inspired by him. I took him with me to establish a shipyard in Oregon. We had one of the most marvelous honeymoons that anyone could hope to get in life. We drove all through California and Oregon. He was with me for four or five years and now we are still good friends.

Question: Do you have regrets that these relationships always prove to be short-lived, three or four years at most? Have the boys always been established by then?

Four years at the most. No, I have no regrets; always, these boys have turned out to be somebody. One boy is one of the greatest nuclear physicists of America. Another is a great engineer. Did I introduce you to George whom I took from Italy to America? He was in my own home for four years, the same age and a great friend of one of my sons. I took him with me to Sicily and we stayed in a large hotel near Palermo. There we had a wonderful honeymoon. How can you regret a wonderful affair such as that?

If, later this evening, you come to the building where I live, I will introduce you to a boy whom I have brought up from the age of thirteen. He is now sixteen. Naturally, we are just friends now, but he is still one of the most lovable boys you could hope to meet.

ONE Institute Extension Lectures:
Philosophy

February 1, 1958 (#14) "Resolved that 'Homosexual Living is Better Than Heterosexual'," a panel discussion.

January 31, 1959 (#26) "Classical Boy Love and Modern Civilization," by Mario Palmieri, M.S., Ph.D.

May 7, 1961 (#50) "What is Maturity?" by D. B. Vest.

July 27, 1962 (#58) "Whither the Homophile Movement?" by Custis Dewees.

June 7, 1964 (#89) "Contrasts in Morality: U.S. and Abroad," by Dr. Dean Franklin.

January 29, 1966 (#104) "Ethics for the Homophile," by Donald Lucas.

May 5, 1968 (#130) "Public Morality, Legal Morality, Homophile Morality," by Charles J. Cozzetta.

June 6, 1974 (#196) "A Philosophy for Non-Procreative Sexuality," by Lester Kirkendall.

January 26, 1980 (#259) "Our Goals as Human Beings," by Myra Riddell, MSW.

June 7, 1981 (#274) "A Feminist Viewpoint," by Harriet Perl.

April 7, 1991 (#361) "Moral Issues of Homosexuality," by Tom Johnson, Ph.D., Professor of Philosophy, Pierce College, Los Angeles. Video cassette in Audiovisual Collection of ONE's Baker Memorial Library.[11]

---

[11] See also Appendix, 13-1: ONE Institute Graduate School of Homophile Studies. Philosophy 510/610 "Questions of Morality and the Homophile Lifestyle."

PART III

ONE INSTITUTE TODAY

CHAPTER 14

HOMOPHILE STUDIES: SUMMARY

T he preceding chapters five through thirteen are the testing ground for Homophile Studies. Is there such a thing? Or, is it just a random flicker on the screen of scholarship?

At the time the Education Planning Committee originally chose nine fields for close examination, it was because these disciplines had arrogated to themselves the claim to be possessors of definitive information about homosexuality. The Committee had neither any thought nor was it then aware that the ancient pantheon of the great gods in Egypt was also, ninefold, an ennead. Nor did the fact that the Greeks in their shrewd analyses of thought and culture had assigned definitive roles to the Nine Muses influence the Institute's choices. We leave to others all speculations about numerology and archetypes, choosing instead to get right down to taking a one-by-one look at those nine areas chosen for study, keeping clearly in mind the immutable law of logic that there can in reality be no such thing as an isolated discipline.

HISTORY. The chapter begins with a 1957 student paper on Heliogabalus as an illustration of student work during the Institute's second year of classes, followed by a student report of a lecture by polymath D. B. Vest, which can in retrospect be seen as an early outline of his book, *The Five Ages of Man.*

In a syllabus and article, "Homosexuality in History," this Editor drew attention, among other matters, to the discovery that there were at least ten specific areas of human behavior which in past periods have often revealed traces of Homophile behavior.

Excerpts from the Harry Hay article drew attention in considerable detail to religious and social fermentation already under way during the Neolithic Revolution. It was this pre-scientific period that saw the world-wide spread of the mystique of the Mother Goddess cults on Earth over which it was believed that she ruled. As Hay reports, there already were regulations about semen, coitus, purification by water, and countless other aspects of conduct, many of which are still with us today.

ONE Institute doctoral student, Hardman, demolishes for all time the faulty scholarship which attributes the advent of homophobia to Judeo-Christian or even later influences. He traces its beginnings to as early as the reign of Hammurabi, but also reports that more permissive folk practices were still widespread over mediaeval Europe as late as the 18th century. His paper concludes with an introduction to the challenging record of Mamluke rule in Egypt, with its form of institutionalized pederasty.

Papers by both faculty member Kepner and ONE Institute doctoral student Lombardi offer evidence of Homophile influences from earliest times in German history, which culminated in the open declarations of Ulrichs and his followers in the latter part of the 19th century.

Student papers by Coates on lesbians during the Nazi period and Booher on the great growth of Homophile organizations in post World War II Germany illustrate the range of ONE Institute inquiries.

SOCIOLOGY.   In his 1958 review of a then new sociological textbook, ONE Institute Dean Thompson unerringly exposed the fatal flaw in sociological theory which, while claiming to offer definitions of society, relegated the millions of Homophiles as being not a part of society, but mere "deviants, from crime broken families."

In his article on "Culture," faculty member Underwood raised questions which have resurfaced repeatedly throughout the Movement's history and continue to create controversy today.

This Editor's "The Sociology of Homosexuality" follows Thompson in rejecting sociological theories which created a virtual "Caste of Untouchables," the sex deviants, as a way of dealing with levels of social analysis quite beyond their means at the time. It was recommended that the profession start over again by doing basic examinations of the field of actual human behavior. Primate behavior among man's near relatives was suggested as a good place to begin.

The sociological side effects which followed the 1961 ONE Midwinter Institute merits special notice, including the extensive statistical tables which are given in full. The Kepner report of a lecture by sociologist Fradkin, which focused upon this survey, summarizes a number of the issues.

An unprecedented academic joint study project, four semesters of sociology classes given by ONE Institute faculty member, Dorr Legg, and California State University at Long Beach Professor Fradkin, is offered as an example of what can be accomplished on such a cooperative basis.

The closing section on Laud Humphrey's valuable years of association with ONE Institute, his lectures and classes, shows vividly how much was lost by his untimely early decease.

PSYCHOLOGY. The chapter opens with an account of steps by which ONE from the earliest days became involved in psychotherapy in the form of peer counseling. The role of pioneer, Charles Rowland, is described as are the early and deeply influential associations with Dr. Evelyn Hooker and psychiatrist Dr. Blanche M. Baker.

One result of ONE's long continued association with Evelyn Hooker is the fortunate possession of a hitherto unpublished interview of her by ONE Institute faculty member, Laud Humphreys. This interview has been included in full because of its very personal summarizing of decades of the continuing evolution of psychological views about homophilia and her remarkable role in that evolution.

Peer counseling and Dr. Baker's part in ONE's many years of such work is given detailed notice as is the active participation in ONE Institute's development by clinical psychologist Dr. Ray Evans. His part in nationwide educational counseling assistance for masters and doctoral students from universities all over the country is described. Close affiliation and cooperative counseling programs with the Southern California Council on Religion and the Homophile are also briefly reported.

ONE Institute has no hesitancy in claiming to have played a significant part in the salutary changes which have so greatly altered the field of psychology since the 1950s.

LAW. In the eyes of Homophile men and women in the early 1950s, Law was the dragon which must be slain. How to do this was the problem. ONE found itself embroiled in attacks by the dragon early on by the mere fact of existing. True to form from ONE's standpoint, the problem was seen to be basically one of education. It is for such reasons that ONE Institute has viewed its role not as a strategy of protests, marches, and sit-ins, but as taking away the very weapons from the enemy through education.

Most notable early success, one with national impact, was the U.S. Supreme Court's 1958 decision that *ONE Magazine* was not obscene and that the U.S. Mails be thereby ordered to transmit copies of *ONE Magazine* forthwith, a victory for the free flow of ideas and discussion in obedience to the Constitution of the United States.

The "Post Office Case Byproduct," was a formal approach to an educational analysis of the encrustations of theory which have adhered to Law. The financial request which was made was not granted, but the training in preparing the application provided a syllabus for further study of Law and its theoretical foundations.

The "Homosexual Bill of Rights," 1961 Midwinter Institute program, has already been mentioned for its unexpected applications to sociology, but Law had been its intended concern. The ONE Institute classes, which prepared for this event and the subsequent controversies, did much to affect the direction of the whole Homophile movement with impact upon hundreds who had never heard of ONE or seen any of its publications.

Another legal action was the formal launching in 1964 of a foundation to serve as a channel for financial programs of giving by individuals and foundations. This foundation (ISHR) has brought continuing benefits, and illustrates how Law can be directed into constructive Homophile pursuits.

Lively interest in legal matters kept a steady stream of articles on legal topics appearing in all of ONE's publications. The unusual number of them is shown in a selected bibliography included later in the chapter. While bibliographies on Law are numerous and generally well prepared, a bibliography from the Homophile point of view may not be so easily found. The list of Extension Lectures on the subject is long and virtually a course in the study of the philosophy of Law.

RELIGION. In this chapter the slow pace of change in religious attitudes toward sexual behavior is explored. Class discussions took note of the very long period in social development during which the cause of pregnancy was not known. Sex acts were therefore judged by quite different rules than in more recent times.

Until very recently, theorizing about male/female polarity has been based on the assumption that hormonal effects easily observable in the animal kingdom applied also to humans. Religious interpretations of such primitive, pre-scientific reasoning call for examination. If males and females are not drawn toward each other by biological laws, how much current religious theory about sexual relations can be considered valid?

Faculty member Underwood calls for rational approaches to religion. Faculty member Kepner raises familiar inconsistencies brought to light in examining the records of various religious traditions worldwide.

This Editor's "A Moral Imperative" focused narrowly upon specific complaints against specific church bodies in their responses to the

Homophile Community, and added a call to put their house in order.

"Lot, Sodom, Onan and Paul" was ONE Institute Lecturer Monwell Boyfrank's homespun and quirky look at those four *vis-a-vis* the Homophile question.

On following pages is the historical account of the brave attempt by mainline Protestant church groups to bridge the gap between themselves and the Homophile community. "The Council on Religion and the Homophile" is a record of this several year effort which fell victim to gradual depletion as various denominational groups chose to go their own non-ecumenical ways.

BIOLOGY. The papers excerpted for this chapter reach such a pitch of controversy as to suggest that they are at the very center of theory and concern in Homophile Studies. The insistent and continued challenging of this particular scientific discipline throughout class discussions and the papers which have resulted seem to confirm this supposition. What seemed inexcusable to several of the inquirers has been the complacent willingness of an entire scientific field to conduct its massive scientific enterprises quite content with an inherited road map accepted without question as valid. This road map defines the duty of Biology to faithfully observe and report the bio-processes by which organisms come into being, go through a process of maturation, and then replicate. Other inquiries have been ruled irrelevant if not indeed disruptive to the pristine simplicity of this scientific enterprise.

Is there some Darwinian mandate which forbids asking if the Galapagos scenario is adequate to account for phenomena once the record moves beyond the lower orders and on to homo sapiens?

Is it possible that self-preservation and replication are not fully explanatory to all individuals? Here the biologists fail in not being able to locate within the human organism any fixed developmental law, or tropism, which invariably turns the genders toward each other for the purpose of replication. Among plants and simpler animals, this does indeed seem to be true, but observation indicates that this is by no means universally the rule among humans. Some of the D. B. Vest papers in this chapter raise very penetrating questions about such matters.

Biologists' thinking seems to have been fixated for so long at a level in which replication and self-preservation are the only impelling forces worth noting that genetic altruism and other more recent inquiries are seen as hardly deserving mention. For the man (or the Homophile) in the street, to raise such points risks being considered unbelievably naive. However, in Homophile Studies, with no particular awe for labels of any sort, both asking and expecting considered answers to questions has become a habit. To avoid being regarded as merely contentious and little more, it should be understood that in biology and the other academic disciplines under discussion here the concern of Homophile Studies is for shortcomings of method and theory concerning the Homophile sector only. Other aspects of these disciplines are not under review in these pages.

ANTHROPOLOGY. Unlike any of the preceding areas of study, anthropology approaches, studies, and records Homophile behavior directly among peoples all over the world. This openness has made anthropology an attractive topic with promise of offering much for Homophile Studies. In fact, the Ford & Beach, *Patterns of Sexual Behavior* (1951), was one of the earliest and most comprehensive known tabulations of variations in attitudes toward homosexuality from a worldwide list of cultures. They reported cultural attitudes ranging from those completely opposed to homosexual behavior to those somewhat tolerant, and a surprising number which gave homosexual behavior complete approval for all males, at least as a developmental phase.

Cross-cultural reporting has now been so extensive that there is a risk of becoming overly absorbed in a romanticized view of other peoples and other times. It needs to be emphasized that each of the field studies reported and the relevant folk tales developed out of a very special set of circumstances and a very specific time frame, which, however attractive, may offer little insight or application for society today.

Another cautionary note is that substantially all of the folk customs reported reflect pre-scientific levels of thinking. A very large percentage of these "folk theories" rest upon assumptions such as the so called "Third Sex Theory." Others imply sex role inversion: the presence of one identity in a body of the opposite sex. There are all manner of mythologic and fanciful variations on such hypotheses.

A goal for Homophile Studies is to discover usable values applicable to men and women of today. Anthropology provides many opportunities for examining the variety of ways in which societies have developed their value systems. The accidents and circumstances of such developments have set the directions for many of the attitudes and ideals by which we still live today.

A culture's thinking and decisions about sexual behavior are essential concerns in Homophile Studies. How have these decisions been made? For example, humans have always been aware that, as with animals, one part of their kind gives birth; the others do not. Equally fundamental, the menstruation phenomenon has from earliest times been the occasion for fears and various taboos, as recorded in folk tales and the Bible. These are only some of the ways by which the female body has been accorded a unique place in human thinking. It should be noted, however, that although invariably accorded such specific attention, births have not always of themselves been welcome where subsistence problems were acute. What does seem clear is that some degree of female mystique has always been present, and that the concept of life has long been identified with the female body to which a special role has been accorded.

A complementary male mystery would be expected to be present, especially where hunting was an important aspect of survival, progressively less so in regions where plentiful fruits and plant life made hunting of secondary importance or as agriculture became more important. The male phenomenon of erection and its pleasurable potentials have been basic in human experience. This says nothing, however, as to where and how such pleasure might be sought. Biological evidence has already indicated that there is no physiological compulsion that it must be sought only from female bodies.

Pre-scientific thinking may in some instances have assumed this to be true, but pre-scientific thinking can be notoriously misleading and unreliable. Where, then, have we derived the seemingly unshakable conviction that pleasure between two human bodies can only properly be sought between male and female? For such answers we must turn to both history and religion. Each of those fields supplies examples of humanity's painful efforts to discover how natural forces act, and how these effect human welfare. There has always been an irrepressible penchant for leaping to conclusions which go far beyond what evidence supports. Thus, entire systems of supposition and belief have emerged, some of which live on and on for millennia without challenge.

Anthropology presents us with such examples of customs and taboos with which groups have managed to create reasonably workable living patterns that have only tenuous connection with what could be called reality. Within all such complex value systems, Homophile Studies regard sexual customs and practices to be of primary significance as rich resources for analyzing human behavior.

LITERATURE & THE ARTS.   Their freedom both to deal with the world around us or to completely turn their backs upon the world of daily experience gives literature and the arts a force and power uniquely their own.   With their artistic skills, writers command techniques for influencing thinking which give literature its unique, almost other-worldly powers.   On the one hand it can command subtle emotional resources for denigrating homoerotic inclinations while glorifying erotic relationships between the sexes.   Yet it also has the capacity for creating idealized situations.   Greek mythology contains countless such affirmative examples at all levels from the love of Zeus for beautiful young Ganymedes to many others throughout classical and later literatures.

Homophile Studies make no claims to special insights in emphasizing the vast emotional powers literature and the arts exercise in influencing and virtually framing entire cultures.   These are standard topics for study in the schools.   What is pointed out, however, is the massive suppression of the quite abundant examples of homoerotic themes in literature and the arts in favor of an obsessive emphasis upon the polarity of male to female attractions.   This censorship has been so sweepingly effective, for example, as to render nearly unthinkable a song or song cycle by a major composer on love between two men or two women.   How could these be *real* themes is the implication?

Recently, there has been modest retrieval of poetry on such themes and a modicum of attention paid to larger scale works.   It is as if both scholars and writers find impediments or mental blocks in their ability to acknowledge fully that such topics are valid, in a sense comparable to having a graduate seminar on the genesis of the Tristan and Isolde legends.   Why is this so?

Homophile Studies always insist that no one field can begin to answer such questions.   The causes lie in the deep recesses of anthropological, religious, and historical thinking from past centuries which in turn, derive their force from hidden pre-scientific flights of fancy now hardened into dogma through long continued repetition.   For better answers perhaps Philosophy will be able to help us uncover the roots of the ambiguities.

PHILOSOPHY.   The primary utility of philosophy for Homophile Studies is its emphasis on asking questions then questioning the answers. "Be always skeptical" is the first rule of philosophy when it comes to knotted and emotionally complex questions of relations between the sexes, of feelings and judgments of feelings handed down with the authority and power of law. Philosophy urges the Homophile scholar to be forever dubious, forever challenging the "wisdom of the ages" which lies so heavily over great areas of human behavior. Plunging headlong into battle, the Homophile scholar asks questions about human conduct considered to have been settled long ago.

The counsel of Philosophy is the bold and rude, "By whose authority?" Suspicious of Cartesian self-centered navel-watching, a sociological and relativistic "Man is the measure of all things" sounds more congenial. On that basis the organism becomes the point of beginning for the first battle in the "nature vs. nurture" controversy.

Psychologists of certain persuasions dismiss all "anecdotal evidences" from historians and anthropologists as hopelessly unscientific. Faced by such controversies the advice of Philosophy is: simplify, focus upon specific questions felt to be of most immediate concern.

For example, has what is today called love, erotic love between opposite sexes, existed for all time? Admittedly, a procreative urge with some people (perhaps socially fostered at times) has roots within the bios itself. The male/female nexus, well designated "the war between the sexes," seems to have emerged in part from a transmutation of troubadour religious poetry and songs about the Virgin Mary into a more generalized celebration of woman, all women.

Rolling backward a few millennia to the beginnings of agriculture and the rapid spread of Mother Goddess cults, a time celebrated by some feminist theoreticians as one of great harmony and equity, the question must be asked if this is not where some of today's troubles began.

The mystical veneration of woman as source of all life and fertility and doyen of the Earth, added to this the associated cult mysteries which included the requirement that the male must mate with her lest terrible consequences come upon the community, bring an element of force into play. Male votaries of some of the goddesses even castrated themselves with sharp stone knives to remove the offending male evidences from their bodies.

Such a heightened sense of magical values associated with women's bodies, and the commandment that the male sex organs become subservient to such requirements as the Mother Goddess was said to demand, led to a divided society: woman as an all inclusive entity and males whose requirement was to protect and serve the female principle as the very embodiment of life. Is not the genesis of a patriarchal reaction already visible in such a framework?

Philosophy emphasizes the human weakness for adding to some nucleus of fact, wild speculations and hypotheses. The next step then is to refine the whole construct, endowing it with assumed values where no values exist. In Homophile Studies the imperative is to identify such reliable nuggets as can be found and then clear away the thickets of sheer senseless reification such as have piled up through the ages.

This brief summary of what ONE Institute has been doing and an overview of what ONE Institute faculty and students have produced brings us to the next step, what of the future? What goals and directions can be envisaged as projects for the years ahead?

CHAPTER 15

WHAT OF THE FUTURE?

I n looking toward the future, two major areas for investigation need to be considered: (1) Comprehensive Reform of traditional studies of Homophilia and (2) Radical Critiques and Revisions of methods and assumptions long considered trustworthy and reliable.

(1) COMPREHENSIVE REFORM.   Essential working tools are bias-free translations of texts from other languages and periods. Unfortunately, in some of these texts, genders have been altered to conform to what the translator considered appropriate relationships. In other cases meanings have been obscured by the use of euphemisms for behavior the translators found objectionable. Whether done consciously or through inability to believe that a text in question meant what it said, meanings have been subverted. A whole new lexicon or glossary is needed for arriving at the true meanings of many words and phrases. Watch out for: *lewd, weak, dissolute, companion, favorite, friend, bohemian, decadent, fop, dandy, Arcadian, epicene, thigh, groin* – the list of the many disparate attempts to translate such terms clearly and accurately goes on and on.

Another much-needed working tool is a comprehensive Biographical Dictionary. A number of limited beginnings have been made,[1] but a more thorough database approach is now needed. Endless disputes as to inclusion and exclusion should be bypassed for the present, leaving refinements for later decision. With such a Dictionary in hand, compilations of names of persons in the arts, sciences, and political realms who have made great contributions to humanity become possible. For far too long ignorant and intentional scholarly misconduct has touted the importance of famous individuals while refusing to acknowledge their personal status. This sort of free ride can no longer be tolerated, giving credit to society in general to which it is not entitled. To make public the wide range of fields to which Homophile men and women have contributed is merely to give credit where credit is due.

Such truth-telling will undoubtedly lead to revisions of many episodes in history and make a good start at breaking "the conspiracy

---

[1] "Our Homophile Heritage," ONE Institute 1984, 15 pp. (ONE's Baker Memorial Library & Archives)

of silence" which for centuries has thwarted proper evaluation of the Homophile component in society.

These few suggestions are but examples of scholarly obligations which should be taken for granted and regarded as merely routine. The next phase is far more difficult and will be distasteful or repellent to some. In approaching this phase, some words of caution are needed. ONE Institute is in no way providing answers to difficult questions. Nor is it indulging in Utopian or science fiction.

(2) RADICAL REVISIONISM.   It should be noted here that in the following examinations of Paleolithic developments, access to information has been constrained by the relative accessibility of records drawn primarily from African and European evidence. Not more than passing notice can be given to what may be even more limited information from Asia and the Pacific.

Is radical revision needed? As we look at the society which existing methods have produced, improvements would seem to be very much needed.   Family and marriage admittedly suffer from serious dysfunction. News reports tell of divorce, battered women, drug abuse, and children murdered. Streets of our cities are conspicuously littered with the homeless and mentally disturbed. Alcoholism and use of drugs have become widely endemic.

Authority figures tell us that such things have always existed and that, while amelioration and piecemeal improvements are possible, the basic problem is an overreaching and ill-defined something called "The Human Condition."

Readers of the preceding pages are well aware that serious complaints have been lodged against each of nine major fields of human expertise under study. First, the most serious of such charges points to fundamental errors in thought systems which claim to embrace society as a whole while totally ignoring the very existence of millions of Homophile men and women.

How can such flawed assumptions claim status as responsible scholarship or as having scientific standing of any sort? If the basic assumptions are wrong, so will be the conclusions. No deluge of footnotes can change that fact. Why then senselessly and compulsively follow along the old and familiar grooves of inquiry? Might it not seem to make sense to ask some very basic questions which apparently are not being asked?

From the point of view of humanity as a whole, perhaps the most flagrant of these questions is, *do we really know what men and women are?* To put it bluntly, the mythical man from Mars who might ask that question would soon be flooded with such a jumble of bits and pieces from our collective past, ancient mythologies, folk axioms, and speculative "leaps of faith" as to cause him to run for the safety of his spaceship.

For those of us confined to this planet, we at ONE Institute asked ourselves, what sort of questions did our remote ancestors ask during their efforts to keep alive? All manner of fears and mysteries confronted them daily. How did I get here? Who are we?

Many dawn stories of which traces can still be found speculate that creation begins with a male. Such mythologies have been found in many parts of the world and in widely different cultures. They all share a concept of maleness as self-sufficient and rudimentary. Was this some patriarchal plot? It is doubtful that Paleolithic man had much time for political enterprises. How could this maleness concept have seemed so natural and believable? Humans were certainly well aware that there was a portion of society which was "Not Male."

As keen observers of the animals they hunted, they observed the same division among animals, but the value systems which they were slowly and pragmatically constructing had also noted that males were generally stronger and larger than "Not Males." Moreover, males never experienced some of the physical handicaps which at times inexplicably beset those others. Males were at any time able to go out after the food by which the group mainly lived. Early on, males acquired remarkable skills of forest lore and technical expertise in tool making. Did not all this mean that males were the preservers of life itself for the community?

The "Not Males" sometimes mysteriously swelled up and gave birth to young for reasons not then understood. Ethology tells us that, in the entire kingdom of mammals, birth is considered to be highly important. Paleolithic man felt much the same. Although zealously protecting the young, those early scientific pragmatists were well aware that in times of severe attack the young might have to be abandoned to predators. Birth was not then considered as irrevocably sacred.

As reasoning beings, humans also realized that a new birth was not an unmixed blessing whenever food supplies were scarce and uncertain. Infanticide sometimes occurred. Some of the earliest records mention this as an occasional practice. Social constructs such as today's evaluations of the sanctity of human life, the morality of abortion, or birth control, were late arrivals arising from changed value systems quite foreign to Paleolithic mankind. It should not be forgotten that this period lasted much longer in human history than what has taken place since.

During this formative period, a very disturbing and mysterious occurrence was exhibited by the "Not Males:" at times they bled. An illness perhaps, a premonition of death? Caution was called for in coming into contact with such unexplained dangers. As late as the Old Testament, admonitions and taboos regarding this menstrual phenomenon were many and severe.

Another strange occurrence which Lower Paleolithic scientists tried to understand was the phenomenon of erection, voluntary or involuntary. Did the involuntary event come from some unseen force? Was it beneficent, or in some way dangerous, even though it could lead to pleasure? If some outside force was sending this manifestation, perhaps only the voluntary form was legitimate? Satisfactory answers for such parts of the value systems they were devising with so much difficulty were sought with great and urgent fear.

Modern hormonal studies tell us that human animals have no such object-oriented urges corresponding to the estrus cycle among lower animals. Thus, human bodily contacts are biologically non-specific in their orientation. Certain male-to-male contacts had a highly pleasurable component. Bodily contacts with "Not Males" might also afford pleasure, but there could always be concern about violation of taboos in such risky encounters.

A further question about lower Paleolithic belief systems: Was there a "phallus fraternity" with rules and a rationale known only to those who could qualify? In that regard, what is to be made of the penis sheaths still worn today in some parts of the world? Anthropologists report what they believe to be explanations, but we learn that such explanations are not always definitive.

Further difficulties of interpretation are found concerning the rock carvings and paintings, petroglyphs, which feature phallic representations in so many parts of the world. These vary from very crude representations often difficult to decipher to the magnificent high art in the caves of Altimira, Lascaux, and other sites. Many of them represent humans as nothing but stick figures engaged in the hunt. Yet a great many show erections. What was the association between erections and hunting? Explanations have been few and mostly unpersuasive.

Finally, what of the future of Homophile studies? The suggestions in the preceding pages are but a few of the lines of inquiry which call for study. To raise further issues at this point seems premature.

Flagrant pre-scientific errors were made as humanity struggled on from the Upper Paleolithic into the Neolithic Revolution. Great changes which would affect all future history regarding the roles of both men and women began to emerge. The tangled legends and Mother Goddess mythologies must be approached only with thorough and careful research.

Questions such as: Did Paleolithic women willingly commit themselves into socially counter-productive philosophical positions which have enslaved all women ever since? Can real liberation ever be achieved without alarmingly radical corrections throughout many layers of such dogmas? The questions are so many that it may be best to master Paleolithic matters before venturing into the seductive environs of the Neolithic Great Mother, where complications lurk without number and where many of today's problems about sexual matters had their genesis.

FINANCING HOMOPHILE STUDIES. The course followed at ONE Institute has been very simple and by no means ideal. From the start the policy has been that support should come not from public agencies but from sources which believe that such work merits support.

ONE Institute believed that while public funds have great allure, in practice the funding body has a tendency to determine policies; as the old adage has it, "whoever pays the piper calls the tune." Modern bureaucracy has tended to become so complicated that even ordinary requirements for filling out forms and paper work may sometimes overshadow the work to be attempted.

Income from student tuitions, benefits, fund raisers and the like have been only enough to meet a few of the needs. The progress of ONE Institute has therefore been lamentably slow. Quick solutions have not yet been found. The number of those to whom the work seems important and valuable remains small, despite some very generous and welcome exceptions. Grants from several foundations have been of modest dimensions, usually designated for some specific purpose. A small handful of faithful friends has remembered the Institute in their wills. It does not seem pleasing, however, to think of having to wait around for people to die. Adequate financing for ONE Institute's ambitious academic and research objectives has continued to elude the Institute's Board of Governors.

THE CENTER FOR ADVANCED STUDIES. Such post-doctoral facilities exist in many parts of the country and serve valuable purposes. However, they do imply financial resources which are devoutly to be wished for but which have not yet been available. There have been few donors with a sense of loyalty to a social group strong enough to elicit the level of financial support required to maintain a program of this sort.

ONE Institute's spacious campus and buildings have from time to time brought scholars for whom the Institute's small staff cannot at present provide adequate services. Nevertheless, the Institute continues to do what it can with those resources presently available to it and hopes to be able it to do much more in the future, as society shows increased appreciation for Homophile Studies. In time it most certainly will.

PART IV

APPENDIX

INDEX AND TOPICAL GUIDE

Invitation, Knights of the Clocks Social Event, 1951 (ONE's Baker Memorial Library & Archives)

Hosts at this "Wedding Anniversary" were two members of the "Knights of the Clocks, Inc." Guests were a comfortable mix of races and assorted personal relationships including both men's Beverly Hills employers and their families.

You are invited to attend

Gene and Edward

Fourth Anniversary Party

on Saturday, May the Twelfth

nineteen hundred and fifty-one

at 1170 East 34th Street

Los Angeles, Calif.

from 9 o'clock in the evening until 3 a.m.

PLEASE PRESENT INVITATION

APPENDIX, 1-1a

ONE, Incorporated. Articles of Incorporation & By-Laws, 1953. (ONE's Baker Memorial Library & Archives)

1953 Edition

--

Official Documents

of

O N E, I N C O R P O R A T E D

Founded: Los Angeles, California
October 15, 1952

A R T I C L E S   O F   I N C O R P O R A T I O N

Filed: With Secretary of State, Sacramento, California — February 7, 1953

Charter: Granted by the State of California — May 27, 1953

B Y - L A W S

Filed: With Secretary of State, Sacramento, California — October 16, 1953

———

November, 1956

APPENDIX, 1-1b

ONE, Incorporated. Articles of Incorporation & By-Laws, 1953. (continued)

ARTICLES OF INCORPORATION

OF ONE, INCORPORATED

On this day we, the undersigned, have associated ourselves for the purpose of forming a non-profit corporation under and pursuant to the laws of the State of California, and do certify as follows:

I.

NAME

That the name of the corporation shall be ONE, INCORPORATED.

II.

PURPOSES

A. PRIMARY PURPOSES:

That the specific and primary purposes for which this corporation was formed are to publish and disseminate a magazine dealing primarily with homosexuality from the scientific, historical and critical point of view, and to aid in the social integration and rehabilitation of the sexual variant.

B. GENERAL PURPOSES:

That the general purposes for which this corporation is formed, in addition to those enumerated above, are as follows:

1. To publish and disseminate magazines, brochures, leaflets, books and papers concerned with medical, social, pathological, psychological and therapeutic research of every kind and description pertaining to socio-sexual behavior.

.2. To sponsor, supervise and conduct educational programs, lectures and concerts for the aid and benefit of all social and emotional variants and to promote among the general public an interest, knowledge and understanding of the problems of such persons.

3. To stimulate, sponsor, aid, supervise and conduct research of every kind and description pertaining to socio-sexual behavior.

4. To promote the integration into society of such persons whose behavior varies from current moral and social standards and to aid the development of social and moral responsibility in all such persons.

5. To lease, purchase, hold, have, use and take possession of and enjoy any personal or real property necessary for the uses and purposes of the corporation, and to sell, lease, deed in trust, alien or dispose of the same at the pleasure of the corporation, and for the purposes and uses for which said corporation is formed and to buy and sell real or personal property and to apply the proceeds of the sale, including any and all income, to the uses and purposes of the corporation.

APPENDIX, 1-1c

ONE, Incorporated. Articles of Incorporation & By-Laws, 1953.
(continued)

6. To do any and all other acts, things, business or businesses in any manner connected with or necessary, incidental, convenient, or auxiliary to any of the objects hereinbefore enumerated or calculated, directly or indirectly, to promote the interest of the corporation.

III.
NON-PROFIT CORPORATION

That this corporation does not contemplate the distribution of gains, profits, or dividends to the members thereof and is organized pursuant to Part I of Division 2 of Title 1 of the Corporations Code of the State of California.

IV.
PRINCIPAL OFFICE

The county of the State of California where the principal office for the transaction of the business of this corporation is to be located is Los Angeles County.

V.
FIRST DIRECTORS

That the names and addresses of the persons who are to act in the capacity of directors until the selection of their successors are:

MARTIN BLOCK	1061 $\frac{1}{2}$ N. St. Andrews Los Angeles, California
DALE JENNINGS	1933 Lemoyne St. Los Angeles, California
TONY REYES	221 S. Bunker Hill Ave. Los Angeles, California

The number of persons named above shall constitute the number of directors of the corporation until changed by an amendment to the by-laws increasing or decreasing the number of directors as may be desired.

VI.
MEMBERSHIP

That the authorized number and qualifications of members of this corporation, the different classes of membership, if any, the property, voting and other rights and privileges of each class of membership, and the liability of each or all classes to dues or assessments, and the method of collection thereof shall be set forth in the by-laws of this corporation.

VII.
BY-LAWS

That the by-laws of this corporation shall be adopted by the directors named in the Articles of Incorporation and may thereafter be amended or repealed by means provided in the by-laws.

IN WITNESS WHEREOF, the persons who are to act in the capacity of first directors of the corporation have hereunto set their hands this 7th day of February, Nineteen Hundred and Fifty-three.

MARTIN BLOCK   DALE JENNINGS   TONY REYES

APPENDIX, 1-1d

ONE, Incorporated. Articles of Incorporation & By-Laws, 1953. (continued)

BY-LAWS

As provided in Article VII of the "Articles of Incorporation of ONE, Incorporated," as filed with the Secretary of State, Sacramento, California, October 16, 1953, we, the undersigned Directors of said corporation do hereby adopt the following By-laws:

ARTICLE I, Board of Directors

    A. As provided in Article V, "Articles of Incorporation of ONE, Incorporated," the "First Directors" shall "act in the capacity of directors until the selection of their successors."

    B. Three Directors shall be elected at the Annual Meeting, January 1954 and at each third annual meeting thereafter.

    C. A majority of the members present and voting shall be necessary to elect a Director.

    D. Should a Director resign, or the position become otherwise vacant, the remaining Directors shall appoint a member to serve as a Director until the following Annual Meeting, at which time an election shall be held to fill the unexpired term.

ARTICLE II, Officers

    A. The Directors shall annually elect a chairman, a vice chairman, and a secretary-treasurer, who shall also be chairman, vice chairman, and secretary-treasurer respectively of the Corporation.

    B. Duties of Officers.

        1. The Chairman shall preside at all Director's and Corporation meetings. He shall annually report to the members on the affairs of the Corporation.

        2. In the absence of the Chairman, the vice chairman shall act in the capacity of chairman.

        3. The secretary-treasurer shall:

            a. Keep minutes of the Corporation and Director's meetings.

            b. Prepare and file such official reports for the Corporation as may be required.

            c. Submit a financial report to the members annually.

    C. In the event of a vacancy in any office the Directors shall fill the vacancy not later than at the monthly Director's meeting following the date of the vacancy.

ARTICLE III, Meetings

    A. The Annual Meeting of the Corporation shall be held in January of each year.

    B. Regular meetings of the Board of Directors shall be held once each month.

    C. Special meetings of the Corporation, or of the Board of Directors, may be called by any officer, providing three days' written notice shall have been given each member thereof.

    D. The Board of Directors may invite persons other than Directors to attend any of its meetings.

    E. Failure to attend an Annual, or other, corporate meeting, shall render a member liable to dismissal from the corporation, at the discretion of the Board of Directors. Absence from two consecutive meetings of the Board of Directors shall automatically dismiss a Director from his office, the remaining Directors concurring.

    F. Meetings shall be conducted in accordance with Robert's Rules of Order, except as herein provided.

ARTICLE IV, Members

    A. The number of voting members, including Directors, shall not exceed nine.

    B. Should a member resign, or the position otherwise become vacant, the Board of Directors shall propose a name, or names, to fill the vacancy at the Annual Meeting next following the date when the position became vacant. At least two-thirds of the members present and voting shall be necessary to elect a member. Failing this affirmative vote, the vacancy shall remain until the following Annual Meeting.

    C. For reasons deemed sufficient, a member may be removed from membership

APPENDIX, 1-1e

*ONE, Incorporated. Articles of Incorporation & By-Laws, 1953.
(continued)*

by the unanimous vote of the Directors present and voting at any regular Director's meeting, provided said member shall have been notified of the intended action prior to the meeting and shall have been invited to appear and speak in his own behalf.

D. Duties of Members:

1. The Corporation will hold each member responsible for the satisfactory execution of the duties assigned to him.

2. A member may be named by the Board of Directors as head of a department. He shall make reports to the Directors of the activities of his department at their request.

a. A head of a department may submit to the Board of Directors recommendations concerning his department for adoption by the Board as corporate policy.

b. A head of a department may submit to the Board of Directors names of persons recommended for employment in his department.

E. Special Non-voting Members.

1. Privileges and duties of non-voting Annual Members shall be determined by the Board of Directors and announced at each Annual Meeting for publication in the February issue of ONE Magazine.

2. Privileges and duties of non-voting Contributing Members shall be determined by the Board of Directors and announced at each Annual Meeting for publication in the February issue of ONE Magazine.

3. Privileges and duties of non-voting Associate Members shall be determined by the Board of Directors and announced at each Annual Meeting for publication in the February issue of ONE Magazine.

4. Non-voting Life Members are entitled to receive a life-time subscription to ONE Magazine, with duties and other privileges to be determined by the Board of Directors and announced at each Annual Meeting for publication in the February issue of ONE Magazine.

5. The privileges of non-voting Honorary Membership may be extended by the Board of Directors to persons rendering signal financial or other services to the Corporation.

ARTICLE V, Dues and Assessments

The Board of Directors shall fix the amount of dues and assessments, if any, and the terms of payment thereof, for the various classes of members and announce the same at each Annual Meeting for publication in the February issue of ONE Magazine.

ARTICLE VI, Financial Policies and Compensation

The Board of Directors shall determine the fiscal policies of the Corporation and fix all rates of compensation and salaries to be paid to Directors, officers, members, employees, or others.

ARTICLE VII, Employees

Employees shall be engaged, and their respective duties determined, by the Board of Directors solely.

ARTICLE VIII, Amendments

A two thirds affirmative vote of the members present and voting at any Annual Meeting shall be necessary to amend these by-laws, provided notice of the proposed change shall have been given each member at least one month previously.

- - - - - - - - - - -

APPENDIX, 1-2

Advertising Flier, pub. 1952. (ONE's Baker Memorial Library & Archives)

IS A DEVIATION FROM ALL OTHER MAGAZINES

Designed to be enjoyed by everyone, it frankl; brings into the open a subject that is seldom treated with dignity; objective research or laudable levity. Respectable without primness, honest without causing embarrassment, it written for readers of all ages and for accept ance in every home. Its aim is mutual under standing and stimulation for everyone regard less of race, creed or political conviction.

ONE'S origin came out of the taboo on homosexuality which has stymied research and forbidden public discussion in all media unless somberly clinical or hysterically bigoted. It has imposed social silence under the name of "propriety". This silence has al lowed public unawareness of gross trespasses on hu man rights by both private persons and public agencies. ONE speaks for millions of men and women all over the world. ONE speaks to everyone.

ONE's contents include the following: humor, science, literature, sports, the arts, philosophy, history and the law from its special viewpoint. ONE's accent is on factual information. Its contributors include authorities in all fields as well as unheard writers whose work has previously been denied publication.

Watch for the first issue of 1953 appearing early in January. Yearly subscriptions are two dollars and single issues twenty cents.

YOUR CHECK IS AN INVESTMENT IN TRUTH.

Name...

Street..

City...Zone.....State.............

I want a year's subscription....................................

I want..........copies of the next Issue........................

I want to make a contribution of...............................

ONE, incorporated
post office box 5716
los angeles 55, california

APPENDIX, 1-3

ONE Magazine, Representative Articles, v.I, 1953.

Staff. "Letter to You," no 1, January, pg.3.

Jennings, Dale. "To be accused, is to be Guilty," no.2, February, pp.10-13.

Staff. "The Mattachine," no.2, February, pp.18,19.

_____ "The Law," no.2, February, pp.21-22.

Cory, Donald Webster. "An Address Delivered to the International Committee for Sexual Equality," no.2, February. pp.2-11.

Volk, Elwin. "The Law," no.3, March, pp.14-16.

_____ "The Law," no.4, April, pp.14-16.

Jennings, Dale. "Where are You Going," no.5, May, pp.2-4.

Cory, Donald Webster. "Can Homosexuals be Recognized?" no.9, September, pp.2-4.

Vest, D.B. "Evolution's Next Step," no.11, November, pp.5-9.

Barr, James. "Death in a Royal Family," no.12, December, pp.11-13.

APPENDIX, 1-4

ONE Magazine, Representative Articles, v.II, 1954.

Julber, Eric. "And the Law," no.1, January, pp.13,14.

Jennings, Dale. "Miami Junks the Constitution," no.1, January, pp.16-21.

Staff Women. "The Feminine Viewpoint," no.2, February, entire issue.
Freeman, David L. "Who is this Man?" no.3, March, pp.16-18.

Julber, Eric. "The Law: a Discussion of Entrapment," no.4, April, pp.7-8.

Pedersen, Lyn. "England and the Vices of Sodom," no.5, May, pp.4-17.

Krell, Arthur. "We Need a Great Literature," no.5, May, pp.19-23.

Staff. "Religion and the Homosexual," no.6, June, entire issue.

Pedersen, Lyn. "In Paths Untrodden: A Study of Walt Whitman," no.7, July, pp.4-15.

Armon, Virginia and Howard Russell. "The Oedipal Complex," no.11, November, pp.9-11.

APPENDIX, 1-5

1955 Midwinter Institute. Letter of announcement and invitation, (ONE's Baker Memorial Library & Archives)

, incorporated

232 south hill st.

los angeles 12, california

January 12, 1955

Corporation Members,
Subscribers & Guests

Dear Friends:

We invite you to attend, on January 29, 1955, a busy day of events which has been planned so that we may get to know you better and that you may take active part in some of our diversified work. The following program can give you only a hint of the interest and value which have been packed into each of the sessions.

Morning Session - open to voting and nonvoting Members -

11:00 Annual Meeting of the Corporation - Reports and business.
12:30 Informal luncheon.

Afternoon Session - THE 1955 MIDWINTER INSTITUTE

2 - 5 Admission by Registration Card only

"Looking Inside Our State Hospitals - The Sexual Psycopath" Howard Russell, Los Angeles, Psychologist (Special Education Services).

"The Homophile in Society," Dr. G. Th. Kempe, Utrecht, Holland, Criminologist & Sociologist. (Paper to be read).

Intermission.

"A Psychiatric Evaluation of Homosexuality; Causative Factors and Therapeutic Suggestions," Blanche M. Baker, M.D., Ph.D., San Francisco, Psychiatrist.

Annual Banquet - Admission by Advance Reservation only.

7:00 Dinner

"How ONE Started - An Historical Sketch," by a founder.
"Previews of 1955 - The Magazine; Library; Social Services."
"Some Legal Problems," by ONE's attorney.
"An Exciting New Book," for spring publication by the Book Department.

Registration and Reservations must be made promptly so that cards may be sent you in advance. None will be available on the day of the sessions. Location of the meetings will be given on the cards. If you wish to bring guests, please list their names. We very much hope you can be with us on this important occasion.

Cordially yours,

ONE, INCORPORATED
by Board of Directors

APPENDIX, 1-6a

Suggested Prospectus for Division of Education. (ONE's Baker Memorial Library & Archives)

page -1-

SUGGESTED PROSPECTUS FOR DIVISION OF EDUCATION
(INSTITUTE OF ANDRO-CYNIC HUMANITIES)
(INTERMEDIATE)
(INTERGRADE)
(ISOPHYLLIC)   MAY 17 1955

I. OBJECTIVES

    A. Long Range Goal...to restore the maximal in-balance of reciprocal social contribution between the Homophilic Minority and its Parent Community, by:

        1. Establishing a permanent federation of study institutes, at the University level,- to explore, evaluate, and integrate into universal social consciousness a constructive appreciation of the singular utilitarian contributions and potentials of the Homophilic culture in the evolution of Civilization;

        2. Creating progressive ways and means by which both the Minority and the Parent Community may prepare themselves to integrate these singular potentials to the greatest advance of the whole Community.

    B. Immediate Goal ...to germinate conceptual horizons of the long term project by providing preliminary leadership-grooming programs oriented to current levels of Minority interest awareness: by-

        1. Responding to the need to lay the groundwork for social integration, in terms of developing an awareness of social responsibility and obligation, at levels which begin to reflect and reveal the generative potentials of the Minority's own special culture;

        2. Responding to the need for vocational re-orientation and training programs enabling our Minority to pursue and enjoy,constructively,uninhibitive opportunities to realize each his own potential;

        3. Providing an immediate approach to Vocational re-orientation in the nature of Avocational or Hobby-ist workshops and seminars which may, in addition, provide grass-roots laboratories in the stimulation of social responsibility through cooperation;

        4. Providing informal areas for the germination of conceptual horizons,by both Parent and Minority groups, through the set-up of four-to-six week discussion courses in a Survey of Homophilic Humanities.

II. SUGGESTED PROCEDURES

    A. Towards the awareness of social responsibility

        1. Engender in all work committees a sense of fraternal sponsorship in the products of the Corporation:

            a. At all affairs and parties given by committee individuals, the magazine ... in terms of subscriptions and services... should be featured, the Barr Publication promoted, and the tambourine passed for stamp money.

APPENDIX, 1-6b

Suggested Prospectus for Division of Education. *(ONE's Baker Memorial Library & Archives)* *(continued)*

page -2-

II. A. 1.

    b. Individuals capable of contributing special event parties should be encouraged to do so in terms of evening affairs oriented towards raising amounts between $10.00 to $20.00 a piece. Sample affairs might be:
      (1. Chamber-Music Evening   (4. Treasure Hunt
      (2. Music Discussion Evening   (5. Barbecue
      (3. Special Recipe Party   (6. Special TV Event

    2. At the work-committee and "friends" level, a box-top competition should be promoted... concerning, at the moment, the publication of "A Game of Fools".

      a. The competition to secure the greatest quantity of advance orders.

      b. the "box-top" to be the competitor's own addressographed envelope from a recent copy of ONE.

      c. Board to survey facilities available at the wholesale level, for interesting prizes:

        (1. some kind of travel, or vacation gimmick, <u>retailing</u> at $100.00

          (a. qualification for this prize.....10 orders or more

        (2. some sort of cultural self-improvement facility such as an oil or photography portrait study; 5 sessions in piano coaching, 5 swimming and/or diving lessons, 5 sessions in ceramic-making or whatever is available.

          (a. personal sevices rendered to be evaluated at $10.00/hr.
          (b. qualification for this prize .... 5 orders or more.

        (3. gift certificate on Home furnishings (including fabrics), books, or records, <u>retailing</u> at $25.00

          (a. qualification for this prize ....all comers

      d. Publications Division of ONE, Inc., to give a wind-up affair for the campaign to declare the winners, utilizing the occasion as a rally for whatever new participation projects are in process.

      e. Moneys earned through the sale of Game of Fools, over and above expenses, to be set aside as the reserve-core for future publications.

    3. Individuals, who exhibit capabilities as future discussion chairmen and teachers, should be encouraged to institute privately-run seminars ... topical and/or participatory in character.... at, say a buck a throw. Seminars might be:
      (a. Adventures in listening   (c. Adventures in Design
      (b. Adventures in Anthropology   (d. Adventures in Cookery

APPENDIX, 1-6c

Suggested Prospectus for Division of Education. (ONE's Baker Memorial Library & Archives) (continued)

---

page -3-

II.
  B. Cashing on the popularity of "DO-IT-YOURSELF" projects, set up a series of short-term, semi-participatory, independently-run workshopsx in three categoriesx established at $1.00 per session:

    1. First category.... <u>Designs for Living</u>,- a set of four 2-hour sessions introducing and surveying the techniques of (say):

        a. Interior Decoration   g. Photography
        b. Furniture Design   h. Metal &/or plas-
        c. Ceramics   tic Sculpture
        d. Fabric design & weaving
        e. Architecture
        f. Architectural Models

    2. Second Category... <u>Designs for Recreation</u>,- a set of four 2-hour sessions introducing the techniques and surveying the preliminary requirements for:

        a. Folk Dance Group   f. Public Speaking
        b. Chamber Music Group   g. Diction
        c. Sketching Group
        d. Choral Group
        e. Theater Arts

    3. Third Category ... <u>Designs for Social Knowledge</u>,- a set of four 2-hour sessions presenting group selected topical discussions to promote further exploration of:

        a. Anthropology   f. Homophile Humani-
        b. History of Design   ties
        c. History of Architecture
        d. Social History of Music
        e. Techniques of Piano

    4. All funds derived from these sessions, over and above that needed for session material expenses to be <u>donated</u> to One Inc., publishing fund.

  C. On the basis of the above-run independent sessions, donated to the credit of ONE INC., xxxxxx convoking a conference of all participants towards the launching of a full-fledged Corporation Institute of Humanities:

    1. Major session to be participated in by all students and session chairmen with the objective of setting up a more permanent curricula at both elementary and advanced levels.

    2. Summary session for potential discussion and/or workshop leaders to lay groundwork for organized coordination.

    3. Windup Institute Demonstration and Party to:
        a. acquaint project personnel with each other
        b. drum up enthusiasm for the full-scale institute
        c. raise funds and pledges for institutional promotion.

APPENDIX, 1-6d

Suggested Prospectus for Division of Education. (ONE's Baker Memorial Library & Archives) (continued)

5-16-55

MAY 1 9 1955

FUND DRIVE TO PROMOTE $10,000.00,
(as the first lap in a 5 year $50,000 goal.)

THE WATCH-WORD (even as with the old Citizen's Committee against entanglement) is AUDACITY!

A. Dispense with the head-ache of the "Game of Fools" publication costs by securing advance Purchase Orders from, say, 100 book-stores and "factoring" or discounting same against a bank loan to 85% of the Purchase Order's value.

B. Utilize Mattachine's example and develop a campaign to invest in the "Minority's own printing plant", a FREEDOM FOR HOMOEHILE PRESS, which can always "roll" for the Minority's own guidance, its own best interests, and its own defense....come what may!

   1. Objective....to raise $10,000.00 as the initial reserve for this project:

     a. by direct gift
     b. by soliciting non-voting associations

   2. Promote motivations by:

     a. bleeding the current Canadian photo-publishing campain to suggest how, if this happened here, it could scare off printers from handling our "counter-offensive" as well as our magazine in general, and refuse use the standard ad-vance credits on which most business must be done.

     b. re-hash the Miami Story to illustrate the same thing

     c. warn that press and book censorhip of publication can happen here.

   3. Campaign suggestions,-engineered on a six-months basis: (joak:-"Now is the time for all good summer soldiers to come ...)

     a. Direct-mail program,- objective $5,000.00

       (1. a real heart-throb in deathless prose to a selective list......for gifts
       (2. a rally-your-brothers mobilizer to a second selected list of those who, thru' such activity, might develop as useful corp "associates".

     b. A folding money promotion in the Magazine proper, with the objective - $2,500.00

       (1. engineered to a six-months cumulative tempo like the Rheingold Blitz.
       (2. Perhaps sectioned off into topical components like....
        (a. August....buy-the-varityper month
        (b. September ... buy-the-linotyper month

     c. Personal activities program:

       (1. Switch the Box-Top Competition,suggested in my Educational Prospectus, this to this project, and raise goals accordingly objective,- $1,000.00

APPENDIX, 1-6e

Suggested Prospectus for Division of Education. (ONE's Baker Memorial Library & Archives) (continued)

B. 3. c.

¶2. Utilize the summer vacations for a March-Of-Quarters Drive;- objective,-$500.00 in small change

    (a. bevies of beautiful boys beating the beaches and shaking cans for quarters, (also dimes, pennies, and slugs)

    (b. special parties' program on individually-run small scale lever: beach parties, treasure-hunts, wienie roasts, "coming-out" balls, etc.

(3. Corporation to run a big year-end pre-Xmas Bazaar: objective,- $1,000.00

    (a. To wind up box-top competition and award winners.

    (b. Entertainment in part by specialty groups (if any) offshot from educational programme.

    (c. Raffle off, or auction off, specialty or valuable merchandise which may have been donated in lieu of cash.

    (d. Bazaar to include some of the features of its church traditional models:
        (i. cake competition and raffle
        (ii. pie ditto
        (iii. hawking of home-made crafts such as jams, pickles, ash-trays, what-nots, falsies, bustles, and drags.
        (iv. chances

    (e. Bazaar to be engineered and oriented in terms of 250-500 attendance, at $1.00 admission, and the net of $1,000.00 over all expenses.

        Respectfully submitted

In one hull of a rush (when the boss isn't looking)

Harry Hay

APPENDIX, 2-1

1956 Midwinter Institute and Fourth Annual Meeting. Letter of announcement and invitation. (ONE's Baker Memorial Library & Archives)

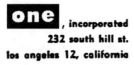, incorporated

232 south hill st.

los angeles 12, california

January 6, 1956

Members of the Corporation,
Subscribers & Guests

Dear Friends:

    You are invited to attend ONE'S MIDWINTER INSTITUTE & Fourth Annual Meeting, to be held in Los Angeles, January 27 & 28. The theme of this unique event in the field of education will be: "American Homosexuals, 1950 - 1955."

P R O G R A M

Friday Evening, January 27 - 8:00 FOURTH ANNUAL MEETING

    Reports, Business, Announcements.
    Open to voting and non-voting members only.

Saturday Morning, January 28 - 10:00 1956 MIDWINTER INSTITUTE

    "The New Look in America Since 1950" A brief statement of the
    Institute's theme - the remarkable series of recent social changes
    concerning the homosexual.
    "The Mattachine Foundation," by one of its Founders.
    "The Mattachine Society, A Report," by Ken Burns, President
    (& members of the Society).

Saturday Afternoon, January 28 - 2:00

    "Two Signposts of Change: QUATREFOIL (Barr) & THE HOMOSEXUAL IN
    AMERICA (Cory), a brief paper.
    "The National Association for Sexual Research, Its Program,"
    by Steve Potter, President (& members of the Association).
    "ONE, Incorporated: Education-Publishing-Research-Social Service,"
    by its officers and staff.

    We are hoping to see you at these sessions. Please fill out and mail TODAY
the following registration blank. ALL REGISTRATIONS MUST BE MADE BY MAIL. Cards
of admission will be mailed to you approximately one week before the meetings.
Address of the meetings will be included.

                                        Cordially yours,

                                        ONE, Incorporated
                                        by Board of Directors

───
    Registration Blank for 1956 Midwinter Institute & 4th Annual Meeting

Name (I am over 21 years of age)_____

Street Address_____

City_____ State_____

    Enclose Registration fee $1.00 for subscribers; $2.50, for others.
    Voting & non-voting Members will receive their cards without fee.

APPENDIX, 2-2a

Program, 1957 Midwinter Institute, "The Homosexual Answers His Critics." (ONE's Baker Memorial Library & Archives)

P R O G R A M

1 9 5 7 MIDWINTER INSTITUTE

"T H E H O M O S E X U A L A N S W E R S H I S C R I T I C S"

January 26
MORNING CHAIRMAN, Ricky Linn

10:00 A.M. WELCOME from ONE, Incorporated
by Ann Carll Reid, Board of Directors

CENSORSHIP & CIVIL LIBERTIES
by Dr. Eason Monroe, Secy., Southern
California American Civil Liberties Union

HOW HOMOSEXUALS CAN COMBAT ANTI-HOMOSEX-
UALISM. (Written for the Midwinter Institute by Albert Ellis, Ph.D., Psychologist, New York City.

ANTHROPOLOGY LOOKS AT THE HOMOPHILE - An
Introduction. By Henry Hay, Los Angeles

12:00 Noon: Luncheon at Embassy Grill (Optional)
(Cost, about $1.00)

AFTERNOON CHAIRMAN, Ricky Linn

2:00 P.M. THE EDUCATION DIVISION OF ONE, Incorporated
by Don Slater, Board of Directors

"CROSS-FIRE FROM THE CRITICS" - Special
Feature, Direction by Bob Hannum.

15-Minute Intermission

THE HOMOSEXUAL ANSWERS HIS CRITICS
Panel of Students and Faculty of ONE
Institute.

QUESTIONS. As many written questions answered as time permits.

5:00 P. M. ADJOURNMENT

APPENDIX, 2-2b

Program, 1957 Midwinter Institute, "The Homosexual Answers His Critics." (continued)

PROGRAM OF 1957 Midwinter Institute, Continued

EVENING: Toastmaster, Bob Hannum

7:30 P.M. ANNUAL BANQUET

ONE'S YEAR
by Ann Carll Reid, Chairman, ONE, Inc.

THE CIRCLE OF SEX
by Blanche M. Baker, Ph.D., M.D. Psychiatrist, San Francisco, and Gavin Arthur,
San Francisco.

- - - - -

January 27

MORNING

10:00 A.M. BRUNCH - Daughters of Bilitis

11:00 A.M. BRUNCH - Mattachine Society
                    2302 W. 11th St., Rear Apt. Upstairs
                              (Cost, $1.00)

AFTERNOON

3:00 P.M. DRAMATIC READINGS
          a New Play, MAMMA DOLL, by James Barr

          TEA

5:00 P.M. ADJOURNMENT UNTIL 1958.

APPENDIX, 2-3

ONE Institute. Presenting a Symposium: How Homosexuality Fits In, November 11-17, 1957, (ONE's Baker Memorial Library & Archives)

O N E I n s t i t u t e

232 south hill street   los angeles 12, california   MIchigan 6983

P R E S E N T I N G

        A SYMPOSIUM: HOW HOMOSEXUALITY FITS IN
        November 11 - 17, 1957   at 465 Geary Street,
           Studio 30, San Francisco, Calif.

        SPONSORED BY THE DAUGHTERS OF BILITIS

Monday   8-10 PM   SQUAW-MEN & AMAZONS
                 Some Sex Customs of Our Ancestors

Tuesday   "   THE GLORY THAT WAS GREECE
                 Men & Women Who Made It Great

Wednesday   "   THE "NEW ATHENS" IN AMERICA
                 Some Intellectual & Social Currents Examined

Thursday   "   MORES & MORALS
                 Femininity, Masculinity, & Philosophy

Friday   "   IS YOUR BODY HOMOSEXUAL ?
                 Evidence From Biology & Medicine

Saturday   "   THE TWILIGHT OF THE GODS
                 Disaster, or Decadence ? Germany as Example

Sunday   3-5   PM   THE CURSE OF EVE & THE CURSE OF SODOM
                 Religious Doctrines Down Through the Ages

     "   7-9   HOMOPHILE ORGANIZATIONS: WHERE ARE THEY HEADED ?
                 Roundtable & coffee - open to those attending
                 at least three of the previous sessions.

The first four sessions will be conducted by W. Dorr Legg, Acting
Director;   the following three by James Kepner, Jr., Instructor.

TUITION: Eight sessions, $ 10; any three, $ 5; single session $ 2.
        Make checks payable to ONE, Inc., or Daughters of Bil-
        itis, 693 Mission Street, San Francisco 5, California.
....
           E N R O L L M E N T   B L A N K

Name ....

Street Address ....

City ....Zone............

I am over 21 .... Signed

the Education Division.............ONE, Inc.

Founded 1952

APPENDIX, 2-4a

Midwinter Institute [1958] Theme: Homosexuality - A Way of Life.
(ONE's Baker Memorial Library & Archives)

M I D W I N T E R   I N S T I T U T E

THEME: HOMOSEXUALITY — A WAY OF LIFE

February 1

    10:00 A.M.   REGISTRATION

    10:30 A.M.   RESOLVED: HETEROSEXUAL LIVING IS BETTER
    THAN HOMOSEXUAL.   Chairman, Dr. M. C. Thompson

        AFFIRMATIVE — Dr. Arthur E. Briggs, Attorney
                    Howard Russell, Psychologist

        NEGATIVE —   V. C. Vostwald, Graduate Student,
               ONE Institute
               Lyn Pedersen, Associate Editor,
        ONE Magazine

    12 Noon.   INFORMAL LUNCHEON

    2:00 P.M.   ROUNDTABLE DISCUSSIONS. First session

        GROUP A — IS HOMOSEXUALITY A SOCIAL NECESSITY?
        Chairman, Jack Roust, Student, ONE Institute

            1.   Does society need non conformists?
            2.   Questions of overpopulation.
            3.   Is the heterosexual enough for a balanced
        and progressive society?
            4.   Are homosexuals better qualified for
        certain jobs?

        GROUP B — DO HOMOSEXUALS HAVE COMMUNITY RESPONSI-
        BILITIES? Chairman, Don Rifle, Anthropologist

            1.   Does everyone have social obligations?
            2.   As members of a minority are there
        special obligations?
            3.   Should we obey "bad" laws?
            4.   Should homosexuals police their own group?

        GROUP C — PROMISCUITY: WRONG OR RIGHT?
        Chairman, R. F. Lynd, Foreign Missionary

            1.   Religious views.
            2.   Is it a psychological or biological
        necessity?
            3.   Social and legal dangers.
            4.   Can it hold a partnership together?

APPENDIX, 2-4b

Midwinter Institute [1958] Theme: Homosexuality - A Way of Life.
(continued)

3:15 P.M.   INTERMISSION

3:30 P.M.   ROUNDTABLE DISCUSSION. Second session

GROUP D - SHOULD HOMOSEXUALS GET MARRIED?
Chairman, Don Plagman, Parent

    1. Will it aid adjustment?
    2. Is it fair to the other partner?
    3. Is bisexual living desireable?
    4. Will it harm the children?

GROUP E - THE LESBIAN PARTNERSHIP
Chairman, Dawn Frederics, ONE Magazine Staff
Artist

    1. The "butch" and "femme" tradition
    2. Drinking
    3. Finances
    4. Social life

GROUP F - THE OLDER HOMOSEXUAL.
Chairman, Fred Frisbie, Engineer

    1. Gerontology - newest "life science"
    2. Single living - social life
    3. The partnership
    4. Finances

4:45 P.M.   ADJOURNMENT

5:00 P.M.   COCKTAIL HOUR. Host - Rudy

7:00 P.M.   SYMPOSIUM (The Banquet)

ONE AND THE SUPREME COURT, by ONE's Attorney

THE PATTERNS OF SPARTA, a dramatic portrayal
by Miss Rachel Rosenthal (from "The Corn King
and The Spring Queen" by Naomi Mitchison)

"GYMNOPEDIES" incidental music by Satie

APPENDIX, 2-4c

Midwinter Institute [1958] Theme: Homosexuality - A Way of Life. (continued)

February 2

    3:00 - 5:00 P.M.   FIRESIDE TEA

        HOW ABOUT RELIGION AND THE HOMOPHILE?
        Hosts - "The Heavenly Twins"
        Chairman, Julian Underwood, ONE Institute
        Instructor

            1. The Orthodox Christian Churches
            2. Other Christian Groups
            3. Oriental based Religions
            4. Philosophical Groups

APPENDIX, 2-5a

1959 Midwinter Institute... "Mental Health and Homosexuality."
(ONE's Baker Memorial Library & Archives)

1959 MIDWINTER INSTITUTE

AND

7TH ANNUAL BUSINESS MEETING

January 30   —   February 1, 1959

ONE INCORPORATED

232 South Hill Street   --   Los Angeles

ONE CONFIDENTIAL   *VOLUME IV, NO. 1*

APPENDIX, 2-5b

1959 Midwinter Institute... "Mental Health and Homosexuality."
(continued)

BUSINESS MEETING

Friday, January 30, 1959

8:00 P.M.   I   READING OF MINUTES, by the Secretary

II   REPORTS
ONE Magazine, by Alison Hunter, Women's Editor
and Eve Elloree, Art Director
ONE Institute Quarterly: Homophile Studies, by James Kepner, Editor
and Dawn Frederic, Art Editor
Promotion Committee, by Sten Russell, Chairman
Library, by Leslie Colfax, Librarian
Education Division - ONE Institute. by W. Dorr Legg, Director
Circulation Committee, by James Kepner
Social Service Division, by Don Plagman, Committee Member
Book Service, by Don Slater, Manager
Board of Directors, by the Chairman

III Unfinished and New Business

IV   Adjournment

V   Reception - Home of R. H. Stewart

1959 MIDWINTER INSTITUTE

"MENTAL HEALTH AND HOMOSEXUALITY"

Fred Frisbie, Chairman

Saturday, January 31, 1959

9:00 A.M.   Registration and Exhibition of Books for sale

9:30 A.M.   HOMOPHILE MOVEMENTS IN UNITED STATES TODAY - Progress Reports
Daughters of Bilitis, by Del Martin, President, San Francisco
Mattachine Society, Inc., by Rick Hooper, Chairman, San Francisco
ONE. Incorporated, by James Kepner, Jr., Vice Chairman

10:30 A.M.   TOWARD BETTER MENTAL HEALTH - Roundtable Discussions
Group A.   Adjustment—Through Partnership. Moderators, Lawson and Plagman
B.   Creative Expression as Therapy. Miss Dawn Frederic
C.   Must Christians Live With Guilt? Right Rev. Thomas Martin
11:15 A.M.   Group D.   Sex Repression and Mental Health, Moderator, Ron Argall
E.   Should Men and Women Homosexuals Associate? Mrs. V. Vostwald
F.   Is it Unnatural to be Homosexual? James Kepner, Jr.

12:00 Noon   Luncheon
Address, 'ACCEPTING MIDDLE AGE.' ' Dr. T. M. Merritt, PhD, Dean Emeritus.
ONE Institute

APPENDIX, 2-5c

1959 Midwinter Institute "Mental Health and Homosexuality."
(continued)

2:00 P.M.   MENTAL HEALTH AND HOMOSEXUALITY - A Panel Discussion
Chairman: Eric Julber, Attorney, Los Angeles
Blanche M. Baker, M.D., PhD., Psychiatrist, San Francisco
Trent E. Bessent,PhD. Chief Clinical Psychologist, Metropolitan
    State Hospital, Norwalk, California
W. Dorr Legg. A.B., B.M., M.L.D., Director, ONE Institute
Vita S. Sommers, PhD , Clinical Psychologist, Los Angeles

3:30 P.M.   INTERMISSION

3:45 P.M.   PSYCHODRAMA 'A Mental Health Problem Demonstrated' with audience
participation, conducted by William F. Baker, A.B., San Francisco

5:00 P.M.   RECESS

Saturday, January 31, 1959

6:00 P.M.   COCKTAIL HOUR

7:00 P.M.   ANNUAL BANQUET, Toastmaster, Don Slater
INTRODUCTIONS
AN IMPORTANT ANNOUNCEMENT
Address: CLASSICAL BOY LOVE AND MODERN CIVILIZATION,
    by Dr. Mario Palmieri, M.S., PhD.

Sunday, February 1, 1959   Samson De Brier, Chairman

2:00 P.M.   TEA AND POETRY - Presented by the Department of Literature and
Creative Arts, ONE Institute

    S I   Poems from the Greek Anthology
    The Sonnets of Michelangelo

    II   Traditional Spanish Dances, by Antonio Reyes

    III Some Modern Poems

    IV A Special Feature

    V INTERMISSION

    VI THE MOON QUEEN - An Oriental Fantasy, in One Act,
    by Doyle Eugene Livingston - A First Performance

    VII TEA

5:00 P.M.   ADJOURNMENT UNTIL *1960!*

APPENDIX, 2-6a

January 28-31, 1960, The Education Division of ONE, Inc. Presents its Sixth Midwinter Institute, Theme: "The Homosexual in the Community." (ONE's Baker Memorial Library & Archives)

January 28-31, 1960

The EDUCATION DIVISION of ONE, INC.,

Presents Its

SIXTH

MIDWINTER

INSTITUTE

Theme: "THE HOMOSEXUAL IN THE COMMUNITY"

ADVANCE REGISTRATION IS REQUIRED

APPENDIX, 2-6b

January 28-31, 1960, The Education Division of ONE, Inc. Presents its Sixth Midwinter Institute, Theme: "The Homosexual in the Community." (continued)

The EDUCATION DIVISION of ONE, INC., Presents Its

SIXTH MIDWINTER INSTITUTE

in conjunction with the

EIGHTH ANNUAL BUSINESS MEETING of ONE, INC.

Theme: "THE HOMOSEXUAL IN THE COMMUNITY"

to be held at ONE's Offices (entrance, 233 S. Broadway) and at the NEW HOTEL CLARK, in downtown Los Angeles
January 28-31, 1960

PROGRAM

THURSDAY

8:00 p.m. Final Class in Sociology of Homosexuality. HS 200. Topic. "Homosexuality and Overpopulation." Visitors Welcome. Fee, $1.

FRIDAY

10:00 a.m. MEMBERS' DAY. Open House to Friends of ONE. No fee. Slides and Tapes Activities of Homophile Organizations.

12:00 noon Luncheon ("Dutch Treat").

1:30 p.m. Orientation Workshop on Local Problems, for benefit of out-of town Members.

8:00 p.m. ONE's 1960 Annual Business Meeting

10:30 p.m. Reception for Members and Guests

SATURDAY
1960 MIDWINTER INSTITUTE

9:00 a.m. Registration

9:45 a.m. Welcome: James Kepner, Jr., Chairman of ONE, Inc.

10:00 a.m. PANEL DISCUSSION: **"The Homosexual in the Community."**
Rev. Stephen H. Fritchman, First Unitarian Church, Los Angeles.
Dr. Zoltan Gross, Ph.D. Psychologist, Beverly Hills.
David Miller, M.A., Teacher, San Francisco.
Charles Rowland, Personnel Manager, Los Angeles.
Moderator: Miss Helen Sanders, former president, Daughters of Bilitis.

12:00 noon LUNCHEON.
Introductions.
Address: Eric Julber, ONE's Attorney. "Community Standards and ONE Magazine's Editorial Policies."

2:00 p.m. Paper: "Normative Factors and Cultural Determinants in the Dynamics of Homosexual Pairing." W. Dorr Legg, Director, ONE Institute.
Research Paper: Value Conflicts and Value Congruence of a Homosexual Group in Heterosexual Society." Evelyn Hooker, Ph.D. Dept of Psychology, U.C.L.A.

ROUNDTABLE DISCUSSIONS: Groups meeting concurrently.
A. Regulated Homophile Mating: Key to Social Approval?
B. Coming to Terms With Current Social Values
C. Is There a Place for Homophiles in Community Life?
Roundtable Summary, with Dr. Hooker, Mr. Legg and chairmen of the three roundtables.

5:30 p.m. Cocktail Hour (drinks not included in admission price).

7:00 p.m. ANNUAL BANQUET
Introductions and Announcements.
Address: Dr. Eason Monroe, executive director, American Civil Liberties Union of Southern California
Poetry readings.
A group of gay folk songs sung by Lisa Ben.

SUNDAY

11:00 a.m. MEET DR. BAKER.

2:45 p.m. GAME OF FOOLS: American Premiere Performance of James Barr Fugate's hard-hitting play about four homosexuals in a trap. Fourth Annual Presentation of the Drama Department of ONE INSTITUTE.

PRICES

$11.50 for Entire Saturday Program (including Luncheon and Banquet) and Play.
Reduced Rate for Couples: $10 per person.
Special Rates for Members. (See January Conf.).
Prices for Individual Sessions.

Saturday Registration $2.50
Saturday Luncheon 2.75
Banquet 6.00
Game of Fools 2.40

Dr. Baker session, $2.50 (separate from rest of program)
Thursday and Friday Sessions will be held at ONE's Offices.
Saturday Sessions will be held at the NEW HOTEL CLARK, 426 S. Hill Street
Place for Sunday Sessions and Receptions to be announced.

ADVANCE REGISTRATION IS REQUIRED
Address all mail to: **ONE, Inc., 232 South Hill Street, Los Angeles 12, Calif.**

APPENDIX, 2-7a

ONE Institute of Homophile Studies, 1959-1960 Announcement and Schedule of Classes. (ONE's Baker Memorial Library & Archives)

ONE INSTITUTE OF HOMOPHILE STUDIES

1959
1960

209 S BROADWAY

announcement and schedule of classes

The Education Division of One, Inc.
Vol. IV No. 1

Education is one of the purposes for which ONE, a non-profit California corporation, was organized. Its charter calls for "dealing primarily with homosexuality," through research, "educational programs," publications and other means as enumerated.

HISTORY AND ORGANIZATION

ONE's Education Division sponsored its first public meetings in January, 1955. These Midwinter Institutes, repeated annually since that date, have presented lectures by psychiatrists, psychologists, attorneys, as well as panels and roundtable discussions, and literary, dance and dramatic features representing homophile interests by other means. These Institutes have attracted visitors from various parts of the United States, Canada and overseas.

The response to these programs encouraged ONE to consider providing for serious academic study of homosexuality on a continuing basis. A committee of the Education Division was appointed, during the summer of 1956, to make a study of the situation and report.

Its report enumerated as deficiencies felt to characterize existing university facilities for the study of homosexuality: (1) academic timidity concerning an admittedly "touchy" subject; (2) lack of budget support, resulting in extreme superficiality of such little work as was being attempted; (3) the largely either Freudian or medical bias of most research; (4) professional reluctance to approach the topic objectively; (5) the consequent unscientific levels prevailing, with a few honorable exceptions.

APPENDIX, 2-7b

ONE Institute of Homophile Studies, 1959-1960 Announcement and Schedule of Classes. (continued)

While recognizing the immense difficulties presented by its proposal for a full-fledged Institute of Homophile Studies, and the severe shortage of funds for new projects, the committee felt that delay would only aggravate the difficulties. It recommended that a beginning be made at once.

The Corporation studied, and adopted, the report. A Board of Trustees was appointed to have administrative responsibility over ONE Institute of Homophile Studies. Officers were appointed to conduct its general academic and routine business: a Dean, for academic matters; a Director for administrative affairs; a Secretary.

LOCATION AND FACILITIES

The Los Angeles Metropolitan Area offers unique cultural and educational resources favorable to homophile studies. Evidence of this is found in the remarkable development here of organizations and publications concerned with homosexuality. The world's earliest lesbian magazine was founded here. The earliest interracial homosexual organization was founded in Los Angeles, as was the only organization known to have been devoted primarily to the legal problems of homosexuals. Both of the largest existing American organizations, ONE and t h e Mattachine Society, were founded in Los Angeles.

The presence of the movie industry and its off-shoot TV, of a very large number of vigorous little theater groups, of an extensive musical life, of art galleries and colonies, the vast libraries of the city and the several major universities in the area, give a particular cultural flavor to the region which has often been misunderstood by those conventionally oriented. Unusually large populations of oriental, negro and Spanish speaking peoples further ensure the cultural diversity and liberalism of the area.

Resources of particular value to the student of homophilia are the Huntington Library's collection of erotica, one of the world's largest; the Clark Memorial Library's great collection of Oscar Wilde

papers and other items: the Gertrude Stein collection in another library.

ONE's own library is a rapidly growing collection of specialized materials, containing a large section of biographies of noted homophiles, of non-fiction, both scientific and otherwise, and of homophile fiction in several languages. A small slide collection is continually being added to, as is the uncatalogued mass of periodical and newspaper items available for special projects.

The library is open to students for reading. Books may be withdrawn by Friends of ONE, by others where special permission is granted.

CLASSES AND INSTRUCTION

Classes were first given in the fall semester of 1956, open only to staff members of the Corporation. The semester was devoted to a rapid survey of the general position of nine subjects (law, sociology, religion, etc.) in regard to homosexuality. This course was repeated the following semester and opened to the public.

Beginning in the fall of 1957, classes have been given as described below. Approximately two hundred and fifty persons have enrolled or attended the classes. In addition to the regular classes a lecture series by resident or visiting experts in various fields has broadened the scope of the instruction. Several hundred persons have attended these lectures and those given at the Midwinter Institutes.

A standard numbering system such as is used by many universities has been adopted for identification of the various subjects offered. Students with any level of previous education may attend, although their benefits from class work will depend largely on the degree of background they may possess. The subject matter is designed to afford the student greater understanding of the social and personal aspects of homosexuality with a view to lessening tensions and conflicts wherever these exist.

APPENDIX, 2-7c

ONE Institute of Homophile Studies, 1959-1960 Announcement and Schedule of Classes. (continued)

DESCRIPTION OF COURSES

HS - 100   INTRODUCTION TO HOMOPHILE STUDIES. What is homosexuality? How does it fit into the scheme of things? A critical examination of how biology, anthropology, sociology and psychology view these questions. *(Omitted in 1959-60)*

HS - 101   INTRODUCTION (continued). Summaries of the attitudes toward homosexuality expressed in historical studies, law, literature, religion and philosophy. Some general theories of homosexuality evaluated. *(Omitted in 1959-60)*

HS - 130   LANDMARKS IN HOMOPHILE LITERATURE. Outstanding literary works by homophiles, or about homosexuality, from Homer to Proust. The "gay novels" of Vidal, Barr, Vin Packer and others. For the student seeking a general knowledge of the field. *Wednesday evenings, 8-10.* Slater.

HS - 200   THE HOMOSEXUAL IN AMERICAN SOCIETY. A sociological examination of the well-adjusted homosexual. How homosexuality is accomodated or rejected by the various elements of American social structure. Problems and the quest for solutions. *Thursday evenings, 8-10.* Legg.

HS - 201   SOCIOLOGY (continued). Social maladjustments of the homosexual. Rough trade, the hustler, drag queens, vice cops, blackmail, crime, alcoholism, personality disorganization, suicide. Corrective proposals. The programs of the various homophile movements. *Thursday evenings.* Legg.

HS - 210   HOMOSEXUALITY IN HISTORY. Contrasting social attitudes in paleolithic and neolithic times; emerging customs and institutions. Attitudes toward homosexuality in Mesopotamia, Egypt, India and China. Greece and some of its great homophile figures. *(Omitted in 1959-60)*

HS - 211   HISTORY (continued). The rise and decline of Rome. The clash of pagan and Christian sex attitudes. The story of Inca and Aztec homosexuality. Modern European history. Homophilia in United States. *(Omitted in 1959-60)*

HS - 251   THE ORTHODOX FREUDIAN TEXTS ON HOMOSEXUALITY. A close examination of the text of Freud's little known but basic early volume, *Three Essays on the Theory of Sexuality*, to see how the initial analysis of homosexuality by Freud stands up today. Also, how it compares with the theories of both orthodox and schismatic Freudians. *Tuesday evenings, 8-10. (Spring Semester only)* Kepner.

HS - 310   HOMOSEXUALITY IN MODERN GERMAN HISTORY. A survey of the influence of homosexuals and homosexuality on the tragic modern history of Germany, tracing the effects of German sexual mores and vagaries upon American life. Stories from the exciting lives of many famed German homosexuals. Illustrated with slides. *Tuesday evenings, 8-10.* Kepner.

APPENDIX, 2-7d

ONE Institute of Homophile Studies, 1959-1960 Announcement and Schedule of Classes. (continued)

FEES

For each course, per semester $15; for those who are Friends of ONE, $10. Visitors are invited to attend single sessions. Fee, $1.

OFFICERS AND FACULTY

Thomas M. Merritt, Dean Emeritus.
W. Dorr Legg, Director.
Alison Hunter, Secretary.

James Kepner, Jr.. Instructor in History and Psychology.
W. Dorr Legg, A.B., B.M., M.L.D., Associate Professor of Sociology.
Thomas M. Merritt, Ph.D.. Professor Emeritus of Philosophy.
Donald Slater, A.B., Instructor in Literature.

CALENDAR

1959	September	16	Fall semester begins
	November	26	Thanksgiving holiday
	December	23	Christmas holiday begins
1960	January	5	Classes resume
	January	28	Semester ends
	January	29-31	Sixth Annual Midwinter Institute
	February	9	Spring semester begins
	June	10	Semester ends

EXTENSION CLASSES

Interest in the work of ONE Institute expressed by those living in other cities has already occasioned the giving of extension classes in the fall of 1957 in San Francisco, and in Denver in the summer of 1959.

It is hoped that at some future date methods may be devised for offering courses by mail for those living at a greater distance from the Institute. No practical way of handling this demand has yet been worked out.

PUBLICATIONS

ONE Institute Quarterly of HOMOPHILE STUDIES is the official publication of the Institute. It carries articles by faculty members, students, and other writers who have done work in the field. Annual subscription to the Quarterly is $3.50; single copies $1.

APPENDIX, 2-8a

ONE Institute of Homophile Studies...Presents Its Seventh Midwinter Institute, Thursday, January 26-Sunday, January 29 [1961], Theme: "A Homosexual Bill of Rights." (ONE's Baker Memorial Library & Archives)

ONE INSTITUTE OF HOMOPHILE STUDIES

The Education Division of ONE, Inc.

Presents Its

SEVENTH MIDWINTER INSTITUTE

Thursday, January 26 - Sunday, January 29

Theme: "A Homosexual Bill of Rights"

A Group-Participation Project in Homophile Education

ONE INSTITUTE:

Board of Trustees

George Mortensen, Chairman
Don Slater, Vice Chairman
W. Dorr Legg, Treasurer

Officers

Dr. Thomas M. Merritt,
    Dean (Emeritus)
W. Dorr Legg, Director
Robert Gregory, Secretary

The Seventh Midwinter Institute was planned and developed as a class project in HS-260, "The Theory and Practice of Homophile Education." This Seminar has met two or more hours per week since September, 1960, preparing plans for the Institute.

Host Committee

Joe Aaron, Chairman
Ron Argall
Miss Sten Russell
R. H. Stuart

*   *   *

ONE CONFIDENTIAL   Vol. VI Number 1
                        January, 1961

APPENDIX, 2-8b

ONE Institute of Homophile Studies...Presents Its Seventh Midwinter Institute, Thursday, January 26-Sunday, January 29 [1961], Theme: "A Homosexual Bill of Rights." (continued)

SCHEDULE OF EVENTS

THURSDAY, January 26, Final Class, Fall Semester, ONE Institute - HOMOSEXUALITY IN HISTORY.

8:00-10:00 PM "Byzantine Sex Laws and Repressions," Associate Professor, W. Dorr Legg.

FRIDAY, January 27, WORKSHOP DAY.

10:00-12:00 AM Discussion of procedures to be used on following days in framing the "Bill of Rights;" tabulation of data from questionnaires submitted.

12:00- 2:00 PM Luncheon Period.

2:00- 5:00 PM Continuation of data tabulation; briefing of committee chairmen, secretaries and other participants on their duties during Saturday and Sunday sessions.

5:00- 8:00 PM Dinner Period.

8:00-10:00 PM NINTH ANNUAL BUSINESS MEETING, ONE, Incorporated. For Corporation Members and invited guests of the Corporation only.

The various Thursday and Friday events all held at ONE's offices. Enter through door at 233 South Broadway, Los Angeles; telephone MAdison 4-6983.

SATURDAY, January 28, BILL OF RIGHTS DAY. California Room, Clark Hotel, 426 S. Hill Street, Los Angeles.

9:00- 9:45 AM Registration and Choose- four - Chairman Period.

9:45 AM Address of Welcome, Miss Sten Russell, Associate Editor, ONE Magazine.

10:00-12:00 AM Study by the five Drafting Committees of typical questionnaires and proposals submitted by mail, as follows:

Drafting Committee I. Preamble and Definitions, Chairman, Ron Longworth, Editor, ONE Confidential.

Drafting Committee II. Social Rights, Chairman, Miss Helen Sanders, Charter Member, Daughters of Bilitis.

Drafting Committee III. Religious Rights, Chairman, Professor Alan Hart, faculty member of a nearby denominational college.

Drafting Committee IV. Scientific Questions and Overpopulation, Chairman, William F. Baker, San Francisco.

Drafting Committee V. Legal Rights, Chairman, Robert Gregory, Secretary, ONE Institute.

APPENDIX, 2-8c

ONE Institute of Homophile Studies...Presents Its Seventh Midwinter Institute, Thursday, January 26-Sunday, January 29 [1961], Theme: "A Homosexual Bill of Rights." (continued)

12:00- 2:00 PM   Buffet Luncheon and Informal Exchange of Ideas.

2:00- 3:30 PM   Compilation by each Drafting Committee of material found pertinent to its section of the Bill; no additions to be made after 3:30 Recess period.

3:30- 3:45 PM   Recess Period.

3:45- 5:00 PM   Preparation of the outlines for their respective portions of the Bill by each of the five Drafting Committees.

5:00- 9:30 PM   Adjournment of work sessions; dinner period.

From 10:00-12:00 AM, and from 2:00-5:00 PM, Saturday, Don Slater, Editor, ONE Magazine, will be available for interviews concerning ONE; SocialService inquiries. For appointment see Mr. Slater. No other staff member will be available for personal interviews.

During the work sessions Saturday and Sunday members of HS-260, Seminar, will be available to answer questions concerning areas of interest of the various Drafting Committees, or other problems of Committee jurisdiction.

9:30-   PM   Reception - for Guests of the Institute only. Host: R. H. Stuart

Cocktails.

Entertainment:
      Hank's Mad Marionette's.
      Lod Andre, Song Stylist and Composer.

SUNDAY,   January 29, ADOPTION DAY,   Clark Hotel

11:00   AM   Continental Breakfast; free-for-all discussion.

1:00- 4:00 PM   Drafting of the five sections of the Bill, for presentation at the Banquet; each Drafting Committee to prepare and adopt its own section (by Committee acclamation, or by majority vote, as preferred).

4:30   PM   ANNUAL BANQUET, Garden Room

Moderator: W. Dorr Legg, Director, ONE Institute
Commentators:
      Dr. Evelyn Hooker, U C L A, Psychologist;
      Herbert Selwyn, Jr., Attorney;
      Miss Del Martin, Editor, THE LADDER;
      Hal Call, Editor, MATTACHINE REVIEW.

A Tribute: "Blanche M. Baker, M.D., Ph.D.,— Retrospect and Forecast." William F. Baker.

ADJOURNMENT

APPENDIX, 2-9a

Tenth...Midwinter Institute, Los Angeles, California, January 26-28, 1962. (ONE's Baker Memorial Library & Archives)

Tenth Anniversary Celebration

1952 **one** 1 9 6 2

"A mystic bond of brotherhood makes all men one."
—Thomas Carlyle

TEN YEARS OF HOMOPHILE RESPONSIBILITY AND LEADERSHIP

ANNUAL BUSINESS MEETING of ONE, INC.

MIDWINTER INSTITUTE

Los Angeles   California.

J A N U A R Y 26 - 28, 1962

APPENDIX, 2-9b

Tenth...Midwinter Institute, Los Angeles, California, January 26-28, 1962. (continued)

C O M P L E T E   P R O G R A M

Friday, January 26th, 1 9 6 2

2:00 P.M.	welcome to 1962 Midwinter Institute, George Morten-son, Chairman, ONE, Incorporated.
2:15	"This was Dr. Baker," a tape from the first Institute.
2:45	"Toward Understanding - The Blanche M. Baker Founda-tion," William F. Baker, San Francisco.
3:15	Intermission
3:30	Open House in ONE's Library, hosted by the staff.
4:00	Evelyn Hooker, Ph.D., UCLA psychologist and Don Slater, Editor, ONE Magazine, discuss homosexuality. Tape of an August 28, 1959, K P F K broadcast.
5:00	Adjournment
8:00 P.M.	TENTH ANNUAL BUSINESS MEETING OF O N E, INCORPORATED. Open to Members of the Corporation (including "Friends of ONE) and invited guests.
	Minutes of the previous meeting. Treasurer's Report, read by Lois Mitchell, book-keeper. A 10-Year Summary of Business Operations, William Lambert, Business Manager. ONE Magazine Report, Don Slater, Editor. Art Department Report, Eve Elloree, Director. Circulation Report, Hal Schmoll, Assistant. Promotion Department Report, Joe Aaron, Chairman. Librarian's Report, read by George Neal, Assistant. Social Service Division Report, read by Don Slater. Education Division Report, W. Dorr Legg, Director, ONE Institute. Book Department Report, Don Slater, Manager. The Chairman's Report for 1962, George Mortenson.
	Election of New Members. New Business. Adjournment.
10:30	Reception, for the Members and their guests. Home of P. H. Stuart, a "Friend of ONE."
	Saturday, January 27th, 1 9 6 2
9:30 A.M.	Tickets and registration.
	THEME: 10 YEARS OF LEADERSHIP AND RESPONSIBILITY, (I)
10:00	"ONE, Incorporated, 1952 - 1962," George Mortenson.
10:20	"ONE Institute, Its Challenge," W. Dorr Legg, students.
11:00	"You and the Law, 1952 - 1962," William E. Glover, Secretary, Social Service Division.
11:20	Case Histories from ONE's Social Service Files, Don Slater.

APPENDIX, 2-9c

Tenth...Midwinter Institute, Los Angeles, California, January 26-28, 1962. (continued)

Saturday Continued

12:15 P.M.   LUNCHEON. Joe Aaron, presiding.

Introductions.
"Whither the Homophile Movement ?" Curtis Dewees,
New York City, long a member of the Mattachine Society.

2:00   THEME: THE AMERICAN HOMOPHILE MOVEMENT.

The League for Human Rights. Chicago, 1925.
VICE VERSA. Los Angeles, 1947-1948, Lisa Ben, Editor.
Knights of the Clock. Los Angeles, 1949-1954,
Lorenzo Wilson, a past President.
Mattachine Society & Foundation. Los Angeles, 1950-
1953, Henry Hay, a Founder; Dr. Wallace de Ortega
Maxey, Fresno, a former Board Member.
Mattachine Society, Inc. Los Angeles, 1953 to date.
Ron Argall, a past President; Don Lucas, President;
Hal Call, Editor, THE MATTACHINE REVIEW, San Francisco.
National Association for Sexual Research. Los Angeles
1954-1957.
Daughters of Bilitis. San Francisco, 1955 to date.
Jaye Bell, President, San Francisco; Helen Sanders,
Los Angeles, Vice President.
The Philodemians. Boston, 1961, to date.
The Janus Society. Philadelphia, 1961, to date.

3:30   Intermission.

3:45   THEME: 10 YEARS OF LEADERSHIP AND RESPONSIBILITY (II).

"ONE, Voice of the U. S. Homosexual, Don Slater,
Manager, Publications Division; Donald Webster Cory,
Contributing Editor, ONE Magazine 1953-1955.

ONE's Research Activities: Marcel Martin, Ph.D.,
Associate Editor, ONE Magazine; description by Mrs.
Suzanne Prosin, San Fernando State College graduate
student of her research project; preliminary report
on ONE Institute sociological questionnaire; Ray
Evans, Ph.D., clinical psychologist, "Abstracts
Department," ONE Institute Quarterly.

5:00   Cocktail Hour. (Price of drinks not included in tickets)

6:30 P.M.   ANNUAL BANQUET. Martin Block, first Chairman of
ONE, presiding.

INTRODUCING: More Makers of ONE.
Guy Rousseau, originator of the name ONE.
Geraldine Jackson, earliest woman staff member.
A message from Dale Jennings, Editor, 1953-1954.
Samson, "discoverer" of Ann Carll Reid. Eve Elloree,
and Eric Julber.
Ann Carll Reid, former Editor, ONE Magazine.
Eve Elloree, Art Director from 1953 to date.

APPENDIX, 2-9d

Tenth...Midwinter Institute, Los Angeles, California, January 26-28, 1962. (continued)

<u>Saturday Continued</u>

Thomas M. Merritt, Ph.D., Dean (Emeritus) ONE Institute
Sten Russell, writer, Editorial & Corporation, 1954-61

ADDRESS: "Toward a Rational Approach to Homosexuality"
Donald Webster Cory, New York City, author "The Homosexual in America," 1951, and other books.

<u>Sunday, January 28, 1 9 6 2</u>

11:45 A.M. BRUNCH, at home of "friend of ONE," R. H. Stuart.

12:30 P.M. THEME: THE HOMOPHILE SEEKS A RELIGIOUS FOCUS, Sten Russell, presiding.

The Church of One Brotherhood. Los Angeles, 1955 - 1958, Milan Charles, former member.
"The Sexual Background of the Dead Sea Scrolls," Rev. Claude Lane, San Francisco.

3:00 Antonio Reyes, a Founder of O N E Presents -

AN AFTERNOON AT THE THEATER

Master of Ceremonies: Rolando

Opening - The Ballet Rolando

1. Mike Rusk   "I've Got a Crush on You."
           "The Boy Next Door."
2. Rita Stroska   "Spanish Lace."
3. Ramonin   Guitar Solo.
4. Sola   "La Macarena."
5. Rita Stroska   You Do Something Me."
6. Lisa Ben   "I'm in Love With Someone"original
           "That Old Gang of Mine" parody.
7. Peter Oliver Kilman Dialogues from "The ZooStory."
8. Hank   His Gepetto Marionettes.

Intermission

9. The Rolando Dancers.
10. P. E. Britton   Poetry Reading
11. John Borragon   "Melody in F."
12. Al Hart   "I Don't Care." - Costume.
13. Mike Rusk   "Let's Do It."
           "Hold Me, Thrill Me, Kiss Me."
14. Anabella & Juanico "Afro-Cuban Fire."
15. Lisa Ben   "Promise You Wont Go." original
           "There Again."   "
           "Cruising Down the Boulevard."
           "Frankie and Johnnie." parody.

Finale - Ballet Rolando.

APPENDIX, 2-10a

The Education Division of ONE, INC., Presents Its 1963 Midwinter Institute, Theme: "New Frontiers in the Law." (ONE's Baker Memorial Library & Archives)

The **EDUCATION DIVISION** of **ONE, INC.,**

Presents Its

1963

MIDWINTER

INSTITUTE

Theme: "NEW FRONTIERS IN THE LAW"

ADVANCE REGISTRATION IS REQUIRED

APPENDIX, 2-10b

The Education Division of ONE, INC., Presents Its 1963 Midwinter Institute, Theme: "New Frontiers in the Law." (continued)

The EDUCATION DIVISION of ONE, INC., Presents Its

1963 MIDWINTER INSTITUTE

in conjunction with the

ELEVENTH ANNUAL BUSINESS MEETING of ONE, INC.

MEMBERS DAY

FRIDAY, January 25th, 1963
3 - 5 PM, OPEN HOUSE, for The Friends of ONE, at the offices.
8:00 PM, 11th Annual Business Meeting, ONE, Incorporated. Reports, Elections, Discussion.
10:30 PM, Reception For The Friends of ONE.
Unveiling of Memorial Plaque (BOJI) of Dr. Blanche Baker, by William F. Baker, San Jose.

MIDWINTER INSTITUTE
SATURDAY, January 26, 1963
9:45 AM, Registration. Tickets: Joe Aaron, William E. Glover, Chairman, W. E. "Dane"Mohler, Jr
10:00 AM, "ONE Institute Examines New Frontiers in the Law," Thomas M. Merritt, PhD, Dean (Emeritus) ONE Institute.
10:30 AM, "Why Reforms Are Needed, Part I,"W. Dorr Legg, Director, ONE Institute.
10:50 AM, "Why Reforms are Needed, Part II," Hal Call, President Mattachine Society, San Francisco.
11:15 AM, "Some Social Attitudes Blocking Legal Reform."

12:00 Noon, ANNUAL LUNCHEON - Chairman, Ann Carll Reid, Editor ONE Magazine, 1954-57.
"Man's Law and God's Laws," Father James G. Jones, Director St. Leonard's House, Chicago.
2:00 PM, Chairman, Herbert Selwyn, Jr., "The Right to Be Free From Unreasonable Search," Frank W. Wood,Jr., Hollywood Defense Attorney.
3:00 PM, Intermission
3:15 PM, PANEL: "Public Vs. Private Rights," Attorney from Southern California A.C.L.U. Attorney William Kraker, Beverly Holls, Legal Administrative Asst., "Dane"Mohler, Jr., L.A. Attorney Herbert Selwyn,Jr., L.A. MODERATOR Chuck Thompson, Detroit, Michigan.

5:00 PM, Adjournment.
5:30 PM, Cocktail Hour.
7:00 PM, ANNUAL BANQUET. Toastmaster: James Kepner, Jr., Los Angeles, Editor ONE Institute Quarterly, 1958-60.
"The Double Standard Moral Code as an Instrument of Corruption, Persecution and Abuse of Power," Attorney Morris Lowenthal, San Francisco.

SUNDAY, January 27, 1963
11:30 AM, FELLOWSHIP BREAKFAST
Chairman, William F. Baker, "A Chaplain's Inside View of St. Leonard's House and of Prison," Father James G. Jones,

ONE INSTITUTE OF HOMOPHILE STUDIES

announcement and schedule of classes
1962-63 academic year

HS-134 Drama Workshop. Reading and dramatic presentation of homophile poetry and plays. Coaching in self-expression. Thursday evenings, 8-10, Finley.
HS-130 Writing for Publication. The special problems of writing for the American and European homophile press. Individual consultation and group discussions. Hours to be arranged. Slater.
HS-137 Second semester continuation of HS-130. Slater.
HS-140 Library. Workshop. Classification and use of scientific works and fiction in the homophile field, cataloguing, bibliographical research. Tuesday evenings, 8-10, Slater.
HS-212 Homosexuality in History. Specialists, scientific and philosophical trends, emergence of a worldwide social movement. Monday evenings, 8-10, Legg.
HS-213 Homosexuality in History, Second semester continuation of HS-212. Analysis of programs and ideology of homophile organizations in U. S. and abroad. Monday evenings, 8-10. Legg.

FEES
The fee for each course per semester is $15.00. Visitors are invited to attend single sessions if they wish. The fee for these is $1.00.

2256 Venice Boulevard, Los Angeles 6, California

APPENDIX, 2-11

*1966 Midwinter Sessions. (ONE's Baker Memorial Library &
Archives)*

1966 MIDWINTER SESSIONS

Jan.

28 8 PM Annual Business Meeting, ONE, Inc.

   10 PM Reception in Home of Member

29 9 AM Registration - ONE Auditorium

   10 AM Panel:-"The Homophile Movement."
            Harold Sarle, Moderator

   11 AM "What Can We Do For Those In Trou-
            ble?" Rev. A. Smith, Methodist

   12 PM NOON RECESS, Lunch at Mannings

    2 PM "Ethics for the Homophile," Don Lu-
           cas, Secy., SF Mattachine Society

    3 PM Panel:- "The Total Human Being."
           Ray Bradbury, famed author; Rev. R.
           Ohlson, Presbyt., Herbert Selwyn,
           atty. Robert Earl, Moderator

    5 PM "Mad, Mad, Mad Puppets," by Hank

    6 PM Cocktail Hour, Hollywood (optional)

    7 PM 1966 Annual Banquet. Hollywood Roo-
           sevelt Hotel. Address: "ONE, Inc.,
           Today," Atty. Hillel Chodos, ONE's
           legal counsel. Address: "If Illin-
           ois Changed The Laws, So Can Your
           State," Paul Goldman, eminent Chi-
           cago atty. & TV personality, legal
           counsel for "ONE in Chicago."

30 11 AM Brunch & Open House at "The Twins"
           with their famed collection of an-
           tiques and art work.

    3 PM Panel: "How To Find Your True Self;
           The Search for Identity." Mary-Faith
           Albert, writer, housewife & mother;
           Rev. L. Jondahl, Campus Pastor, Cal
           State College at L.A.; James Kep-
           ner, Jr.,Editor, PURSUIT & SYMPOS-
           IUM. Gregory Carr, Moderator.

    5 PM Private Dinner Parties

    8 PM Special Gala Performance, INSTANT
           THEATER, by Rachel Rosenthal, King
           Moody & Cast. Improvisations & the
           absurd. Entire Horseshoe Theater
           reserved for ONE. Coffee hour af-
           ter the show.

APPENDIX, 2-12a

The Education Division of ONE, Inc., Institute of Homophile Studies, Presents Its 11th Midwinter Institute, Theme: "New Insights into Homosexuality," January 31-February 2, 1969. (ONE's Baker Memorial Library & Archives)

The EDUCATION DIVISION of ONE, INC.,

INSTITUTE OF HOMOPHILE STUDIES

Presents Its

IITH

MIDWINTER

INSTITUTE

Theme: "NEW INSIGHTS INTO HOMOSEXUALITY"

January 31 - February 2, 1969

APPENDIX, 2-12b

The Education Division of ONE, Inc., Institute of Homophile Studies, Presents Its 11th Midwinter Institute, Theme: "New Insights into Homosexuality," January 31-February 2, 1969. (continued)

P R O G R A M

Friday, January 31, 1969

8:00 P.M. SEVENTEENTH ANNUAL BUSINESS MEET-
ING OF ONE, INCORPORATED; Friends
of ONE & Guests
Minutes
Reports - Treasurer
Education Division
*Research Division (given Sat.AM)
Publications Division
Social Service Division
"ONE of Chicago"
"ONE in Detroit"
"ONE in New York"
Baker Memorial Library
Public Relations
House & Hospitality Committee
Board of Directors
Old Business
New Business - Election of New Members
Election of Board of Di-
rectors (Term 1969-72)
Other
Adjournment
Reception for Friends of ONE & Guests

Saturday, February 1, 1969

9:30 A.M. Registration & Tickets
10:00 A.M. Opening of 11th Midwinter Institute by Robert Earl, President, ONE, Inc.
*"ONE's Research Program: A Report"
"Interview with Dean (Emeritus) of ONE
Institute, Thomas M. Merritt, Ph.D." (Taped January 12, 1969)
"Research Design for a Study of Homosexual Males," by ONE Institute Director,
W. Dorr Legg
12:00 NOON Adjournment of Session

12:30 P.M. Buffet Luncheon
"Transvestism, Transsexualism & Homosex-
uality," by UCLA Gender Identity Clinic
Director Richard Green, M.D.

2.

APPENDIX, 2-12c

The Education Division of ONE, Inc., Institute of Homophile Studies, Presents Its 11th Midwinter Institute, Theme: "New Insights into Homosexuality," January 31-February 2, 1969. (continued)

2:00 P.M. "A Study of 388 North American Homosexual Males," by Institute for the Study of Human Resources Research Asst., J. M. Underwood
Intermission
Panel Discussion of paper:
  by psychiatrists Richard Green, M.D., (UCLA), Richard Parlour, M.D. (Claremont) Asst. Prof. of Sociology Barry Dank, Cal State College (Long Beach)
    Moderator: Fred Selden, Secy. "ONE of Chicago"

6:00 P.M. No host cocktail hour
7:00 P.M. Midwinter Banquet
        Entertainment
8:30 P.M. "The Varieties of Homosexual Expression," by Mattachine Society President Harold Call, illustrated by color slides and movie.

Sunday, February 2, 1969

11:30 A.M. Fifth Annual Meeting, Institute for the Study of Human Resources

1:30 P.M. Registration & Tickets
2:00 P.M. "Studies in Personality Characteristics of Several Hundred Homosexual Males," by Asst. Prof. of Psychology (UCLA) Peter Bentler, Ph.D.
Intermission
Panel Discussion of paper:
  by psychiatrist Martha Kirkpatrick, M.D. (UCLA); clinical psychologist Fred Goldstein, Ph.D.; Associate Prof. of Criminology, Cal State College (Long Beach) Howard E. Fradkin, Ph.D.; Associate Professor of Sociology (Santa Monica City College) Kenneth Poole
    Moderator: Attorney Herbert Selwyn

Reception by ONE's House & Hospitality Committee

Adjournment of Midwinter Institute

3.

APPENDIX, 2-13a

1972 Midwinter Institute, Program. (ONE's Baker Memorial Library & Archives)

OPENING SESSION

ONE's AUDITORIUM, 2256 VENICE BOULEVARD, LOS ANGELES
FRIDAY EVENING, JANUARY 28, 1972, AT 8 O'CLOCK

Welcome to the Midwinter Sessions, President of ONE, Inc,
 Robert Earl
Members of the Southern California Council on Religion &
 the Homophile and Others
Moderator: Joe Gilgamesh, Member ONE's Board of Directors

THE GAY CHALLENGE TO RELIGION & THE CHURCHES

Reverend Troy Perry, Pastor Metropolitan Community Church,
 Los Angeles
RESPONDING PANEL:
Father Howard, Roman Catholic Priest
Reverend Marjorie Likins, Youth & Campus Ministry, United
 Church of Christ
Reverend Alex Smith, Formerly Director, Methodist Downtown
 Service Center
Reverend Kenneth Wahrenbrock, Downey Methodist Church

RECEPTION

Hosted by ONE's House & Hospitality Committee, Chairman
 Fred Freedman; Libations Expert, Luis

SECOND SESSION

SATURDAY MORNING AT 10 O'CLOCK

Presented with the Cooperation of the Institute for the
 Study of Human Resources
Moderator: W. Dorr Legg, Director ONE Institute of Homo-
 phile Studies

COUNSELING HOMOSEXUALS: A REPORT & DISCUSSION

"The Seattle Counseling Center for Homosexuals," Robert Dei-
 sher, M.D.
RESPONDING PANEL:
Martha Kirkpatrick, M.D., Psychiatrist, Westwood Village
Michael McLane, M.S., Psychologist, Pasadena
Myra Riddell, M.S.W., Clinical Social Worker, Beverly Hills
Richard Parlour, M.D., Psychiatrist, Montclair

LUNCHEON BREAK AT 12 O'CLOCK

APPENDIX, 2-13b

1972 Midwinter Institute, Program. (continued)

THIRD SESSION

SATURDAY AFTERNOON AT 1 O'CLOCK

Presented with the cooperation of the Erickson Educational
    Foundation

PART 1

Moderator: Robert Earl, Instructor ONE Institute

AN INDICTMENT OF THE AMERICAN EDUCATIONAL SYSTEM

by Jim Kepner, Instructor, ONE Institute

RESPONSES & COMMENTARY:

Howard Fradkin, Ph. D., Associate Professor of Sociology,
    California State College at Long Beach
Senior & graduate psychology students from Long Beach State
Other ONE Institute students
Audio-visual tapes of Institute class sessions

PART 2

IMPLICATIONS OF SOME CURRENT RESEARCH PROJECTS

Peter Bentler, Ph.D., Professor of Psychology, UCLA
Vern Bullough, Ph.D., Professor of History, San Fernando
    Valley State College
Barry Dank, Assistant Professor of Sociology, California
    State College at Long Beach
Kenneth A. Poole, Ph.D., Professor of Sociology, Santa Mon-
    ica City College

THE 1972 MIDWINTER BANQUET

JANUARY 29, HILTON HOTEL, 930 WILSHIRE BLVD. LOS ANGELES

Cocktail Hour (no host) 6:30 PM, The Los Angeles Room

Banquet, 7:30 PM, The Golden State Room
Host: ONE Incorporated, Robert Earl President

MENU

Mixed Green Salad Imperial

Boned Breast of Capon, Sauce Chasseur

Rice O'Brien   *Broccoli Polonaise*

Mile High Ice Cream Pie   Sauce Fraisette

Coffee

APPENDIX, 2-13c

1972 Midwinter Institute, Program. (continued)

```
* * * * * * * * * * * * * * * * * * * *
         Gay Folk Songs  by Lisa Ben
         Dramatic Sketches  & Dance

      Ralph Lucas, Chairman ONE's Drama Group
      & Players from SPREE Drama Workshop

             Songs: Pat Rocco
             Accompanist Bob Mitchell

   Greetings & Introductions, W. Dorr Legg, Emcee

   THE PEOPLE TELL THEIR STORY
         HOW IT ALL BEGAN -- AND WHY
              THE PAINS AND GAINS OF GROWING UP
                  A THIRD DECADE GETS UNDER WAY
                  * * * * * * * * * * * * * * * * * * * * * * * * *
```

AN ANNOUNCEMENT:

    Reed Erickson, President, Erickson Educational Foundation
Baton Rouge, Louisiana

FIFTH SESSION

SUNDAY AFTERNOON, JANUARY 30, 1972

AT THE PURPLE LION - SUNSET AND LA BREA

Host: Eli Pomoh, ONE, Incorporated Voting Member
Brunch: Served from 12:30 to 1:45 PM

Moderator: Herbert Selwyn, ONE's Attorney

SOME RIGHTS & MANY WRONGS

Phyllis Z. Deutsch, Attorney, Beverly Hills
Dave Glascock, President Gay Community Alliance
Steve Schock, Board Member California Committee for Sex Law
    Reform
Frank A. Wood, Attorney, Los Angeles

TWENTIETH ANNUAL BUSINESS MEETING OF ONE, INCORPORATED

                Robert Earl, President
                Bob Marks, Vice President
                John Bresee, Secretary Treasurer

REPORTS

ELECTION OF NEW VOTING MEMBERS

ELECTION OF BOARD OF DIRECTORS TO SERVE UNTIL JANUARY 1975

OLD & NEW BUSINESS

ADJOURNMENT

APPENDIX, 2-14a

Institute for the Study of Human Resources, Forum on Variant Sex Behavior, June 7-9, 1974. (ONE's Baker Memorial Library & Archives)

Institute for the Study of Human Resources

An Operating Foundation, Established in 1964

• •

2256 VENICE BOULEVARD, SUITE 203, LOS ANGELES, CALIFORNIA 90006

Telephone: (213) 735-5257

FORUM ON VARIANT SEX BEHAVIOR

JUNE 7-9, 1974

Research papers, workshop sessions and field trips to give physicians, social workers, psychologists, counselors, clergy, teachers and other professionals a concentrated overview of up-to-date information and recent developments concerning some of the less well-known types of sex behavior. Distinguished experts will contribute original papers, clinical findings and research data on transsexualism, incest, transvestism, sado-masochism, fetishism, male and female homosexuality.

FRIDAY, JUNE 7

2:00 PM	Welcome to the FORUM, Vern L. Bullough, Ph.D., Vice President of the Institute; "A Philosophy for Non-Procreative Sexuality," Lester A. Kirkendall, Ph.D., Professor of Family Life Emeritus, Oregon State University, Corvallis; "The Transsexual Experience," a panel of postoperative female-to-male and male-to-female transsexuals. Chairman Zelda Suplee, New York City, Director Erickson Educational Foundation.
3:30 PM	Intermission
3:45 PM	Workshops on Transsexualism: (1) Psychiatric Considerations, Martha Kirkpatrick, M.D., psychiatrist; (2) Medical Aspects, a physician; (3) Social Adjustments After Surgery, Daniel Lynden, Director International Transsexual Guidance;
5:00 PM	Field Trip Orientation, W. Dorr Legg, M.L.D., Coordinator of Institute Educational Programs. Registrants may enroll in up to three conducted field trips to a wide range of sex variant institutions. Some groups will be restricted to from four to eight persons; registrations will be closed when the quotas are filled.
7:00 PM	Dinner at a gay restaurant, food and drinks not included in registration fee;
8:00 PM	Religious services at Temple Beth Chayim Chadashim; Reception and discussion at the home of a long-term male couple;
9:00 PM	A lesbian bar (women only); a leather bar (men only); a dancing bar; a transvestite show; a bar for older males; the beer bar.

SATURDAY, JUNE 8

9:00 AM	"Incest, Some Recent Data," Howard E. Fradkin, Ph.D., Professor of Sociology, California State University/Long Beach; "Fetishism & Sado-masochism Between Males," Bernie Prock, graduate student in psychology, one-time male prostitute; "Transvestism," Virginia Prince, Ph.D., Editor TRANSVESTIA.
11:00 AM	Intermission
11:15 AM	Panel with the above speakers: Chairman Dr. Lester A. Kirkendall.

APPENDIX, 2-14b

Institute for the Study of Human Resources, Forum on Variant Sex Behavior, June 7-9, 1974. (continued)

SPECIAL ADDED FEATURE

12:30 PM	Luncheon (not included with registration fee).
	Introductions
	"Sex Variants and the Double Standard of Law Enforcement," attorney Albert Gordon.
	A longtime fighter for human rights, Mr. Gordon recently brought suit as a taxpayer in the nine Superior Courts of Los Angeles County against Los Angeles Police Chief Edward Davis and Sheriff Peter Pitchess, in a unique legal strategy aimed at unfair police practices.
2:30 PM	Chairman, Barry M. Dank, Ph.D., Associate Professor of Sociology, California State University/Long Beach;
	"Newsex and Ambisexuality," Laud Humphreys, Ph.D., Professor of Sociology, Pitzer College, Claremont;
	"Sources of Hostility Toward Sex Variants," Vern L. Bullough, Ph.D., Professor of History, California State University/Northridge.
3:45 PM	Intermission
4:00 PM	Panel Discussion: "Male & Female Homosexuality," the above speakers; psychotherapist Bernice Augenbraun, M.S.W.; psychotherapist Myra Riddell, M.S.W.
5:00 PM	Adjournment.
6:30 PM	No Host Cocktail Hour

BANQUET

7:30 PM	"The Institute for the Study of Human Resources: 1964-74"
	Introductions
	Entertainment
	"Saying Some Things About a Friend of Mine," Christopher Isherwood, author; Trustee of the Institute;
	"Reminiscence and Forecast," Evelyn Hooker, Ph.D., Chairman NIMH Task Force on Homosexuality; formerly Professor of Psychology, UCLA.

SUNDAY, JUNE 9

11:00 AM	Morning Services at Metropolitan Community Church, established in 1968, to be open to sex variants not welcomed by other denominations; now with over sixty branches in the U.S. and abroad.
12:00 Noon	Tour of the Church Facilities
1:00 PM	Brunch hosted by ONE Institute of Homophile Studies;
2:30 PM	Open House, Daisy Borden Harriman Research Library;
	Conducted by Library staff;
4:00 PM	Adjournment of the FORUM.

APPENDIX, 2-15a

Institute for the Study of Human Resources, Seminar: "Sex, Role & Gender," March 7-9, 1975. (ONE's Baker Memorial Library & Archives)

Institute for the Study of Human Resources

An Operating Foundation, Established in 1964

2286 VENICE BOULEVARD, SUITE 202, LOS ANGELES, CALIFORNIA 90006
Telephone: (213) 735-5252

SEMINAR: "SEX, ROLE & GENDER"

March 7-9, 1975

This training program of Continuing Education is designed especially for social workers, nurses, physicians, therapists, counselors, clergy and others whose practice includes persons having atypical sexual orientation and interests. The sessions feature original papers, clinical reports, panels of experts, roundtable discussions, workshops on specific problem areas and conducted field trips. This highly specialized training seminar can be taken for one hour of college credit by arrangement with the School of Social & Behavioral Sciences, California State University, Northridge.

PROGRAM CO-ORDINATORS

Vern L. Bullough, Ph.D., Professor of History,
California State College, Northridge.
Howard E. Fradkin, Ph.D., Professor of Sociology,
California State College, Long Beach.
W. Dorr Legg, M.L.D., Director, ONE Institute
of Homophile Studies, Los Angeles.

FRIDAY, MARCH 7

6:30 PM	Registration for those attending the dinner.
7:00 PM	Dinner at a gay restaurant; location will be shown on your tickets.
8:00 PM	Welcoming Address: Professor Bullough, Institute Vice President.
8:45 PM	"Objectives of the Field Study Program," Dorr Legg, Chief, Institute Educational Research Section.
9:00 PM	Unit I Field Trip: gay bar and a gay dance club. Unit II Field Trip: Lesbian bar (women only) and gay dance club.

SATURDAY, MARCH 8

The Severance Room, 2936 West 8th Street, Los Angeles

9:00 AM	Panel: "Sex, Role & Gender." Varying presentations of the theme by therapists, transsexuals and a transvestite.
10:30 AM	Intermission
10:45 AM	Paper: "A Hormone Research Progress Report," a doctoral student.
11:00 AM	Roundtable Discussions of the morning's Panel; three groups will be convened.
12:30 PM	Luncheon Break

APPENDIX, 2-15b

Institute for the Study of Human Resources, Seminar: "Sex, Role & Gender," March 7-9, 1975. (continued)

Saturday, March 8 (Continued)

2:30 PM   Paper: "Toward a Counseling Center Program," Professor Fradkin, Institute Board of Directors.

3:00 PM   Workshops on Guidance, Adjustment & Special Problems:
                 Section I —   Sex Reassignment: Some Social, Psychological & Medical Aspects.
                 Section II —   Sadomasochism Between Males.
                 Section III —   Pedophilia: Taped Interview, followed by discussion.
                 Section IV —   Transvestism will be the entire subject of the Unit I Field Trip at 8:30 PM, hence no afternoon workshop.

5:00 PM   Adjournment for Afternoon

6:30 PM   Dinner at a different gay restaurant; location will be shown on your tickets.

8:30 PM   Unit I Field Trip: Meeting of a transvestite organization; visit to a transvestite nightclub.

9:00 PM   Unit II Field Trip: Gay bar for older men; a different gay dance club.

SUNDAY, MARCH 9

11:00 AM   Morning Service, Metropolitan Community Church, 1050 South Hill Street, Los Angeles.

3:00 PM   "Sex, Role & Gender," closing lecture, speaker to be announced; ONE Institute Auditorium, 2256 Venice Boulevard, Los Angeles.   MISS CHRISTINE JORGENSEN

4:30 PM   Coffee Hour and Open House in Daisy Borden Harriman Research Library, same address.

REGISTRATION BLANK

Registration $25; $35 for 1 hour university credit; $15 for students currently enrolled in a college or university; a few student scholarships available. Registration provides attendance at all sessions; one conducted Field Trip each evening; no meals, drinks or transportation included. Dinner prices in gay restaurants usually range from around $3.50 up.

I wish to attend dinner at my own expense Friday evening _____ ; Saturday evening _____ .

I wish to be assigned to Field Trip Unit _____ Friday evening; Unit _____ Saturday evening; roundtable & workshop assignments will be made during the sessions.

Name _____

Street _____

City _____ State _____ Zip _____

Make checks payable to Institute for the Study of Human Resources, Suite 203, 2256 Venice Boulevard, Los Angeles, California 90006; Tel. (213) 735-4357.

APPENDIX, 2-16a

ONE's 1978 Midwinter Institute, "A Search for Our Roots, Gay Life & Liberation - 1860-1960," January 27-29, 1978. (ONE's Baker Memorial Library & Archives)

ONE'S 1978 MIDWINTER INSTITUTE

A Search for Our Roots
Gay Life & Liberation — 1860-1960

January 27-29, 1978

Friday & Saturday at ONE Center, 2256 Venice Blvd, Los Angeles, near Weste

```
Friday 8 PM:    Welcome by Joe Gilgamesh, President, ONE, Inc.
Jan 27          A PANEL:  FOUR OF OUR PIONEERS: FORERUNNERS OF THE MOVEMENT.
                - KARL HEINRICH ULRICHS, "John the Baptist" of the German
                  Homophile Movement, by MIKE LOMBARDI
                - EDWARD CARPENTER, Prophet of Gay Liberation in England,
                  by BISHOP MIKHAIL ITKIN
                - NATALIE CLIFFORD BARNEY, a One-Woman Gay Movement in
                  France from 1896-1972, by JIM KEPNER
                - HENRY GERBER, Forerunner of America's Homophile Movement
                  from 1925-1972, by JIM KEPNER
        10 PM:  SOCIAL HOUR

Saturday 9 AM:  OPENLY GAY IN AMERICA, 1776-1918  by JIM KEPNER
Jan 28
       10 AM:   recess
       10:15:   A PANEL:  THE WAY WE WERE:  PERSONAL REMINISCENCES OF THE
                FORTIES & FIFTIES
                participants to be announced
                Chairman, Milt Sanford

       12:00    lunch break
                coffee & tea will be available
                box lunches can be had from several nearby places

        2 PM:   HISTORICAL SKETCH:  GAY LIFE IN MEXICO
                DAVID LENNOX, Tulane University

        3:00:   break

        3:15:   A PANEL:  WAY BACK IN THE TWENTIES & THIRTIES, PERSONAL
                REMINISCENCES
                Chairman: George Mortenson
                Writer Harry Otis
                Lieut. Dorothy Putnam
                W. Dorr Legg
                others
```

to counter the widespread view that gay life only came out in the open in the last two or three decades

APPENDIX, 2-16b

ONE's 1978 Midwinter Institute, "A Search for Our Roots, Gay Life & Liberation - 1860-1960," January 27-29, 1978. (continued)

26th annual meeting
of ONE, INC.

SUNDAY
JAN 29   To be held in honor of the newly formed Council -- ONE in Long
             Beach at THE CHANDELIER, 4205 Atlantic Ave., just north of
             Carson, Long Beach

   1 PM: BUFFET BRUNCH

   2 PM: ONE's 26th Annual Meeting
            Reports of the Departments & Divisions
            President's Talk
            New Business
            Election of New Trustees _
            Election of Board of Directors

   4 PM: Adjournment

   4:30:   Film: ONE WORLD TRAVEL CLUB 1977 Tour: Japan, Taiwan, Hognkong
            Bangkok, Singapore, Manila. Produced & narrated by Harold
            Call, President of Mattachine Society, San Francisco.

   5 PM: Cocktail hour
======= ======= ======= ======= ======= ======= ======= =======

All who have heard Harry Otis lecture or read any of his hilarious gay
travel stories will understand that the audience would have liked to hear
more of his tales of gay life in New York during Prohibition days,
of drag balls with thousands dancing and upper-class hanky panky, with
some pretty big names being mentioned. Not any lesss enthralling was
Lieutenant Dorothy Putnam having at four-score just renewed her driver's
chauffer's, ambulance and truck-driver's licenses. She told of wild
escapades while at a private girl's school, of her acquaintanceship
with Amelia Earhart, and many war-time experiences at a time when there
were only the men's tearooms provided. Dorr Legg told of the waterfront
bar (a courtesy designation) in a Southern port city where young homosexuals danced with both the sailors who came there and the resident
girls and everyone was perfectly comfortable about it all; of his good
fortune in "coming out" not by any of the customary routes but into the
middle of a well-established little "community" of all age ranges and
little of the bitchiness and in-fighting he later came to know about.

The 26th Annual Business Meeting, held for the first time out of Los
Angeles in honor of the newly formed "ONE in Long Beach Council" opened
with a delightful brunch and then proceeded with reports from the officers of the Corporation, chairmen of the many Divisions & Departments
which perform ONE's wide range of activities. The texts of these reports will be available for the Trustees and the top two classes of
Members. Excerpts will be published in these pages whenever there is
room. A number of guests were present, including Ken Burns who served

APPENDIX, 2-17a

ONE Annual Meeting [and] Program, [1980] Midwinter Sessions.
(ONE's Baker Memorial Library & Archives)

APPENDIX, 2-17b

ONE Annual Meeting [and] Program, [1980] Midwinter Sessions. (continued)

F R I D A Y   E V E N I N G   J A N U A R Y   2 5
A T   8   P. M.

O N E   C E N T E R   2 2 5 6   V E N I C E   B L V D

Call to Order, President Bob Marks
Reading of Minutes, Secretary Ed Gilbert & Treasurer
Treasurer's Report
Library & Archives, Librarian David Moore
Social Service, Jesse Jacobs
Education, ONE Institute Director Dorr Legg
Research, Chairman Ed Gilbert
Publications, Geraldine Jackson
ONE Enterprises (Benefits), Joe Gilgamesh
Councils (Chapters)
ONE in Long Beach, President Murray Anderson
Others Included in President's Report
Hospitality Committee, Chairman Fred Freedman
President's Report
Discussion of Reports & Questions
Election of Trustees to servie three years
Election of Director to fill one year term
Other New Business
Adjournment of Business Session
Reception - Cocktails - Coffee

Parking on Venice Boulevard is recommended

APPENDIX, 2-17c

ONE Annual Meeting [and] Program, [1980] Midwinter Sessions.
(continued)

SATURDAY, JANUARY 26, 1980

Hyatt House Plaza, 3515 Wilshire Boulevard, LA

9:00 A. M. Registration

10:00   "   Welcome to Midwinter Sessions, President

OUR GOALS AS CITIZENS IN SOCIETY

Moderator: Past President Robert Earl

Presentation and Discussion by
Representatives Civil Rights Groups,
Democratice & Republican Clubs

Questions & Discussion

12:00   "   Noon Break

1:30 P. M. Welcome to Afternoon Sessions

OUR NEEDS & GOALS AS HUMAN BEINGS

Moderator: Myra Riddell, MSW
SouthernCalifornia Women for Understanding

Presentation and Discussion by
Representatives of lesbian groups,
Religious groups, Service Organizations

3:30   "   Coffee Break

4:00   "   OUR OUTREACH TO SOCIETY

Moderator: Fr. Dwain Houser, PhD

Presentation and Discussion by ONE, Inc.
& ONE Institute, Professional &
Teacher Groups; Media (In Touch &
Others)

5:30   Adjournment for Afternoon

APPENDIX, 2-17d

ONE Annual Meeting [and] Program, [1980] Midwinter Sessions. (continued)

SATURDAY JANUARY 26, 1980

Hyatt House Ballroom, 3515 Wilshire Boulevard, LA

7:00 Cocktail Hour - No Host

8:00 BANQUET

           Spinach Salad with Mushrooms

           Filet Mignon

           Duchesse Potatoes

           Vegetable

           Rolls

           Frozen Cocoanut Ball, Chocalate Sauce

           Coffee

WE'RE ON OUR WAY

Master of Ceremonies, Gene Touchet, PhD

Introduction of Officials & Guests
The Moderators Summarize the Day's Sessions
Bob Earl, Myra Riddell, Dwain Houser

Keynote Speaker: Attorney Richard Kaplan,
               Co-Chair of M E C L A

one incorporated

FOUNDED 1952

A non-profit corporation formed to publish a magazine dealing primarily with homosexuality from the scientific, historical and critical point of view . . . books, magazines, pamphlets . . . to sponsor educational programs, lectures and concerts for the aid and benefit of social variants, and to promote among the general public an interest, knowledge and understanding of the problems of variation . . . to sponsor research and promote the integration into society of such persons whose behavior and inclinations vary from current moral and social standards.

APPENDIX. 2-18a

Mattachine Society, Inc. Department of Education, presents a series of lectures and a panel program by the ONE, Institute of Homophile Studies, Education Division of One, Inc., Los Angeles. Mattachine Seminar Series, San Francisco - August 12 to September 2, [1959], inclusive. (ONE's Baker Memorial Library & Archives)

Mattachine Society, Inc.

DEPARTMENT OF EDUCATION
Carl B. Harding, Director

presents

a series of lectures and a panel program

by the

ONE INSTITUTE
OF HOMOPHILE STUDIES

Education Division
of One, Inc. *Los Angeles*

MATTACHINE SEMINAR SERIES
San Francisco — August 12 to September 2, inclusive

APPENDIX. 2-18b

Mattachine Society, Inc. Department of Education, presents a series of lectures and a panel program by the ONE, Institute of Homophile Studies, Education Division of One, Inc., Los Angeles. Mattachine Seminar Series, San Francisco - August 12 to September 2, [1959], inclusive. (continued)

announcement and schedule of classes

By special arrangement with One, Inc., Los Angeles, six lectures and a concluding panel discussion program will be presented by the faculty of ONE INSTITUTE OF HOMOPHILE STUDIES, the Education Division of One, Inc., as the third event in the Mattachine Seminar Series for 1959-1960. These will be held in the Society's offices on 3rd floor, 693 Mission Street on Friday evenings and Saturday afternoons from Aug. 12 through Sept. 2 in accordance with the schedule which follows.

Advance registration is urged immediately. Fees for the course and for individual lectures are listed below. Attendance is open to any person over 21 years of age. Single lectures may be attended upon payment of the fee at the door.

A great deal of research and preparation for each topic has been undertaken by each of the three faculty members in charge. These topics all represent a serious examination of significant material related to the orientation, adjustment and acceptance of the homophile in our adult society; however, many attitudes surrounding current moral standards will be questioned in the light of actual behavior practices past and present.

These lectures will be of particular benefit to persons in fields of sociology, psychology, mental health, correction, law enforcement, religion and law itself, as well as to anyone seeking a more rational understanding of homosexuality as opposed to the purely emotional reaction.

SESSION I: Friday, Aug. 12   James Kepner, Instructor

8-10 P.M.: THE CAUSE OF SEX DEVIATION: A FRANK LOOK AT FREUD

Are homosexuals competent to evaluate psycho-analytic writings? How do Freud's theories affect the lives of homosexuals? What did Freud say about the cause of homosexuality? Did Freud consider homosexuality a perversion or a neurosis? Does this agree with what psychoanalysts say today? How did Freud relate inversion to his general theory? Was Freud's approach scientific? Does his theory hold up?

APPENDIX. 2-18c

Mattachine Society, Inc. Department of Education, presents a series of lectures and a panel program by the ONE, Institute of Homophile Studies, Education Division of One, Inc., Los Angeles. Mattachine Seminar Series, San Francisco - August 12 to September 2, [1959], inclusive. (continued)

SESSION II: Saturday, Aug. 13   James Kepner, Instructor

2-4 P.M.: THE HOMOSEXUAL INFLUENCE IN CONTEMPORARY HISTORY

Is homosexuality of any historical significance? How do homosexuals influence history? How does current history influence homosexuals? Is the current homosexual movement of any historic significance? What individual homosexuals figure largely in world affairs? Is western morality undergoing any change important to homosexuals? Is there a world trend toward toleration?

SESSION III: Friday, Aug. 19   D. Slater, Instructor in Literature

8-10 P.M. THE SATYRICON OF PETRONIUS: Masterpiece of Debauchery

Nero's Rome: Petronius: arbiter of elegance, scientist of pleasure; *Satyricon*: satirical novel; Translations compared; Weakness of flesh, foible of mind; and Are today's hot novels really hot?

SESSION IV: Saturday, Aug. 20   D. Slater, Instructor in Literature

2-4 P.M.: JAMES BARR: AMATEUR PROPAGANDIST—an examination of the opinions and beliefs of Barr from a study of *Quatrefoil:*

Barr's favorite characters and ideas; A Greek ideal; Reaction to the established church: The romantic love affair; the masculine homosexual; and Mr. Barr's lack of experience.

SESSION V: Friday, Aug. 26   W. Dorr Legg, Associate Professor of Sociology

8-10 P.M.: HOMOSEXUALITY, CRIME AND SOCIAL DISORGANIZATION

Homosexuality examined as a system of social breakdown. How has sociology arrived at this concept? Is society breaking down, or is it merely changing? Is the homosexual a minority group; a deviant group? The homosexual criminal. The homosexual and his friends. Is the homosexual most at home in the underworld? Does homosexuality breed criminality?

SESSION VI: Saturday, Aug. 27   W. Dorr Legg, Associate Professor of Sociology

2-4 P.M.: REPRESSION, BISEXUALITY & MARRIAGE: WAYS OF ESCAPE

Is continence good for society? Self-imposed abstinence; in reli-

APPENDIX. 2-18d

Mattachine Society, Inc. Department of Education, presents a series of lectures and a panel program by the ONE, Institute of Homophile Studies, Education Division of One, Inc., Los Angeles. Mattachine Seminar Series, San Francisco - August 12 to September 2, [1959], inclusive. (continued)

gious orders. Is sublimation possible; desirable? The theory of bisexuality as balanced sexuality. Is bisexuality a myth? The use of bisexuality as a smokescreen. The social and economic uses of marriage. Marriage as a hideout. What about the wife (or husband) and the children?

SESSION VII: Friday, Sept. 2   ONE Institute Faculty Members

7-8:30 P.M.: DO HOMOPHILE STUDIES HAVE ANY PRACTICAL VALUE?

Arguments: General education is all anyone needs. Theoretical discussions aren't going to accomplish anything. Why should I study about homosexuality anyhow? What good will it do me? You must have authorities to teach the courses. I am well adjusted and don't need to study.

FEES

Complete series of six lectures and final panel program...... $10.00
Any three events—lectures and/or panel program............ $5.00
Door Admission to any single lecture or panel program....... $2.00

(Advance registration urged immediately so that adequate seating arrangements can be made. Send cash, check or money order with coupon below)

- -

Mattachine Society, Inc.
Department of Education
693 Mission Street
San Francisco 5, California

Please enroll me as indicated for the Mattachine Seminar Series of One Institute lectures as announced in this folder, for which I enclose the appropriate fees. I am over 21 years of age.

   ENTIRE SERIES $10.00
   THREE EVENTS (list dates) $5.00

                                                    (Signed)
Name ——————————————————————————————

Address ————————————————————————————

City————————————— Zone——— State—————————

APPENDIX, 2-19

One Institute Comes Again - to Chicago ... 1971. (ONE's Baker Memorial Library & Archives)

ONE Institute
Comes Again   -   to Chicago

The following series of six one-hour Extension Classes will be given at the Activity Headquarters of *ONE of Chicago*, 2201A North Clybourn Avenue, April 19-21, 1971, by ONE Institute Director, W. Dorr Legg, who will also be lecturing at Northwestern University during his stay in Chicago.

SCHEDULE OF CLASSES

Monday, April 19,   8 PM: IS HOMOSEXUALITY INBORN?

                       9 PM: SOME PSYCHOLOGICAL ARGUMENTS EXAMINED

Tuesday, April 20,   8 PM: RELIGION: FRIEND, OR FOE?

                       9 PM: HOMOSEXUALS WHO MADE HISTORY

Wednesday, April 21, 8 PM: A MINORITY STARTS DEFINING ITSELF

                       9 PM: BRIGHT HOPES FOR THE FUTURE & SOME
                                PITFALLS

A similar series of Extension Classes was first given in Chicago in February, 1963 with very good attendance. It was from these meetings that interest was aroused which resulted in the organizing of *ONE of Chicago*.

Professor Legg now returns to attend and take part in the 7th Annual Banquet of this important branch of *ONE - The National Homophile Organization*. He will speak briefly about the above classes and make some announcements about other matters at the Banquet, to be held April 17, at 7 PM, in the Skyline Room of the Sherman Hotel.

He hopes many of you will be there, and looks forward to greeting old friends at that time. You are urged to attend both the gala Banquet and the classes, for they have been carefully designed to help each individual better understand himself and those with whom he comes in contact.

Your prompt advance reservations will help defray travel costs for this trip, and will be appreciated.

------ ------ ------ ------ ------ ------ ------ ------ ------

I enclose $_____   ($1 for each one-hour class)

Name _____

Address _____

City _____   State _____ Zip_____

APPENDIX, 2-20a

ONE of Chicago, Goals and Objectives, Adopted March 1967. (ONE's Baker Memorial Library & Archives)

ONE of Chicago

Goals and
Objectives

Adopted March 1967

APPENDIX, 2-20b

ONE of Chicago, Goals and Objectives, Adopted March 1967. (continued)

ONE OF CHICAGO is an organization formed as a regional council of the Outreach Program of ONE, Incorporated of California and is devoted to integrating the homophile into a pluralistic society.

> In February 1963, during a series of lectures given in Chicago by a professor from ONE Institute, the possibility of organizing a council of Friends was discussed. In November, 1965, the Friends of ONE living in Chicago, guided by a board member of ONE, Incorporated, formed a regional council, known as ONE of Chicago. ONE, Incorporated is a non-profit California corporation founded for the purpose of spotlighting and understanding one of the least known, most pressing and disturbing problems confronting society--that of individuals whose sexual orientation is at variance with the currently accepted mores. Friends of ONE are "special non-voting members" who are helping ONE attain its objectives through active participation and support. Article IV, Section E, paragraphs 1-5 of the By-Laws of ONE, Inc., provides for the organization of regional councils.

ONE OF CHICAGO strongly advocates improving the public image of the homophile by actively disseminating positive information based on fact rather than exclusively correcting false statements and impressions.

> The general public has long maintained an ill conceived stereotyped image of the homophile. ONE of Chicago knows this to be greatly distorted and has set about to change this situation by demonstrating--not with marches, pickets and sit-ins--but with everyday personal examples of how to be integrated into society as the majority of homophiles desire.

> All too frequently the homophile remains silent and puts up little or no resistance to the violation of his civil rights and personal dignity. ONE believes these rights would be violated far less frequently if accurate knowledge of the homophile were more generally accepted and if greater effort to correct these injustices were exerted.

ONE OF CHICAGO contends that the homophile's response to his sexual orientation is one of the variations of meeting a basic human need and should be accepted.

> ONE maintains that acceptance of the homophile's sexual response should be within the same framework as any other sexual response which by current practices provides for the protection of youth, prohibits the use of force, and limits participation to consenting adults in private. ONE discourages excessive overt actions which tend to attract undue attention, thus causing prejudicial criticism of the group.

APPENDIX, 2-20c

ONE of Chicago, Goals and Objectives, Adopted March 1967. (continued)

ONE OF CHICAGO actively supports causes for the betterment of society in general and the homophile in particular by encouraging adequate and accurate representation of our views in local, state, and national government, and by encouraging cooperation among homophile organizations in order to attain maximum unity of purpose.

Many other organizations have programs which can be considered beneficial toward improving the social conditions of the homophile. ONE of Chicago, to gain mutual strength and unify our determination, extends encouragement to these organizations when their activities relate to the intentions of ONE, Inc.

Responsible citizenship requires awareness of legis-lative programs and participation in taking necessary measures to secure laws which will deprive no one of his human rights. These measures include voting with careful consideration for officials in elections, informing these representatives of your views through appropriate means, furnishing factual information to support these views, and being constantly alert to maintain legislative progress.

ONE OF CHICAGO attempts to keep its members well informed regarding the latest developments and research in the humanities and sciences, relating the homophile to these endeavors by providing a forum for interesting informative programs and provocative discussions.

At regular meetings interesting programs are presented-- usually by speakers who provide the latest information in their field of endeavor as it relates to the homophile.

Because of the nature of the daily situations which confront the homophile and the lack of practical, con-structive understanding in these situations, a forum is provided for open discussion and sharing of experiences. From these discussions general information is evolved which could be applied individually.

ONE OF CHICAGO furnishes a framework for social and philanthropic activities with an intent to emphasize mutual interests of its members.

By organizing the Friends of ONE, a framework is created for social activities which satisfy some of the needs of the homophile and which are compatible with the contempo-rary standards of society.

ONE OF CHICAGO, as a Midwest representative of ONE, Incorporated of California, supports and participates in the various divisional programs of ONE, Incorporated along with national and international aspects of the homophile movement.

The Friends of ONE in the Midwest have put in motion activities which are intended to advance the various divisional programs of ONE.....Education...Publication... Research.....Social Services.

APPENDIX, 2-21

ONE of Chicago presents a Lecture by Mr. Antony Grey of London, England, on Sex, Morality and Happiness. (ONE's Baker Memorial Library & Archives)

ONE of Chicago

presents

A LECTURE BY

Mr. Antony Grey

of London, England

on

Sex, Morality and Happiness

Monday, October 30 – 8:00 P.M.

at

THE CHURCH OF OUR SAVIOUR
530 West Fullerton Parkway
Chicago, Illinois

Mr. Grey is secretary of both the homophile organizations of England and is probably the individual most responsible for implementing the Wolfenden Report.

FOR FURTHER INFORMATION PHONE
FR 2-8616

DONATION $1.00

APPENDIX, 4-1

ONE Institute Graduate School of Homophile Studies... Philosophy 500 Homophile Studies, an Analytic Method, 1981 Fall Schedule. (ONE's Baker Memorial Library & Archives)

ONE *Institute Graduate School of Homophile Studies*

2256 VENICE BOULEVARD LOS ANGELES CALIFORNIA 90006-5199 TELEPHONE (213) 735-5252

PHILOSOPHY   500   HOMOPHILE   STUDIES
AN   ANALYTIC   METHOD
1981   fall   schedule

This is the Basic Core Course required of all the Graduate School students. It provides in outline form an overview of the multidisciplinary approach to the field of sex variance followed in Homophile Studies.

Each of nine disciplines which contain information concerning sex variance is briefly examined: to what extent does its particular viewpoint provide useful insights ? Are its methods of study well adapted to the task or in some respects yielding questionable results ? What answers can each discipline provide ? Which fall outside its scope ?

Biology, anthropology, history, religion, law, psychology, sociology, literature and philosophy are each examined in this way to orient students and prepare them for more detailed later studies in their own areas of special interest.

Two class hours weekly and one in consultation with faculty. Each student will select from the above nine one topic for outside reading and for a paper. The paper will be given presentation in class and discussed. Monday evenings 8 - 10 P. M., Legg. Non-credit students may audit the class sessions as HS-100.

* *

October   5 Opening Session: the subject matter of Homophile Studies.

          12 Biology's answers: Is variance congenital: conditioned ?

          19 Anthropology examines simpler societies for the answer.

          26 Early history tells a very complicated story.

November   2 Modern history is a record of contradictions.

           9 Comparative world religions and their world views.

          16 Christianity in the modern world.

          23 What is law:Does it lead, or follow ?

          30 Law in the age of technology.

December   7 Psychology looks at "the mind."

          14 Psychiatry takes psychology back to biology.

          21 Sociology offers still another perspective.

January   4 Literary insights and visions.

          11 Philosophy struggles with good and bad, right and wrong.

          18 Concluding Session.

Applications, requests, and inquires may be directed to the Assistant Dean for

Student Affairs, ONE Institute Graduate School, 2256 Venice Boulevard,

Los Angeles, CA, 90006-5199

APPENDIX, 4-2a

ONE Institute Graduate School of Homophile Studies, [History 500] Homosexuality in History: Outline. [Spring 1982] (ONE's Baker Memorial Library & Archives)

ONE *Institute* Graduate *School of Homophile Studies*

2256 VENICE BOULEVARD LOS ANGELES. CALIFORNIA 90006-5199   TELEPHONE (213) 735-5252

HOMOSEXUALITY IN HISTORY: OUTLINE

Course: Hist 500 (500)
Term: Spring 1982
Time: Wed. 6:30-9:00 pm.
Place: ONE Inst.
Instructor: Dorr Legg, MLD; Dean

Purpose of course is to train both non-specialist students, as well as history majors, in the methodology of the multi-disciplinary application of a particular field to developing the theory of homophile studies. The attempt is made to discover the origins of social attitudes and institutions which have formed society as it is today, following contemporary research emphasis on the sex behavior of birds and nonprimate mammals as contributing hypotheses to monkey and ape studies (See Hrdy, The Woman that never evolved, 1981); material considered essential to an understanding of prehistory.

S E S S I O N S

February 3   The distinctions between "Homophile Studies" as a self-
              contained field and "Gay Studies," or, "The Psychology
              of Homosexuality" and other approaches anchored within
              the traditional university curriculum.

       10   The predecessors of man: ethology, primate studies. See,
              on the primate diogram, "Almost too late man has real-
              ized that his own behavior and social structure are
              understandable only as a variant of a basic "primate
              diogram" or way of life. (J. Loy, review Social groups
              of monkeys, apes and men. Chance & Jolly, 1970); see
              also, Behavior of vervet monkeys & other cercopithe-
              cines, Struhsaker, Science: June 2, 1967; Knuckle-walk-
              ing and the problem of human origins, Tuttle, Science:
              November 21, 1969; The social life of baboons, Washburn
              & DeVore, Scientific American, June 1961; In praise of
              the achieving female monkey, Lancaster, Psychology To-
              day, September 1973.

       17   From hominids to man. Traces in glacial and inter-
              glacial Pleistocene from archaeological evidence. See,
              fossils and the mosaic nature of human evolution, Mc-
              Henry, Science: October 31, 1975; World Prehistory, Clark,
              1961; Puzzling out man's ascent, Time: November 7, 1977;
              Prehistory, Hawkes, 1965.

       24   Paleolithic humans: climatic influences, hunting sub-
              sistence; nomadic or cavedwelling patterns and the dev-
              elopment of sex roles by functional and environmental
              factors. Sexual attitudes as determined by pre-scientific
              (cause of pregnancy not known) undifferentiated behavior
              (male-female, male-male, female-female), evidence of con-
              temporary sex behavior value systems remaining undocumented
              and primate homosexual behavior being well-documented
              human homosexual behavior cannot be dismissed. See Clark:

APPENDIX, 4-2b

ONE Institute Graduate School of Homophile Studies, [History 500] Homosexuality in History: Outline. [Spring 1982] (continued)

       & hawkes above; also reports on living Paleolithic groups;
Into the stone age, Newsweek; February 17, 1969; Living
stone age, Time, January 5, 1959; The ancient world of a
war-torn tribe, Life, 1963.

March 3 New technologies bring a new age, the Neolithic; moving
from random food-gathering to cultivation; the decline of
nomadism and dependence on hunting; gradual development
of houses, villages, the property concept, food storage,
pottery; new female roles as woman too becomes a provider
in addition to "creating life;" new mythologies and pre-
scientific idealogies started to evolve. Male & female
roles become more differentiated as the theoretical concept
of "woman" grew more detailed: both male & female "mystery"
traditions took form ,eventually becoming established
cults. With the decline of group total dependence on the
males and the numerical decrease of available game unting
began to take the form of aggression and thieving to gain
goods & supplies; male and female roles further divided
into functions considered "suitable" for each. See again,
Clarke & Hawkes, above; also, G. Childe, Man makes himself.

     10 The tempo of social change and technical invention increases
bringing larger populations and the pressure for still more
changes. Tool-making moves from exclusive dependence on
wood, bone and stone to an advanced technology utilizing
copper. The Neolithic as a culture style, rather than a
question of dating, emerges in various parts of the world
at widely divergent times, spreading the Mother Goddess
cults world-wide, gradually becoming the Mesolithic. Man
moves from savagery to barbarism to civilization and history
arrives. See: C. Dawson, Dynamics of world history; C.
Davidson, Story of prehistoric civilization; L. Cottrell,
The anvil of civilization; G. Childe, What happened in
history; H. Frankfort, The birth of civilization in the
near east, 1956.

     17 The lands between the rivers; the rapid evolution of an
almost modern world with literature, law, philosophy,
language & writing, cities and highly formulated religions.
See, C. Ceram, Secret of the Hittites, 1956; G. Coutenau,
Everyday life in Babylonia and Assyria; G. Goodspeed,.Hist-
ory of the Babylonians and and Assyrians, 1927; S. Kramer,
From the tablets of Sumer, 1956; F. Frankfort, Before
philosophy, 1949; M. Moscati, Ancient Semitic Civilization,
1957; E. Chiera, They wrote on clay, 1938; C. Wooley, The
Sumerians; I. Gaster, The oldest stories in the world, 1952.

     24 Continuation of "the fertile crescent" story. Same refs.

     31 The near east continued & concluded.

April 7 No class; Spring vacation.

     14 New themes and emphases from Egypt and the Nile Valley.

     21 India; the Aryas; Hinduism (a focus on sex); Buddhism.

     28 China, the Middle Kingdom comes next on stage.

     5 Japan, a thousand years without changes; samurai homophilia.

     12 Research papers due. Summary: What have we seen thus far ?

APPENDIX, 4-3a

ONE Institute Graduate School of Homophile Studies, Sociology 500 (600) Theoretical Concepts in the Sociology of Homosexuality. (ONE's Baker Memorial Library & Archives)

ONE INSTITUTE
3340 COUNTRY CLUB DRIVE LOS ANGELES, CALIF. 90019 • (213) 735-5252

ONE Institute Graduate School of Homophile Studies

THEORETICAL CONCEPTS IN THE SOCIOLOGY OF HOMOSEXUALITY

Course: Soc 500 (600),
Term: Spring 1982
Time! Tues. 5:30-8:00 pm.
Place: ONE Inc.
       2256 Venice Blvd.
       Los Angeles, CA 90006
Instructors: Laud Humphreys, Ph.D.
              Brian Miller, Ph.D. can.

Course Description:
This seminar is concerned with a critical examination of
the theoretical and empirical literature dealing with the
various approaches to the sociology of homosexuality. The
course is divided into two parts. The first part will
deal with symbolic interactionist concerns relating to
homosexuality. Here will be addressed such issues as
societal reactions to homosexuality, and gay identity
development. The second part of the course will deal with
structural and social-psychological theories of sexual
oppression. In this section will be discussed Marxian and
Freudian views of the restriction of life chances, and the
development of strategies to cope with domination.

Required Texts and Readings:

Kenneth Plummer, SEXUAL STIGMA: AN INTERACTIONIST ACCOUNT.
       London: Routledge & Kegan Paul, 1975.
Barry Adam, THE SURVIVAL OF DOMINATION: INFERIORIZATION
       AND EVERYDAY LIFE. New York: Elsevier, 1978.

Xeroxed handouts will be distributed to the class to supplement certain areas of the texts. It is expected that students
will familiarize themselves with this material.

Course Organization:
The course will be organized around a series of lectures and
class discussions roughly paralleling the organization of the
texts. Students are expected to contribute heavily and critically to class discussions. Grades will be based on the
following: Two in-class, essay-style examinations on readings
and lectures, and a formal, library-research paper.

"A mystic bond of brotherhood makes all men one:..." Carlyle.

APPENDIX, 4-3b

ONE Institute Graduate School of Homophile Studies, Sociology 500 (600) Theoretical Concepts in the Sociology of Homosexuality. (continued)

Evaluation:
Course grades will be distributed in the following way:
1. Seminar participation   10%
2. In-class examinations   40%
3. Research paper   50%

Office Hours:
You are expected to consult with the instructors periodic-
ally during the term, particularly with respect to the
development of your major paper. We will be available
before and after class or by appointment. Our residence
phone number is 213-658-7690. It is connected to an answering service so you may leave a message if we are not in.

Class Schedule (Tentative):

Feb.	2	Intro. To Course & Symbolic Interaction Theory	
	9	Interactionist View of Sexual Variance	Plummer, P. 3-90
	16	Homosexual Development I	Plummer, P. 93-121
	23	Homosexual Development II, Coming out Gay careers	Plummer, P. 122-153 Xerox, Cass
Mar.	2	Collective Gay Reactions	Plummer, P. 154-174
	9	Sociology of the Closet	Plummer, P. 175-196
	16	Coping with Stigma (Goffman)	Xerox, Humphreys
	23	In-class Exam	
	30	Structural Theories & Homosexuality	Adam, Chap. 1
Apr.	5-9	Spring Vacation: No Classes	
	13	Restriction of Life Chances	Adam, Chap. 2
	20	Oppression & Consciousness	Adam, Chap. 3
	27	Managing Domination	Adam, Chap. 4
May	4	In-class Exam	
	11	Summary & Conclusions; Research Papers Due	

APPENDIX, 4-4

Literature 501. (Transcribed from original in ONE's Baker Memorial Library & Archives)

ONE Institute Graduate School
Literature 50I: Literature
Pre-History to Renaissance
Drs. Richard Follett and Gene Touchet

September 8:   Course Overview and Egyptian Literature

September 15: Biblical Literature: *Genesis* 19:1-29 (cf. *Judges* 19); *Leviticus* 18:22 & 20:13 (Holiness Codes); *The Book of Ruth*; David and Jonathan in I & II *Samuel*

September 22: Biblical Literature: *Romans* I:26, I *Corinthians* 6:9-10, I *Timothy* I:9-10 & Boswell, esp. Appx. I

September 29: Greek Literature: Achilles and Patrocles in *The Iliad* – Greek arete

October 6:   Greek Literature: Sappho & Women's Poetry in *Patriarchies*

October 13:   Greek Literature: 5th century Greek Writings, esp. *The Symposium*

October 20:   Greek Literature: *The Greek Anthology*

October 27:   MIDTERM EXAMINATION IN CLASS

November 3:   Roman Literature: Catullus, Martial, and other poets *The Satyricon*

November 10: Augustine and Early Church Patriarchs

November 17: Medieval Literature (especially as translated and available in Boswell)

FINAL PAPER PROSPECTUS DUE FROM EACH STUDENT BY THIS DATE

November 24: Thanksgiving Vacation

December 1:   Medieval Literature: Further readings from Boswell

December 8:   Chaucer: "The Pardoner's Tale"

December 15: FINAL PAPER PRESENTATIONS: 75% on paper, 25% on presentation min. 15 pages M.A. program; 25 pages Ph.D. program. 1. Research based; 2. From course materials; 3. Only Turabian of MLA Handbook styles.

APPENDIX, 4-5a

*ONE Institute Graduate School, Religion 500 - Religion 600,
Religion and Sexual Minorities. (ONE's Baker Memorial Library &
Archives)*

```
                   ONE INSTITUTE GRADUATE SCHOOL
                     Religion 500  -  Religion 600
                   Religion and Sexual Minorities
                        Dr. Dwain E. Houser


                            Syllabus


September 13   Course Overview

September 20   Basic Concepts of Religious Thought/ Principles of Comparative
               Religion.

September 27   The Dawn of Belief.  (Prehistoric Religion and the Premative
               Religions of America, Africa and Australasia.)

October 4      The Ancient World.  (Sexual views of Egyptian, Babylonian, Hittite,
               Assyrian, Greek, Norse, Celtic, and Roman Religion and Myth.)

October 11     Hinduism

October 18     Buddhism

October 25     MIDTERM EXAMINATION

November 1     Islam

November 8     Judaism

November 15    Christianity (Early Christian and Roman Medieval)

November 22    Christianity (Protestantism)

November 29    Modern American Religious Expression.  (Mainline Chirstian, Funda-
               mentalism, Roman Catholic, Eastern Sects, Mormans and other religious
               views that affect the homosexual)

December 6     Metropolitan Community Church and Gay Caucuses in the Churches

December 13    RESEARCH PAPER (Oral presentation of student's research)

December 20    FINAL EXAMINATION


REQUIRED READINGS:  At least five issues of the following periodicals:
Affirmation/Gay Mormons, Affirmation/United Methodists for Lesbian and Gay
Concerns, Apostolos, Bondings, Concord (formerly The Gay Lutheran), Dignity,
FCGC Newsletter, GALA Review, The Gay Christian, Gay Synagogue News, G'vanim,
In Unity, Integrity Forum, More Light, SDA Kinship, United Church Coalition
for Gay Concerns Newsletter, Voice of the Turtle, Evangelicals Concerned Newsletter,
Axios.  In addition all class assigned Biblical and Religious Text sources.
```

APPENDIX, 4-5b

ONE Institute Graduate School, Religion 500 - Religion 600, Religion and Sexual Minorities. (continued)

ONE INSTITUTE GRADUATE SCHOOL
Religion 500 - Religion 600
Religion and Sexual Minorities
Dr. Dwain E. Houser

Barth, Karl. Church Dogmatics. Volume III, Part 4. Edinburgh: T & T Clark, 1961.

Boswell, John. Christianity, Social Tolerance, and Homosexuality: Gay People in Western Europe from the Beginning of the Christian Era to the Fourteenth Century. Chicago: University of Chicago Press, 1980.

    -- , The Epic of Gilgamesh

Horner, Tom. Eros in Greece: A Sexual Inquiry. New York: Privately Printed, 1978.

Kiefer, Otto. Sexual Life in Ancient Rome. Trans. by Gilbert and Helen Highet. London: Routledge and Kegan Paul, 1934.

Kirk, Jerry. The Homosexual Crisis in the Mainline Church: A Presbyterian Minister Speaks Out. Nashville, Tennessee: Nelson, 1978.

Mc Neill, John J. The Church and the Homosexual. Mission, Kansas: Sheed, Andrews and McMeel. 1976.

    -- , Kama Sutra

Al-Nahli, Killab Al Bah

Moore, Paul, Jr. Take a Bishop Like Me. San Francisco: Harper and Row. 1979.

Arbiter, Petronius. The Satyricon

Goodich, Michael. The Unmentionable Vice: Homosexuality in the Late Medieval Period. Santa Barbara, California: Ross-Erikson, 1979.

APPENDIX, 4-6

ONE Institute Graduate School of Homophile Studies, [Psychology 565] Homosexuality and Psychotherapy. (ONE's Baker Memorial Library & Archives)

ONE Institute Graduate School of Homophile Studies

HOMOSEXUALITY AND PSYCHOTHERAPY

Term: Spring 1983
Time: Tues 5:30-8:00 pm.
Place: ONE Inc.
     2256 Venice Blvd.
     Los Angeles, CA 90006.
Instructor: Brian Miller

Course Description:
This seminar is concerned with a critical examination of the
theoretical and clinical literature on the various
approaches to the issue of homosexuality and psychotherapy.
The course is divided into two parts. The first part will
deal with a short history of the relationship between the
dicipline of psychology and homosexuality. Various theories
of psychotherapy will be discussed and how they view homosexuality.

The second part of the course will deal with actual case
histories of homosexuals seeking psychotherapy and appropriate interventions. Various therapeutic techniques will
be discussed and assessed in light of the above theories.

Required Texts and Readings:

Woodman, N.J. & Lenna, H.R. COUNSELING WITH GAY MEN AND WOMEN.
    San Francisco: Jossey-Bass, 1980.

Xeroxed handouts will be distributed to the class to supplement
certain areas of the texts.

Course Organization:
The course will be organized around a series of lectures and
class discussions roughly paralleling the organization of the
text. Students are expected to contribute heavily and critically
to class discussions. Grades will be based on the following:
One in-class, essay-style examination on readings and lectures,
seminar participation, and a formal, library-research paper.

Evaluation:
Course grades will be distributed in the following way:
1. Seminar participation 10%
2. In-class examination 40%
3. Research paper 50%

APPENDIX, 4-7

Course Outline, 1983: History 560: Germany Since the Mid-19th Century: A Study of Political Pathology. (ONE's Baker Memorial Library & Archives)

ONE *Institute Graduate School of Homophile Studies*

2256 VENICE BOULEVARD LOS ANGELES, CALIFORNIA 90006-5199   TELEPHONE (213) 735-5252

HISTORY 560: Germany Since the Mid-19th Century; a Study of
Political Pathology
Dorr Legg, Dean, ONE INSTITUTE; Spring 1983; Monday
5:30 - 8:00 P.M.

S Y L L A B U S

January	24	A People, but Not a Nation
	31	Intellectual Ferments of the 1850s.
February	7	Bismark, Midwifes an Empire.
	14	Stirrings of Homosexual Liberation.
	21	Washington's Birthday; Class Omitted.
	28	Love/Hate Thy Neighbor, a German Paradox.
March	7	Homosexual Intrigues at Court & Conflicts Ahead.
	14	War Shakes the Reich's Foundations.
	21	The Weimar Interlude: Homosexual Liberation & Unrest.
	28	The Hitler Phenomenon is Born. A Genetic Deformity ?
April	4	Mobs, Chaos & Holocaust.
	11	Can a Broken Nation Live Again ?
	18	Homosexuality in Germany Today.
	25	Is the German "Case History" Useful To Us ?
May	2	Final Exam.
	9	Discussion of Class Papers.

R E Q U I R E D   R E A D I N G S

John Lauritsen & David Thorstad, The Early Homosexual Rights Movement.
James D. Steakley, The Homosexual Emancipation Movement in Germany.

R E C C O M E N D E D   R E A D I N G S

ARCADIE (French) Index searches.
Robert Asprey, The Panther's Feast.
Magnus Hirschfeld, Sexual History of the World War.
Christopher Isherwood, The Berlin Diaries.
DER KREIS (German) Index Searches.
Louis P. Lochner,   The Goebbels Diaries.
Peter Neuman, The Black March.
Werner Richter, The Mad Monarch.

APPENDIX, 4-8

Awarding of Degrees Ceremony [January 29, 1984] (ONE's Baker Memorial Library & Archives)

THE   MILBANK   MANSION

You are invited to attend an afternoon CONVOCATION and OPEN HOUSE in beautiful and historic Milbank Mansion on the Campus of ONE Institute of Homophile Studies, 3340 Country Club Drive, Los Angeles, beginning at 2:30 pm, Sunday, January 29, 1984, for the

AWARDING OF DEGREES CEREMONY

Master of Arts in Homophile Studies
Deborah Ann Coates
Paul David Hardman
Michael Anthony Lombardi

This will be a first in educational history for student specialists in this new field of academic studies, offered nowhere else in the world but at Los Angeles' own ONE Institute. Do not miss the opportunity to take part in this historic occasion.

Following the Convocation ceremony, there will be Open House in ONE's Baker Memorial Library in Milbank Mansion. Guests may then proceed to Arlington Hall on the same Campus to visit exhibitions prepared by ONE Institute staff and various committees of ONE Incorporated, including the special Art and Museum collections.

Events of the afternoon will conclude with a showing of movies and slides taken during ONE World Travel Club Tours of Europe and other parts of the world. Refreshments will be served.

Enter the Campus through Arlington Avenue Gateway, just south of Country Club Drive, parking on the tennis court and in the garage area. Exit will be by the Van Ness Gateway ONLY. Arlington Gateway will be open at 2:00 pm.

APPENDIX, 5-1a

History 561: German Homophile Movement..., Syllabus. (ONE's Baker Memorial Library & Archives)

ONE Institute Graduate School of Homophile Studies

HISTORY 561: GERMAN HOMOPHILE MOVEMENT
           Michael A. Lombardi, Ph.D.
           Spring Term 1985
           Wednesdays 6:30 - 9 p.m.

S Y L L A B U S

(1)	Feb	13	1730 to Hoessli
2		20	Early Ulrichs
3		27	Late Ulrichs
4	Mar	6	1869 and the Sexologists
5		13	Hirschfeld and the Turn-of-the-Century
6		20	Second Empire
7		27	Third Empire
8	Apr	3	Midterm
9		10	German Influence on the British
10		17	German Influence on the Americans
11		24	1968/1969 §175 Abolished
12	May	1	Contemporary Research
13		8	Mystery Guest Lecturer
14		15	German Film in Homophile Context
15		22	Final

R E Q U I R E D   R E A D I N G S

One item from reading list; brief oral report

APPENDIX, 5-1b

History 561 German Homophile Movement, Syllabus. (continued)

ONE Institute Graduate School
READING LIST
(proposed)
[GERMAN HOMOPHILE MOVEMENT]
[Lombardi, Spring 1985]

I. EIGHTEENTH CENTURY (1730'S HOLLAND)

Hamilton, Mark. <u>My Brother's Image.</u> New York: Avon Books,
1983.

Lombardi, Michael A. <u>Emanuel Valk: The Trial of A Gay
Preacher in 18th-Century Holland.</u> Los Angeles: Urania
Manuscripts, 1984.

Roemer, L.S.A.M. <u>Uranism in the Netherlands till the
Nineteenth Century with Special Emphasis on the
Numerous Persecutions of Uranians in 1730: A Historic
and Bibliographic Study.</u> Trans. Michael A. Lombardi.
Los Angeles: Urania Manuscripts, 1978.

II. NINETEENTH CENTURY

Benkert, Karoly Maria. <u>Paragraph 143 of the 1851 Prussian
Penal Code and its Preservation as Paragraph 152 in the
1867 Penal Code of the North German Confederation.</u>
Trans. Michael A. Lombardi. Los Angeles: Urania
Manuscripts, 1982.

Kraft-Ebing, Richard von. <u>Psychopathia Sexualis.</u> [1882]

Meier, Karl. <u>Heinrich Hoeszli: On the 100th Year of His
Death.</u> Trans. Michael A. Lombardi. Los Angeles: Urania
Manuscripts, 1982.

Symonds, John Addington. <u>Studies in Sexual Inversion:
Embodying: A Study in Greek Ethics (1883) and A Study
in Modern Ethics (1891).</u> N.p.: Privately printed,
1928.

III. KARL HEINRICH ULRICHS: PRIMARY LITERATURE

Ulrichs, Karl Heinrich. <u>Araxes: A Call To Free The Nature Of
The Urning From Penal Law.</u> Trans. Michael A. Lombardi.
Los Angeles: Urania Manuscripts, 1981.

Ulrichs, Karl Heinrich. <u>A Casket Of Cypress Wood: Lyric
Poetry In Memory Of Ludwig II.</u> Trans. Michael A.
Lombardi. Los Angeles: Urania Manuscripts, 1983.

APPENDIX, 5-1c

History 561 German Homophile Movement, Syllabus. (continued)

Ulrichs, Karl Heinrich. Formatrix: Anthropological Studies
On Uranian Love. Trans. Michael A. Lombardi. Los
Angeles: Urania Manuscripts, 1981.

Ulrichs, Karl Heinrich. Inclusa: Anthropological Studies On
The Sexual Love Between Men. Trans. Michael A.
Lombardi. Los Angeles: Urania Manuscripts, 1979.

Lombardi, Michael A., trans. Karl Heinrich Ulrichs: Letters
To His Kinsfolk. Los Angeles: Urania Manuscripts, 1978.

Lombardi, Michael A., trans. Karl Heinrich Ulrichs: Letters
To His Publishers And Other Correspondence. Los
Angeles: Urania Manuscripts, 1985.

Ulrichs, Karl Heinrich. Manor: A Novella. Trans. Michael A.
Lombardi. Los Angeles: Urania Manuscripts, 1980.

Ulrichs, Karl Heinrich. Memnon I: The Sexual Nature of the
Man-Loving Urning. Trans. Michael A. Lombardi. Los
Angeles: Urania Manuscripts, 1984.

Ulrichs, Karl Heinrich. Raging Sword (Gladius Furens).
Trans. Michael A. Lombardi. Los Angeles: Urania
Manuscripts, 1977.

Ulrichs, Karl Heinrich. Refuge Of Hope (Ara Spei). Trans.
Michael A. Lombardi. Los Angeles: Urania Manuscripts,
1983.

Ulrichs, Karl Heinrich. Rod Of Freedom (Vindicta): Battle
For The Freedom From Prosecution Of The Love Between
Men. Trans. Michael A. Lombardi. Los Angeles: Urania
Manuscripts, 1980.

Ulrichs, Karl Heinrich. Vindex: Social-Juridical Studies On
The Sexual Love Between Men. Trans. Michael A.
Lombardi. Los Angeles: Urania Manuscripts, 1979.

IV.   ULRICHS: SECONDARY LITERATURE

Ambach, Juerg. Karl Heinrich Ulrichs: One Of Our First
Pioneers. Trans. Michael A. Lombardi. Los Angeles:
Urania Manuscripts, 1983.

Kennedy, Hubert. "Karl Heinrich Ulrichs: Pioneer of
Homosexual Emancipation." 2 Parts. Body Politic,
March, 1978, pp. 23-25; April, 1978, pp. 24-26.

APPENDIX, 5-1d

History 561 German Homophile Movement, Syllabus. (continued)

Kennedy, Hubert. "The 'Third Sex' Theory of Karl Heinrich
    Ulrichs." Journal of Homosexuality, 6, Nos. 1/2
    (1980/81), 103-111.

Lombardi, Michael A., trans. Sacred Forest (Nemus Sacrum):
    Uranian Poetry by Karl Heinrich Ulrichs. Los Angeles:
    Urania Manuscripts, 1981.

Lombardi, Michael A. The Translation of the Writings of Karl
    Heinrich Ulrichs. Los Angeles: Urania Manuscripts,
    1984.

Lombardi, Michael A., trans. Two Letters By Karl Heinrich
    Ulrichs To Paul Heyse. Los Angeles: Urania Manuscripts,
    1984.

Nash, Paul J. "Karl Heinrich Ulrichs' Manor: A Fiction." Los
    Angeles: Urania Manuscripts, 1982.

Nash, Paul J. "Karl Heinrich Ulrichs: A Monument In Gay
    Literature." Los Angeles: Urania Manuscripts, 1982.

Persichetti, Nicolo. In Memory Of Karl Heinrich Ulrichs.
    Trans. Michael A. Lombardi. Los Angeles: Urania
    Manuscripts, 1982.

V.   TWENTIETH CENTURY

Carpenter, Edward. The Intermediate Sex: A Study of Some
    Transitional Types of Men and Women. 1906; rpt.
    London: George Allen & Unwin Ltd., 1952.

Hiller, Kurt. On the Question of Terminology. Trans. Michael
    A. Lombardi. Los Angeles: Urania Manuscripts, 1982.

Hirschfeld, Magnus. "Adaptation Treatment of Homosexuality
    (Adjustment Therapy)." Trans. Henry Gerber. ONE
    Institute Quarterly, V, Nos. 2-4 (1962), 41-54.

Hirschfeld, Magnus. "Classification of Homosexuals as to Age
    Preferences and Sex Acts." Trans. Henry Gerber. ONE
    Institute Quarterly, V, No. 1 (Winter 1962), 20-29.

Mann, Klaus. Andreas Receives a Visitor. Trans. Michael A.
    Lombardi. Los Angeles: Urania Manuscripts, 1982. [With
    an essay on George by Paul J. Nash]

APPENDIX, 5-1e

History 561 German Homophile Movement, Syllabus. (continued)

VI.   WEIMAR REPUBLIC (1917-1933)

Steakley, Jim. "Iconography of a Scandal: Political Cartoons
      and the Eulenburg Affair." Visual Communication, 9,
      No. 2 (1983), 20-51.

VII. THIRD EMPIRE (1933-1945)

Heger, Heinz, The Pink Triangle.

Lenz, Reimar. The Wholesale Murder of Homosexuals in the
      Third Reich. Trans. Michael A. Lombardi. Los Angeles:
      Urania Manuscripts, 1979.

Rector, Frank. The Nazi Extermination of Homosexuals. New
      York: Stein and Day, 1981.

Tielman, Rob. The Persecution of Homosexuals in the Second
      World War in the Netherlands. Trans. Michael A.
      Lombardi. Los Angeles: Urania Manuscripts, 1979.

Venema, Adriaan. The Persecution of Homosexuals by the
      Nazis. Trans. Michael A. Lombardi. Los Angeles: Urania
      Manuscripts, 1979.

VIII. LESBIANS

Faderman, Lillian, and B. Eriksson, eds., Lesbian-Feminism
      in Turn-of-the-Century Germany. Bales City, MO: Naiad
      Press, 1980.

Faderman, Lillian. "The Morbidification of Love Between
      Women by 19th-Century Sexologists." Journal of
      Homosexuality, 4, No. 1 (1978), 73-90.

Quataert, Jean H. Reluctant Feminists in German Social
      Democracy (1885-1917). New Jersey: Princeton
      University Press, 1979).

Rueling, Anna. "What Interest Does the Women's Movement Have
      in Solving the Homosexual Problem?" (1906); trans.
      Michael A. Lombardi. Los Angeles: Urania Manuscripts,
      1977.

IX.   REFERENCE WORKS

Bullough, Vern, et al. An Annotated Bibliography of
      Homosexuality. New York: Garland Publishing, Inc.,
      1976. [Vol.I Science; Vol.II Fiction]

APPENDIX, 5-1f

History 561 German Homophile Movement, Syllabus. (continued)

Dannecker, Martin. <u>Theories of Homosexuality.</u> Trans. David Fernbach. London: Gay Men's Press, 1981.

Kepner, Jim. <u>Becoming A People: A 4,000-Year Gay and Lesbian Chronology.</u> Los Angeles: National Gay Archives, 1983.

Lauritsen, John and David Thorstadt. <u>The Early Homosexual Rights Movement (1864-1933).</u> New York: Times Change Press, 1974.

Steakley, Jim. "The Gay Movement in Germany." <u>Body Politic,</u> 9 (1973), 14.

Steakley, Jim. <u>The Homosexual Emancipation Movement in Germany.</u> 1975; rpt. Salem, New Hampshire: The Ayer Company, 1982.

APPENDIX, 6-1a

Sociology Bibliography. (Transcribed from original in ONE's Baker Memorial Library & Archives)

Sociology Bibliography

Texts Consulted, A Partial List.

Gordon W. Allport, *The Nature of Prejudice* (New York: 1958).

Robert Cooley Angell, *Use of Personal Documents* (New York: Social Responsibility Council, 1945). [Nephew of Charles H. Cooley, this editor's college professor.]

Howard S. Becker, *The Other Side* (New York: 1964).

Emory S. Bogardus, *The Development of Social Thought* ((New York: 1955).

Marshall B. Clinard, *Sociology of Deviant Behavior* (New York: 1957).

Charles H. Cooley, *Social Organization* (New York: 1904, 1942).

S. Eldridge, *Fundamentals of Sociology* (New York: 1950).

Evelyn Hooker, "The Homosexual Community," in John H. Gagnon and William Simon (eds.), *Social Deviance* (New York: 1967).

S. Koenig, *Principles of Sociology* (New York: College Outline Series).

A. A. Kroeber, *The Nature of Culture* (New York: 1955).

Ralph Linton, *The Tree of Culture* (New York: 1955).

Robert K. Merton, *Social Theory & Social Structure* (Chicago: 1949).
_____ *Sociology Today* (Chicago: 1959).

W. F. Ogburn and M. F. Nimkoff, *Sociology* (Boston: 1950).

Robert Park, *Introduction to the Science of Sociology* (Chicago: 1931).

Talcott Parsons, *The Social System* (Glencoe: 1951).
_____ and E. A. Shils, *Toward a General Theory of Action* (New York: 1937).

J. Tudor Rees, *They Stand Apart* (London: 1955).

Aymor Roberts, *Forbidden Freedom* (London: 1960).

M. Schofield, *Sociological Aspects of Homosexuality* (London: 1965).

P. Sorokin, *The American Sexual Revolution* (Boston: 1956).
_____ *Society, Culture and Personality* (New York: 1947).

APPENDIX, 6-1b

Sociology Bibliography. (continued)

William Grahamn Sumner, *Folkways* (New York: 1907, 1940).
_____ and J. C. Kellar, *The Science of Society* (New York: 1927).
Donald S. West, *Homosexuality* (London: 1955).
Gordon Westwood (pseud. N. Schofield), *Society and the Homosexual* (New York: 1953).
_____ *A Minority* (London: 1960).
K. L. Wolff, *Sociology of Georg Simmel* (Glencoe: 1950).
Kimball Young, *Sociology* (New York: 1940).
P. V. Young, *Scientific Social Surveys* (New York: 1956).

Other Authors Reviewed:

R. N. Anshen
L. L. Barnard
Broom and Selznick
S. C. Cole
R. M. Frumkin
Gillin
Grinker and Hughes
Hutzler
Clifton R. Jones
G. G. Lenski
Lumley
MacIver
Roucek
H. D. Stein and R. A. Cloward
R. L. Sutherland

APPENDIX, 6-2a

Questionnaire. (ONE's Baker Memorial Library & Archives)

PLEASE FILL OUT THIS QUESTIONNAIRE and return promptly
Your reply will be a help is the drafting of

A HOMOSEXUAL BILL OF RIGHTS

-- the theme for ONE's Seventh Midwinter Institute, January 26-29, 1961 in Los Angeles.
A WIDE RANGE OF VIEWS AND OPINIONS WILL SERVE TO MAKE THIS A TRULY REPRESENTATIVE DOCUMENT. ATTACH EXTRA PAGES IF YOU WISH TO EXPRESS YOUR IDEAS AT GREATER LENGTH.

I. What general rights are now denied by:

a. Current religious attitudes

b. Social attitudes

c. Legal codes

d. Scientific theories

II. Are laws being widely enforced by "extra-legal" methods?

Professional groups.

Are you active in church work.   How long.

Has religion been a problem.

Are you interested in sports.   Politics

Business.   Farming.

Pets.   Literature

Music.   Art.   Theater.

Other.

Do you ever buy physique photos ___ Moderately.

Extensively.

Would you like homosexual pen pals

How often do you have sex ___ Is this adequate

Is sex a problem to you

Do you consider yourself effeminate (males)

Do you consider yourself masculine (females)

How do you regard you ___ What role do you prefer

Have you ever been arrested for homosexual activity _ Convicted

Served time ___ How long ___ Have you ever been blackmailed.

Beaten up ___ How Often ___ Robbed

ONE incorporated

232 south hill street   los angeles 12, california

APPENDIX, 6-2b

Questionnaire. (continued)

Age — Male — Female — Heterosexually married —

How long ——— Children ——— Divorced —

How Long ——— Homosexually married ———

How Long ——— Previous such connections -

Length of each ——— Your Education: Grammar school:

High School ——— College - Degrees

Fields of specialization - -

Present Employment (type) - -

How Long - Previous Employment (type) -

How long -

Do you rent - Own your own home — How long have you

lived there - ——— How long at former address -

To describe the economic status of those replying, what is your monthly

income ——— Present state of your health -

Have you ever had serious illness ——— What -

Have you ever been under a psychiatrist's or psychoanalyst's care —

How long - In a mental institution - How long -

Do you smoke - Has drinking ever been a problem -

In what way — - How long —

Are you active in homophile work -

In Civic or Philanthropic work Which -

III. What limits should be placed upon public behavior of homosexuals?

IV. What specific rights should homosexuals have?

V. What form should the proposed "Bill" have?

VI. How should it be used when completed?

VII. Will you help to prepare it?

VIII. Do you plan to attend the Midwinter Institute in January?

IX. Have you a preference as to the work activity you would like during the sessions?

CONCERNING THE FOLLOWING QUESTIONS...

In documenting the Institute's work it will help to know something about the persons who favor particular approaches to such a "Bill." Answers to the following questions are optional and will be used for tabulations only. No identification will be made between personal data submitted and the attitudes expressed other than for statistical purposes.

APPENDIX, 6-3a

ONE INSTITUTE, 1967-1968, HS-222, Sociology Seminar. (ONE's Baker Memorial Library & Archives)

---

1 9 6 7   O N E   I N S T I T U T E   1 9 6 8

HS-222, Sociology Seminar - - - - - - - - - - - - - - - - - - First Semester Outline
                                    (Underwood)

(Informal Studies of Groups of North American Homophiles Males, Applying Elementary Statistical Principles to Data Obtained From Various Questionnaire Surveys. Knowledge of
Statistical Mathematics NOT Required.)   - - - - - -

GENERAL SOCIOLOGICAL & STATISTICAL REFERENCES:-

Contemporary Sociology, Joseph S. Roucek (Ed.), Philosophical Library, N. Y., 1958
Scientific Social Surveys & Research, Pauline V. Young, Prentice-Hall, N. J., 1958
Introduction to the Theory of Statistics, Yule & Kendall, Hafner, N. Y., 1950

- -
September, 1967, Wednesdays, 8:00 P.M., 13, 20, 27.

  I. The 1960 "Questionnaire Project," - origin & subsequent development.
 II. A Review of pp. 3 & 4, with some sample responses.
III. A Study of the Data Fields:
      1. Psychological (a) General psychological (b) Psychosexual.
      2. Sociological (a) General sociological (b) Sociosexual.
 IV. Possible relations between sexual & psychosexual data, and other types of data.
  V. Structural vs. dynamic approaches to social studies. (Present Institute studies
     are structural.) (Possible uses for the dynamic approach in homophile studies.)
 VI. Subjective vs. behaviorist approaches to psychological studies. (ONE INSTITUTE's
     homophile social studies make use of subjective psychological data as an aid to
     explaining the social structure.)
VII. BACKGROUND SCIENTIFIC CONSIDERATIONS:
      1. Experimental vs. statistical methods.
         a. Physical science & the experimental method; physical nature "loosely coupled;"
            studies proceed via the "closed system," the "controlled experiment," the
            "mathematical statement" (examples, Boyle's Law, Ohm's Law, etc.).
         b. Social science & the statistical method; social environment (social institu-
            tions, customs, traditions) "tightly coupled," involving large numbers of
            interlocked causes, economic, geographic, ethnic, political, psychological,
            etc.; "closed systems" & "controlled experiments" impossible to construct;
            studies must begin with end-facts, with circumstances "as they are," i.e.,
            with "data," assembled from various sources & organized in various ways,
            hoping to infer true social causes from a sufficient study of effects.
         c. Statistics are quantities, interpreted as measures, or proportions. Statis-
            tics must therefore be based on numerical data. Social science studies do
            not stop with general speculations about (for example) "the purposes and
            results of education in modern democratic societies." As with all other sci-
            ences, they must support their studies and conclusions with numbers, in this
            case, numbers indicating "how many students, reaching how many degrees or le-
            vels of education, in how many schools, with how many teachers," etc. Obvi-
            ously, these quantities will not create, and do not stand for, much less
            guarantee actual educational values; but they must be present to supply prac-
            tical social dimensions and measures of these values, and as an aid in under-
            standing them, and in forecasting their probable effects.

- -

APPENDIX, 6-3b

ONE INSTITUTE, 1967-1968, HS-222, Sociology Seminar. (continued)

ONE INSTITUTE, 1967-68; HS-222 Sociology Seminar, First Semester Outline

October, 1967, Wednesdays, 8:00 P.M., 4, 11, 18, 25.

I. Types of Questionnaires, & Techniques of Questioning (Using the "X" Questionnaire, and the 1960 & 1967 Questionnaires as examples.)
   1. The Unstructured Questionnaire a) definition b) purposes
   2. The Structured Questionnaire a) definition b) purposes
      A. The closed (categorical) question
      B. The open (free response) question
   3. Problems of Communication
      a. Language & Syntax
      b. Frame of reference (in which terms used or questions asked are to be understood).
      c. Sequence of questions
   4. Forms of response
      a. Alternate choice
      b. Multiple choice
      c. Check lists; fill-ins
      d. Open end questions
   5. Subjective questions & responses. Usefulness of; hazards of.
   6. Concrete or factual questions. How much or many; what took place; when; where.
   7. Securing quantitative data. Value of estimates, approximations; averages; exact quantities.

II. Three Major Treatments & Uses of Data in Social Studies (and their application to existing homophile data).
   1. Descriptive (or comparative) statistics. Based on simple enumeration, as a census, a birth-count, death-count. These are recorded from quite ancient times. As fluctuations in such counts (from time to time, or from place to place) became subjects of serious scientific speculation and study, there developed a new approach to data, known as:-
   2. Analytical Statistics. This involved the development of much criticism and theory as to methods of:-
      a. Assembling and classifying data
      b. Interpretation of "frequencies" (number of times a certain object or other datum is counted), with respect to the "universe" (total group) being studied.
      c. Determining "parameters" (measures of central tendency; of dispersion), as a means of making data tell something about what is "dominant" or "typical" in a group under study; mean or average; median; moment.
      d. Obtaining samples of a group, as a basis for reaching conclusions about the total group. (Basic question:- "What section of the group which I want to study do I really have?"); "random" sampling; "controlled" sampling.
      e. Reaching conclusions from given data. The "null"hypothesis; the ad hoc hypothesis, ("Figures don't lie, but liars can figure"). Absence of a priori hypothesis as the chief weakness or danger of analytical statistics.
   3. Formal Research Statistics. The remedy for defects in theory and practice of analytical statistics. The a priori hypothesis; the use of "statistical inference" in determining how well a hypothesis explains the data. Recognition that statistical analysis cannot create hypotheses, but only test the value of an a priori or "working" hypothesis. Both scientific attitude and method involves continued willingness to apply and test assumptions. In science, there is only one "fundamental article of faith" - "faith in the universality of cause and effect."

APPENDIX, 6-3c

ONE INSTITUTE, 1967-1968, HS-222, Sociology Seminar. (continued)

ONE INSTITUTE, 1967-68; HS-222, Sociology Seminar, First Semester Outline

November, 1967, Wednesdays, 8:00 P.M., 1, 8, 15, 29.
December, 1967, Wednesdays, 8:00 P.M., 6, 13.

I. Application of Descriptive, Analytical, and Formal Research Methods to Homophile
Psychological and Sociological Data (as illustrated in the work of a recognized
"out-group" practitioner of each).

   1. Kinsey, A.:- The Descriptive Method (Ref: Sexual Behavior in the Human Male)
   2. Bieber, I.:- The Analytical Method (Ref: Homosexuality)
   3. Hooker, E.:- The Formal Research Method (Refs: "Anthropological and Cross-Cul-
           tural Aspects of Homosexuality;" Sexual Inversion, Judd Marmor
           (Ed.), 1965. "The Adjustment of the Male Overt Homosexual;" The
           Problem of Homosexuality in Modern Society, Hendrik M. Ruitenbeck
           (Ed.), 1963. "An Empirical Study of Some Relations Between Sexual
           Patterns and Gender Identity in Male Homosexuals;" Sex Research,
           John Money (Ed.), 1965. "The Homosexual Community;" Sexual
           Deviance, Gagnon & Simon, (Eds.), 1967.)

II. Application of Descriptive, Analytical, and Formal Research Concepts and Methods
to Data Obtained by the "In-Group" Homophile Surveys. (Specifically the Questionnaire
Data available at ONE Institute.)
   1. Kinds of Data Available
      a. Sociological, psychological.
      b. Insufficiency of "quantified" data.
   2. Purposes for which original data was obtained, and further data sought.
      a. Descriptive, as a basis for constructing a realistic "group profile."
      b. Formal Research, as a means of testing various assumptions and hypotheses
         (some presumedly fallacious) related to homosexuality and homosexual beha-
         vior.
   3. Additional psychological and sociological data needed;
      a. From childhood & adolescent periods; familial data.
      b. Self-projective data.
      c. More specifics in educational, cultural and recreational areas.

III. Effectiveness of "In-group" (over "out-group") Surveys of the Homophile Population
Predicated On:-
   1. Use of in-group language
   2. Familiarity with in-group mores
   3. Sympathy with in-group problems and values, with consequent minimization of
      resistance, antagonism, suspicion, etc., over furnishing data.
   4. Wider spectrum of contacts available, both as to kind and quantity.

- -

January, 1968, Wednesdays, 8:00 P.M., 3, 10, 17, 24

   I. Workshop Tabulation & Basic Statistical Derivations (using data from 41 respondents to the "X" Questionnaire).
   II. Semester Review, using oral examination and discussion methods.

- -

APPENDIX, 6-3d

ONE INSTITUTE, 1967-1968, HS-222, Sociology Seminar. (continued)

ONE INSTITUTE, 1967-68; HS-223, Sociology Seminar, Second Semester Outline

February, 1968, Wednesdays, 8:00 P.M., 7, 14, 21, 28

   I. THE 1960 QUESTIONNAIRE - Criteria for Evaluating the Basic Data, and the Elimina-
       tion of Certain Data; Review & Interpretation of the Basic 18-Category Data Distri-
       butions with the Derived Statistics (from the entire sample of 388 respondents).

- -

March, 1968, Wednesdays, 8:00 P.M., 6, 13, 20, 27

   I. Special Distributions Within A Sample Group; Purposes; Methods.

   II. Special Distributions & Their Interpretations from the 1960 Questionnaire:-
       1. Psychiatric Cases
       2. Alcoholism Cases
       3. Religious Attitudes (positive, negative, indifferent)
       4. Sex Role Preferences (M, F, MF)
       5. Gender Identifications
       6. Other Completed or Possible Distributions

   III. Workshop Distribution Project (to be selected)

- -

April, 1968, Wednesdays, 8:00 P.M., 3, 10, 17, 24

   I. Statistical Correlations; Their Purposes; Methods.

   II. Correlations & Interpretations from the 1960 Questionnaire:-
       1. Age, with:
          a. Career length
          b. Sex role preference; sex frequency
          c. Gender identification
       2. Physique Photo & Pen Pal Interests with:
          a. Age
          b. Sex role preference & frequency
          c. Gender identification
       3. Sex Role Preference with Gender Identification; with career and marriage data;
          with other psychological and sociological data, including data on social con-
          flicts.

   III. Workshop Correlation Project (to be selected)

- -

May, 1968, Wednesdays, 8:00 P.M., 1, 8, 15, 22
June, 1968, Wednesdays, 8:00 P.M., 5 & 12 (end of Second Semester)

   I. Workshop Questionnaire Project. The construction of a comprehensive psychological
       and sociological Questionnaire, built upon the existing questionnaires, using all
       data areas included in these. Emphasis on "self-projections," also adolescent &
       pre-adolescent sex and familial experiences. (Ref: The Bieber Questionnaire)

   II. First & Second Semester Review, using oral examination & discussion methods.

APPENDIX, 6-4a

Basic Percentage Tables. (ONE's Baker Memorial Library & Archives)

SOCIOLOGICAL & ATTITUDES SURVEY - 288 North American Male Homosexuals (1961 Questionnaire Data)
(I. S. H. R.)   (Sociological & Other Objective Data)

CATEGORY	# of Respondents	% of Respondents	NOTES AND COMMENTS
AGE Rnge { High	--	--	21 yrs
Median	--	--	71 yrs
Mode	--	--	34.8 yrs
Low	--	--	30.0 yrs
EDUCATION College Grad.+	206	53.2	Median yrs. schooling, 15.12; 90 with Postgraduate Studies, leading to 51 M.A.'s (13.1% of 388), and 30 Doctorates (7.7%). (Cf. U.S. Adult male pop. or 54,134 million, with 10.6 median yrs. school-ing; College Grads. 8%, H.S. Grads. 41%; a projected 2.5% with M.A.'s, 0.5% with Doctorates for a comparable age bracket, based on 1963 data for degrees conferred on males 21+yrs.)
H.S. Grad.	158	40.7	
Below	24	6.1	
Total	388		
CAREER (other than student)			No unskilled farm or other labor represented. Un-der "I.", Fine Arts comprises 42 individuals (11.5%) and Technical, 46 (12.6%). (Cf. U.S. Bureau of Labor figures in the same categories for a compara-ble population:- I. 29.2%; II. 15.6%; III. 55.2%. These approximations also exclude the farming occu-pations, and general unskilled labor.) In ONE's tabulation, "clerical & sales" combined under the single heading "Mercantile."
I. Professional, Tech-nical, Management, Proprietors, Fine Arts...............	208	58.3	
II. Clerical & Sales.....	128	34.2	
III. Crafts, Trades, Oper-atives, Service.....	28	7.5	
Total	364		
INCOME ($800+/month)	48	12.6	"None" includes 10 non-earning students and 26 job-less. Approx. per capita yearly income based on 345 earners:- $6,588/yr. (Cf. U.S. figures on per capita income for adult males from non-Government wages & salaries, $4500 yr. excl. 14-21 age group)
($400 - 800)	185	48.6	
($100 - 400)	112	29.4	
None	36	9.4	
Total	381		
HOME OWNERSHIP (+)	142	36.6	(Cf. 1960 figures for U.S. gen. pop:- 32.797 mil-lion adults of both sexes occupying own home, or 30.8% of total adult population.)
MARRIAGES, Hx: Respondents reporting 0	166	42.8	278 Individual marriages; maximum 7 mar. per per-son, 30 yrs. max. length per mar.; median lgth 5.8 yrs.; 97 - 5+ yrs., 11 - 15+ yrs., 5 - 25+ yrs.
" -1 yr only	33	8.5	
" 1 Yr & +	161	41.5	
Non-responsive	28	7.2	
Total	368		
Het. Respondents Rptg. 0	284	73.3	4 reported 2 mar.; min. lgth. 2 mos.; max. 33 yrs.;

APPENDIX, 6-4b

Basic Percentage Tables. (continued)

SOCIOLOGICAL & ATTITUDES SURVEY (I. S. H. R.)

MARRIAGES, Het., Cont'd.

Respondents rptg. 1 or more, any length......	73	18.7	Median, 10.1 yrs.; 54 - 5+ yrs., 22 - 15+ yrs., 3 - 25+ yrs.. "No sex relations" specified in 3, 1 of whom stated wife was lesbian.
Non-responsive..........	31	8.0	
	388		

COMPARISON TABLE: 276 Hx. & 76 Het. Marriages & their reported status as of Questionnaire return:—

	Homosexual	Heterosexual
Current:.......	113; Median length	...40; Median length, 14.2 yrs.
Terminated:...;	163; " "	...;36*; " 6.5 yrs.
%	(of 276):...... 59%	(of 76):........: 47%

*By divorce, 29 (38%); by separation, 7 (9.2%)

COMPARISON TABLE: 1960-63 data on 200,000 Divorces (Gen. Pop. 22 States) with Homophile Sample:—

	(Het. Div.) General population	(Hx. Sep.) Homophile Sample*(Het. Div.)
Median Mar. Length............	7.1 yrs.	........3.1 yrs..........6.5 yrs.
Approx. proportion to total Mar.....	1 in 4	........3 in 5..........1 in 3

*47 of 76 Het. Mar. were childbearing, 5 children in 2 mar., 4 in 3, 3 in 8, 2 in 12, and 1 in remainder. 22 (46.8%) of the 47 marriages were broken in spite of children. Strong association (I2>20, P<.001)seems indicated between the 40 current Het. mar. and absence of Hx. mar. There were 30 of these, or 75% of the total; whereas of 36 terminated Het. mar., 28 showed prior or subsequent incidence of Hx. mar. Strong association (I2>11, P<.001) also seems indicated between the 40 current Het. mar. and top (Prof.& Administrative) career status, in line with long-observed phenomena of male homophiles entering heterosexual marriage as concession to career ambition. (See special tables on marriage for other relevant data.)

PSYCHIATRIC HISTORIES

3 mos.+ of treatments*......	69	17.8	(See special tables on these psychiatric sates)
Under 3 mos.............	30	7.7	
None..........	289	74.5	
	388		

*Includes 9 with symptoms of alcoholism.

SYMPTOMS OF ALCOHOLISM

	26	6.7	Public Health Service estimates place incidence of actual plus incipient alcoholism in the general adult population as high as 8 - 10%.

SOCIAL CONFLICT AREAS (Arrests, Robbings, Beatings, Blackmailings). Respondents rptg. incidence of one, some or all......

	185	47.8	Of the 185, 85 were involved in multiple types of incidents, so that altogether there were reports of 304 incidents of one type or another, of which 78 (25.8%) were arrests, 130 (42.8%) were robbings, 64 (20.8%) were beatings, & 32 (10.6%) blackmailings. Repetitions of same type of incident not recorded.

APPENDIX, 6-4c

Basic Percentage Tables. (continued)

SOCIOLOGICAL & ATTITUDES SURVEY (I.S.H.R)

(Psychosexual and Other Subjective Data)

Category		N	%	Notes
SEX FREQUENCIES (per wk.)	0-1	66	22.5	14.5% Percentages at immediate left are/from derived *Sexual Behavior in the Human Male*, Table 40. They in-
6xwk. or less but over 2Xmo. tabulated as "medium" range.	1-2	79	27.0	24.4 clude ages 15-20, the range of biggest frequen-
	2-3	46	15.7	20.6 cy according to Kinsey, which is not represen-
	3-4	52	17.7	15.9 ted in ONE's sample. They also include all
	4-5	12	4.1	8.9 forms of sexual outlet. Kinsey's median fre-
	5-6	5	1.7	5.3 quency for ages 21-70 (from Table 44), 1.35;
	6-7	5	1.7	3.2 mean, 1.95. (Cf. Ibid., Chap. 21, and Kinsey's
	7+	28	9.6	7.2 conclusions from his survey that frequencies
Non-resp. or indeter-minate - 95. Median, 2.04; Mean, 2.64; Mean Deviation, 1.62; Standard deviation, 2.075.		295		mean, 1.95. of homosexual outlet run considerably below those for all forms of sex outlet (esp. heterosexual). It is assumed that few, if any, of ONE's sample would rate below 4 in the Kinsey scale.
SEX ROLE PREFERENCE	Male	148	45.2	(Cf. also special table on psychiatric cases in ONE's sample.)
"	Female	56	17.1	Cf. the Bieber Study (106 psych. cases):—
"	M-F	124	37.7	Insertors 35.9%
		328		Insertees 31.1
GENDER IDENTIFICATION	Masc.	293	75.5	Either 23.6
"	Fem.	32	8.2	N-Resp. 9.4
"	M-F	63	16.3	
		388		Note differences with corresponding sex role pre-
HEALTH	Excellent	131	33.8	ferences above.
"	Good	229	59.0	
"	Fair	25	6.4	
"	Poor	3	0.8	
		388		
PHYSIQUE PHOTO INTEREST	+	267	69.0	
		288		
PEN PAL INTEREST	Positive	219	56.4	
"	Indiff.	52	13.4	
"	Negative	117	30.2	
		388		
RELIGIOUS ATT.	Positive	150	38.9	
"	Indiff.	219	56.8	
"	Negative	16	4.3	
		385		

APPENDIX, 6-4d

Basic Percentage Tables. (continued)

SOCIOLOGICAL & ATTITUDES SURVEY (I.S.H.R.)

CIVIC & SOCIAL INT. +	154	40.3
HOBBY & RECREATIONAL		
" " Extensive	68	17.5
" " Average	266	68.7
" " Negligible, None	54	13.8
SPORTS INTEREST +	172	44.3

APPENDIX, 6-4e

Basic Percentage Tables. (continued)

SPECIAL TABLE NO. I

(Psychiatric Cases)
Median Age - 31.5

69 Respondents having history of 3 mos. or more psychiatric treatment (median length of treatment - 1 yr. 3 mos.)

KEY TO READING COLS. 1, 2, & 3 IN THIS & SUBSEQUENT TABLES:-

Col. 1 - #/# is the proportion between number of respondents in category listed at left (within the special subject group), and total number of respondents (within the special subject group);

Col. 2 - #/# is the corresponding proportion for respondents in the remainder of the sample (i.e., excluding the subject group).

Col. 3 - Col. 1-Col. 2, after reducing each to %, and retaining algebraic sign. (The complete 2X2 contingency table may be reconstructed from Cols. 1 & 2 by calculation of the remaining 1st & 2nd order frequencies. The sum of the denominators from each column = N. EXAMPLE, Item (11), Symptoms of Alcoholism:- 9/69; 17/319; + 7.7 (13.0-5.3)Remaining cell frequencies are 60 & 302, N=388.)

NOTES:-
(a) C (contingency coefficient) has been calculated only for values of P ≤ .30;
(b) The derivation (and thus the sign) of Col. 3 quantities depends on assignment of the 1 degree of freedom to the numerator of Col. 1. A negative sign may be read as positive (or a + as -) for the NON-subject group by transposing the columns of the contingency table, assigning the 1 degree of freedom to the numerator of Col. 2. The attributes presently studied frequently make this transposition advisable, as a means of expressing suggested contingencies more intelligibly.

		1	2	3	χ^2	P Between	C =
	EDUCATION						
1.	Post-Grad.	14/68	76/318	- 3.3	.343		$\sqrt{\frac{\chi^2}{N+\chi^2}}$
2.	Coll-Grad.	23/68	93/318	+ 4.6	.558	.50-.30	
3.	13-16	16/68	84/318	- 2.9			
4.	thru 12	9/68	49/318	- 2.2			
5.	below 12	6/68	16/318	+ 3.8			
	CAREER						
6.	Top*	20/65	110/309	- 4.8	.552	.50-.30	
7.	Fine Arts	9/65	33/309	+ 3.2			
8.	Mercantile	24/65	104/309	+ 3.2			
9.	Technical	7/65	39/309	- 1.9			
10.	Trades & Skilled Labor	5/65	23/309	+ 0.3			
11.	SYMPT. ALCOHOLISM	9/69	17/319	+ 7.7	5.570	.02-.01	.1190
	INCOME						
12.	High	7/53#	41/292	- 0.8	.026		
13. (4/00 - 800)	Medium	27/53	158/292	- 3.2	.180		
14.	Low	19/53	93/292	+ 4.0	.327		

*Incl. all professional, administrative, executive careers.
#Excludes 16 Jobless reporting no income. The association table for joblessness in this group is based on 16/69; 10/312; +19.9%. χ^2 > 20, P < .001.

APPENDIX, 6-4f

Basic Percentage Tables. (continued)

	1	2	3	x^2	P Between	C
(Special Table - Psychiatric Cases, cont'd)						
15. HOME OWNERSHIP +	14/67	128/313	-20.0	9.434	.01-.001	.1555
MARRIAGES, Hr.						
16. None	31/63	136/300	+ 3.9			
17. -Yr.	10/63	23/300	+ 8.3			
	41/63	159/300	+12.1	3.069	.10-.05	.0916
18. Yr.+	22/63	141/300	-12.1	"	"	"
Hat.						
19. Any Length +	10/64	63/293	- 5.9	1.117	.30-.20	.0558
SOCIAL CONFLICT INCIDENCE*						
20. One, some, all +	39/69	146/319	+10.7	2.630	.20-.10	.0820
SEX FREQUENCY						
21. High	12/64	19/283	+12.0			
22. Low	22/64	68/283	+10.4			
	34/64	87/283	+22.4	11.510	P <.001	.1791
23. Medium	30/64	196/283	-22.4	"	"	"
SEX ROLE PREF.						
24. Male	31/61	117/267	+ 7.0	.982	.50-.30	
25. Female	10/61	46/267	- 0.8			
26. M-F	20/61	104/267	- 6.2			
GENDER IDENT.						
27. Masc.	49/69	244/319	- 5.5	.920	.50-.30	
28. Fem.	7/69	25/319	+ 2.3			
29. M-F	13/69	50/319	+ 3.2			
HEALTH						
30. Xlnt-Good	59/69	301/319	- 8.9	6.636	P = .01	.1296
31. Fair-Poor	10/69	18/319	+ 8.9	"	"	
(Xlnt Alone)	(13/69)	(118/319)	(-18.2)			
32. PHYS. PHOTO INT.+	50/69	217/319	+ 4.5	.520	.50-.30	.0366
33. PEN PAL INT. +	45/69	174/319	+10.7	2.627	.20-.10	.0820
34. RELIG. ATTIT. Pro	24/69	126/316	- 5.2	.617	.50-.30	.0400
35. CIVIC & SOCIAL INTERESTS +	29/69	125/315	+ 2.3	.129		
HOBBY & REC. INT.						
36. Extensive	18/69	50/319	+10.4			
37. Average	39/69	227/319	-14.7	5.640	.02-.01	.1197
38. Neglig.	12/69	42/319	+ 4.3			
39. SPORTS INT. +	30/69	142/319	- 1.0	.024		

*Of the four types of social conflict, taken singly or in combination, the
Robbing/beating combination appears among the greatest number of respondents
in this group. The tabular quantities are:- 11/69; 16/319; +11.0; X^2=10.467,
.01>P>.001; C=.1621; (11 is number of respondents involved). As to kind,
beatings (19 occurrences reported), show the highest rate of incidence, the
tabular quantities being:- 19/67; 45/237; +9.4; X^2=2.7590; .10>P>.05;
C=.0948

APPENDIX, 6-4g

Basic Percentage Tables. (continued)

SPECIAL TABLES CONTINUED. (In the following tables, only those categories are listed where the data yields levels of significance at or within .30).

SPECIAL TABLE #2
(Male Sex Role Pref.)

148 Respondents, Median Age - 36.1 yrs.

	1	2	3	X2	P Between	C
EDUCATION						
1. 13+ but 16-	48/146	38/180	+11.8	5.744	.02-.01	.1315
CAREERS						
2. Top	55/146	52/168	+ 6.7	1.568	.30-.20	.0705
3. Technical	14/146	26/168	- 5.9	2.435	.20-.10	.0271
INCOME						
4. (400-800) Medium	79/137	78/153	+ 6.7	1.300	.30-.20	.0670
5. MARRIAGES, Het. -	114/137	126/166	+ 7.3	2.433	.20-.10	.0892
SEX FREQUENCY						
6. High	9/138	19/163	- 5.2	2.335	.20-.10	.0877
7. Low	33/138	52/163	- 8.0	2.353	.20-.10	.0880
	42/138	71/163	-13.2	5.488	.02-.01	.1338
GENDER IDENT.						
8. Masc.	130/148	123/180	+19.5	17.511	P<.001	.2251
9. Fem.	4/148	22/180	- 9.5	10.084	.01-.001	.1727
10. M-F.	14/148	35/180	-10.0			
11. PHYSIQUE PHOTO +	95/148	128/180	- 6.9	1.787	.20-.10	.0736
PEN PALS Int.						
12. +	79/148	111/180	- 8.3	2.274	.20-.10	
13. -	52/148	46/180	+ 9.6	3.556	.10-.05	.1035
14. CIVIC & SOCIAL +	67/148	67/179	+ 7.9	2.058	.20-.10	.0791
15. HOBBIES & REC.Ext	29/148	26/180	+ 5.2	1.543	.30-.20	.0684
16. SPORTS INT. +	69/148	71/180	+ 7.2	1.709	.20-.10	.0720

SPECIAL TABLE #3
(M-F Sex Role Pref.)

124 Respondents, Median Age - 34.13 yrs.

	1	2	3	X2	P Between	C
1. EDUCATION - Coll. Grad & Post Grad	74/124	93/202	+13.7	5.719	.02-.01	.1313
2. ALCOHOLIC SYMPT.+	3/124	19/204	- 6.9	5.858	.02-.01	.1324
GENDER IDENT.						
3. Fem.	5/124	21/204	- 6.3	4.144	.05-.02	.1117
4. M-F.	24/124	25/204	+ 7.2	3.060	.10-.05	.0961
5. HEALTH Xlnt&Good	118/124	184/204	+ 5.0	2.605	.20-.10	.0887

MALE SRP's showed borderline (.50> P >.30) contingencies, positive, for psychiatric disturbances(+4.2%), social conflict involvement (+4.9%), homosexual marriage (+4.9%) & home ownership (+3.7%). MF's showed similar contingencies, negative for psychiatric disturbances (-4.0%), positive for het. marriage (+4.0%)

APPENDIX, 6-4h

Basic Percentage Tables. (continued)

(SPECIAL TABLES, CONT'D)

SPECIAL TABLE #4
(Female Sex Role Pref.)

56 Respondents - Median Age, 33.3

	1	2	3	x^2	P Between	C
EDUCATION						
1. College Grad. & Post Grad.	22/56	145/270	-14.4	3.860	.05-.02	.1080
2. H.S. Grad.	13/56	38/270	+ 9.1	2.935	.10-.05	.0945
CAREER						
3. Top	12/51	95/263	-126	3.015	.10-.05	.0975
4. Technical	9/51	31/263	+ 5.9	1.319	.30-.20	.0645
INCOME						
5. (800+) High	9/44	27/246	+ 9.4	3.084	.10-.05	.1025
6. (400-800) Med.	18/44	139/246	-15.6	3.655	.10-.05	.1115
7. SYMPT. ALCOHOL.+	7/56	15/272	+ 7.0	3.622	.10-.05	.1045
SEX FREQUENCY						
8. High	8/52	20/249	+ 7.4	2.757	.10-.05	.0953
9. Low	21/52	64/249	+14.7	4.576	.05-.02	.1224
	29/52	84/249	+22.1	8.904	.01-.001	.1695
GENDER IDENT.						
10. Masc.	28/56	225/272	-32.7	28.185	P<.001	.2813
11. Fem.	17/56	9/272	+27.1	46.550	P<.001	.3525
12. M-F.	11/56	38/272	+ 5.6	1.176	.30-.20	.0598
13. HEALTH Fair/Poor	7/56	19/272	+ 5.5	1.935	.20-.10	.0766
14. PHYSIQUE PHOTO +	44/56	179/272	+12.8	73.652	P<.001	.4282
PEN PALS INT.						
15. +	37/56	153/272	+ 9.8	1.838	.20-.10	.0747
16. -	11/56	87/272	-12.3	3.376	.10-.05	.1009
17. CIVIC & SOCIAL +	16/56	118/271	-14.9	4.301	.05-.02	.1139
18. HOBBIES. REC.Negl.	11/56	34/272	+ 7.2	2.001	.20-.10	.0778
19. SPORTS INT. +	17/56	123/272	-14.8	4.192	.05-.02	.1123

FEMALE SRP's indicate borderline (.50>P>.30) contingencies, positive, for mercantile (clerical & sales) careers (+6.5%), and for heterosexual marriage (+6.2%).

Comparing the three SRP's, the M's and F's (as might be anticipated?) are at contrary extremes in a number of categories, even where contingency indices are not strong; while the MF's stand out as an average, or balance, with indicators for association failing to reach appreciable levels of signifiance in most categories.

APPENDIX, 6-4i

Basic Percentage Tables. (continued)

(SPECIAL TABLES CONT'D)

SPECIAL TABLE #5

203 Respondents reporting (a) Hx. marriages only, (b) Hx. and Het. marriages, and (c) Het. marriages only, Tabulated for the following selected categories:- Gender ID, Sex Role Pref., Sex. Frequency, 3 mos.+ psychiatric care, physique photo interest, owner of residence, and presence of top career status.

Hx. Marriages only (yr.+), 130 respondents

	1	2	3	x^2	P Between	C
1. SEX ROLE PREF. Male	57/113	23/64	+14.5	3.470	.10-.05	.1387
2. SEX FREQUENCY Medium	92/114	44/68	+16.0	5.780	.02-.01	.1754
3. PHYSIQUE PHOTO +	77/130	55/72	-17.2	6.625	.01	.1782
4. OWNS RESIDENCE +	54/128	46/72	-21.7	8.678	.01-.001	.2039
5. TOP CAREER +	43/130	33/72	-12.7	3.211	.10-.05	.1251

Hx. and Het. Marriages, 31 Respondents

1. GENDER IDENT. M-F	2/31	26/171	- 8.8	1.680	.20-.10	.0908
2. SEX FREQ. High	7/29	15/153	+14.3	4.716	.05-.02	.1590
3. OWNS RESIDENCE +	19/31	81/169	+13.4	1.870	.20-.10	.0964

Het. Marriages only, 42 respondents

1. GENDER IDENT. M-F	8/42	20/160	+ 6.5	1.194	.30-.20	.0766
2. SEX ROLE PREF. Male	12/37	68/140	-16.2	3.077	.10-.05	.1306
3. M-F	18/37	50/140	+13.0	2.069	.20-.10	.1059
4. SEX FREQUENCY Low	11/39	13/143	+19.1	9.883	.01-.001	.2260
5. Med.	24/39	112/143	-16.8	4.570	.05-.02	.1565
6. PHYSIQUE PHOTO +	34/42	98/160	+19.7	5.701	.02-.01	.1655
7. OWNS RESIDENCE +	27/41	73/159	+20.0	5.184	.05-.02	.1589
8. TOP CAREER +	22/42	54/161	+18.9	5.048	.05-.02	.1565

APPENDIX, 8-1a

A Study of the Civil Rights Status of Homosexuals under the Existing Laws of the Several States. (ONE's Baker Memorial Library & Archives)

A S T U D Y O F T H E

C I V I L R I G H T S S T A T U S

O F H O M O S E X U A L S u n d e r t h e

E X I S T I N G L A W S O F T H E

S E V E R A L S T A T E S

ONE, Incorporated
Room 328
232 South Hill Street
Los Angeles 12, California

April, 1957

APPENDIX, 8-1b

A Study of the Civil Rights Status of Homosexuals under the Existing Laws of the Several States. (continued)

A Study of the Civil Rights Status of Homosexuals Under the Existing Laws of the Several States.

INTRODUCTION

Authorities estimate that there are more than ten million homosexual men and women in the United States, and at least thirty million more whose occasional homosexual acts would make them liable under current laws.

In considerable numbers, these American citizens find themselves being prosecuted under the provisions of a complicated, sometimes contradictory, and extremely varied body of statutes - the "sex laws."

So far as is known, no comprehensive study has ever been made of the civil rights of this large segment of the population, or of their personal and social character, or of their cultural relationship to American society generally.

It is proposed that a three-fold inquiry be made:

(1) Of such violations of civil rights of these citizens as may occur in the administration of present sex laws;

(2) Of conflicts and inconsistencies to be found among various statutes;

(3) Of the larger question of the constitutional status of the sex laws themselves.

SECTION I - Need for Definitions

The law nowhere defines "a homosexual" or a "homosexual act." State laws merely define, often in an ambiguous way, certain sex acts considered criminal, usually without reference to the sex of either party to the act.

Such sex acts are variously termed "sex perversion," "sodomy," "the crime against nature," "gross indecency," "bestiality," or "unnatural" or "abominable" sex acts, and under prevailing definitions may be committed between members of the same or opposite sex.

The term "sex psychopath" may involve any kind of sex orientation; and is variously defined in various states. It is also variously interpreted by psychologists making the application. The entire definition of "irresponsibility" in relation to psychosis seems at present to be extremely confused.

SECTION II - Statistics & Problems of Interpretation

Estimates of the numbers of homosexual men and women in the United States are currently based upon public surveys of the sort conducted by the late Dr. Kinsey, as well as upon public records connected with law enforcement, hospitals and other institutions. (Kinsey-type surveys have been criticized on methods of sampling, on methods of interrogation, and on methods of projecting data. Statistics based upon public records have also been criticized, but on grounds that they are confined to a non-representative class of homosexual - namely, the severely maladjusted and disturbed type.)

Statistics permitting a comprehensive evaluation of the American homosexual, including a representative proportion of well-adjusted homosexuals, have so far never been gathered. Statistics based merely on the incidence of homosexual ACTS do not adequately define or describe the CLASS as a whole. Critiques of a more SUBJECTIVE nature, and involving other areas of social behavior, must be brought to bear.

APPENDIX, 8-1c

A Study of the Civil Rights Status of Homosexuals under the Existing Laws of the Several States. (continued)

SECTION III - Concepts about the Homosexual Explicit or Implicit in
          The Laws.
    Concepts of: aberration, criminality, immorality, abnormality,
neurosis, disease, perversion, psychosis, unnatural tendencies, degeneracy, etc., examined from parallel texts by various authorities (anthropologists, biologists, psychoanalysts, psychiatrists, legislators,
judges, the clergy).
    Study of the application (as provided in certain statutes) of
these theoretical concepts, for purposes of: "Adjustment" (of the homophile to his or her own condition), or "cure" (reorientation into
heterosexual patterns).

SECTION IV - Can the Concepts (listed in Section III) be Factually
          Validated? Have They Been So Validated?
    Statistical Analysis:
    A. What are the actual facts concerning homosexuals as to:- age
levels, education, race, religion, vocational records, financial status, heterosexual marriages (children?), health, politics, homosexual
mateships ("marriages"),hobbies, other personal interests?
    B. What are the public records concerning this class as to:- ar-
rests (on homosexual charges – on other charges); nature of prison experience, if any; nature of mental hospital records, if any; military
history, if any? How do such statistics relate to the total number of
homosexuals? How do they contrast with similar figures for the general population?

SECTION V - Laws Applicable to Homosexual Acts & Persons
    A. Texts of the laws of the 48 States, District of Columbia, &
Territories; years of their adoption.
    B. Civil Service Regulations (local, state, federal); military
regulations and procedures; FBI procedures (security regulations);
status of teachers.
    C. Special applications of:- disorderly conduct laws; vagrancy
and assault laws; disturbing the peace; registration of sex offenders.

SECTION VI - Application of these Laws to the Homosexual
    A. Arrests of homosexuals under these laws, by states.
    B. Convictions for homosexual offenses (misdemeanor, felony) by
States.
    C. Sentences: fines (amounts); prison terms (lengths); repeaters.
    D. Inconsistent application of laws to male, as against female
offenders.
    E. Hospital commitments of homosexuals by states; authority for
commitment; terms; treatment; releases; recidivists.
    F. Survey, by states, of court rulings, decisions, and degree of
enforcement of the sex laws.

SECTION VII. - Legal Precedents & Their Antecedents
    A. What precedents for current American sex laws are to be found
in:- American legal history; English law; Christian Church law; pre-
Christian religious law; sex laws of other countries?
    B. What are the extra-legal antecedents of sex laws affecting the
homosexual, under relevant aspects of Anthropology, Biology, Litera-

APPENDIX, 8-1d

A Study of the Civil Rights Status of Homosexuals under the Existing Laws of the Several States. (continued)

ture, Religion, Politics, Psychology, Sociology, etc. - thought in
these fields presumed as supporting or in some way affecting modern
legislation?
    C. What social mores (extra-legal) create difficulties for the
homosexual? Prejudices; masculine-feminine distinctions; minority
status (if any). What extra-legal factors militate against equitable
administration of, or revision of, the sex laws?

SECTION VIII - Preliminary Analysis of Sex Laws & Civil Rights
    A. Analysis of sex laws in relation to State Constitutions; the
Constitution of the United States.
    B. Civil status of sex offenders (misdemeanants, felons) as to:-
voting rights; ownership of real and other property; business licenses;
employment; residence requirements.
    C. What are the presumed purposes of the laws? Are these purpo-
ses being achieved? Does the law restrain homosexual acts; protect
society; improve the homosexual; create a criminal class?
    D. General estimates of the workability, fairness, and enforce-
ment potential of the present laws.

SECTION IX - The Concept of Civil Rights
    A. History of the concept; natural law; common law; bodily rights
of the person; "higher" law (the politico-philosophical concepts of
human rights).
    B. American theories of freedom:- rebellion, non-conformity,
rights of minority groups, the right to be "wrong."
    C. Constitutional basis for our laws; underlying moral presump-
tions; common law limitations on the Rights of States; the Declaration
of Independence - its legal status, if any; the Bill of Rights; the
"forgotten" Ninth Amendment; Supreme Court rulings on the rights of
unpopular minorities.

SECTION X - Civil Liberty Infringements
    Statistical examinations of civil liberty infringements in enfor-
cing sex laws; due process; enforced testimony (psychological tests);
entrapment; registration; rules of evidence; the testimony of accom-
plices.

SECTION XI - Present Extent of Studies & Information in This Area
    A. Sex law studies of the various State Legislatures.
    B. Proceedings and recommendations of:- The American Law Insti-
tute; The American Bar Association; American Medical Association Committee on Forensic Medicine; Church of England Moral Welfare Council;
the Roman Catholic Church (in England).
    C. Changes in the laws of New York State.
    D. Experience under changed laws in Denmark, Sweden, Holland,
Switzerland, Poland.
    E. Experience of countries employing the Code Napoleon.
    F. Studies made by independent research authorities:- Kinsey,
Ellis, et al.

SECTION XII - Related Issues
    A. Juvenile delinquency; authority of State over children and

APPENDIX, 8-1e

A Study of the Civil Rights Status of Homosexuals under the Existing Laws of the Several States. (continued)

their welfare.
    B. Standards and patterns of masculinity, femininity.
    C. Obscenity laws & publishing rights.
    D. Blackmail, suicide, murder, assault & battery - as incidental
to the present legal status of the homosexual.
    E. Financial and social LOSSES to the homosexual under present
status.
    F. Class reaping financial and social GAIN from present laws.

SECTION XIII - Conclusion
    Analysis of the entire concept of sex laws from the viewpoints
of:- Constitutional law; natural law; higher law; common law - based
on summaries of all preceding material.

SECTION XIV - Recommendations
    A. Proposals for rational revision of the sex laws.
    B. Proposals for programs aimed at achieving this goal.

SECTION XV - Appendix & Bibliography.

- - - - -

APPENDIX, 8-2a

General Instructions For All Drafting Committees. Seventh Midwinter Institute, 1961. (Transcribed from original in ONE's Baker Memorial Library & Archives)

General Instructions For All Drafting Committees

A. *Interest Areas.* The following outlines are intended as guides only, and as descriptive of particular Interest Areas. It is to be expected that other topics will be suggested. Care should be exercised in making sure that topics added do not infringe upon the Interest Areas of other Drafting Committees. In case questions of this nature arise members of the Study Seminar, HS-260, will be available during all work sessions for consultations concerning demarcation of Interest Area boundaries.

B. *Definitions of Terms Used.* Whenever it becomes necessary to have a term defined for use in the Bill, all Committees are directed to apply to Drafting Committee.

C. *Procedures.* Each Committee shall proceed in general as follows:
1. Familiarize itself with questionnaires and proposals mailed in.
2. Make a list of all proposals deemed appropriate to the Committee's Interest Area.
3. Prepare an outline from the points to be covered in section of Bill assigned to Committee.
4. Write text of Committee's section of the Bill.
5. Present to Annual Banquet, Chairman reading the text.
6. Discussion of submissions by Banquet Commentators.

D. *Length of Texts.* Each Committee's submission shall not exceed three hundred and fifty words, the whole Bill to be further reduced to about one thousand words before publication.

E. *Personnel.* Each Drafting Committee will have a Chairman and a Secretary. Other committee members are to choose for themselves the group they wish to work with. It is expected that they will then continue right through with this committee; committee-hopping is to be discouraged.

F. *Uses for the Bill.* In addition to the text submitted, each Drafting Committee is asked to add a concise list of proposed uses to which the Bill might be put, Committees acting independently in this respect.

G. *Appendix.* Material collected by any Drafting committee felt to be appropriate as references, addenda, citations, statistics, etc., should be appended to the Committee's other submission for possible inclusion in a published Appendix to the Bill.

APPENDIX, 8-2b

General Instructions For All Drafting Committees. Seventh Midwinter Institute, 1961. (continued)

H. *Questionnaires and Letters.* Tabulation and analysis of questionnaires and letters concerning the Bill of Rights will be continued during the Spring Semester of HS-261, meeting Monday nights, 8-10; also, preparation of this material for publication will be undertaken by this Education Seminar.

Duties And Suggested Topics For Drafting Committees

Drafting Committee I.

Preamble And Definitions

A. To supply, on request from other Drafting Committees, "official definitions" of terms as they are to be understood for use in the Bill of Rights.

B. To establish a working definition, for purposes of the Bill, of the groups or classes of persons to whom the Bill shall be said to refer.

C. To prepare a Preamble to the Bill.

D. Suggested topics for consideration:

1. The right of non-conformity; the right of choice (free will); the line between individual and group rights.

2. Do homosexuals have the right to demand the status of a minority group? Must the wishes of the majority be accepted? The right to civil disobedience.

3. Can democratic voting procedures determine moral and ethical questions? Does the State have authority to prescribe sex behavior? Do homosexuals have the right to set up their own standards of sex behavior – as individuals, as a group?

Drafting Committee II.

Social Rights

A. To prepare and present the section of the Bill dealing with social rights and responsibilities.

B. To give particular attention to problems concerning women;

APPENDIX, 8-2c

General Instructions For All Drafting Committees. Seventh Midwinter Institute, 1961. (continued)

C. Suggested topics for consideration:

1. Work rights – The right to employment without discrimination in either private or public capacity; the right to military service without prejudice or penalty.

2. Fiscal rights – The right to equal insurance privileges; to own and bequeath real or personal property on an equal footing with other portions of society; the right to inheritance; equal tax rights; to own and conduct businesses on equal footing with others.

3. Social rights – To choose one's mode of dress; to determine suitable public and private behavior; to participate freely in community affairs and public life; to social facilities and privileges (dancing, sports, etc.).

4. Family rights – The right to parental respect and understanding; the right to social equality with heterosexual brothers and sisters; the right to have children, if desired.

5. Personality rights – The right to be free from social discrimination; the right to be free from social contempt; freedom from slander.

Drafting Committee III

Religious Rights

A. Duty of this Committee is to prepare the section of the Bill dealing with the religious rights of homosexuals.

B. Suggested topics for consideration:

1. Doctrinal rights. The right to be theologically evaluated as are other members of society; the right to be as free from religious denunciation as anyone; the right to have homosexual love accorded no lower rank than heterosexual love.

2. Institutional rights. The right to take active part in church work; to hold church offices without prejudice; to equal treatment as a church member.

3. Rights of equity. the right to be free of religiously-imposed mask-wearing (hypocritical behavior); the right to equal treatment by both clergy and organizations, i.e., to official attitudes and conformity with actual practices.

General Instructions For All Drafting Committees. Seventh Midwinter Institute, 1961. (continued)

---

4. The right to church-approved homosexual marriage for those who wish it.

5. The right to freedom from religious interference (for the non-religious).

Drafting Committee IV

Scientific Questions And Overpopulation

A. To prepare the section of the Bill dealing with rights homosexuals seek from the sciences (and social sciences).

B. To give particular attention to the rights of homosexuals in relation to the current world-wide population "explosion."

C. Suggested topics for consideration:

1. The right to have scientific study of homosexuality freed of value judgments; the right to have scholars study human behavior without censoring out homosexual factors; the right to free, frank, scientific reporting.

2. The right to have homosexuality studied objectively, i.e., without an ever-present heterosexual frame of reference; the right to have homosexuality presented as simply a mode of behavior, not a deviation, a variation, perversion, inversion, etc.

3. The right to serious, scientific treatment of the role of the homosexual concerning overpopulation; eugenics, artificial insemination.

4. The right to impartial sex education of young people concerning homosexuality; the right to require scientists to fearlessly seek out and present factual information on the topic to adolescents; the right to demand objectivity from social scientists and case workers concerning the topic.

5. The right to defense from faulty court testimony by psychologists, psychiatrists, etc.

APPENDIX, 12

Letter from Mary Renault to Donald J. Leiffer, dated 23rd May '58.
(ONE's Baker Memorial Library & Archives)

```
                                112 Fairway,
                                Durban North,
                                Natal, S.Africa.          23rd May '58


Dear Mr Leiffer,
                Your shot in the dark did eventually reach the target,
taking in three continents instead of two.  I hope you have not been
thinking too dimly of me for the delay; it has only just got here, and
gave me a lot of pleasure.  The praise of people who have experienced
themselves the situation one has tried to deal with in a book, is most
of all worth having.  Besides which, it is good, five years after a book
has appeared, to find it still making a fresh impact on someone; it makes
one feel a bit less ephemeral than one thought.

        I agree with you about the Ralphs and the Bunnies; too bad it's the
latter who put up a united front and make all the noise.

        Thank you for asking me to meet you in England.  I should have been
delighted to, if I had been there.  Thank you so much for writing.

                                Yours sincerely,

                                Mary Renault.
```

APPENDIX, 12-1a

Homophile Literature 500. (Transcribed from originals in ONE's Baker Memorial Library & Archives)

Homophile Literature 500
January-May, 1982
Drs. Gene Touchet and Richard Follett
syllabus issued 2/25/82

25 February: Emily Dickinson, Hart Crane, Horatio Alger: selected works Stephen Wright, ed., Different, esp. Anderson, "Hands," and James, "The Pupil"

4 March: Radclyffe Hall, The Well of Loneliness Gay/Lesbian Theoretical Perspectives: Dennis Altman, Homosexual: Oppression and Liberation

11 March: Crew and Norton, guest editors, "The Homophobic Imagination: An Editorial," College English (November 1974) Karla Jay and Allen Young, eds., Lavender Culture, especially Young, p.23; Jay, p.48; Saslow, p. 215; Parts Six and Seven.

18 March: STUDENT PRESENTATIONS of non-English literatures

25 March: Continuation of Gay/Lesbian Literary/Political Theories from readings above and additional sources to be provided in lecture/discussion (For example, you may wish to see Jeanette Foster's discussion of lesbian literature and C.A. Tripp's discussion of censorship.)

1 April: Lillian Faderman, Surpassing the Love of Men, entire text but be sure to read Section III.B. "When It Changed" before the class discussion.

8 April: SPRING BREAK — No Class Meeting

15 April: TERM PAPER IDEAS DUE: Class discussion of term paper topics, sharing of ideas, suggestions for resources, etc. Written precis desired but not required. Continuation of discussion of literary perspectives

22 April: Rita Mae Brown, Rubyfruit Jungle and Six of One

29 April: John Rechy, The Sexual Outlaw

6 May: Felice Picano, ed., A True Likeness: Lesbian and Gay Writing Today, specific selections to be announced

13 May: Sally Gearhart, The Wanderground

20 May: SHARING OF STUDENT PAPERS IN CLASS — FINAL CLASS MEETING

APPENDIX, 12-1b

Homophile Literature 500. (Transcribed from originals in ONE's Baker Memorial Library & Archives)

Homophile Literature 500
Dr. Michael Lombardi
Homophile Literary History & Survey

I. Ancient

Babylonia: *Gilgamesh* (2,000 B.C.) – first written record of homophilia – Jealous Goddess Ishtar vs Enkidu & G.

Greek – Plato: *Symposium & Phaedrus* (580 B.C.)

Venus Urania, Greek Goddess of Homophiles, "pais" [boy], i.e. "young warrior"

Sappho: *Poetry* (580 B.C.) Sapphic Love, The Isle of Lesbos

Roman – Virgil: *Eclogues* (37 B.C.) Corydon & Alexis

Petronius: *Satyricon* (66 A.D.)

Roman Homophile life

II. Judeo-Christian

Bible: Ruth & Naomi – *Ruth* I:16-17 (1312 B.C.) "Whither thou goest..."

David & Jonathan – *I & II Samuel* (1063 B.C.) "Passing the love of women..."

The Sodomites: *Genesis* 19 – "So we may know them..."; *I Kings* 15:12 – "Male cult prostitutes"

The Homophobe: Paul – *Romans* I:26 – "Men committing shameless acts with men"; *Cor.* 6:9 – "Nor Homosexuals" [false translation]

Legislation: *Leviticus* 18:22; 20:13 (550 B.C.) – "You shall not lie with a male...", "They shall be put to death."

Justinian (538 A.D.) – Combined Cannon & Roman Law, "They cause earthquakes, famine and plague."

Emperor Charles V (1932) The "Carolina" used Justinian as reference

Homophile Literature 500. (continued)

III. Asian

Seventeenth century: Ihara Saikaku, Women Who Loved Love (1682-83) Gay Life In Japan

Contemporary – Yukio Mishima, *Writings* (Compare to Gide, Proust)

IV. British

Medieval – Chaucer – "The Pardoner's Tale" (1387-1400)

Elizabethan – Shakespeare – *Sonnets* (1592-1602)

Marlow – *Hero and Leander* (1593)

Milton – *Sycidas*; *Sonnet To Diodati* (ca.669-74)

Eighteenth century – Mary Wollstonecraft, *Mary, A Fiction* (1888-89) 1st lesbian novel by a woman

Nineteenth century – Lord Byron, *Writings* (1800-03)

O. Wilde, *Writings* – His Trial, 1892

T. E. Lawrence (of Arabia), *Seven Pillars Of Wisdom* (1926)

D.H. Lawrence, *Aaron's Rod* (1922)

Uranians: J. A. Symonds, *Modern Ethics*–Ulrichs' disciple (1891)

E. Carpenter – *Intermediate Sex, Iolaus & Poetry*

William Johnson "Cory", *Poetry*

Dr. Edwin Emannuel Bradford, *Poetry*

Digby Dolben, *Poetry*

Modern – Joseph Conrad, *Victory* (1915)

W. Somerset Maugham, *Writings*

W. H. Auden, *Writings*

C. Isherwood, *I Am A Camera;* adaptation: "Cabaret" (Berlin Early 1930's)

Bloomsb'ry – Virginia Woolf, *Writings*

E. M. Forster, *Maurice* (1913-14, 1971) Cambridge Homophile life

Legislation – Henry VIII (1525-34) "Hanging for Buggery"

Wolfenden Report (1957) – for decriminalization

APPENDIX, 12-1d

Homophile Literature 500. (continued)

V. German
   Eighteenth century – Pyra & Lange – *Poetry*
   Legislation – Legal tracts / dissertations
   Neo-Classicists (Uranians) – Hoeszli – *Eros* (Cult. Hist.) (2
        Vols, 1834/36)
   Zschokke – *Eros* (1859) (novella)
   Legislation – Bavarian Code Napoleon (1813)
   Gay King of Wuerttemberg (1860's) Non persecution /
        prosecution
   143 (Prussia, before 1869), 152 (North German Confedera-
        tion, 1869), Par. 175 (Second Empire to 1968/9)
   Karl Heinrich Ulrichs (pseud. Numa Numantius), *Raging
        Sword, Poetry* & fiction (1862-80)
   Healthy Homosexual – M. Dannecker
   The romanticists' emphasis on the holy right of subjectivity
        and individualism also led to increasing emancipa-
        tion of women – Dorothea Schlegel,   Bettina
        Brentano, Friederich, the Great.
   Nineteenth century – Kleist, *Penthesilea* (1808) (drama)
   Platen, *Diary / Poetry* (1819-21) – Platen-Heine conflict;
        Jew & gay baiting
   Grillparzer, *Libussa* (1872), *Sappho* (1818) (Drama)
   Aimee Duc, *Are They Women?* (novella) (1901)
   Symbolism – Stephan George, *Poetry* (1892)
   George Circle – Maximillian Affair did not go into Inner
        Exile, applauded by Nazis
   Realism – Paul Heyse, *Alcibiades*
   Freud, *Essays* (1904-05)
   Biology – Dr. Benedikt Friedlaender, *Platonic Love* (1909)
   Pederasty – Thomas Mann, *Death In Venice*
   Fin-de-Siecle Decadence (1912)
   Contemporary – Clara Viebig, *Daughters Of The Rhineland*
   Robert Musil, *Young Toerless* (1906)

APPENDIX, 12-1e

Homophile Literature 500. (continued)

V. German (continued)
Wilhelm Schaefer, *Winckelmann's Death*
Hans Henny Jahnn, *The Wooden Ship* (1937) – murder
mystery & bloodbrotherhood
Helmut Heiszenbuettel, *D'Alemberts End* (1970)
Hubert Fichte, *Novels*
Alexander Ziegler (Switzerland), *Labyrinth*
Hirschfeld Group – Magnus Hirschfeld
Annual for Sexual Intermediaries (1898-1923); Henry
Gerber, *Translations*
Adolf Brand, *Der Eigene* (The Special, 1896-1929)
Publications – *Der Kreis* (The Circle; Switzerland)
Activism – Klaus & Erika Mann, *Writings*
Kurt Hiller, *Writings* (1908) – founder of "Activism"
Third Empire – H. Heger, *Pink Triangle*
M. Sherman, *Bent, a Play.*

VI. American
Nineteenth century – Melville, *Typee* (1846-47)
Bayard Taylor, *Joseph and his Friend* (1870–earliest gay
novel in English)
Adhesiveness – W. Whitman, *Calamus* (1855-56)
The mighty calls to freedom of W.W. were indicative of the
new trend... Under the influence of W., American
literature turned... distinctly American...
Willa Cather, *My Antonia*
Radcliffe Hall, *Well Of Loneliness* (1928)
Gertrude Stein, *Writings*
E. Dickenson / Sue Gilbert, *Poetry & Letters*
Djuna Barnes, *Writings* (1928)
Hart Crane, *Writings*
Natalie Barney, *Writings*

Homophile Literature 500. (continued)

VI. American (continued)
Anäis Nin, *Writings*
Edward Prime (pseud. Xavier Mayne), *Imre* (1908) – Prime
    is the father of American Homophile literature, Noel
    Garde
Adrienne Rich, *Writings*
Helen Rose Hull, *The Labyrinth* (1923)
Blair Niles, *Strange Brother* (1931) – Harlem background
G. Vidal, *City and the Pillar* (1948)
Tennessee Williams, *One Arm* (1948)
James Baldwin, *Giovanni's Room* (1956) – (1st Homophile
    novel by a black person)
Armistead Maupin, *Writings*
Joseph Hansen, *Writings* – murder mysteries, many pub-
    lished in *ONE Magazine*
Military – James Barr, *Quatrefoil; Game of Fools*, a play
The Kinsey Report (1948) – Medical
Periodicals – *ONE* (1953-67) – 1st openly Homophile
    magazine; *One Institute Quarterly* (1958-72) –
    Homophile studies
Legislation – 647(A) PC – sodomy laws
VII. French
Legislation – *Code Napoleon* (1789) – no anti-gay law
Modern – Genet, *Writings*
Proust, *Cities of the Plain* (1921-22)
Simone de Beauvoir, *The Second Sex*
Verlaine, *Sappho*
Baudelaire, *Lesbos*
Renée Vivien, *Writings* (1904)
Colette, *Writings* (1904-05)
Gide, *Corydon* (1911; *Nouvelle Revue Française* (1909)

APPENDIX, 13-1a

*ONE Institute Graduate School of Homophile Studies. Philosophy 510/610
"Questions of Morality and the Homophile Lifestyle." (ONE's Baker Memorial
Library & Archives)*

ONE INSTITUTE
3340 COUNTRY CLUB DRIVE LOS ANGELES, CALIF. 90019 • (213) 735-5252

ONE Institute Graduate School of Homophile Studies

COURSE: Philosophy 510/610
              Questions of Morality and the Homophile Lifestyle

TERM: Spring 1982

PLACE: ONE Inc., 2256 Venice Blvd., Los Angeles, CA 90306

INSTRUCTOR: Dwain E. Houser, Ph.D.

COURSE DESCRIPTION: This seminar is concerned with ethical
problems within same-sex relationships from a historic perspective,
as well as a personal level. The first part of the course will
address itself to the various ethical theories and moral philosophy which have historically been used to judge homosexual
relationships and out of which many lifestyle problems have arisen.
The second half of the course will focus on specific ethical
criteria by which the homophile community and individual homosexuals may wish to evaluate themselves with the intent of laying
the foundations for a homosexual ethic.

REQUIRED READINGS:

Edward Batchelor, Jr. Homosexuality and Ethics. New York: The
     Pilgrim Press, 1980.

John Boswell. Christianity, Social Tolerance and Homosexuality.
     Chicago: The University of Chicago Press, 1980.

Additional handouts will be distributed to the class and a reading
list will emerge as the course proceeds. Students are expected to
familiarize themselves with all material mentioned in class and
suggested by the instructor.

COURSE ORGANIZATION: The seminar will be organized around a series
of lectures and class discussions, supplemented with outside and
textual readings. Students are expected to contribute heavily and
critically to class discussions. Grades will be based on two
in-class essay style examinations and a formal research paper of
about 15 pages.

"A mystic bond of brotherhood makes all men one..." Carlyle.

APPENDIX, 13-1b

ONE Institute Graduate School of Homophile Studies. Philosophy 510/610 "Questions of Morality and the Homophile Lifestyle." (continued)

CLASS SCHEDULE:

Week	Topic
1	Introduction to the course
2	Nature and scope of a value system
3	Ethical relativism vs. authority (subject/object in ethical evaluations)
4	Homosexuality and nature
5	Homosexuality and pleasure
6	Homosexuality and religious ethical ideals I
7	Homosexuality and religious ethical ideals II
8	In-class exam
9	Situational ethics and contextual ethics in the modern gay and lesbian community
10	Spring vacation (no class)
11	Self-realization and ethics
12	The basis of social responsibility in the gay and lesbian community
13	The basis of personal homosexual morality
14	In-class exam
15	Summary: Research papers due

APPENDIX, 13-1c

ONE Institute Graduate School of Homophile Studies. Philosophy 510/610 "Questions of Morality and the Homophile Lifestyle." (continued)

PHILOSOPHY 510/610   Questions of Morality and the Homophile Lifestyle
Spring 1982
MID-TERM EXAMINATION

Instructions: This exam is designed to provid opportunity for maximum self-expression. It is open book, and although length is not a criteria, the student is expected to cover the answers to the questions in some depth. To this end 24 hours has been given to complete the exam (Due in the Deans office at 4 pm, Thursday, March 25, 1982). This exam is counted as 25% of your final grade. Good luck.

1. Jeremy Bentham (1748-1832) said, "I am a selfish man, as selfish as any man can be. But in me somehow or other, as it happens, selfishness has taken the form of benevolence." What school of ethics does such a statement reflect, and how do you relate the ideas of that school to the future ethical developments in Homosexual lifestyles?

2. How does science fit into an authoritarian view of ethics, and as such, what are the hidden pitfalls in appealing to scientific discovery in establishing ethical standards?

3. From your reading and class discussion, how has religion (especially Judeao-Christian religion) hampered personal ethical standards among gay men and women?

INDEX

Abstracts Department, ONE Institute Quarterly 172
Adult sexual re-socialization 169
Age of Freud 12
Albany Trust 60
Alcoholism 133, 138, 140, 144, 202
American Civil Liberties Union 1, 21, 36
American Psychiatric Association 161
American Psychological Association 160
Arcadie 58
Arena Three 60
Argo, Jack [pseud.], see Werres, Johannes
Armon, Virginia 177
Awarding of degrees 77

Baker Memorial Library 21, 27, 30, 40, 53, 56, 60, 159, 236
Baker, Dr. Blanche M. 19, 33, 44, 157, 172, 319
Baker, William F. 18, 186
Barazoku 63
Barr, James 37, 180, 263, 293
Basic Percentage Tables 130, 428-436
Ben, Lisa [pseud.] 40, 263
Benjamin, Dr. Harry 32, 172
Bentler, Peter 45, 47
Berlin 61
Bibliography Project 41, 50, 53-55, 285, 291
Bieber, Irving 42, 137, 169
Bird, Merton 1, 3
Block, Martin 3
Boston Institute of Homophile Studies 48
Boswell, John 48
Boyfrank, Monwell 99, 212, 305, 306, 321
Bradbury, Ray 43
Buenos Aires 66
Bullough, Vern L. 1, 54, 55
Burckhardt, Rudolf 57, 97
Burnside, John 129

Center for Advanced Studies 5, 332
Center for the study of sexuality 167
Child molestation 65
Child-raising, modern 127
China's two histories 68
Cities of the plain 93
Civil rights 1, 38, 179, 182, 183, 185, 209, 437-441
Clinical entity 160
Coates, Deborah A. 105
College credit 70
Conger, Richard [pseud.], see Legg, W. Dorr
Conspiracy of Silence 37, 79, 328
Conspiratorial caution 66
Corbin, Joan 16, 180
Cory, Donald Webster [pseud.], see Sagarin, Edward
Council on Religion and the Homosexual (CRH) 209
Counseling Center 176
Counseling the Homosexual 43, 45
Cowboys in Colorado 49
Crowther, R. H. [pseud.], see Underwood, Julian "Woody"
Cultuur en ontspannings Centrum (C.O.C.) 25, 26, 58, 59, 98
Cutler, Marvin [pseud.], see Legg, W. Dorr

Dank, Barry M 45, 130
Darr, Jane [pseud.], see Barr, James
Daughters of Bilitis 32, 39, 186, 187, 209-211
Delos 62
Deviant behavior 35, 125
Diploma mills 73
Division of Education Planning Committee 22, 28
Dominant males 126

Elcano, Barrett W. 55
Elloree, Eve [pseud.], see Corbin, Joan
Erickson Educational Foundation 47, 53, 145, 176
Ethnocentric racism 63
Etiology 169, 173
Evans, Dr. Ray 130, 172, 175, 176, 196, 226, 319
Extension classes 4, 30, 32, 33, 49, 357
Extension Lecture Series 4

Farley, Morgan 40, 263, 265
Fenelon, Fania 105
Final Report of the Task Force on Homosexuality 159, 161, 167, 168
Finocchio's 162
First homosexual university 70
Flowers for picking 65
Follett, Richard J. 76
Forbundet av 1948 56
Fradkin, Howard E. 45, 72, 142, 145, 318
Frederic, Dawn 52
Frederick the Great 10, 36
Freeman, David [pseud.], see Rowland, Charles
Freud, Sigmund 12, 14, 37, 176, 233
Frisbie, Frederic 99

Garde, Noel I. 85
Gay Liberation, Birth 1
Gay researchers 164
Gender identification 135, 139, 144
Gerber, Henry 99
Gibson, John D. 54
Goldman, Paul 43
Goldstein, Fred J. 5
Graduate student assistance 175
Greece 62
Green, Dr. Richard 5
Grey, Antony 59
Guyon Society 146

Hafiz 101, 104
Hamburg 61
Hardman, Paul D. 96, 248
Hay, Henry (Harry) 2, 19, 27, 89, 95, 117, 238, 258, 317
Heard, Gerald (D.B. Vest) 18, 83, 229, 230, 235, 317, 321
Heliogabalus 80
Heterosexual Assumption, The 42, 215
Hirschfeld, Magnus 12-14, 23, 24, 30, 57, 61, 97, 100, 101, 103, 292
History nodes 88

Holocaust, Homosexual, see Homophile Holocaust
Homoaffectionalism 95
Homophile (the word) 23, 25-27
Homophile Education Project 38
Homophile Holocaust 36, 98, 108
Homophile movement: United States 119
Homophile movement:Europe 80, 97, 99
Homophile movement:Germany 99, 101, 108, 112, 414-419
Homophile movement:Holland 98
Homophile movement:Switzerland 57
Homophile movement:United States 32, 46, 179, 320
Homosexual (the word) 23, 25, 101, 103
Homosexual Bill of Rights, Drafting Committees 38, 322, 442-446
Homosexual Bill of Rights, Questionnaire 128-145, 422, 423
Homosexual Culture 117, 122
Homosexual marriage 132, 138, 143, 180
Homosexual Minority 117, 118, 120, 121, 123, 161
Homosexuality in History 31, 80, 84, 86, 99, 317
Hooker Report, see Final Report of the Task Force on
        Homosexuality
Hooker, Dr. Evelyn 18, 36, 44, 48, 145, 157, 171, 176, 319
Houser, Dwain E. 71, 74
Humphreys, Laud 72, 76, 159, 161

Incest 147
Inquisition, The 67
Insel, [Die] 97
Institute for the Study of Human Resources (ISHR) 4, 41, 71-74,
        173, 224, 225, 284, 320, 384-387
International Congress for Sexual Equality (ICSE) 110, 292
Isherwood, Christopher 13, 24, 48, 61, 176
Islamic gap 62

Jennings, Dale 2, 3
Jones, Father James G. 40, 187
Jorgensen, Christine 48, 172
Julber, Eric 18, 33, 180, 181, 184

Kaplan, Richard 49
Kepner, James L. Jr. 21, 27, 32, 36, 39, 52, 53, 55, 97, 142, 184,
    201, 211, 221, 318, 320
King, Brian 57
Kinsey Effect, The 14
Kinsey Scale 36, 59, 163
Kinsey, Alfred C. 14, 24, 67, 160, 215
Kirkpatrick, Dr. Martha 45
Klopfer, Bruno 163
Knights of the Clocks 1, 339
Krafft-Ebing, Richard von 11, 101-103
Kreis [Der] 25, 57, 97, 110, 292

Legg, W. Dorr 2, 3, 27, 31, 43, 52, 71-73, 75, 76, 89, 128, 145,
    204, 211, 214, 248, 318
Legman, Gershon A. 55
Leiffer, Don 27
Lesbianism 105, 168, 169, 177, 271
Lombardi, Michael H. 103, 104, 318
London 60
Lowenthal, Morris 40, 185, 187

Maier, Karl 57
Mailer, Norman 262
Marmor, Judd 42, 161
Mattachine Society 2, 19, 49, 117-119, 157, 163, 211, 213, 215,
    238, 292, 396
McKenzie, Compton 38
McNeil, Merritt A. 265, 271, 275
Medical Model, The 11
Merritt, Dr. Thomas M. [pseud.], see Thompson, Dr. Merritt M.
Midwinter Institute, 1955 18, 346-351
Midwinter Institute, 1956 19, 352
Midwinter Institute, 1957 29, 353, 354
Midwinter Institute, 1958 33, 356-358
Midwinter Institute, 1959 33, 359-361
Midwinter Institute, 1960 36, 362-363
Midwinter Institute, 1961 38, 128, 185, 368-370, 442
Midwinter Institute, 1962 40, 371-374
Midwinter Institute, 1963 40, 187, 375, 376

Midwinter Institute, 1966 42, 377
Midwinter Institute, 1969 130, 378-380
Midwinter Institute, 1970 46
Midwinter Institute, 1972 47, 381-383
Midwinter Institute, 1978 49, 388, 389
Midwinter Institute, 1980 49, 390-393
Minorities Research Group 60
Moore, David G. 56, 71-73
Morin, Stephen 170

Nazi dykes 106
Nazis 14, 24, 25, 56, 61, 98, 99, 108
Neal, K. O. [pseud.], see McNeil, Merritt A.

Oedipus Complex 87, 176
One finger joint 67
One Institute of Graduate Studies 70, 72, 73, 403-413, 422, 426,
     449, 455
ONE Institute of Homophile Studies 4, 16
ONE Institute Quarterly 52, 171, 172, 286
ONE Magazine 16, 343-345
ONE of Chicago 50, 398-402
ONE, Incorporated 3, 41, 338-342
ONE, Inc. Education Division 19, 347-351
Otis, Harry 49, 286

Palmieri, Dr. Mario 33, 309
Parlour, Dr. Richard R. 45
Pedersen, Lyn [pseud.], see Kepner, James L. Jr.
Peer Counseling 43, 155, 157, 171, 176, 319
Perry, Rev. Troy 58
Physique photo interest 135, 139
Pink Triangles 98
Platen-Hallermuende, Count August von 101
Police approval 57
Poole, Kenneth 45
Positive gay identity 170
Postmaster of Los Angeles 17

Reid, Ann Carll [pseud.], see Wolf, Irma "Corky"
Renault, Mary 262, 446
Reyes, Antonio 3
Rio de Janeiro 65
Rocco, Pat 57-59, 146, 286
Role inversion 64
Rorschach technique 158, 163, 174
Rosenthal, Rachel 33, 43, 263
Rousseau, Guy [pseud.], see Whitaker, Bailey
Rowland, Charles 117, 153, 156, 319
Rush, Stella 82, 186, 211
Russell, Sten [pseud.], see Rush, Stella

Sagarin, Edward 40, 117
Sampson, Chet 50
Sao Paulo 65
Schliemann, Heinrich 9
Selden, Fred 45
Selwyn, Herbert 72, 211
Sex frequencies 134, 139, 140
Sex itself 127
Sex role 134, 135, 139, 140, 143, 144, 242, 322
Sex, Role and Gender 48, 386, 387
Slater, Don 3, 34, 37, 53
Smith, A. E. [pseud.], see McNeil, Merritt A.
Social disorganization 125
Social justice 165
Social setting 163, 164
Society of Anubis 46
Sociology of Homosexuality 28, 34, 36, 123, 318
Southern California Council on Religion and the Homophile 210
Stonewall Bar 1

Taiwan 63
Terminology 23
Teubal, Savina 47
Third sex theory 101, 103, 322
Thompson, Chuck [pseud.], see Sampson, Chet
Thompson, Dr. Merritt M. 22, 27, 29, 30, 34, 35, 52, 118, 187, 235, 285, 304

Touchet, Gene 72, 75
Transsexual theory 104

Ulrichs, Karl Heinrich 10, 102, 104, 318
Underwood, Julian "Woody" 21, 27, 42, 45, 54, 119, 122, 130, 296,
      318, 320
Uranism 104

Van Leeuwen, Jaap 26
van Santhorst, Arend [pseud.], see Van Leeuwen, Jaap
Variant sexual behavior 47, 384, 385
Vest, D. B. [pseud.], see Heard, Gerald
Visual Kama Sutra 67
Vriendschap 25, 26, 292

Werres, Johannes 59, 97, 109-111
Whitaker, Bailey 3
Williams, Walter 72
Wolf, Irma "Corky" 16
Wolfenden Committee Parliamentary Report on Homosexuality 38,
      60, 198, 292
Women of ONE, The 17